Open Generative Syntax

Editors: Elena Anagnostopoulou, Mark Baker, Roberta D'Alessandro, David Pesetsky, Susi Wurmbrand

In this series:

1. Bailey, Laura R. & Michelle Sheehan (eds.). Order and structure in syntax I: Word order and syntactic structure.

2. Sheehan, Michelle & Laura R. Bailey (eds.). Order and structure in syntax II: Subjecthood and argument structure.

3. Bacskai-Atkari, Julia. Deletion phenomena in comparative constructions: English comparatives in a cross-linguistic perspective.

4. Franco, Ludovico, Mihaela Marchis Moreno & Matthew Reeve (eds.). Agreement, case and locality in the nominal and verbal domains.

5. Bross, Fabian. The clausal syntax of German Sign Language: A cartographic approach.

6. Smith, Peter W., Johannes Mursell & Katharina Hartmann (eds.). Agree to Agree: Agreement in the Minimalist Programme.

7. Pineda, Anna & Jaume Mateu (eds.). Dative constructions in Romance and beyond.

ISSN: 2568-7336

Dative constructions in Romance and beyond

Edited by

Anna Pineda

Jaume Mateu

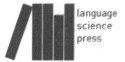
language
science
press

Pineda, Anna & Jaume Mateu (eds.). 2020. *Dative constructions in Romance and beyond* (Open Generative Syntax 7). Berlin: Language Science Press.

This title can be downloaded at:
http://langsci-press.org/catalog/book/258
© 2020, the authors
ISBN: 978-3-96110-249-5 (Digital)
         978-3-96110-250-1 (Hardcover)

ISSN: 2568-7336
DOI:10.5281/zenodo.3744254
Source code available from www.github.com/langsci/258
Collaborative reading: paperhive.org/documents/remote?type=langsci&id=258

Cover and concept of design: Ulrike Harbort
Typesetting: Ahmet Bilal Özdemir, Anna Pineda, Carla Bombi, Sebastian Nordhoff
Proofreading: Alec Shaw, Amir Ghorbanpour, Aniefon Daniel, Brett Reynolds, Christopher Straughn, Esther Yap, Jeroen van de Weijer, Lachlan Mackenzie, Mario Bisiada, Jean Nitzke, Sauvane Agnès, Sean Stalley, Sebastian Nordhoff, Sophie Ellsäßer, Stefan Schnell, Tom Bossuyt
Fonts: Libertinus, Arimo, DejaVu Sans Mono
Typesetting software: X⅃LATEX

Language Science Press
Xhain
Grünberger Str. 16
10243 Berlin, Germany
langsci-press.org

Storage and cataloguing done by FU Berlin

Contents

Dative constructions across languages: An introduction

Anna Pineda
Sorbonne Université

Jaume Mateu
CLT-Universitat Autònoma de Barcelona

1 Presentation

1.1 Interest of the volume

The present volume offers a comprehensive account of dative structures across languages –with an important, though not exclusive, focus on the Romance family. As is well-known, datives play a central role in a variety of structures, ranging from ditransitive constructions to cliticization of IOs and DOM-marked DOs, and including also psychological predicates, possessor or causative constructions, among many others. As interest in all these topics has increased significantly over the past three decades, this volume provides an overdue update on the state of the art. Accordingly, the chapters in this volume account for both widely discussed patterns of dative constructions as well as some that are relatively unknown.

1.2 Structure of the volume

The book is organized into four main parts, comprising 15 papers, preceded by an overview by M. Cristina Cuervo. This contribution offers a cross-linguistic perspective on applicative heads, which over the past years have been widely assumed to be licensers of dative arguments cross-linguistically.

 Anna Pineda & Jaume Mateu. 2020. Dative constructions across languages: An introduction. In Anna Pineda & Jaume Mateu (eds.), *Dative constructions in Romance and beyond*, iii–xiii. Berlin: Language Science Press. DOI:10.5281/zenodo.3744254

PART I is dedicated to analyzing datives in the context of ditransitive constructions, with focus on identifying the well-known *Double Object Construction.*

The literature on Double Object Constructions (e.g. *John gave Mary the book),* which is typically focused on English, is very rich (Oehrle 1976; Kayne 1984; Larson 1988; Jackendoff 1990b,a; Pesetsky 1995; Harley 2002, among many others). The three main analyses found in the literature which account for constructions with dative arguments, particularly ditransitive constructions, stipulate:

1. an extra structure above the lexical V (see Baker 1988; 1997, Marantz's (1993) Applicative Hypothesis for Bantu and English, Anagnostopoulou (2003) for Greek, Miyagawa & Tsujioka (2004) for Japanese, or Miyagawa & Jung (2004) for Korean, a.o.);

2. an extra structure inside the lexical V (Small Clause, Kayne 1984; Zero Morpheme, Pesetsky 1995); and

3. a proposal reconciling the two approaches mentioned above by distinguishing Low and High Applicatives (Pylkkänen 2002), which hypothesizes the existence of extra structure above the VP for High Applicatives (those for which the interpretation does not involve a Goal argument) and extra structure inside the VP for Low Applicatives (those for which the interpretation involves transfer of possession).

Since Pylkkänen's work on Applicatives in English, Finnish and Japanese, the use of these syntactic heads has been further developed and has given rise to works on many languages (McGinnis 2001 for Albanian and Icelandic, Cuervo 2003 for Spanish, McIntyre 2006 for German, Fournier 2010 for French, Pineda 2013; 2016; 2020a for Catalan). Additionally, more types of Applicatives have been proposed (for example, Cuervo's (2003) Affected Applicatives).

One of the most important implementations of Applicatives involves a particular type of ditransitive construction, the aforementioned Double Object Construction (DOC), as in English *John gave Mary the book.* Although DOCs have been traditionally considered to be absent in Romance languages (Holmberg & Platzack 1995; Kayne 1984), over the past decades several researchers have claimed that Spanish indeed has this construction (Masullo 1992; Demonte 1995; Romero 1997; Bleam 2003). On the basis of Pylkkänen's (2002) aforementioned work on applicatives, the existence of DOCs in Spanish has again been argued to be correct (Cuervo 2003). This proposal has been since extended to other Romance languages, such as French (Fournier 2010), Portuguese (Torres Morais &

Salles 2010), Romanian (Diaconescu & Rivero 2007) and Catalan (Pineda 2013; 2016; 2020a).

However, while the existence of DOCs, usually assumed to be mediated by applicative heads, is widely established in the study of English ditransitive constructions (Baker 1988; Marantz 1993; Pylkkänen 2002; 2008), their presence in other language families remains highly controversial, especially in the realm of Romance languages. Thus, it is generally assumed for English that an applicative head is the backbone of the DOC (1), introducing the IO in its specifier position and relating it to the DO, in its complement position (2):

(1) John gives Mary the book.

(2)

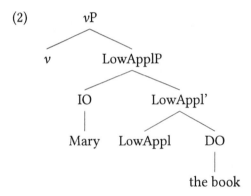

For Romance languages, it has been argued that the DOC pattern, with an applicative head, is also attested. This gives rise to two different perspectives: those identifying the DOC with clitic-doubled ditransitives (see e.g. Cuervo 2003) and those arguing that the presence or absence of dative clitic doubling is not structurally relevant for DOCs (see e.g. Pineda 2013; 2016; 2020a). That is, there is no consensus as to whether a doubling dative clitic is a *sine qua non* condition for Romance DOC. Romance languages offer an interesting landscape from which to consider a doubling dative clitic in ditransitive constructions. While this construction is possible in Spanish, Catalan and Romanian, it is impossible in French, Portuguese and Standard Italian. Moreover, doubling is compulsory in some American varieties of Spanish (Río de la Plata / Chile / Caracas) (Parodi 1998; Senn 2008; Pujalte 2009) and Trentino (Cordin 1993). Another point of controversy has to do with the (non-)existence of an English-like dative alternation (*John gave Mary the book, John gave the book to Mary*) in Romance. Most of the aforementioned authors defend the existence of two different ditransitive constructions, the double object one (with clitic doubling) and the prepositional one (without clitic doubling), featuring structural differences (opposite c-commanding relations between objects) and semantic differences (successful transfer of possession or not). However, Pineda (2013; 2016; 2020a) challenged this claim by showing that the purported structural and semantic differences between clitic-doubled and non-clitic doubled ditransitives constructions are not as robust as suggested. This assertion brings Romance clitic-doubling languages such as Spanish, Catalan or Romanian (for the latter, see also von Heusinger & Tigău (2020) close to non-doubling languages, such as French, Italian and Portuguese, for which the existence of two structural relations between the objects of ditransitive sentences has been acknowledged in the literature (see Harley 2002; Anagnostopoulou 2003; Fournier 2010, and Boneh & Nash 2011 for French; and Giorgi & Longobardi 1997; McGinnis 2001; Harley 2002 for Italian).

In the present volume, this issue is tackled, with special attention extended to the situation in Portuguese, by ANA CALINDRO. This author discusses whether a particular diachronic change in the expression of indirect objects (generalization of *para* 'to' in ditransitive constructions) in Brazilian Portuguese distinguishes this language from other Romance languages. She treats the structural representation of ditransitives in this language by dispensing with applicative heads and instead making use of a p head (Svenonius 2003; 2004; Wood 2012) and the i^* single argument introducer proposed by Wood & Marantz (2017).

The situation of Portuguese and Spanish ditransitives is also analyzed by PAULA CÉPEDA & SONIA CYRINO. These authors explore the causes and the consequences of the two linear orders (DO>IO and IO>DO) allowed for the DO and the IO in Spanish, European Portuguese and Brazilian Portuguese ditransitives. They conclude that arguments supporting a DOC analysis for ditransitive constructions in these languages are inconclusive on both semantic and structural grounds. They argue that the two previously mentioned orders are derivationally related via an information structure operation.

Romanian ditransitives are also discussed in detail in this volume. ALEXANDRA CORNILESCU provides an account of the binding relations between the DO and the IO in Romanian ditransitives, focusing on the grammaticality differences triggered by clitic doubled IOs, differentially marked DOs and clitic doubled DOs. The data discussed in her paper, which have otherwise received scant attention, lead the author to propose a derivational account for ditransitive constructions to explain these differences.

Finally, French, Italian and Catalan ditransitives are also considered in the volume. In the paper by MICHELLE SHEEHAN, the author argues that ditransitives in these languages have two underlying structures so that a DP introduced by 'a/à' can be either dative, akin to the English DOC, or locative, akin to the English *to*-dative construction. SHEEHAN bases her claims on the relations between objects with a focus on Person Case Constraint (PCC) effects. The author contrasts PCC effects in ditransitives and in *faire-infinitive* causatives, providing evidence that such effects are not limited to clitic clusters, as previously suggested for Spanish by Ormazabal & Romero (2013). In causatives, clitics also trigger PCC effects because the *a/à* is unambiguously dative.

The debate regarding the existence or absence of an English-like dative alternation, with a DOC and a *to*-dative construction, has received interest outside Romance linguistics. Accordingly, the volume includes an exhaustive account of Russian ditransitives, by SVITLANA ANTONYUK. This author proposes that the well-known binary distinction between DOC and the prepositional *to*-counterpart is insufficient for Russian and a ternary distinction is needed. She formulates her claim on the basis of Russian quantifier scope freezing data, which demonstrate that Russian ditransitive predicates are not a homogeneous group, but rather subdivide into three groups with distinct underlying structures.

PART II is dedicated to other dative constructions, including possessor and experiencer constructions and related structures. The study of possessor datives is tackled from three different perspectives. First, in EGOR TSEDRYK's paper, the focus is extended to predicative possession and possessive modality in Russian, which allows both the dative ('Vanja$_{DAT}$ be$_{EXIST}$ this book') and the locative ('At Vanja$_{GEN}$ be$_{EXIST}$ this book') to occur with the existential BE. The dative has a directional meaning (possible possession), opposed to stative inclusion of the locative (actual possession). This construal of the dative is furthermore extended to modal necessity of imperfective infinitive constructions ('Vanja$_{DAT}$ to get up early tomorrow'). Finally, building on the part-whole relation (possessum ⊆ possessor) described by dative (*give the books ⊆ to the woman*) and genitive possessors (*the books ⊆ of the woman*), as well as the reverse relation (possessor ⊇ possessum) found with instrumentals *the woman ⊇ with the books*, a discussion is offered by LUDOVICO FRANCO & PAOLO LORUSSO on the instances of such inclusive relations in the aspectual domain, when continuous/progressive tenses are combined with dative (*Gianni is at hunt* 'Gianni is hunting') or instrumental (*They eat with honey* 'They are eating honey') morphemes in different languages, such as Italian or Baka. Additionally, experiencer constructions are analyzed by ANTONIO FÁBREGAS & RAFAEL MARÍN, with focus on the stative meaning that characterizes dative experiencers with Spanish psychological verbs (compare *A Juan le preocupan las cosas* 'To John CL$_{DAT}$ concern.3PL the things' stative *vs. Juan se preocupa por las cosas* 'John CL$_{REFL}$ concerns.3SG for the things' dynamic). A semantic characterization of datives as not denoting a full transference relation, but only a boundary, allows one to account for the stativity associated with experiencer datives. This contrasts with other prototypical values of datives such as recipients or goals, which are claimed to denote a transfer and are therefore dynamic.

PART III contains two proposals regarding applicative heads, which recently have been considered a cross-linguistic licenser of dative arguments. Building on Pylkkänen's 2002; 2008 analysis of high and low applicatives, two proposals are advanced. The first, based on Bantu data, is elaborated by MATTIE WECHSLER. This author proposes the existence of a 'super high' applicative, and argues that (at least in Bantu) applicative heads are underspecified regarding their height. In the second proposal, which is based on data from Chukchi, West Greenlandic and Salish, DAVID BASILICO advocates for a different syntax of the low applicative head, which permits one to account for the presence of an antipassive morpheme in applicative constructions.

PART IV focuses on the study of case alternations involving dative case. A wide range of structures where case alternations occur are considered in this volume. Within the Romance family, alternations involving dative case are attested with agentive verbs whose single complement is dative or accusative-marked (see Fernández Ordóñez 1999 and Sáez 2009 for Spanish, Ramos 2005; Morant 2008; Pineda & Royo 2017 and Pineda (2020b) for Catalan, Ledgeway 2000 for Neapolitan, Troberg 2008 for French (on a diachronic perspective), and Pineda 2016 for a comprehensive Romance view including Catalan, Spanish, Asturian and Italian varieties). In the present volume, a related case of variation is analyzed by ADAM LEDGEWAY, NORMA SCHIFANO & GIUSEPPINA SILVESTRI, where dative in the marking of the IO with agentive verbs alternates with genitive case, in constructions such as *I told* [GEN/DAT the boy] *to go* or *I spoke* [GEN/DAT *the mayor*]. The data discussed come from Southern Italian varieties, where the Romance-style dative marking (*a* 'to') alternates with a Greek-style marking (*di* 'of').

Another instance of case alternation involving dative case involves psychological predicates (Belletti & Rizzi 1988), where the experiencer may show dative or accusative case in several Romance languages (see for example Cabré & Mateu 1998; Pineda & Royo 2017 and Royo 2017 for Catalan, and Fernández Ordóñez 1999 for Spanish). In the present volume, CARLES ROYO offers an exhaustive account of dative/accusative alternations with psychological predicates in Catalan varieties, and analyses the connection between the case alternation and the causative vs. stative nature of the construction.

Variation involving dative structures in Catalan is further explored in the contribution of TERESA CABRÉ & ANTONIO FÁBREGAS who examine the notion of dative from a morphological perspective. Catalan dialectal differences between Valencian and non-Valencian varieties suggest an analysis of the notion of dative as non-monolithic. Whereas the dative clitic exponent *li* in Valencian Catalan is case-marked with dative, the corresponding *li* in non-Valencian Catalan is claimed to correspond to a locative adverbial embedded under D (thus *l+i*), the locative element being attested independently in these varieties as *hi* (both in the plural dative clitic, *els hi* 'them$_{DAT}$', and in strictly locative contexts, *Hi sóc* 'I am there'). The consequences of this dialectal divide for clitic combinations are also explored.

In the Romance context, dative/accusative alternations are also closely connected with the so-called *leísmo*, the use of dative clitics for DOs, and *loísmo/laísmo*, the use of accusative clitics for IOs. These phenomena are the object of a study by RITA MANZINI, who compares the realization of Romance *a*-DPs (including Goal arguments of (di)transitive, Goal arguments of unergative verbs, and differentially marked objects of transitive verbs) and their compatibility with a cliticized dative form. In *leísta* varieties, a dative clitic is used not only for Goal arguments, but also for differentially marked objects. However, in *loísta/laísta* varieties, accusative clitics are used not only for differentially marked objects but also for Goal arguments of unergative verbs. Both phenomena are exemplified using data from Spanish and Southern Italian varieties. MANZINI offers a unified account of Standard Spanish, as well as *leísmo* and *loísmo/laísmo* patterns in Spanish and Italian varieties, arguing that the case array may be set differently for lexical DPs and for clitics, the latter being optionally associated with DOM (whose syntactic structure of embedding is the same as *typical* dative arguments) and therefore giving rise to *leísmo*.

Finally, beyond the Romance linguistic domain, a well-studied language with case variation involving the dative is Icelandic, where dative/accusative has been extensively analyzed (see for example Barðdal 2001; 2008; Svenonius 2002; Maling 2002; Jónsson & Eythórsson 2005). The present volume also offers a contribution in this line of research, with particular attention extended to the degree of predictability of the use of dative case. JÓHANNES GÍSLI JÓNSSON & RANNVEIG THÓRARINSDÓTTIR analyze Icelandic case alternations in marking the object of borrowings and neologisms, and assess the conditions that motivate the use of the dative case, at the expense of the default accusative case, in the context of these novel transitive verbs.

Acknowledgements

The edition of this collection of papers has been supported by the research project of Ministerio de Ciencia e Innovación FFI2017-87140-C4-1-P.

References

Anagnostopoulou, Elena. 2003. *The syntax of ditransitives: Evidence from clitics.* Berlin: Walter de Gruyter.

Baker, Mark C. 1988. *Incorporation: A theory of grammatical function changing.* Chicago, IL: Chicago University Press.

Baker, Mark C. 1997. Thematic roles and syntactic structure. In Liliane Haegeman (ed.), *Elements of grammar*, 73–137. Dordrecht: Kluwer.

Barðdal, Jóhanna. 2001. *Case in Icelandic: A synchronic, diachronic and comparative approach.* Lund: University of Lund. (Doctoral dissertation).

Barðdal, Jóhanna. 2008. *Productivity: Evidence from case and argument structure in Icelandic.* Amsterdam: John Benjamins.

Belletti, Adriana & Luigi Rizzi. 1988. Psych-verbs and θ-Theory. *Natural Language & Linguistic Theory* 6(3). 291–352. DOI:10.1007/BF00133902

Bleam, Tonia. 2003. Properties of double object construction in Spanish. In Rafael Núñez-Cedeño, Luis López & Richard Cameron (eds.), *A Romance perspective on language knowledge and use: Selected papers from the 31st Linguistic Symposium on Romance Languages (LSRL)*, 233–252. Amsterdam: John Benjamins.

Boneh, Nora & Lea Nash. 2011. When the benefit is on the fringe. In Janine Berns, Haike Jacobs & Tobias Scheer (eds.), *Romance languages and linguistic theory 2009: Selected papers from 'Going Romance' Nice 2009*, 19–38. Amsterdam: John Benjamins.

Cabré, Teresa & Jaume Mateu. 1998. Estructura gramatical i normativa lingüística: A propòsit dels verbs psicològics en català. *Quaderns: Revista de traducció* 2. 65–81.

Cordin, Patrizia. 1993. Dative clitic doubling in trentino. In Adriana Belletti (ed.), *Syntactic theory and the dialects of Italy*, 130–154. Torino: Rosenberg/Sellier,

Cuervo, María Cristina. 2003. *Datives at large.* Cambridge, MA: Massachusetts Institute of Technology. (Doctoral dissertation). https://dspace.mit.edu/handle/1721.1/7991.

Demonte, Violeta. 1995. Dative alternation in Spanish. *Probus* 7(1). 5–30. DOI:10.1515/prbs.1995.7.1.5

Diaconescu, Rodica & María Luisa Rivero. 2007. An applicative analysis of double object constructions in Romanian. *Probus* 19(2). 209–233.

Fernández Ordóñez, Inés. 1999. Leísmo, laísmo y loísmo. In Ignacio Bosque & Violeta Demonte (eds.), *Gramática descriptiva de la lengua española*, 1317–1398. Madrid: Esposa.

Fournier, David. 2010. *La structure du prédicat verbal: Une étude de la construction à double objet en français.* University of Toronto. (Doctoral dissertation).

Giorgi, Alessandra & Giuseppe Longobardi. 1997. *The syntax of Noun Phrases: Configuration, parameters and empty categories.* Cambridge: Cambridge University Press.

Harley, Heidi. 2002. Possession and the double object construction. *Linguistic Variation Yearbook* 2(1). 31–70.

Holmberg, Anders & Christer Platzack. 1995. *The role of inflection in scandinavian syntax.* New York: Oxford University Press.

Jackendoff, Ray. 1990a. On Larson's treatment of the double object construction. *Linguistic inquiry* 21(3). 427–456.

Jackendoff, Ray. 1990b. *Semantic structures.* Cambridge: MIT Press.

Jónsson, Jóhannes Gísli & Thórhallur Eythórsson. 2005. Variation in subject case marking in Insular Scandinavian. *Nordic Journal of Linguistics* 28. 223–245.

Kayne, Richard S. 1984. *Connectedness and binary branching.* Dordrecht: Foris.

Larson, Richard K. 1988. On the double object construction. *Linguistic Inquiry* 19(3). 335–391.

Ledgeway, Adam. 2000. *A comparative syntax of the dialects of Southern Italy: A minimalist approach.* Oxford: Blackwell.

Maling, Joan. 2002. Það rignir þágufalli á Íslandi [It rains dative in iceland]: Verbs with dative objects in icelandic]. *Íslenskt mál og almenn málfræði* 24. 31–105.

Marantz, Alec. 1993. Implications of asymmetries in double object constructions. In Sam A. Mchombo (ed.), *Theoretical aspects of Bantu grammar*, 113–150. Stanford, CA: CSLI Publications.

Masullo, Pascual J. 1992. *Incorporation and case theory in Spanish: A crosslinguistic perspective.* University of Washington. (Doctoral dissertation).

McGinnis, Martha. 2001. Variation in the phase structure of applicatives. *Linguistic Variation Yearbook* 1(1). 105–146.

McIntyre, Andrew. 2006. The interpretation of German datives and English have. In Andre Meinunger Hole Daniel & Werner Abraham (eds.), *Datives and other cases*, 185–211. Amsterdam: Benjamins.

Miyagawa, Shigeru & Yeun-Jin Jung. 2004. *Decomposing ditransitive verbs*. Proceedings of the Seoul International Conference on Generative Grammar. 101-120.

Miyagawa, Shigeru & Takae Tsujioka. 2004. Argument structure and ditransitive verbs in Japanese. *Journal of East Asian Linguistics* 13. 1–38.

Morant, Marc. 2008. *L'alternança datiu/acusatiu en la recció verbal catalana*. València: Universitat de València. (Doctoral dissertation).

Oehrle, Richard. 1976. *The grammatical status of the English dative alternation*. Cambridge, MA: Massachusetts Institute of Technology. (Doctoral dissertation).

Ormazabal, Javier & Juan Romero. 2013. Differential object marking, case and agreement. *Borealis: An International Journal of Hispanic Linguistics* 2(2). 221–239.

Parodi, Teresa. 1998. Aspects of clitic doubling and clitic clusters in Spanish. In Albert Ortmann Ray Fabri & Teresa Parodi (eds.), *Models of inflection*, 85–102. Tübingen: Niemeyer.

Pesetsky, David. 1995. *Zero syntax: Experiencers and cascades*. Cambridge, MA: MIT Press.

Pineda, Anna. 2013. Double object constructions and dative/accusative alternations in Spanish and Catalan: A unified account. *Borealis: An International Journal of Hispanic Linguistics* 2. 57–115.

Pineda, Anna. 2016. *Les fronteres de la (in)transitivitat: Estudi dels aplicatius en llengües romàniques i basc*. Barcelona: Institut d'Estudis Món Juïc. Published and revised version of the doctoral dissertation.

Pineda, Anna. 2020a. Double object constructions in Romance: The common denominator. *Syntax*.

Pineda, Anna. 2020b. From dative to accusative: An ongoing syntactic change in Romance. *Probus: International Journal of Romance Linguistics* 32(1). 129–173.

Pineda, Anna & Carles Royo. 2017. Differential Indirect Object Marking in Romance (and how to get rid of it). *Revue Roumaine de Linguistique* 4. 445–462.

Pujalte, Mercedes. 2009. *Condiciones sobre la introducción de argumentos: El caso de la alternancia dativa en español*. Universidad Nacional del Comahue. (Master's thesis).

Pylkkänen, Liina. 2002. *Introducing arguments*. Massachusetts Institute of Technology. (Doctoral dissertation).

Pylkkänen, Liina. 2008. *Introducing arguments* (Linguistic Inquiry Monographs 49). Cambridge, MA: MIT Press.

Ramos, Joan Rafael. 2005. El complement indirecte; L'alternança datiu/acusatiu. *Estudis romànics* 27. 93–112.

Romero, Juan. 1997. *Construcciones de doble objeto y gramática universal.* Madrid: Universidad Autónoma de Madrid. (Doctoral dissertation).

Royo, Carles. 2017. *Alternança acusatiu/datiu i flexibilitat semàntica i sintàctica dels verbs psicològics catalans.* Barcelona: Universitat de Barcelona. (Doctoral dissertation). https://www.tdx.cat/handle/10803/523541.

Sáez, Luis. 2009. Applicative phrases hosting accusative clitics. In Héctor Campos Ronald P. Leow & Donna Lardiere (eds.), *In little words: Their history, phonology, syntax, semantics, pragmatics, and acquisition,* 61–73. Washington: Georgetown University Press.

Senn, Cristina Rita. 2008. *Reasuntivos y doblado del clítico: En torno a la caracterización del término "casi - nativo".* Ottawa: University of Ottawa. (Doctoral dissertation).

Svenonius, Peter. 2002. Icelandic case and the structure of events. *The Journal of Comparative Germanic Linguistics* 5. 197–225. DOI:10.1023/A:1021252206904

Svenonius, Peter. 2003. Limits on P: Filling in holes vs. Falling in holes. *Nordlyd* 31(2). 431–445. DOI:10.7557/12.13

Svenonius, Peter. 2004. Adpositions, particles and the arguments they introduce. In Eric Reuland, Tammoy Bhattacharya & Giorgos Spathas (eds.), *Argument structure,* 63–103. Philadelphia, PA: John Benjamins.

Torres Morais, Maria Aparecida & Heloísa Salles. 2010. Parametric change in the grammatical encoding of indirect objects in Brazilian Portuguese. *Probus* 22(2). 181–209.

Troberg, Michelle Ann. 2008. *Dynamic two-place indirect verbs in French: A synchronic and diachronic study in variation and change of valence.* Toronto: University of Toronto. (Doctoral dissertation).

von Heusinger, Klaus & Alina Tigău. 2020. Dative clitics in Romanian ditransitives. In Adina Dragomirescu, Alexandru Nicolae, Adnana Boioc & Stefania Costea (eds.), *Selected papers from Going Romance 31, Bucharest.* Amsterdam: John Benjamins.

Wood, Jim. 2012. *Icelandic morphosyntax and argument structure.* New York, NY: New York University. (Doctoral dissertation).

Wood, Jim & Alec Marantz. 2017. The interpretation of external arguments. In Roberta D'Alessandro, Irene Franco & Ángel J. Gallego (eds.), *The verbal domain,* 255–278. Oxford: Oxford University Press. DOI:10.1093/oso/9780198767886.001.0001

Chapter 1

Datives as applicatives

María Cristina Cuervo

University of Toronto

This work investigates dative arguments within a theory of applicative arguments. The focus is on what dative arguments have in common as a class — well beyond the most typical datives in ditransitive constructions — and as subcases of applied arguments, as found in both languages with a rich case system, and languages without overt case marking.

A typology of applicative constructions that directly associates with dative arguments is developed. The various subtypes of applicatives are derived from a restricted set of structural properties and syntactic-semantic features (the type of complement of the Appl head, the dynamic/stative nature of its complement, and the presence/absence of an external argument, and of a verbal head above the applicative).

The various interpretations of applied arguments (e.g., possessors, bene/malefactives, recipients, experiencers, affected, causees) are configurationally derived, and do not require encoding as part of the denotation of the applicative head beyond the traditional, minimal notion of Appl as introducing an argument "oriented" towards its complement. This richness of interpretations sets applied arguments apart from the narrow range of interpretations for arguments of v/Voice, on the one hand, and the practically unconstrained interpretations of arguments of lexical verbs/roots, on the other.

1 Datives and applicatives

1.1 Introduction

Dative arguments appear in many languages as the third morphological case, after nominative and accusative, or ergative and absolutive. Although the most common role of datives seems to be that of indirect object with transitive verbs

María Cristina Cuervo. 2020. Datives as applicatives. In Anna Pineda & Jaume Mateu (eds.), *Dative constructions in Romance and beyond*, 1–39. Berlin: Language Science Press. DOI:10.5281/zenodo.3776531

— typically as recipients — arguments in dative case can combine with all classes of predicates, and can express sources, experiencers, possessors, benefactives, malefactives, causees, locations, affectees, non-volitional agents or dispositionals. Both inter- and intra-linguistically a dative argument can alternate with accusative, genitive, and nominative DPs, or with prepositional phrases.

It is possible to consider that such variety of meanings and constructions prevents us from finding a common core, and that dative case can be unpredictable, or a default case. There has been, however, a lot of work seeking unification either at the semantic or the syntactic levels. Sometimes the unification has proposed that all true datives are extensions of prototypical indirect objects in ditransitive constructions.

In this work I present an approach to the investigation of dative arguments within a theory of applicative arguments. In order to develop this approach, I start with the hypothesis that dative arguments are applicative arguments, and focus on the syntactic context into which an applicative head is merged, with particular attention to certain properties of the complement and the head that selects the applicative phrase. This is done for two reasons:

- the belief that both the complement structure and the structure immediately above the applicative are relevant for a typology of applicative constructions that accounts for their syntax and provides a base on which to develop a systematic account of their crosslinguistic distribution;

- the belief that dative/applicative arguments — like subjects and unlike direct objects — have structural meanings; that is, that their interpretation is predictable (beyond certain idiosyncrasies related to the meaning of verbal roots) on the basis of their structural position and properties of the licensing head.

By studying dative structures as applicatives — that is, employing the theoretical, empirical and methodological tools employed for the study of applicative constructions — it is possible to explore generalizations and theoretical proposals that can abstract away from case marking, word order and other language-particular morphosyntactic properties.

Another crucial issue that applicatives bring to the forefront is the head that licenses a dative argument, questioning the assumption that datives, as internal arguments, are licensed by the verb. In a language like Spanish, for instance, in which a dative argument can appear with practically any kind of verbal predicate (Cuervo 2003, see §3 below), an approach to licensing of datives on the basis of lexical properties of verbs is not tenable. The study of datives as applicatives provides a framework which can potentially capture all datives as a class, beyond their shared morphology, in terms of the type of licensing, while allowing for restricted variation in terms of structural position and thematic interpretation.

What emerges, then, is a broader approach to the study of dative constructions which, while it takes case seriously and ponders what all dative arguments have in common (beyond the most typical datives in ditransitive constructions), also disregards case and considers what subsets of dative arguments have in common with arguably similar constructions marked by various cases (Finnish) or not marked by case at all (Bantu). Studying datives as applicatives places the investigation in the context of an articulated theory of argument licensing heads, which is an independently needed component in a general theory of syntax.

I discuss below various parallels between applicatives and datives, and, in §2, potential counterarguments to analyzing datives as applicatives. A typology of applicative constructions that directly associates with dative arguments in many languages is developed in §3. In §4 I illustrate how the various subtypes of applicatives (and datives) are derived from a restricted set of structural properties and from syntactic-semantic features of the applicative head. The various interpretations of applied arguments are configurationally derived, and do not require encoding as part of the denotation of the applicative head. Dative experiencers, in §4.4, are presented in a case study on the domains which contribute to the morphosyntactic properties and interpretation of these dative-applicatives. Conclusions are presented in §5.

1.2 Datives as applicatives

Although not all applicatives are datives and not all datives are applicatives, both involve the notion of an argument distinct from canonical or 'core' arguments (i.e., subjects and objects), which nevertheless exhibit characteristics of "regular" arguments.[1] Intra- and inter-linguistically, both applicatives and datives are characterized by morphosyntactic properties that span various constructions and interpretations.

When we ask the central question of what type of argument dative arguments are, we note that they can be similar to objects in properties of word order, case,

---

[1] As a reviewer points out, applied arguments are characterized as "non-core" arguments as opposed to canonical subjects and objects. Later, I will discuss the distinction of core/non-core as a distinction between selected arguments (core) and extra, non-selected arguments (non-core), assumed in other work.

and cliticization. They also can be similar to subjects in their interpretation being quite regular and structurally determined, mostly falling within the realm of possession, location/direction and affectedness.[2]

In their syntactic behaviour and their syntactic interpretation, dative arguments display strong parallels with applicatives, which are argued to be licensed as specifiers of a specialized functional head, like subjects, but usually pattern with objects in case licensing, object agreement, and movement in passive.

Datives also seem to occupy a category between direct objects and arguments of adpositions. That is exactly what applicatives seem to be as well (at least morphologically): the (direct) objects of a derived verb, or of a predicate which includes an incorporated adposition.

Another property common to datives and applicatives is their ability to participate in varied argument structures under the same guise, and to receive a wide range of thematic interpretations. As such, the challenge of providing a unified account of datives and applicatives includes developing an analysis rich enough to account for this latitude, while constrained enough to derive their particular interpretations in particular constructions, as well as the attested cross-linguistic variation.

Much of the work on applicatives in the last thirty years has involved teasing apart different types of applicatives and deriving their interpretations; distinguishing applied objects from prepositional objects (as in studies of the dative alternation); establishing how observed syntactic behaviour (such as word order, movement, scope, etc.) derives from structural properties or, alternatively, from language-particular morphosyntactic coding; determining the source of the applied argument (e.g. is it an independent, specialized head, the result of preposition incorporation, a general transformational rule?). This type of work has also been done for dative arguments both within and outside an applicative framework.

Although there is no general agreement about their defining properties, applicatives have been identified across languages in spite of differences of approach and theoretical persuasion, differences in word order, in morphological marking on the head and the applied DP, in possible interpretations, and in availability with different types of verbs or constructions. In the spirit of Svenonius's

---

[2]I am being very general here. This is not a comprehensive list (the notions of accidental and non-volitional causers and doers, and causees are relevant for many languages, such as Russian, Korean, Spanish, German, Pashto, etc.) and relatively vague notions like these overlap and have various nuances. Issues of interpretations and how they can be derived are discussed in §3 and §4. See also Fábregas & Marín (2020 [this volume]), Franco & Lorusso (2020 [this volume]) , and Tsedryk (2020 [this volume]) for (partial) unification of the semantics of dative arguments.

(2007) work on adpositions, this suggests that applicatives must be a good way for language to do something (e.g., licensing an argument), and a good way of doing something differently (e.g., differently from subject licensors Voice/v, from object licensors Verb/root, and adpositions).

Although crosslinguistic variation in dative arguments might appear less dramatic than variation in applicatives, the general differences in word order, morphological marking on the verb and the argument, and availability and interpretation also apply to datives. It makes sense to ask of datives, as of applicatives, how much of the syntactic and semantic behaviour depends on properties of the licensing head, of the structural environment, of the argument itself, and how much is left to be determined by lexical, idiosyncratic properties of the verb, and knowledge of the world (for approaches quite different from, but still relevant to, those discussed here, see Grimm 2011; Maling 2001). §3 is an attempt to address this central question.

In preparation to addressing this question for datives as applicatives, I discuss some of the arguments that have been presented against taking such an approach.

2 Difficulties in equating datives and applicatives

The need for a theory of dative arguments that accounts for their licensing and interpretation in other than canonical ditransitive constructions is uncontroversial. What remains debatable (and this volume provides good examples of how this issue is alive) is whether such a theory should also account for so-called *canonical ditransitive* constructions.

A central issue in this debate is the contrast between core and non-core arguments, or arguments of the verb versus arguments of a functional head. If such a distinction is made between core and non-core datives, then, in principle, only non-core datives would be applicatives, since all applicatives are, under this definition, non-core.

Another argument for rejecting an applicative analysis of (some) datives is based on a comparison of dative arguments, either intra- or crosslinguistically. The idea is that if a certain type of dative argument differs in syntactic or semantic behaviour from another type of dative which is analyzed as an applicative, then some authors conclude that the contrasting dative cannot be an applicative as well. This is, schematically, the view in Boneh & Nash (2012) for French datives, in Tubino (2012) for Spanish dative causees, Folli & Harley (2006) for Italian benefactives and goals, and Cépeda & Cyrino (2020 [this volume]) for Portuguese datives.

Another counterargument to treating datives as applicatives arises when certain coding aspects of applicative constructions are taken as definitional, such as morphological exponence of argument and head. Snyder (1995) for instance, contrasts double-object constructions — as in English — with dative constructions — as in Spanish — taking them to be different structures. Within Romance, whether the dative *a, pe* or *à* heads a prepositional phrase or signals a dative DP has also been part of the 'datives as applicatives' debates (Sheehan 2020 [this volume]; see Calindro 2020 [this volume] for an analysis of diachronic change of ditransitives in Brazilian Portuguese). For Polinsky (2013), overt morphological marking on the predicate is a crucial property of applicatives, which leads to negating applicative status to most dative constructions. As I have noted in previous work (Cuervo 2015b: 131), the identification of applicatives with a particular morphosyntactic coding, rather than with formal semantic or structural properties, has resulted in common but questionable claims that languages like English, German, Russian, Finnish, Japanese, Basque, Guaraní, Spanish, and Kiowa lack applicative constructions.

Dative arguments fail some diagnostics for applicatives based on certain syntactic asymmetries, and on alternation with prepositional constructions, as discussed in §2.3. Finally, the interpretation of certain datives has also been suggested as a reason not to consider them applicatives, as in the case of agentive causees (Tubino 2012) and experiencers. These semantic, morphological and syntactic difficulties are discussed in turn below.

2.1 Core vs. non-core arguments

One difficulty in identifying dative arguments with applicatives has been the argued contrast among dative arguments between those that appear to be required arguments of the verb, and those that are not. Within Romance, for example, Pujalte (2009) distinguishes between datives with lexically ditransitive verbs such as Spanish *dar* 'give' and *enviar* 'send' from monotransitives such as *comprar* 'buy'; Boneh & Nash (2012) contrast French *à*-datives in canonically ditransitive 'motion' verbs such as *envoyer* 'send' and *dire* 'say' with datives (clitics) associated with verbs such as *massacrer* 'destroy' or *vider* 'empty'. In these two works, the notion of 'core dative' comprises both a notion of 'thematic argument of the verb' and of an 'obligatory' argument DP.

This distinction, however, is problematic. On the one hand, the notion of thematic argument of the verb is vague at best if it is not tightly related to the requirement for the argument to be overtly expressed or some other exclusively syntactic behaviour.[3] With the exception of the verb *give*, which is practically a light verb, and some verbs of direct, physical transfer such as English *hand*, dative recipients can be omitted as easily with canonical ditransitives (1) as with monotransitives (2).

(1) a. Los empleados (le)   enviaron la carta (a la directora).
         the employees 3SG.DAT= sent   the letter DAT the director
         'The employees sent (the director) the letter.'

     b. Il a   dit la vérité (à Jean).
         he has said the truth DAT Jean
         'He told the truth (to Jean).' (Boneh & Nash 2012)

(2) a. Los empleados (le)   compraron un reloj (a la directora).
         the employees 3SG.DAT= bought   a watch DAT the director
         'The employees bought (the director) a watch.'

     b. Il a   acheté des   bonbons (à Jean).
         he has bought INDF.PL candy   (DAT Jean)
         'He bought (Jean) some sweets.'

Although the distinction between lexically ditransitive verbs and monotransitives might be syntactically relevant at some level, that does not mean that when a dative argument appears with a monotransitive the resulting construction must be different from that of a ditransitive like *enviar* 'send' or *poner* 'put'. This is standardly assumed for English: the structure attributed to double-objects related to so-called lexically ditransitive verbs (which take *to*-DPs in their PP variant, such as *send*) is also attributed to double-objects with monotransitives whose PP variant take *for*-DPs (such as *buy*).

There is an additional confusion intertwined in work that argues for an applicative analysis only of non-core datives. It is sometimes the case that differences in morphosyntactic properties have been observed between core and non-core datives. Noted differences concern the case of the applied argument, the exponence of the applicative head (null, or optionally or obligatorily overt), the (im)possibility of the dative to be expressed as a full DP in argument position,and so on. These differences, however, can be the result of there being different subtypes of applicatives within the same language rather than entailing that one

---

[3]See Fernández Alcalde (2014) for further arguments against Pujalte's (2009) distinction between core and non-core datives.

argument is licensed by an applicative head, but the other is not (see Boneh & Nash 2012; Cuervo 2003; 2015a; Diaconescu 2004; Pineda 2016; 2020; Roberge & Troberg 2009, for intra-linguistic morphosyntactic differences among dative/applied arguments).

The other class of dative arguments claimed to be selected, core arguments of the verb, are datives experiencers found with the *piacere*-class, famously analyzed as unaccusative double-object constructions by Belletti & Rizzi 1988.[4] The 'core argument' label makes sense within an analysis like that of Belletti & Rizzi, who propose the two arguments of *piacere*-type verbs are internal arguments of the verb on a par with the internal arguments of canonical ditransitive constructions (double-object constructions). But the parallel between ditransitive constructions and dative experiencer constructions gets blurry when we go beyond the verb *piacere/gustar* 'like' itself and consider psych expressions (e.g. Spanish *dar miedo* 'give fear') and non-psych expressions (e.g. Spanish *quedar bien/mal con* 'go well/badly with'), which cannot be easily analyzed as unaccusative dative experiencer–nominative theme (see Cuervo 2011). The 'core' analysis of these dative experiencers also faces difficulty when predicates beyond *gustar* are considered: *interesar* 'interest', *molestar* 'bother' and *importar* 'matter' can all easily appear without a dative argument, in which case they merely ascribe a property to an entity, without restricting the ascription to a certain individual. The existence of adjectives with the same roots (*interesante* 'interesting', *molesto* 'bothersome', *importante* 'important') similarly suggests that the lexical content of the root does not require licensing of an experiencer argument (see §4.4 for further discussion and an applicative analysis of these constructions).

2.2 Coding properties

Another difficulty in identifying datives as applicatives has been the belief that because applicatives — even low applicatives in double object constructions — are hierarchically higher than the direct object, only languages in which the dative appears linearly before the direct object are languages with applicatives. Numerous studies, however, have shown that the relative word order between a theme and an applicative, or a dative and an accusative DP, is not always a reliable indication of underlying hierarchical asymmetries (Antonyuk 2020 [this volume];

---

[4]This class of psychological predicates corresponds to Belletti & Rizzi's Class III, which comprises verbs like Italian *piacere* and Spanish *gustar* which take a dative experiencer and a nominative theme. The dative argument typically appears preverbally, and the nominative DP after the verb.

Cornilescu 2020 [this volume]; Cuervo 2003; Demonte 1995; Miyagawa & Tsu-jioka 2004; and see McGinnis 2018 for data and discussion).

Morphological marking on the argument DP has also been thought to indicate whether it is an applicative. On the one hand, in the tradition of Bantu studies, applicatives have no case marking. On the other hand, applicatives and double-object constructions have been proposed for languages in which two internal arguments appear with the same case (typically accusative), as argued for English and Korean. There also exist (unambiguously) high applicative constructions (that is, an argument applied to a vP, and therefore not double-objects in Pylkkänen's (2008) sense) in which both the applied and the direct object or causee have accusative case, as argued for Hiaki by Harley (2013). An additional issue concerns the morphological shape of dative case and, potentially, the syntactic category of the dative (DP or PP), particularly in languages in which arguably dative marking is syncretic with an existing adposition, as in the case of Japanese *ni*, Hindi *ko* and Spanish, Catalan, Italian and French *a/à*.

This would seem to leave dative arguments (as well as arguments in other cases, such as allative, adhesive, etc.) as poor candidates for an applicative analysis. Morphological case, however, as arguably a post-syntactic phenomenon, can sometimes obscure underlying syntactic relations, such as hierarchical relations and licensing (McGinnis 2018). Additionally, while languages can vary dramatically in their case systems, variation in argument structure is tightly constrained (Marantz 2013; Wood & Marantz 2017, among others). Finally, dative arguments have been shown to behave as DPs rather than PPs, with dative markers such as Romance *a/à* more akin to a case marker or differential object marker than an adposition (see Calindro 2020 [this volume]; Pineda 2016; 2020; Sheehan 2020 [this volume]).

With respect to morphological marking on the applicative head, for many authors, special marking on the verb is expected; as stated by Polinsky (2013): "It is customary to restrict the designation *applicative* to those cases where the addition of an object is overtly marked on the predicate." This association dates back to Carochi's (1645) original description of Nahuatl "applicative verbs" as "derived verbs", and has been central in Bantu studies. The form of the applicative head, however, is not a definitional property. Applicatives can have more than one form, even in the same language, as is the case of Inuktitut, in which an applicative head can be a verbal affix or be null.[5] Applicative heads can be spelled out by morphology with person features, such as datives clitics in Romance, and verbal

---

[5]The variation between and overt and a null head can also be seen in French, and Catalan and certain varieties of Spanish, as argued by Fournier (2010); Pineda (2016; 2020) respectively.

affixes in P'urhépecha (Moreno Villamar 2018). They have been claimed to take the form of a *dative flag* in Basque (an affix preceding a dative agreement affix on the verb, which signals the presence of a dative argument; see Etxepare & Oyharçabal 2013 and cites within), or cliticized directional pronouns, such as *raa* 'to me/us' in Pashto (Babrakzai 1999).

This brief discussion of morphological properties of applicative constructions across languages shows that there is a continuum of marking from head to the argument: from one extreme being a bound morpheme on the verb (Bantu) to a bound case morpheme on the applied argument (Finnish, Latin) on the other.[6] In the middle, and sometimes in combination, marking can be a verbal clitic (Spanish, Pashto), an adposition, or a case marker.

2.3 Syntactic properties

Some syntactic behaviour associated with certain applicative constructions is usually not found in dative constructions. This is particularly the case for datives in ditransitive constructions.

Low Applicatives in ditransitive constructions have been shown to be asymmetric applicatives: of the two internal arguments, only the applied argument shows a full range of object properties (Pylkkänen 2000: 203).[7] For instance, a low applicative DP is expected to raise in passive, be extracted, require adjacency to the verb, trigger object agreement, and receive the same case as would a direct object of a monotransitive. However, this is not the behaviour of dative arguments in Romance, which typically do not become subjects nor get nominative case in passives, as direct objects do in both transitive and ditransitive constructions. This lack of direct object behaviour, however, can be attributed to particular properties of dative case in particular languages — such as dative being inherent case — which, in turn, interact with passives and movement.

In the case of high applicatives with transitive predicates (symmetric applicatives), object properties are expected to be exhibited by both the internal argument and the applied argument. Again, this is not the case in Romance, but the

---

[6]Roberge & Troberg (2009: 286) expect complementarity between marking on the head or the argument: "We assume that the productive morphological case-marking that existed in Latin made it possible for the [Appl] head to be devoid of overt morphological content."

[7]The association of low applicatives with asymmetric applicatives and high applicatives with symmetric ones — although it has been shown not to hold of several languages in which direct objects retained their object properties in applicative constructions — continues to be used as an argument against applicative analyses of (at least) Romance datives. See McGinnis (2004; 2008) for discussion.

same reservations with respect to this reasoning for low applicatives apply to high applicative constructions.

Dative arguments in Romance and many other languages do perform on a par with DPs standardly analyzed as applicatives on other syntactic properties more directly related to structural position, such as binding, scope, and agreement (Antonyuk 2020 [this volume]; Boneh & Nash 2017; Bruening 2010; Cuervo 2003; Demonte 1995; Pineda 2016; 2020, among others).

On the basis of the arguments for studying datives as applicatives presented in §1.2, and having shown that the arguments against doing this are not compelling, I continue in the next sections to show that the analysis of applicatives directly sheds light on the analysis of dative arguments.

3 Types of datives; types of applicatives

In many languages, dative arguments are compatible with various types of predicates, from ditransitive activity verbs to anticausative change-of-state verbs, and psychological stative predicates. In previous work, I have proposed a classification of predicates that is relevant for a typology of applicatives, which can equally be applied to the study of dative arguments (see Figure 1).

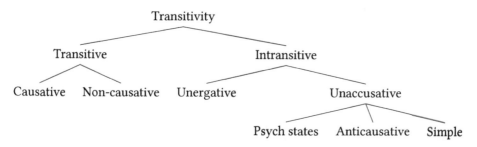

Figure 1: Subtypes of predicates as relevant for a typology of applicatives (Cuervo 2015b: 130)

The classification in Figure 1 predicts some of the contrasts among dative arguments in terms of subtypes of applicatives (such as affected datives with causative verbs versus recipient datives with non-causative transitives). The way the predicates are subdivided, however, does not directly parallel the typology proposed by Pylkkänen (2002; 2008)[8] and later enriched by Boneh & Nash 2011;

---

[8]From this point on, I cite Pylkkänen 2008, but most issues discussed appeared first in Pylkkänen 2002.

Cuervo 2003; 2010; Kim 2011; McGinnis 2001; 2008; McGinnis & Gerdts 2004; Roberge & Troberg 2009, among others. Additionally, the classification based on predicate type does not capture certain proposed implications or correlations among subtypes of applicatives. For instance, if a language allows dative/applicative possessors or recipients with unaccusatives, it also does with transitives, but the reverse does not necessarily hold, as in English. The classification cannot express the intra-linguistic correlation between having (or not having) datives with "lexically" causative verbs (v.g., *break, melt*), and (not) allowing for datives with anticausatives (see Peterson 2007; Cuervo 2015b for discussion).

What is needed is a classification based on structural properties directly relevant for the subtypes of applicatives described in the literature, with the potential to systematically derive the interpretation of the various applicatives/datives, and the "natural classes" of crosslinguistic variation in the availability of applicatives.

In Pylkkänen's work, the crucial distinction in height is actually a distinction between the category or type of the complement of the applicative head.[9] To the basic distinction between applicatives taking nominal complements or entities (LowAppl) and applicatives taking verbal complements or events (HighAppl), further distinctions have been developed, particularly among the verbal complements.

Kim (2011) proposed that in addition to the applicatives which take verbal complements to the exclusion of the subject (vP), there are those which take a larger verbal projection including the subject (VoiceP). This is the case of Peripheral Applicatives which introduce a nominative affectee in Korean and Japanese passives.[10] Tsai (2018) proposes an even higher applicative for Mandarin, which licenses an argument above the inflectional domain and is "involved in the arrangement of the information structure" (Tsai 2018: 18).

Cuervo (2003; 2011; 2015b) proposed that applicative heads taking verbal complements are sensitive to the eventive (dynamic) or stative nature of the vP. Bene-

---

[9]This distinction could be reinterpreted in other terms. For example, McGinnis distinguisges symmetrical and asymmetrical applicatives in terms of phases. See also Boneh & Nash (2017) for a scalar approach to high and low datives in Russian.

[10]In Korean passives, a nominative affectee is the only argument that can trigger honorific agreement with the verb. In the example below, Kim (2012) analyzes *apeci-ka* 'father' as a Peripheral Applicative: a high applicative merged above VoiceP.

(i) apeci₁-ka   Minswu₂-eykey pal-ul   palp-hi-si₁/*₂-ess-t
    father-NOM Minsu-DAT   foot-ACC step-PASS-HON-PST-DECL

'Father₁ was adversely affected by Minsu's stepping on his₁ foot.' (Kim 2012)

factives are prototypical cases of high applicatives taking a dynamic *v*P as complement; experiencers are prototypical cases of high applicatives taking (psychological) stative *v*Ps.

Further, in previous work I have argued that the interpretation of applied arguments not only depends on the (type of) complement of the applicative head and properties of the head, but is also affected by the structure *above* the Appl head.[11] Specifically, I have argued that the interpretation of a high applicative is affected by the structure above the applicative phrase, in particular by whether there is another *v*P above it, embedding or selecting the ApplP, as in the case of Affected Applicatives with (bi-eventive) causatives and anticausatives/inchoatives. For example, Affected Applicatives (3) and Experiencers (4) are both high applicatives which take a stative *v*P as complement; the predictable contrast in interpretation arises from the Experiencers being non-embedded high applicatives (4c) and the Affected Appl being embedded under a dynamic *v*P (agentive v_{DO} in causatives or non-agentive v_{GO} in inchoatives), as in (3c).

(3) Affected datives

    a. With causatives: French
        Le teinturier lui   a   massacré une chemise.
        the dry.cleaner 3SG.DAT= has destroyed a   shirt
        'The dry-cleaner ruined her/his shirt (on her/him).' (Boneh & Nash 2012)

    b. With anticausatives: Spanish
        A   Carolina se   le   rompió la   radio.
        DAT Carolina REFL 3SG.DAT= broke   the radio
        'The radio broke on Carolina.'

---

[11]A reviewer wonders whether this interpretation is countercyclic, and should be restricted to occur within a phase. Indeed, the relevant interpretation discussed here is thematic interpretation at the level of argument structure, which is arguably restricted to the domain limited by VoiceP at the edge. The view that structure above a head is relevant for interpretation, although initially surprising, is compatible with Wood & Marantz's (2017) unification of argument-introducing heads into one, whose distinct interpretations arise as cases of contextual allosemy, that is, configurational meanings within the extended projection of the verb. See below for discussion.

c. Structure of Affected Appl in causatives (Cuervo 2003: 113)

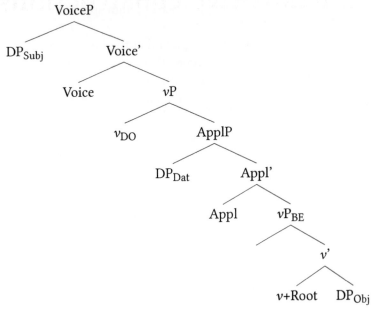

(4) Dative experiencers

    a. A   Rosa le   molesta el humo.
       DAT Rosa 3SG.DAT= bother   the smoke
       'Smoke bothers Rosa.' (Acedo-Matellán & Mateu 2015: 90)

    b. A   Emilio le   parecen difíciles esas decisiones.
       DAT Emilio 3SG.DAT= seem   difficult those decisions
       'Emilio finds those decisions difficult.'

    c. Structure of dative experiencers

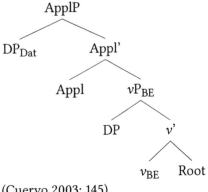

(Cuervo 2003: 145)

This way, Affected Applicatives are distinguished from LowAppl by the structure *below* them: they appear above the root, and take a verbal complement. In turn, they are distinguished from Experiencers by the structure *above* them within the extended verbal projection.

The structure above the applicative is also responsible for the contrast between "instrumentals" and "causees", two types of arguments analyzed as high applicatives taking a dynamic vP as complement. "Causee" is the interpretation assigned to an instrumental high applicative embedded under a dynamic vP (v_{cause} or v_{do}).[12] Unlike an instrumental applicative — embedded directly under Voice which is related to the same event as the agent — a causee is the only external argument related to the embedded event. Although putting together these two types of arguments might initially seem questionable, Jerro observes that "several genetically unrelated and geographically non-contiguous languages have morphological forms that subsume both causative and applicative uses" (Jerro 2017: 752), and proposes for Kinyarwanda a common origin for both types of arguments. Kim (2011) proposes an explanation for the causee-instrumental syncretism in Korean and Niuean arguing that "in morphological causatives, a causer uses a causee as an instrument to make a relevant event take place" (2011: 499). According to Kim, the Niuean instrumental applicative morpheme *aki* introduces the causee under causative *faka-*. She further observes that in Middle Korean morphological causatives, a causee was marked with the instrumental *–(u)lo*, as illustrated in (5), and that an "animate dative DP in morphological causatives and adversity clauses can also be interpreted as an instrument" (Kim 2011: 499).

(5) ai-lo   hwenhi tung-ul   kulk-hi-ko.
     child-ACTIVE.INS cool   back-ACC scratch-i-and

'[I] had$_{caus}$ my child scratch my back cool [i.e. relieving the itch].' (Park 1994, in Kim 2011: 499)

With respect to low applicatives, merged under the verbal root, the distinction between dynamic and stative applicatives also seems to play a role. Pylkkänen defined two sub-types of low applicatives, Low Appl$_{TO}$ and Appl$_{FROM}$, based on languages whose double-object constructions require a transfer-of-possession predicate, such as English and, arguably, Hebrew.[13] These constructions are dou-

---

[12] Some dative causees have been argued to be volitional agents, compatible with agent-oriented adverbials, as in the case of Spanish *hacer*-infinitive constructions (parallel to the French *faire-infinitif*. In this case, there is no agreement whether these should be considered applicatives (as in Torrego 2011) or not (Kim 2011; Tubino 2012). See §4.3 for further discussion.

[13] The verb itself can denote a transfer or it can be a creation verb which is interpreted as a

bly dynamic, in the sense that both the transfer predicate (arguably requiring a PATH structure) and the applicative head encode dynamic relations.

Besides those merged under dynamic verbs of transfer of possession, in some languages a low applicative can also appear under transitive or unaccusative verbs that do not denote *transfer* of possession (either dynamic or stative verbs). This is Cuervo's (2003) LowAppl$_{AT}$, which expresses a non-dynamic possession relation. LowAppl$_{AT}$ can take a DP, a PP or a small clause-type of structure as complement, the applied argument being interpreted as different sub-types of possessors: possessor (6), locative (7), or experiencer (8).

(6) a. DP complement: possessor dative (transitive; French)
    Michel lui   a   lavé   les   cheveux.
    Michel 3SG.DAT= has washed the hairs
    'Michel washed his hair.'

    b. DP complement: possessor dative (unaccusative; Spanish)
    A   la   casa   le   faltan   ventanas.
    DAT the house 3SG.DAT= miss.PL windows
    'The house lacks (some) windows.'

(7) a. DP-PP complement: locative-possessor dative (Spanish).
    Gabi le   puso el   bebé en los brazos a   Emilio.
    Gabi 3SG.DAT= put   the baby in the arms   DAT Emilio
    'Gabi placed the baby in Emilio's arms.'

    b. PP complement: locative-possessor dative (transitive; French)
    Elle lui   a   tiré dans le   ventre.
    she 3SG.DAT= has shot in   the belly
    'She shot her/him in the belly.' (Boneh & Nash 2012)

(8) a. SC complement: experiencer/locative-possessor dative (Spanish)
    Emilio le   puso la   mano encima[14] a   Lucila.
    Emilio 3SG.DAT= put   the hand on.top   DAT Lucila.DAT
    'Emilio laid a hand on Lucila.'

---

transfer event in combination with a LowAppl.

[14]Following Cuervo (2003), I assume here that the particle *encima* acts as the predicate in a small-clause-type of structure, which the applicative head takes as its complement. Unlike there, however, I take the datives in (8) to be low applicatives because they are merged as a complement of the verb. See Acedo-Matellán (2017) for an Affected Appl analysis of spatial datives in Latin.

b. DP complement: experiencer-possessor dative (Spanish)
   A   Emilio le   duele una muela.
   DAT Emilio 3SG.DAT= hurt   a   molar
   'Emilio's molar hurts.'

Sentences in (7) show that a dative argument can be the possessor of a body part or location expressed as the DP complement of a preposition. For (7a), a dative co-appearing with a direct object and a locative PP, one can wonder what the complement of the applicative head is, that is, whether the dative takes the [direct object + locative] or just the locative PP as its complement (as it arguably does in (7b)). While it is true that there is a possession relation between the dative and the locative that excludes the direct object (this is evident in the English translation), the entailment of the sentence is expressed as a possessive construction with the dative as external argument and the theme and locative as internal arguments of *tener* 'have' (e.g. *Emilio tiene el bebé en (los) brazos* 'Emilio has the baby on his arms'). This shows that the part-whole relation between *Emilio* and *the arms* does not require a syntactic relation between the two to the exclusion of the theme *the baby*.[15]

In the examples above, the dative argument is interpreted primarily as the possessor of a body part; in each case, however, there is an "extra" layer of meaning arising from the structure, the meaning of the verb and world knowledge: benefactive (6a), malefactive or affected (7b), locative (6b, 7a), experiencer in (8).

The interpretation that is secondary in the examples above (affected, experiencer) becomes primary — and the possession interpretation is not entailed, although it might arise as secondary — for other types of dative/applicatives. This is the case of dative experiencers, which are possessors of a mental state, as seen in (4), and Affected Applicatives in (3), which are affected by the change of state of an object (expressed as the direct object). In the case of Affected Applicatives, many times the dative argument is also understood as the possessor of that object, and what are termed Affected or Middle Applicatives are sometimes classified as possessors (e.g., Fernández Alcalde 2014; see Cuervo 2003 for arguments to distinguish possessors from affected datives both syntactically and semantically).

As a result of these three distinctions (category of complement, stativity/dynamicity of complement, and embedding structure), a more articulated typology

---

[15]If this were the case, one would expect the entailment to be a location of the theme, expressed as subject, with respect to the dative and PP as internal arguments: *El bebé está en los brazos de Emilio* 'The baby is on Emilio's arms'.

of applicatives can be constructed that accounts for subgroups of applicatives attested in particular languages, as well as the various interpretations that applicative arguments can have inter- and intra-linguistically. Ideally, the typology should also be a good base to account for the morphological form of the Appl head — in particular whether it is overt or null — as well as for the observed syncretisms between applicatives, causatives, adpositions and case markers.

Figure 2 presents a typology of applicatives organized on the basis of configurational properties. As the diagram represents an inventory of Appl heads, it is possible to associate each node in the tree with particular features on the Appl head, both substantive and selectional. Thus, the splits proposed should reflect intrinsic properties of the Appl head or properties of its complement, but should not reflect properties of the structure that appears above the ApplP (which 'selects' the ApplP), as discussed below. Additionally, in an ideal geometry, we would expect that node labels and splits will not repeat within the diagram, and that each division will delineate a particular subtype of Appl. The diagram fulfills this to an important extent, but fails in two places, as discussed below.

The classification in Figure 2 captures Pylkkänen's idea that there are two types of applicatives. The two types are distinguished mainly in terms of their height within the extended verbal projection, in reference to being above or below the verb (specifically the root). This distinction results in the first split between Appls taking a verbal complement, HighAppl, and a non-verbal complement (but not necessarily a DP), LowAppl.[16]

The contrast between dynamicity and stativity is further introduced as a distinction relevant for both applicatives taking verbal and non-verbal complements. Within (non-embedded) high applicatives, this split captures the contrast between BENEFACTIVES and INSTRUMENTALS — related to dynamic events — on one hand, and EXPERIENCERS — related to a state — on the other.[17]

The label EXPERIENCER covers the notion of possessors of (mental) states with psychological or non-psychological predicates (see §4.4 for data and discussion). Among applicatives embedded under a causative, CAUSEES correspond to those taking a dynamic event — analytical causatives in many languages — while AF-

---

[16] I remain agnostic with respect to the existence of applicatives that merge higher than *v*P (such as peripheral applicatives proposed by Kim 2011 and Tsai 2018), as opposed to applicatives found outside the extended verbal domain as a result of movement, and therefore they are not represented in this typology.

[17] As noted by a reviewer, Pylkkänen (2008) argued that benefactive high applicatives can combine with static verbs such as *hold*. This "static verb" is eventive and "dynamic" in the relevant sense, however, as suggested by the reviewer, at least in the context of a benefactive applicative. The notion of "static" is presented in Pylkkänen in opposition to dynamic verbs of transfer.

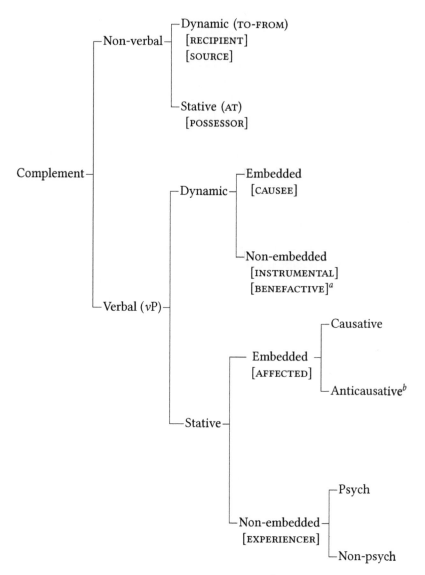

Figure 2: Subtypes of applicatives according to their position in the structure and properties of their complement

---

[a]The label BENEFACTIVE here represents datives with a benefactive, malefactive, or ethical interpretation, as well as "substitutive" applicatives (Peterson 2007).

[b]I assume here a bi-eventive analysis of anticausative constructions whereby a dynamic event — a vP_{GO} expressing the change — embeds a state — a vP_{BE} (see Cuervo 2003; 2015a). Thus, an AFFECTED applicative taking a stative vP as complement is embedded under the dynamic vP both in causative and anticausative constructions.

FECTED are those related to a change of state — lexical causatives in many languages, and anticausatives/ inchoatives.

In light of the fact that their complement is non-verbal, the contrast in dynamicity in LowAppl is encoded as a property of the sub-type of LowAppl head itself (TO and FROM are dynamic for RECIPIENTS and SOURCES, respectively; AT, for POSSESSORS is a stative relation). The contrast between dynamic and stative low applicatives cannot be obtained by simple reference to the embedding verb. Specifically, a stative Appl-AT is compatible with both dynamic, eventive verbs (as for Spanish *wash* and *sell*) and stative verbs (*admire, envy*).[18] In the case of LowAppl, what is either dynamic or stative is the (possessive) relationship between the applicative DP and the theme object DP.

Another distinction is introduced among verbal (high) applicatives: whether the applicative taking a vP as complement is itself embedded under another (dynamic) vP. As mentioned above, CAUSEES and AFFECTED applicatives appear between two vPs, in contrast to, for example, non-embedded BENEFACTIVES and INSTRUMENTALS, which appear between VoiceP and a dynamic vP.

The split between non-embedded Appls and Appls embedded under another vP refers to the structure immediately above the ApplP, that is, to the head the Appl is a complement of. It is unusual for a feature of the Appl head to allude to its selecting head or phrase, and this appears to be an imperfection of the typology.

Another instance of reference to the structure selecting for the Appl could be found in Appls that select a non-verbal complement, that is, LowAppls. The issue is that Appl exclusively appears as a complement of a verb: Appl needs a verbal environment either above or below it, as it is incompatible in the nominal domain. This means that even if we eliminate explicit reference to selecting structure for Appls taking a verbal complement, there will always be implicit reference to a verbal projection above the LowAppl. This property of the classification, rather than being a problem, expresses a central property of applicatives, as opposed to their close relatives, adpositions. In contrast with adpositions, which can typically appear as PP modifiers in the clausal, verbal and nominal domains, Appl is only licensed in a verbal environment. This could be expressed as a feature or variable that needs valuation by a v feature. This proposal accords with Svenonius's (2007) treatment of verbs containing an eventive variable e that is bound by Tense because Appl is like a more restricted Path PP which also "must be linked to verbal structure, hence ultimately bound by tense" (Svenonius 2007: 35).

---

[18]In contrast, a stative verb (e.g., *admirar* 'admire', *faltar* 'lack') is only compatible with a stative applicative (LowApplAT).

As noted earlier, reference to the structure above Appl seems difficult to reconcile with an attempt to capture the various subtypes of applicatives in terms of a geometry of features encoded by the Appl head. These distinctions are better captured by an approach whereby an Appl head is defined as an introducer of an event participant minimally specified as a possessor(-orientation), with its varying interpretations arising contextually. §4 develops this approach by deriving the "typology" in Figure 2 on the basis of configurational properties. Further specification, possibly of a lexical nature, is needed to capture contrasts among low applicatives, and between benefactives and instrumentals.

4 Deriving the sub-types

4.1 Below the verb: Low applicatives

This section briefly discusses the properties of low applicatives which take a non-verbal complement, typically a DP. Arguments of this type of Appl are interpreted as RECIPIENTS, POSSESSORS, SOURCES or LOCATIONS.

The contrast among sub-types of LowAppl has been accounted for in terms of sub-types of heads: TO and FROM for recipients and sources, respectively (Pylkkänen 2008) and AT for possessors (Cuervo 2003).[19] Although dynamicity (or directionality) is at the core of the three sub-types, this constrast cannot be simply derived from differences in the complement of the Appl head, or other configurational properties. As such, the distinction might require encoding as a feature on the applicative head (+/- dynamic, or [Path], for instance); alternatively, the distinction can be captured as a root element associated with the applicative head (as proposed by Wood & Marantz 2017 for high applicatives and Prepositions).[20] Individual languages could, in principle, choose freely among these heads, although TO is the most widespread and basic LowAppl (also the least morphologically marked, Cuervo 2015b).

Although in Pylkkänen (2002; 2008), LowAppl was defined as an applicative merged under a transitive verb expressing transfer of possession, I have shown in previous work that the same relation can take place under unaccusative verbs, as

---

[19]In some languages, including Spanish, locatives and other special arguments can also be expressed as LowAppls.

[20]A reviewer asks whether this difference in encoding is predicted to have empirical consequences. One consequence concerns whether variation in semantics is systematic or unconstrained, which is a central part of my future research. In addition to semantics, intra- and crosslinguistic variation in morphological overtness and shape of heads will be an important topic.

well attested in Spanish with both dynamic verbs (e.g., *crecer* 'grow', *caer* 'fall', *llegar* 'arrive', *doler* 'hurt'$_{\text{Intr}}$) and stative, existential verbs (e.g., *faltar* 'lack', *quedar* 'remain', *sobrar* 'be extra'), contra Baker (1996).

The defining feature of low applicatives is therefore their position as complements of the verb and their possession relation (with an entity or location), rather than the transfer meaning, or the transitivity of the verb. With respect to the category of their complement, LowAppls do not necessarily select a DP: all that is required is that they take a non-verbal complement. As such, cases in which an applicative takes a prepositional phrase or a small clause as complement, as illustrated in (7)–(8), would be cases of low applicatives (LowAppl$_{\text{AT}}$, specifically).

4.2 Benefactives, instrumentals and other dynamic high applicatives

This section discusses the properties of high applicatives which take a dynamic, eventive *v*P as complement, and appear under a Voice head. These high applied arguments are typically interpreted as benefactives, malefactives, or instrumentals.

Benefactives seem to be the most widespread type of high applicatives (Polinsky 2013): applicatives that license an argument related to a dynamic event in a non-actor role. Malefactives and so-called 'ethical datives' can be captured in the same way structurally. The different interpretations could be associated with different subtypes of applicative heads, or could be derived as a combination of a 'factive' meaning of the Appl head, lexical meaning of the verb, and world knowledge. This seems to be the case for 'ethical datives' in Romance (*dativus commodi/incommodi*, see Roberge & Troberg 2009 for discussion of terms for the various datives labelled 'ethical' or 'dative of interest'), in which arguments with the same morphosyntax can be alternatively understood as benefactives (9a) or malefactives (9b); examples from Roberge & Troberg 2009.

(9)   Bene/malefactive applicatives: *v*P$_{\text{DO}}$ complement

    a. Portuguese benefactive
       Elle ligou-lhes   amavelmente a   luz.
       he connected=3PL.DAT kindly   the light
       'He kindly switched on the light for them.'

    b. Italian malefactive
       Gli invitati gli   hanno mangiato tutto quello che   rimaneva
       the guests 3SG.DAT= have eaten   all   that   which remained

nel   frigo.
in.the fridge
'The guests ate everything that was left in the fridge on him.'

Instrumental applicatives have also been assigned the same structural properties, but are thematically related to the event in a more active initiator or actor-like role. If the same position is assigned to instrumental applicatives, then a featural analysis of argument introducing heads could distinguish them from (bene-/male)factives with a +actor/initiator specification. Interestingly, in Kinyarwanda, benefactives and instrumentals are introduced with the same applicative morphology, but contrast in terms of the relative word order between the applicative and the direct object (benefactives appear before, instrumentals after; McGinnis & Gerdts 2004).

Causees are also introduced by an Appl which takes a dynamic *v*P as complement. As we have seen, the contrast between instrumentals and causees reduces in this approach to a contrast between being embedded under another dynamic *v* (Causees) or not (Instrumentals, merged under Voice). Given the semantic and syntactic similarity, and the syncretisms between causatives and instrumentals discussed in §3 for Niuean, Korean and Kinyarwanda, this is a welcome result.[21]

This classification, which considers the structure below and above the Appl head, can also capture "accidental causers" in unaccusative change-of-state verbs (inchoatives), as well as non-volitional agents with activity verbs.

In the case of dative arguments with anticausative predicates, a dative argument is usually ambiguous between an affected reading and an unintentional or accidental causer reading. This is the case for Spanish and German, among other languages. Cuervo (2003; 2014) and Schäfer (2008) propose that the accidental causer reading is the interpretation of a high applicative which takes the bi-eventive inchoative structure as its complement (*v*GO-*v*BE), and which crucially does not merge under an agentive Voice head (example and structure from Cuervo 2003: 166–167).

(10)   a.   Dative with inchoative
          Al   tintorero   se   le   quemaron los pantalones de
          DAT.the dry.cleaner REFL 3SG.DAT= burnt.PL the trousers   of
          Carolina.
          Carolina
          'Carolina's trousers got burnt at the dry-cleaner's.' or
          'The dry-cleaner accidentally burnt Carolina's trousers'

---

[21]Syncretic forms between benefactives and causatives are found in Hualapai (Peterson 2007).

b. Structure of accidental causer high applicative

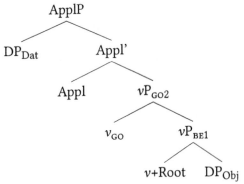

On the same basis, "non-volitional agents" expressed as dative arguments, as in Russian impersonal constructions, could be introduced by a high applicative which takes a dynamic vDO as complement, but no Voice head is projected above it.[22] Except for the structure above them, these arguments are like instrumentals: an entity or individual involved agentively in an event, but without volition (see Skorniakova 2009 for discussion).

(11) Boris-u   xorošo pe-l-o-s'   (# čtoby   zarabota-t' den'gi).
       Boris-DAT.M well   sing-PST-N-REFL   in.order make-INF   money
       'Boris (felt like) singing well in order to make money.' (adapted from Skorniakova 2009: 189)

4.3 Embedded high applicatives: affected applicatives and causees

This section briefly discusses the properties of two kinds of high applicatives embedded under a dynamic, eventive vP: those which take another eventive vP as complement (applied DP interpreted as Causee), and those which take a stative vP (their applied argument interpreted as Affected).

Affected Applicatives are defined as those which appear in change-of-state constructions, both transitive causatives and intransitive anticausative/inchoatives (Cuervo 2003; 2010; 2015a), as illustrated in (3), repeated as (12) below.

(12) a. Le teinturier lui   a   massacré une chemise.
         the dry.cleaner 3SG.DAT= has destroyed a   shirt
         'The dry-cleaner ruined her/his shirt (on her/him).' (Boneh & Nash 2012)

---

[22] Alternatively, a Voice head is projected but it is somehow defective and does not project an argument in its specifier (morphologically expressed as a reflexive).

b. A   Carolina se   le   rompió la   radio.
   DAT Carolina REFL 3SG.DAT= broke   the radio
   'The radio broke on Carolina.'

These applicatives take a state as complement and, in this sense, are the "possessors" of a state. In this they resemble experiencer applicatives, which also relate to a state, as expressed by Figure 2. As possessors or recipients, they can be confused with low applicatives, but two types of evidence suggest a structural as well as an interpretational difference. First, there are languages (e.g., English) in which double objects/low applicatives are productive, but are systematically disallowed in constructions involving an embedded state, such as causative constructions and resultatives (*The storm broke them the radio, *They drank me the teapot empty). Secondly, Affected applicatives do not need to be the possessors of the theme, although a possession relation might be an inferred component of the interpretation (see Cuervo 2003 for further arguments).

As argued in §3, it is the projection above the applicative that distinguishes affected from experiencer applicatives, in particular the fact that there is a dynamic event above Appl that signals the initiation of the state in causatives and inchoatives. An experiencer, by contrast, is the highest argument within the extended verbal projection, as represented in (4c) (see §4.4 for more detailed discussion).

Causees are also derived as a type of high applicative, which, like Affected Appl, is "sandwiched" between two verbal layers.[23] Unlike Affected Appl, Causees take a dynamic, eventive vP as complement. One of the arguments advanced against analysing causees as applicatives has been the interpretation of causees not only as the entity or individual acted upon (or "affected") but also as agentive. This is the semantic argument based on which Tubino (2012) rejects an applicative account of Italian and Spanish causees. In fact, Kim's (2012) conclusion is exactly that the difference in agentivity is what distinguishes high applicatives from arguments of Voice, the contrast being encoded as a feature +/- agentive in the licensing head. Boneh & Nash (2011) also propose that affectedness is the central meaning of applied arguments, while causees are licenced as regular agents, in the specifier of vP.

The framework presented here reconciles the affectedness and the agentivity components of the interpretation of causees. On the one hand, affectedness — a prominent interpretation of causees in the "obligation" reading of causatives

---

[23]In this sense, Causees are a sub-type of Affected Applicatives. However, I reserve the term Affected Appl for those taking a (verbal) state as complement, as a distinction that may be relevant to capture systematic crosslinguistic variation in the availability of applicative constructions.

(as in the Romance *faire-infinitif* constructions, Folli & Harley 2007) — could be derived as the meaning of the High Appl head directly. Alternatively, it can arise as the configurational meaning of an argument that participates in two events: the object of the higher verb *faire* and the 'instrument' or 'bene/malefactive' of the lower predicate, as in Ippolito's (2000) applicative analysis and in Affected Appls. On the other hand, the agentive or 'doer' interpretation of the relation between the dative causee and the lower event can be derived by the applicative being the highest argument within the extended verbal projection of the lower vP (as in accidental causers with unaccusatives, illustrated in (11) above).[24] In other words, agentivity might arise also as the interpretation of an animate argument DP above a dynamic vP for which Voice is not projected.[25] This is possible if the meaning of the applied argument is specified more configurationally than determined by the denotation of the head (see Cuervo 2015b, and Wood & Marantz 2017).

4.4 Dative experiencers as stative high applicatives

This section discusses several structural and semantic properties of dative experiencers as the last type of applicative in the typology schematized in Figure 2: unembedded high applicatives which take a stative vP as complement, and introduce the highest argument in the extended verbal projection (that is, Voice is not projected).

Dative experiencers have received much attention following Belletti & Rizzi's (1988) seminal work on Romance. An important puzzle they recognize is the apparent reversal of the usual thematic mapping: the theme is the nominative subject while the experiencer is coded as object, as illustrated below in Spanish and Pashto. Another important characteristic is the stative nature of dative experiencer constructions.[26]

---

[24] The Voice projection that licenses the causer relates it to a *different* vP, which merges above the applicative, and it is typically spelled out by a causative affix or light verb.

[25] Tollan & Oxford (2018) argue that external arguments of activity verbs can be licensed either as arguments of Voice (for transitives) or v(for unergatives). In a parallel fashion to dative causees receiving an interpretation associated with Voice, dative experiencers as the highest argument within the extended projection of a stative vP also receive an interpretation as the argument of stative Voice: that of holder of a state (Kratzer 1996). See §4.4 for further discussion of experiencer DPs as applied arguments.

[26] Their stative nature has been claimed to cover even cases of eventive interpretations, such as when the verb is in past tense (see Fábregas & Marín 2020 [this volume]), and of psychological expressions with light verbs of movement or transfer of possession (as illustrated in Pashto (14)).

(13) Spanish
      A   Daniela le   gustan las películas suecas.
      DAT Daniela 3SG.DAT= like.PL the movies   Swedish
      'Daniela likes Swedish movies.'
      (Lit. 'Swedish movies are appealing to Daniela')

(14) Pashto
      Meena taa de pradi   khelko na   sharem   wer-z-i.
      Meena DAT of strange people ABL shyness.NOM to.3-go-3
      'Meena feels shy of/from strangers.' (Babrakzai 1999)
      (Lit. 'Shyness goes to Meena from strange people.')

The nature and source of dative case has been debated, but here the two central questions are 1) where does the "experiencer" interpretation come from? and 2) what kind of arguments are dative experiencers?

With respect to their interpretation, experiencer datives with psych predicates have been characterized as possessors or locations, or holders of psychological states. Parsons (1995), for instance, subsumes experiencers as a case of the more general "in-ness relation" of subjects of states: "x is *in* s" by observing that "when the verb is one of psychology or perception, the *in*-ness relation coincides with (...) the Experiencer relation" (1995: 664). For Landau (2010), experiencers are locations of mental states. In de De Miguel's (2015) words, experiencers "combine the values of location and possession" (1995: 243; my translation). This characterization of the meaning of dative experiencers in terms of possessors or locations of states resembles characterizations of stative low applicatives, and makes dative experiencers good candidates for an applicative analysis. Cuervo (2003; 2011) developed a high applicative analysis of dative experiencers: the experiencer DP is external to the state specified by the verbal root, of which the nominative DP is the holder. In this sense, there are two "subjects" in the construction in (15).[27] Dative case and morphological expression of the Appl head as a pronominal clitic are the usual forms for applicative constructions in Spanish.

---

[27]Other evidence that the nominative argument is also a 'subject' is that psychological verbs taking dative experiencers are acceptable without the experiencer, in which case the nominative DP typically appears pre-verbally, as illustrated in (i). See Cuervo 2011 for further arguments and data.

(i) Los ruidos de la calle no importan / molestan / gustan.
     the noises of the street not matter   / bother   / appeal
     'Street noise is not important/ bothersome/ appealing.'

(15)   Dative experiencers as high applicatives (for example (13))

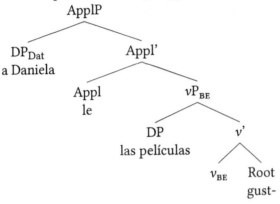

The high applicative analysis contrasts with previous analyses that equate (the initial position of) dative experiencers with datives in canonical ditransitive constructions, whether treated as double-object, incorporation, low applicative constructions or locatives (Belletti & Rizzi 1988; Masullo 1992, among others).[28] Unlike those analyses, (15) expresses the fact that the dative DP is not directly related to the other argument, and that there is no possession relation between the two DPs: crucially, the "possession" relation is between the dative DP and the state (the *v*P complement of the Appl head).

Constructions with experiences datives reveal semantic crosslinguistic variation based on availability of particular constructions. The structure and meaning of the transitive English sentence *Daniela likes Swedish movies* contrast with its translation equivalent in a language with dative experiencers as in (13), in which the psych predicate expresses a property of the nominative argument (*Las películas suecas gustan*, 'Swedish movies are appealing'), a predication that is lacking in the English sentence.[29]

As mentioned earlier, experiencers are related to possessors and (human) locations, but are not taken to be affected arguments. This is consistent with the proposal that affectedness in dative or applicative arguments arises as a configurational meaning involving two verbal layers. However, proposing that dative experiencers are unembedded high applicatives which take a stative *v*P as complement does not directly derive the 'experiencer' interpretation. In principle, the

---

[28] Acedo-Matellán & Mateu 2015, Pujalte 2015 adopt the unaccusative analysis with the dative experiencer as HighAppl and the usual dative case (but change the licensing position of the lower DP).

[29] Not all psych constructions display this variation, however. English also has psych constructions formed with prepositional phrases, such as *to*-DPs with psych predicates such as *appeal, seem,* and *be important.*

interpretation could arise as a result of the lexical meaning of the psych verb, of the denotation of the Appl head or some other specialized head, or the extended verbal configuration as a whole.

It could be argued that the meaning of the experiencer as a specialized type of possessor or location arises from the meaning of the psych verb, in virtue of the dative DP being one of its arguments. Regardless of whether one has any general reservations against a lexically-based approach to argument structure, there are empirical arguments against deriving the interpretation of the dative experiencer from the lexical meaning of a verb. These arguments are presented below from Spanish, but other languages provide similar evidence.

First, not every experiencer is the subject of a *psychological* experience, there also being physical states associated with an experiencer argument, as in (16).[30] Second, intra- and inter-linguistically, many experiencers appear with psychological predicates formed as light verb constructions in which the psych meaning comes from a nominal element, not from the verb, and the dative argument is arguably associated with the light verb, as in (17), and in (14) above. Finally, as noted by Di Tullio (2015), there are dative DPs interpreted as experiencers in combination with idiomatic psychological expressions formed without any psych words, as in (18).

(16) A   Daniela le   aprietan   los zapatos.
      DAT Daniela 3SG.DAT= squeeze.PL the shoes
      'Those shoes are too tight for Daniela.'

(17) A   Daniela le   dan   miedo las tormentas.
      DAT Daniela 3SG.DAT= give.PL fear   the storms
      'Daniela is afraid of storms.' lit., 'Storms give fear to Daniela.'

(18) A   Daniela le   dan   cosa/ no sé   qué las arañas.
      DAT Daniela 3SG.DAT= give.PL thing/ not know.1SG what the spiders
      'Daniela feels uneasy about spiders.'
      Lit., 'Spiders give Daniela stuff/I don't know what' (adapted from
      Di Tullio 2015)

---

[30]The interpretation of the dative in (16) and (19) is not perfectly captured by its English translation. As in the case of other applicatives, such as low and affected applicatives, a dative argument is understood as more than a goal or location, and typically only animate entities are licensed (therefore, the dative in (16) could not be replaced by *the mannequin*) or inanimate entities in a part-whole relation, as in (19b). The contrast between Spanish (16) and its English translation is perhaps similar to the contrast in English between *That is important to Amir/*the lawn* and *That is important for Amir/the lawn*.

These data provide evidence against a lexical source of the experiencer interpretation, since experiencers do not require a lexical psychological verb. An alternative explanation is that the interpretation derives directly from the denotation of a specialized, more functional head, whose contribution is to licence an experiencer both syntactically and semantically (as Voice does for Agents). Within an applicative approach, this head would be the Appl head. It can be proposed that there is a specialized Experiencer 'flavour' or feature specification of HighAppl (as has been proposed for LowAppl in order to derive the recipient, source and possessor interpretation). A specialized head, rather than the verb, as the source of the experiencer interpretation has also been proposed by Landau (2010), and argued by Fábregas & Marín (2020 [this volume]): a prepositional head P which takes the dative DP as its argument and relates it to the state. The non-psychological experiencers illustrated in (16) are potential problems for this "all-in-the-head" approach, since it is not clear whether these cases would require a different P head than the one which combines with psychological predicates. Additional issues arise with arguably experiencer arguments that are hard to classify as either psychological or physical, particularly in the case of inanimate datives, as in (19b).

(19)   a. A   Daniela le   quedan mal los zapatos.
             DAT Daniela 3SG.DAT= stay.PL bad the shoes
             'Those shoes look bad on Daniela.'

       b. Al   regalo le   queda mal ese moño.
             DAT.the present 3SG.DAT= stay   bad that bow
             'That bow looks bad on the present.'

Even more importantly, a problem with the proposal that experiencer is the meaning assigned by a dedicated applicative (or P) head is that, as noted by Wechsler (2020 [this volume]), an unconstrained quantity of different heads would be required to account for the other interpretations. The resulting system would be unable to express or account for the systematicity between the structure of the verbal domain and interpretation of arguments.

A third, intermediate possibility can be developed within a more explanatory applicative analysis: "experiencer" is a configurational meaning which takes into account the Appl head and its position within the extended verbal projection, properties of the complement of Appl, as well as idiosyncratic meanings of vocabulary items, and idiomatic expressions.[31] Ideally, the semantic contribution

---

[31] Such a configurational approach could also be developed on the basis of Landau's (2010) functional P head, but I do not pursue that line here. See Acedo-Matellán & Mateu (2015) for an account of properties of psychological predicates based on characteristics of the root.

of the Appl head is minimal and constant as far as the interpretation of its argument is concerned, although Pylkkänen's (2008) distinction between High and Low in terms of semantic composition must be maintained.

As specifiers of a high applicative, dative experiencers are related to a vP, and share properties with bene/malefactives, instrumentals, causees, and affected applicatives (Figure 2). Unlike bene/malefactives, Affected Appls and causees, experiencers are not typically affected arguments. Unlike instrumentals, experiencers are not related to an event in a 'doer' capacity; if anything, they are closer to undergoers than to agents. Can these different interpretations be derived without postulating "experiencer" directly as the denotation of a particular HighAppl head?

As discussed in §3, experiencers are structurally distinguishable from both Affected Appls and Causees, as represented in Figure 2 by the "embedded/non-embedded" contrast. Since affectedness arises from the applicative argument participating in two (sub)events, the lack of affectedness reading for dative experiencers follows. The contrast between experiencers and bene/malefactives and instrumentals is based, in Figure 2, on the dynamic or stative nature of the complement vP. Stativity is a crucial component of our understanding (or definition) of an experiencer as the possessor of a mental state. Another property of the structure of dative experiencer constructions, however, is crucial: the experiencer is the highest argument, there not being another external argument licensing head (such as v or Voice) above Appl.

In order to test whether these two structural components are needed to obtain an "experiencer" reading (of a high applicative), they should be isolated. First, stative verbs that are not unaccusative, such as Spanish *vivir* 'live', usually appear in unergative structures with a nominative subject alone, or with a locative as well. A dative argument may be added to the sentence with a locative, as in (20).[32]

(20) Emilio le   vive en el jardín (a   Vera).
     Emilio 3SG.DAT= live in the garden (DAT Vera)
     'Emilio is living in Vera's garden (on her).'

The interpretation of the dative argument *Vera* in (20) is not that of an experiencer, but more specifically a bene/malefactive, arguably due to the presence of the external argument, merged above the high applicative, which, in turn, takes a stative vP as complement.

---

[32] The resulting sentence is colloquial, and not accepted by all speakers. In any case, the relevance of the example is the interpretation obtained by those speakers who accept it.

31

The other test is an unaccusative structure in which the dative is the highest argument, but in which the *v*P complement is dynamic rather than stative. Would such dative be interpreted as an experiencer? Fábregas & Marín (2020 [this volume]) probe this question and suggest that a dative argument with a reflexive dynamic predicate is a potential experiencer:

(21) A   Juan se   le   olvidan las cosas (rápidamente).
      DAT Juan REFL 3SG.DAT= forget.PL the things quickly
      'Juan forgets things (quickly).'

This sentence is in present tense, just like the typical stative in (13), but here the present is understood as episodic or habitual, as an activity verb would. Interestingly, what Fábregas & Marín consider an experiencer could be the result of the psychological nature of the predicate in an inchoative structure, in which a dative argument would typically be read as an accidental causer. This highlights the interaction between structural properties and lexical meaning in the interpretation of a dative DP. Note in the examples below how the interpretation of the dative is somewhat different in the absence of a psychological reading of the predicate. In the unintentional causer reading, the underlying structure is that of a high applicative merged above a (non agentive) dynamic *v*PGO (Cuervo 2003; 2014; Schäfer 2008; see §4.2).

(22) A   Juan se   le   pierden / queman las cosas.
      DAT Juan REFL 3SG.DAT= lose.PL / burn.PL the things
      'Juan (accidentally) loses/burns things.'

These data support the view that the interpretation of a (dative) argument as an "experiencer" is better captured as a configurational meaning rather than a meaning dependent on the denotation of a licensing head or a lexical element. In particular, the data show that both stativity of the verbal complement, and absence of an external argument above the dative DP, are crucial components for the experiencer interpretation to arise as the most salient.[33]

---

[33]Kim's (2011) analysis of Korean adversity passives as experiencer *have* constructions (as in English *Peter had the children laugh at him*) is also crucially based on the "affected experiencer" being the highest external argument in the extended verbal domain. Interestingly, these two properties also hold of the arguably other way of licensing experiencer subjects: as Holder arguments licensed by Voice in the context of a psychological predicate, as in *Natasha fears lighting*.

5 Conclusions

The Classical Nahuatl grammarian Horacio Carochi characterized applicatives as those which "orient the action of the verb towards another person, or thing, attributing it to him by way of harm, or benefit, taking it away from him, or putting it on him, or relating it to him in some way or another, as shall be understood through the examples; e.g., *nitlaqua*, 'I eat something'; its applicative is *nictlaquaia in notàtsin*, 'I eat my father something', as if he has fruit, or something else, and I eat it from him...":

> VERBO aplicativo es el que ordena la acción del verbo a otra persona, o cosa, atribuyéndosela por via de daño, o provecho, quitándosela, o poniéndosela, o refiriéndosela de qualquiera manera que sea, como se entenderá por los exemplos; verbi gracia: *nitlaqua*, 'como algo', su aplicativo es *nictlaquaia in notàtsin*, 'como algo a mi Padre', como si tenía fruta, o otra cosa, y se la como. (Carochi 1645: 466)

Carochi's translation of the Náhuatl applicative into Spanish involved the addition of a dative argument (*a mi Padre*, and *se* in *se la como* above), illustrating the overlap between applicative and dative arguments. Although the overlap may be imperfect, it is significant and systematic. The study of datives as applicatives provides a framework to capture datives as a class beyond their morphology in terms of the type of licensing, while allowing for systematic variation in terms of structural position and thematic interpretation.

This broader approach to the study of dative constructions goes well beyond the most typical datives in ditransitive constructions. By putting aside case as a domain where languages can vary, I have focused on what dative arguments have in common as a class and as subcases of applicative arguments, as found in both languages with a rich case system and languages without overt case marking. Going beyond morphosyntactic coding is necessary in the quest to make crosslinguistic generalizations and to articulate a theory of argument structure.

Carochi's (1645) notion of applicatives as derived verbs captures the intuition that there must be some extra piece in a verb that co-occurs with — and licenses — an applied argument. In order to systematically derive the subtypes of dative/applied arguments, it is crucial to take into account the way this extra piece integrates into the extended verbal projection of the clause. In describing its integration, not only the merge position (i.e., the complement) of the Appl head is relevant, but also the dynamic/stative nature of its complement, and the presence/absence of an external argument, and of a verbal head (intruducing a (sub)event) above the applicative. Once such a detailed proposal is developed, broad empirical coverage can be maintained while featural and lexical specification of the Appl head is drastically reduced. This minimal notion of Appl as introducing an argument "oriented" towards its complement accords well with the fact that in so many languages applicatives are expressed as dative arguments, analyzed themselves as an argument "in contact" with the rest of the predicate (Fábregas & Marín 2020 [this volume]) via a directional or locative morpheme, such as Romance *a/à*. Appl is thus akin to the more grammatical adpositions whose complement is interpreted contextually (Svenonius 2007). In this view of semantically underspecified Appl, a distinction remains between applied arguments and arguments of Voice (cf. Wood & Marantz 2017).

The richness of interpretations of applicative and dative arguments, in spite of their being licensed by a functional head with minimal semantics, sets them apart from the narrow range of interpretations for arguments of *v*/Voice, on the one hand, and the practically unconstrained interpretations of arguments of lexical verbs/roots, on the other. Applicatives are, in this sense, an "efficient" way of generating diversity of meaning with limited resources by making use of various properties of the syntactic structures with which they combine.

Abbreviations

The abbreviations used in the glosses of this chapter follow the Leipzig Glossing Rules. Additional abbreviation: HON honorific.

Acknowledgements

I thank two anonymous reviewers for useful comments and suggestions. I am also grateful to Taylor Roberts and the editors of this volume. This work was supported by a Jackman Humanities Institute Fellowship.

References

Acedo-Matellán, Víctor. 2017. Latin datives with prefixed verbs and beyond: A view from the theory of applicatives. *Catalan Journal of Linguistics* 16. 19–49.

Acedo-Matellán, Víctor & Jaume Mateu. 2015. Los verbos psicológicos: Raíces especiales en estructuras corrientes. In Rafael Marín (ed.), *Los predicados psicológicos*, 81–109. Madrid: Visor.

Antonyuk, Svitlana. 2020. The puzzle of Russian ditransitives. In Anna Pineda & Jaume Mateu (eds.), *Dative constructions in Romance and beyond*, 43–74. Berlin: Language Science Press. DOI:10.5281/zenodo.3776533

Babrakzai, Farooq. 1999. *Topics in the syntax of Pashto.* University of Hawaii. (Doctoral dissertation).

Baker, Mark C. 1996. On the structural position of themes and goals. In Johan Rooryck & Laurie Zaring (eds.), *Phrase structure and the lexicon*, 7–34. Dordrecht: Kluwer.

Belletti, Adriana & Luigi Rizzi. 1988. Psych-verbs and θ-Theory. *Natural Language & Linguistic Theory* 6(3). 291–352. DOI:10.1007/BF00133902

Boneh, Nora & Lea Nash. 2011. *High and higher applicatives: The case of French non-core datives.* Somerville, MA: Cascadilla Proceedings Project. 60–68. http://www.lingref.com/cpp/wccfl/28/paper2436.pdf.

Boneh, Nora & Lea Nash. 2012. Core and non-core datives. In Beatriz Fernández & Ricardo Etxepare (eds.), *Variation in datives: A microcomparative perspective*, 22–49. Oxford: Oxford University Press.

Boneh, Nora & Lea Nash. 2017. The syntax and semantics of dative DPs in Russian ditransitives. *Natural Language & Linguistic Theory* 35(4). 899–953.

Bruening, Benjamin. 2010. Ditransitive asymmetries and a theory of idiom formation. *Linguistic Inquiry* 41(4). 519–562. DOI:10.1162/LING_a_00012

Calindro, Ana Regina. 2020. Ditransitive constructions: What sets Brazilian Portuguese apart from other Romance languages? In Anna Pineda & Jaume Mateu (eds.), *Dative constructions in Romance and beyond*, 75–95. Berlin: Language Science Press. DOI:10.5281/zenodo.3776535

Carochi, Horacio. 1645. *El arte de la lengua mexicana con la declaración de los adverbios della.* Mexico: Museo Nacional de México. (Reprint).

Cépeda, Paola & Sonia Cyrino. 2020. Putting objects in order: Asymmetrical relations in Spanish and Portuguese ditransitives. In Anna Pineda & Jaume Mateu (eds.), *Dative constructions in Romance and beyond*, 97–116. Berlin: Language Science Press. DOI:10.5281/zenodo.3776539

Cornilescu, Alexandra. 2020. Ditransitive constructions with differentially marked direct objects in Romanian. In Anna Pineda & Jaume Mateu (eds.), *Dative constructions in Romance and beyond*, 117–142. Berlin: Language Science Press. DOI:10.5281/zenodo.3776541

Cuervo, María Cristina. 2003. *Datives at large.* Cambridge, MA: Massachusetts Institute of Technology. (Doctoral dissertation). https://dspace.mit.edu/handle/1721.1/7991.

Cuervo, María Cristina. 2010. Against ditransitivity. *Probus* 22(2). 151–180.

Cuervo, María Cristina. 2011. Some dative subjects are born, some are made. In Claudia Borgonovo, Manuel Español-Echevarría & Philippe Prévost (eds.), *Selected proceedings of the Hispanic Linguistic Symposium (HLS) 2008*, 26–37. Somerville, MA: Cascadilla Press.

Cuervo, María Cristina. 2014. Alternating unaccusatives and the distribution of roots. *Lingua* 141. 48–70. DOI:10.1016/j.lingua.2013.12.001

Cuervo, María Cristina. 2015a. Causation without a cause. *Syntax* 18(4). 388–424. DOI:10.1111/synt.12115

Cuervo, María Cristina. 2015b. Parameters in argument structure II: Causatives and applicatives. In Antonio Fábregas, Jaume Mateu & Michael T. Putnam (eds.), *Contemporary linguistic parameters*, 123–145. London: Bloomsbury Academic.

De Miguel, Elena. 2015. Los nombres psicológicos: Propuesta de análisis en términos sub-léxicos. In Rafael Marín (ed.), *Los predicados psicológicos*, 211–248. Madrid: Visor.

Demonte, Violeta. 1995. Dative alternation in Spanish. *Probus* 7(1). 5–30. DOI:10.1515/prbs.1995.7.1.5

Di Tullio, Ángela. 2015. Variantes sintéticas y analíticas de los predicados psicológicos. In Rafael Marín (ed.), *Los predicados psicológicos*, 185–210. Madrid: Visor.

Diaconescu, Rodica. 2004. *Romanian applicative constructions*. University of Ottawa. (Doctoral dissertation).

Etxepare, Ricardo & Bernard Oyharçabal. 2013. Datives and adpositions in Northeastern Basque. In Beatriz Fernandez & Ricardo Etxepare (eds.), *Variation in datives: A microcomparative perspective*, 50–95. Oxford: Oxford University Press. DOI:10.1093/acprof:oso/9780199937363.003.0003

Fábregas, Antonio & Rafael Marín. 2020. Datives and stativity in psych predicates. In Anna Pineda & Jaume Mateu (eds.), *Dative constructions in Romance and beyond*, 221–238. Berlin: Language Science Press. DOI:10.5281/zenodo.3776549

Fernández Alcalde, Héctor. 2014. Two types of datives in Spanish: Caused possession vs. Possessor raising. *Acta Linguistica Hungarica* 61(1). 69–90. DOI:10.1556/ALing.61.2014.1.3

Folli, Raffaella & Heidi Harley. 2006. Benefactives aren't goals in Italian. In Jenny Doetjes & Paz González (eds.), *Romance languages & linguistic theory 2004: Selected papers from Going Romance*, 121–142. Amsterdam: John Benjamins.

Folli, Raffaella & Heidi Harley. 2007. Causation, obligation, and argument structure: On the nature of little v. *Linguistic Inquiry* 38(2). 197–238. DOI:10.1162/ling.2007.38.2.197

Fournier, David. 2010. *La structure du prédicat verbal: Une étude de la construction à double objet en français.* University of Toronto. (Doctoral dissertation).

Franco, Ludovico & Paolo Lorusso. 2020. Aspectual datives (and instrumentals). In Anna Pineda & Jaume Mateu (eds.), *Dative constructions in Romance and beyond*, 175–194. Berlin: Language Science Press. DOI:10.5281/zenodo.3776545

Grimm, Scott. 2011. Semantics of case. *Morphology* 21(3–4). 515–544.

Harley, Heidi. 2013. External arguments and the mirror principle: On the distinctness of Voice and v. *Lingua* 125. 34–57.

Ippolito, Michela. 2000. *Remarks on the argument structure of Romance causatives.* Manuscript.

Jerro, Kyle Joseph. 2017. The causative-instrumental syncretism. *Journal of Linguistics* 53 (4). 751–788. DOI:10.1017/S0022226717000044

Kim, Kyumin. 2011. High applicatives in Korean causatives and passives. *Lingua* 121(3). 487–510. DOI:10.1016/j.lingua.2010.10.001

Kim, Kyumin. 2012. Affectees in subject position and applicative theory. *The Canadian Journal of Linguistics / La Revue Canadienne de Linguistique* 57(1). 77–107. DOI:10.1353/cjl.2012.0002

Kratzer, Angelika. 1996. Severing the external argument from its verb. In Johan Rooryck & Laurie Zaring (eds.), *Phrase structure and the lexicon*, 109–137. Dordrecht: Kluwer.

Landau, Idan. 2010. *The locative syntax of experiencers.* Cambridge, MA: MIT Press.

Maling, Joan. 2001. Dative: The heterogeneity of the mapping among morphological case, grammatical functions, and thematic roles. *Lingua* 111(4–7). 419–464.

Marantz, Alec. 2013. Verbal argument structure: Events and participants. *Lingua* 130. 152–168. DOI:10.1016/j.lingua.2012.10.012

Masullo, Pascual J. 1992. *Incorporation and case theory in Spanish: A crosslinguistic perspective.* University of Washington. (Doctoral dissertation).

McGinnis, Martha. 2001. Variation in the phase structure of applicatives. *Linguistic Variation Yearbook* 1(1). 105–146.

McGinnis, Martha. 2004. Lethal ambiguity. *Linguistic Inquiry* 35(1). 47–95.

McGinnis, Martha. 2008. Applicatives. *Language and Linguistics Compass* 2(6). 1225–1245. DOI:10.1111/j.1749-818X.2008.00078.x

McGinnis, Martha. 2018. *Applicatives.* Manuscript.

McGinnis, Martha & Donna B. Gerdts. 2004. *A phase-theoretic analysis of Kinyarwanda multiple applicatives.* http://prism.ucalgary.ca/handle/1880/44523.

Miyagawa, Shigeru & Takae Tsujioka. 2004. Argument structure and ditransitive verbs in Japanese. *Journal of East Asian Linguistics* 13. 1–38.

Moreno Villamar, Itziri. 2018. *Variation in the pronominal clitic system of P'urhépecha-Spanish bilinguals.* Western University. (Doctoral dissertation).

Park, Jeong-Woon. 1994. *Morphological causatives in Korean: Problems in grammatical polysemy and constructional relations.* University of California, Berkeley. (Doctoral dissertation).

Parsons, Terence. 1995. Thematic relations and arguments. *Linguistic Inquiry* 26(4). 635–662.

Peterson, David A. 2007. *Applicative constructions* (Oxford Studies in Typology and Linguistic Theory). Oxford: Oxford University Press.

Pineda, Anna. 2016. *Les fronteres de la (in)transitivitat: Estudi dels aplicatius en llengües romàniques i basc.* Barcelona: Institut d'Estudis Món Juïc. Published and revised version of the doctoral dissertation.

Pineda, Anna. 2020. Double object constructions in Romance: The common denominator. *Syntax.*

Polinsky, Maria. 2013. Applicative constructions. In Matthew Dryer & Martin Haspelmath (eds.), *The world atlas of language structures online.* Leipzig: Max Planck Institute for Evolutionary Anthropology.

Pujalte, Mercedes. 2009. *Condiciones sobre la introducción de argumentos: El caso de la alternancia dativa en español.* Universidad Nacional del Comahue. (Master's thesis).

Pujalte, Mercedes. 2015. Hacia un análisis unificado de los predicados psicológicos estativos en español. In Rafael Marín (ed.), *Los predicados psicológicos*, 111–144. Madrid: Visor.

Pylkkänen, Liina. 2000. What applicative heads apply to. *University of Pennsylvania Working Papers in Linguistics* 7(1.18). 197–210.

Pylkkänen, Liina. 2002. *Introducing arguments.* Massachusetts Institute of Technology. (Doctoral dissertation).

Pylkkänen, Liina. 2008. *Introducing arguments* (Linguistic Inquiry Monographs 49). Cambridge, MA: MIT Press.

Roberge, Yves & Michelle Ann Troberg. 2009. The high applicative syntax of the dativus commodi/incommodi in Romance. *Probus* 21(2). 249–289. DOI:10.1515/prbs.2009.008

Schäfer, Florian. 2008. *The syntax of (anti-)causatives: External arguments in change-of-state contexts* (Linguistik Aktuell = Linguistics Today, v. 126.). Amsterdam: John Benjamins.

Sheehan, Michelle. 2020. The Romance Person Case Constraint is not about clitic clusters. In Anna Pineda & Jaume Mateu (eds.), *Dative constructions in Romance and beyond*, 143–171. Berlin: Language Science Press. DOI:10.5281/zenodo.3776543

Skorniakova, Oxana. 2009. Syntactic and semantic properties of Russian dative "subjects". In Anastasia Smirnova, Vedrana Mihaliček & Lauren Ressue (eds.), *Formal studies in Slavic linguistics*, 166–196. Cambridge: Cambridge Scholars Publishing.

Snyder, William. 1995. *Language acquisition and language variation: the role of morphology*. Cambridge, MA: MIT. (Doctoral dissertation).

Svenonius, Peter. 2007. Adpositions, particles, and the arguments they introduce. In Eric Reuland, Tanmoy Bhattacharya & Giorgos Spathas (eds.), *Argument structure*, 63–103. Amsterdam: John Benjamins.

Tollan, Rebecca & Will Oxford. 2018. Voice-less unergatives: Evidence from Algonquian. In Wm. G. Bennett, Lindsay Hracs & Dennis Ryan Storoshenko (eds.), *Proceedings of the 35th West Coast Conference on Formal Linguistics (WCCFL)*, 399–408. Somerville, MA: Cascadilla Proceedings Project.

Torrego, Esther. 2011. Variability in the case patterns of causative formation in Romance and its implications. *Linguistic Inquiry* 41(3). 445–470.

Tsai, Wei-Tien D. 2018. High applicatives are not high enough: A cartographic solution. *Lingua Sinica* 4(2). 1–21.   DOI:10.1186/s40655-018-0034-y

Tsedryk, Egor. 2020. The modal side of the dative: From predicative possession to possessive modality. In Anna Pineda & Jaume Mateu (eds.), *Dative constructions in Romance and beyond*, 195–219. Berlin: Language Science Press. DOI:10.5281/zenodo.3776547

Tubino, Mercedes. 2012. *Spanish dative causees: Against an applicative analysis*. Barcelona. Paper presented at the 22nd Colloquium on Generative Grammar.

Wechsler, Mattie. 2020. The lexical underspecification of Bantu causatives and applicatives. In Anna Pineda & Jaume Mateu (eds.), *Dative constructions in Romance and beyond*, 241–271. Berlin: Language Science Press. DOI:10.5281/zenodo.3776551

Wood, Jim & Alec Marantz. 2017. The interpretation of external arguments. In Roberta D'Alessandro, Irene Franco & Ángel J. Gallego (eds.), *The verbal domain*, 255–278. Oxford: Oxford University Press. DOI:10.1093/oso/9780198767886.001.0001

Part I

Ditransitive constructions

Chapter 2

The puzzle of Russian ditransitives

Svitlana Antonyuk

University of Graz

In this paper I use the Scope Freezing Generalization (SFG), formulated on the basis of Russian quantifier scope freezing data in Antonyuk (2015) to gain insights into the structure of Russian ditransitives. The paper discusses the finding that Russian ditransitive predicates are not a homogeneous group, but instead subdivide into three distinct Groups, each with its distinct set of properties, with further syntactic evidence supporting the conclusion that these Groups have distinct underlying structures. One of the main findings, suggested by the (revised) SFG and supported by syntactic unaccusativity tests is that a group of Russian "direct objects" are not in fact what they seem, but are instead low Oblique arguments receiving Accusative case from a silent P head.

1 Introduction

The argument structure of ditransitive predicates has been of interests to linguists for quite a long time, with the question of the exact nature of syntactic encoding of ditransitives remaining both a matter of debate and a source of important insights for grammatical theory. Thus, even in English, which has been studied extensively in the generative tradition for over half a century the question of argument structure is far from settled, with novel research ranging in analyses from a derivational Larsonian view (Larson 1988; 2014) to a separate projection view (an applicative analysis of Marantz 1993; decompositional analyses of Pesetsky 1995; Harley 1995; 2002 i.a.) to a derivational reverse-Larsonian view on which the Double Object Construction (DOC) serves as the derivational base for the Prepositional Dative Construction (Hallman 2015). It is not surprising then that in languages that have not been studied as extensively within the generative framework, Russian being one of them, there is little to no agreement on the issue, with a variety of views, schematized in (1) below:

Svitlana Antonyuk. 2020. The puzzle of Russian ditransitives. In Anna Pineda & Jaume Mateu (eds.), *Dative constructions in Romance and beyond*, 43–74. Berlin: Language Science Press. DOI:10.5281/zenodo.3776533

(1) Analyses of Russian ditransitives:

    a. **Dative Goal object originates in Spec, VP position**, assigned Dative case as sister to V' (see Harbert & Toribio 1991; Greenberg & Franks 1991; Franks 1995; Richardson 2007)

    b. **Accusative Theme object is generated in Spec, VP position**, with the Dative originating in the complement position (Bailyn 1995; 2010; 2012; Titov 2017)

    c. **Dative Goal object is assigned case by an Applicative head** (Dyakonova 2005; 2009, following Pylkkänen 2002)

    d. **Non-derivational Dative-higher-than-Theme account** of ditransitives on which datives (locational vs. non-locational) have two distinct underlying structures (Boneh & Nash 2017)

The research summarized here, developed in detail in Antonyuk (2015), offers a way to understand the reason behind such a multitude of views on Russian ditransitives by presenting a novel perspective, different from all of the above in that it discards the underlying assumption of the uniformity of Russian ditransitives and argues instead that Russian ditransitive predicates subdivide into three distinct Groups, each with its own clearly defined set of properties and corresponding differences in syntactic structure. The initial evidence for this proposal comes from quantifier scope ambiguity and scope freezing distribution patterns in ditransitives, supported further by syntactic tests that confirm the underlying structural differences between the three Groups.

The insight about the non-homogeneous nature of Russian ditransitives comes primarily from the scope ambiguity and scope freezing distribution patterns and it should be stressed that the notion of ditransitivity that emerges from this investigation is broader than what is generally assumed. In research on English, for instance, the notion of ditransitivity has been reserved mostly for verbs that undergo Dative shift (the prepositional Dative and the Double Object Construction), as well as the *Spray-Load* alternation. The Double Object Construction and the *with*-variant of the *Spray-Load* alternation are also the constructions that exhibit the scope freezing phenomenon in English (differing in this respect from the scopally ambiguous Prepositional Dative Construction and the Locative Alternant of the *Spray-Load* alternation), with scope ambiguity-scope freezing contrast being treated as one of the properties that characterize ditransitives in English (see, for instance, Bruening 2001, 2010). Current research takes the view that the scope ambiguity - scope freezing contrast is one of the most important properties of ditransitive verbs and moreover, that the scope ambiguity-scope freezing distribution patterns can be used to gain insights into the argument structure of ditransitives. The operative notion of ditransitivity, therefore, has been derived entirely on the basis of which predicates exhibit the scope ambiguity - scope freezing distribution patterns, and that appears to include any predicate which Theta-marks two internal arguments. Thus, the relevant notion of ditransitivity is one that includes both the "canonical" ditransitives which take an Accusative-marked Theme and a Dative-marked Goal internal arguments as well as verbs which include an Accusative-marked Theme and a PP argument or an Instrumental-marked DP or even those where the verbs subcategorizes for two internal arguments which are both realized as Prepositional Phrases.

Turning to data now, despite arguably being identical to English in terms of quantifier scope possibilities and Quantifier Raising properties as far as transitive sentences are concerned (see Antonyuk 2006; 2015, 2019) there are both significant similarities *and* differences once we look at ditransitive sentences. While the important similarity to English is that Russian ditransitives show the same scope freezing effect as do English DOCs and the *with*-variant of the *Spray-Load* construction, the novel Russian data, briefly exemplified in (2)-(7) below, suggest that the range of constructions in which quantifier scope is surface scope frozen in the language is much broader than it is in English. In all of the examples below the sentences in (a) are ambiguous, whereas the sentences in (b) are surface scope frozen.

(2) Russian Equivalent of the PP Dative and the Double-Object Construction:

    a. Učitel' po-dari-l   [kak-uju-to   knig-u]   [každ-omu
       teacher PO-present-PST.M some-ACC.F-IND book-ACC.F every-DAT.M
       student-u]. $\exists\forall/\forall\exists$
       student-DAT.M

       'The teacher presented some book to every student.'

    b. Učitel' po-dari-l   [kak-omu-to   student-u]
       teacher PO-present-PST.M some-DAT.M-IND student-DAT.M
       [každ-uju   knig-u]. $\exists\forall/{*}\forall\exists$
       every-ACC.F book-ACC.F

       'The teacher presented some student with every book.'

(3) Prepositional Ditransitive Construction:

    a. Maša po-trebova-l-a   kak-ie-to   document-y   (s
       Masha PO-demand-PST-F some-ACC.PL-IND document-ACC.PL from
       každ-ogo   posetitel'-a).   ∃∀/∀∃
       every-GEN.M visitor-GEN.M

       'Masha demanded some documents from every visitor.'

    b. Maša po-trebova-la   (s   kak-ogo-to   posetitel'-a)
       Masha PO-demand-PST.F from some-GEN.M-IND visitor-GEN.M
       [každ-yj   document].   ∃∀/*∀∃
       every-ACC.M document.ACC.M

       'Masha demanded every document from some visitor.'

(4) The *Spray-Load* Alternation:

    a. Vanja za-gruz-i-l   [kak-oj-to   vid   sen-a]
       Vania ZA-load-IPFV-PST.M some-ACC.M-IND type.ACC.M hay-GEN.N
       [na každ-yj   gruzovik].   ∃∀/∀∃
       on every-ACC.M truck-ACC.M

       'Vania loaded some type of hay on every truck.'

    b. Vanja za-gruz-i-l   [kak-oj-to   gruzovik] [každy-m
       Vania ZA-load-IPFV-PST.M some-ACC.M-IND truck.ACC.M every-INS.M
       vid-om   sen-a].   ∃∀/*∀∃
       type-INS.M hay-GEN.N

       'Vania loaded some truck with every type of hay.'

(5) The *Clear*-Type Alternation:

    a. Vanja u-bra-l   [neskol'ko tarel-ok] [s   každ-ogo
       Vania U-clear-PST.M several   dish-ACC.PL from every-GEN.M
       stol-a].   ∃∀/∀∃
       table-GEN.M

       'Vania cleared several dishes from every table.'

    b. Vanja u-bra-l   [neskol'ko   stol-ov] [ot   každ-oj
       Vania U-clear-PST.M several-ACC.PL table-ACC.PL from every-GEN.F
       tarelk-i].   ∃∀/*∀∃
       dish-GEN.F.SG

       'Vania cleared several tables of every dish.'

(6) Simple Ditransitives:

 a. Maša zarazi-l-a [kak-oj-to bolezn'-ju] [každ-ogo
  Masha infect-PST-F some-INS.F-IND illness-INS.F every-ACC.M
  pacient-a].   ∃∀/∀∃
  patient-ACC.M
  'Masha infected with some illness every patient.'

 b. Maša zarazi-l-a [kak-ogo-to pacient-a] [každ-oj
  Masha infect-PST-F some-ACC.M-IND patient-ACC.M every-INS.F
  bolezn'-ju].   ∃∀/*∀∃
  illness-INS.F
  'Masha got infected with every illness by some patient.'

(7) "Reflexive Monotransitives" derived from simple ditransitives:

 a. Maša zarazi-l-a-s' [kak-oj-to bolezn'-ju] [ot
  Masha infect-PST-F-REFL some-INS.F-IND illness-INS.F from
  každ-ogo pacient-a].   ∃∀/∀∃
  every-GEN.M.SG patient-GEN.M.SG
  'Masha got infected with some illness by every patient.'

 b. Maša zarazi-l-a-s' [ot kak-ogo-to pacient-a]
  Masha infect-PST-F-REFL from some-GEN.M-IND patient-GEN.M.SG
  [každ-oj bolezn'-ju].   ∃∀/*∀∃
  every-INS.F illness-INS.F
  'Masha got infected with every illness by some patient.'

What is striking about the above examples is that despite all the differences between these sentences, such as changes in the obligatory morphological marking between the two alternating orders in the *Spray-Load* or *Clear*-type alternations or the fact that in some cases one of the internal arguments is realized as a Prepositional Phrase (PP) or, perhaps most strikingly, the "detransitivization" in (7) with scope freezing nevertheless preserved, all the differences notwithstanding, the one constant element in the above pairs is the permuted order of the verb's internal arguments. The Scope Freezing Generalization in (8) captures this fact:[1,2]

---

[1]The SGF in (8) reflects the important assumption that scope ambiguity is the norm and scope freezing is the "marked", special case in need of an explanation.
[2]In this paper I argue, contra Antonyuk (2015), that surface scope freezing observed with di-

(8) *Scope Freezing Generalization (SFG)*, revised (cf. Antonyuk 2015):
Scope freezing results when one QP raises over another to a
c-commanding position within the VP as a result of a single instance of
movement.

In §2 I use the scope data and the SF Generalization as a diagnostic, which suggests a non-homogeneous view of Russian ditransitives according to which they subdivide into 3 distinct Groups. In §3 I discuss syntactic evidence supporting the claim that these groups are distinct. §4 describes which structural possibilities are open for each group of Russian ditransitives, based on observed data patterns. §5 concludes the paper.

2 The basic empirical generalization: 3 classes of Russian ditransitives

Most of the Russian ditransitive constructions can be said to share the property of taking an Accusative (ACC) and a Non-Structural (Inherent) case-marked argument (marked here throughout as OBL for Oblique) that can occur in either order in surface form. The two orders of internal arguments are always truth-conditionally identical, with subtle information-structural distinctions between them. Here the Groups are distinguished according to the effect that word order permutations have on their scope interpretation possibilities. Thus, based on their scope behavior alone, we can distinguish between three distinct classes of ditransitives in Russian, schematized below:

(9) Group 1
ACC > OBL (ambiguous)
OBL > ACC (frozen)

(10) Group 2
OBL > ACC(ambiguous)
ACC > OBL (frozen)

---

transitives and captured by SFG in (8) is a categorically distinct phenomenon from the surface scope *bias* found with cases of scrambling of a QP across a higher QP, as the judgments of surface scope freezing found with Groups 1 and 2 are not similarly affected by Information Structure-relevant phenomena such as prosodically realized Contrastive Focus (Antonyuk & Larson 2016) or by Specificity-related Object Shift, as demonstrated for Ukrainian in Antonyuk & Mykhaylyk (In press).

(11)   Group 3
  ACC > OBL (ambiguous)
  OBL > ACC (ambiguous)

2.1 The three groups exemplified

Group 1 is exemplified by Russian verbs such as *podarit'* ('to present'), which most often selects an Accusative Theme and a Dative Recipient argument:[3]

(12) a. Vospitatel' po-dari-l   [kak-uju-to   igrušk-u]
    caretaker PO-present-PST.M SOME-ACC.F-IND toy-ACC.F
    [každ-omu   rebjenk-u].   ∃∀/∀∃
    every-DAT.M child-DAT.M

    'The teacher presented some book to every student.'

  b. Vospitatel' po-dari-l   [kak-omu-to   rebjenk-u]
    caretaker PO-present-PST.M SOME-DAT.M-IND child-DAT.M
    [každ-uju   igrušk-u].   ∃∀/*∀∃
    every-ACC.F toy-ACC.F

    'The caretaker presented some child with every toy.'

The alternation in (12a,b) resembles the scope freezing pattern of English alternating ditransitives. As we know from English, the THEME > GOAL/RECIPIENT order of quantifiers is ambiguous (13a), allowing either quantifier to be read with wide scope. However, the GOAL/RECIPIENT > THEME order is frozen (13b), allowing only the surface scope interpretation (Larson 1990; Bruening 2001).

(13) a. Alice assigned some exercise to every student.   ∃∀/∀∃
  b. Alice assigned some student every exercise.   ∃∀/*∀∃

(14) presents a non-exhaustive list of verbs whose behavior with respect to the scope freezing diagnostic places them into Group 1:

(14) a. *dat'* ACC/DAT – 'to give (something to.somebody)';
  b. *poobeščat'* ACC/DAT – 'to promise (something to.somebody)';
  c. *zaveščat'* ACC/DAT – 'to bequeath (something to.somebody)';

---

[3]Throughout this paper, the phrase in square brackets represents the argument that cannot be dropped/elided. The one in parenthesis may be omitted while still being implicitly understood.

   d. *najti* ACC/DAT – 'to find (something for.someone)';

   e. *prostit'* ACC/DAT – 'to forgive (something to.someone)';

   f. *napisat'* ACC/DAT or ACC/*k* DAT – 'to write (something to.someone or something to someone)';

   g. *sdelat'* ACC/DAT – 'to do (something to.somebody)';

   h. *predložit'* ACC/DAT – 'to offer (something to.someone)';

   i. *ostavit'* ACC/DAT – 'to leave (something to.somebody)';

   j. *potrebovat* ACC/*s* ACC – 'to demand (something from someone)';

   k. *zaključit' pari* ACC/*s* INS – 'to place a bet with someone'.

The example in (15) presents a Group 2 verb on its two alternating orders. Here, the order on which the Instrumental-marked phrase precedes the Accusative argument is scopally ambiguous, whereas the opposite order of arguments is surface scope frozen.

(15) a. Maša ugosti-l-a (kak-im-to pečen'je-m) [každ-ogo
      Masha treat-PST.F some-INS.M-IND cookie-INS.M every-ACC.M
      rebenka].   ∃∀/∀∃
      child-ACC.M

      'Masha treated every child to some cookie.'

    b. Maša ugosti-l-a [kak-ogo-to rebenk-a] (každ-ym
      Masha treat-PST-F some-ACC.M-IND child-ACC.M every-INS.M
      pečen'je-m).   ∃∀/*∀∃
      cookie-INS.M

      'Masha treated some child to every cookie.'

What differentiates Group 2 from Group 1 is the obvious fact that with Group 2 the surface scope frozen order results when the Accusative argument QP precedes the Oblique-marked QP, whereas with Group 1 the frozen scope results when the Oblique-marked QP precedes the Accusative-marked QP, hence the two Groups are essentially a mirror image of each other with respect to scope.

(16) below presents a number of verbs belonging to this class which showcases its characteristic properties:

(16) a. *oskorbit* ACC/INS – 'to insult (someone with.something)';

    b. *podvergnut'* ACC/INS – 'to subject (someone to.something)';

    c. *izobličit'* ACC/*v* INS – 'to expose (someone in something)';

d. *zaščitit'* ACC/*ot* ACC – 'to protect (someone from something/someone)';

e. *ozadačit'* ACC/INS – 'to perplex (someone with.something)';

f. *obvinit'* ACC/*v* ACC – 'to blame (someone for.something)';

g. *priznat'sja* DAT/*v* ACC – 'to admit (to.someone in something)';

h. *ubedit'* ACC/*v* ACC – 'to convince (someone in something)';

i. *predupredit'* ACC/*o* ACC – 'to warn (someone about something)';

j. *otgovorit'* ACC/*ot* ACC – 'to dissuade (someone from something)';

k. *sprjatat'* ACC/*ot* ACC – 'to hide (someone from someone/something)'.

Finally, there are verbs that behave like neither of the above Groups. With Group 3 predicates the scope is free no matter which internal argument comes first. Consider the example in (17). Here, unlike with the other two Groups, the change in the linear order of quantificational internal arguments yields no truth conditional difference: the sentences remain scopally ambiguous.

(17) a. Maša na-pisa-l-a   [kak-oj-to   slogan]   na každ-oj
          Masha NA-write-PST-F some-ACC.M-IND slogan.ACC.M on every-P.F
          sten-e).
          wall-P.F   ∃∀/∀∃

    'Masha wrote some slogan on every wall.'

    b. Maša na-pisa-l-a   na kak-oj-to   sten-e) [každ-yj
        Masha NA-write-PST-F on some-P.F-IND wall-P.F every-ACC.M
        slogan]
        slogan.ACC.M   ∃∀/∀∃

    'Masha wrote every slogan on some wall.'

(18) below lists some of the verbs that belong to this group:

(18) a. *ostavit'* ACC/*v* ACC – 'to leave (someone/something in something)';

    b. *položit'* ACC/*na* ACC or *v* ACC – 'to put (something on something or in something or somewhere)';

    c. *otdat'* ACC/DAT – 'to give away/to give back (something to.somebody)';

    d. *zapisat'* ACC/ *v* ACC or *na*/P – 'to write down (something in/somewhere or on something)';

e. *vyrastit'* ACC/*v* P – 'to grow (something in/somewhere)';

f. *otpravit'* ACC/*na* ACC – 'to send (something/somebody to something)';

g. *uslyšat'* ACC/*ot* ACC; or *o* GEN/*ot* ACC – 'to hear (about something/ somebody from somebody)';

h. *izvleč'* ACC/*iz* GEN – 'to extract (something from somewhere)';

i. *prisoedinit'* ACC/*k* DAT – 'to annex/to attach (something to something)';

j. *zagnat'* ACC/*v* ACC – 'to corner/to drive (someone in some place/somewhere)';

k. *vstavit'* ACC/*v* ACC – 'to insert (something into something/somewhere)'.

The question that naturally arises then is how to analyze the three Groups, specifically to what should we attribute their differences in scope behavior? Under the results in Antonyuk (2015), where I propose that scope freezing is due to crossing one QP over another in overt syntax and given SFG, the structural expectations for the three Groups of ditransitive predicates are clearly the following:

(19)   Group 1
    V NP-ACC NP-OBL   BASIC ORDER (amb)
    V NP-OBL NP-ACC NP-OBL   DERIVED ORDER (frozen)

(20)   Group 2:
    V NP-OBL NP-ACC   BASIC ORDER (amb)
    V NP-ACC NP-OBL NP-ACC   DERIVED ORDER (frozen)

(21)   Group 3
    V NP-ACC NP-OBL   BASIC ORDER (amb)
    V NP-OBL NP-ACC   BASIC ORDER (amb)

Thus, in Group 1 we expect the frozen NP-OBL > NP-ACC order to reflect raising of NP-OBL overtly over NP-ACC. In Group 2 we expect the frozen NP-ACC > NP-OBL order to reflect raising of NP-ACC over NP-OBL. In Group 3 we have at least two possibilities: either both orders are underived (i.e., base generated) or else one is in fact derived from the other, in a way that results in a configuration that fails to freeze scope.

Before we move on to the structural representations I propose for the three Groups, it is worth asking whether we can independently confirm that the Russian ditransitives do indeed subdivide into the three Groups as discussed above. It turns out there is a number of syntactic tests that the groups differ on. In particular, Groups 1 and 2, which are a mirror image of each other with respect to the scope freezing distribution, also show opposite behavior on a number of tests, briefly discussed below.

3 Syntactic evidence supporting ditransitive classification into three groups

The scope distribution data together with the SFG suggest that the structures of Groups 1 and 2 in particular should effectively be a mirror image of each other. Specifically, while the scope fluidity of ACC > OBL order for Group 1 suggests this is the base order, with the Accusative-marked argument projected higher in the structure, with the opposite order derived by overt QP movement, the scope fluidity of OBL > ACC order for Group 2 verbs suggests the opposite, namely a lower position for the Accusative-marked object. In Antonyuk (2015, 2017, 2018) I have justified the position that the Accusative-marked argument in the latter case cannot be a low direct object but is instead an Oblique argument that originates inside a silent Prepositional Phrase, with the P head case-marking the argument in its complement. Here I will briefly recapitulate the evidence from Antonyuk (2015) supporting this position and then present novel evidence that the low Accusative is indeed not a direct object, but a low Oblique argument.

3.1 The distributive *po* test

A classic test to use when the status of the direct object is in question is due to Pesetsky (1982), who noted that direct objects of transitive predicates and subjects of unaccusative predicates may appear as objects of distributive *po* in Russian, while subjects of transitive and unergative predicates typically may not. Indeed, this test, applied to our examples shows that the objects of Group 2 predicates do not distribute, suggesting structural differences from objects of Group 1 and 3 verbs, which do.

(22) Učitel' po-dari-l   po   tetradk-e   každ-omu
      Teacher PO-present-PST.M DISTR notebook-DAT.F every-DAT.M
      student-u.   Group 1
      student-DAT.M
      'The teacher presented a notebook to every student.'

(23) * Maša ugosti-l-a po   rebenk-u (kak-im-to   pečen'je-m).
        Masha treat-PST-F DISTR child-DAT some-INS.M-IND cookie-INS.M
      'Masha treated each child to a cookie.'   Group 2

(24) Maša na-pisa-l-a   po   slogan-u   na každ-oj   sten-e. Group 3
      Masha NA-write-PST-F DISTR slogan-DAT.M on every-P.F wall-P.F
      'Masha wrote a slogan on every wall.'

3.2 The Genitive of Negation test

Pesetsky (1982) also argued that Genitive of Negation can be used as a test of
unaccusativity in Russian. Applying it to our data we again see a clear dichotomy
between Group 1 and Group 2 verbs:

(25) Učitel' ne po-dari-l   tetradk-i.   Group 1
      teacher NEG PO-present-PST.M notebook-GEN.F
      'The teacher didn't present a notebook.'

(26) * Maša ne ugosti-l-a podrug-i.   Group 2
        Masha NEG treat-PST-F girlfriend-GEN.F
      'Masha didn't treat a friend.'

(27) Maša ne na-pisa-l-a   zapisk-i.   Group 3
      Masha NEG PO-write-PST-F note-GEN.F
      'Masha didn't write a note.'

   The two tests strongly suggest that the direct objects of Groups 1 and 3 predicates behave like true objects while the supposed "direct objects" of Group 2 predicates apparently do not possess properties expected of true direct objects. This
is fully in line with the proposal that the Accusative-marked objects of Group
2 verbs originate low, inside a PP whose null P head assigns lexical Accusative
case.

3.3 Resultative constructions as an objecthood test in Russian

Resultative Constructions have been argued to provide a (deep) unaccusativity test in English (Levin & Rappaport Hovav 1995; cf. Rappaport Hovav & Levin 2001; Kratzer 2005):

(28) a. Dawn pounded the dough flat   (Irvin 2012)
      b. The carrot juice froze solid.
      c. A bottle broke open.

In transitive sentences such as (28a) resultatives can be formed from direct objects only and cannot occur with external arguments or with VP-internal oblique arguments. If the test is applicable to Russian, the prediction, given our results so far, is that only the predicates belonging to Groups 1 and 3 will participate in the formation of a resultative construction. If the "direct object" of Group 2 predicates is indeed not a true direct object, it will not be possible to form a grammatical resultative construction on the basis of Group 2 predicates. The sentences below show that the prediction is correct: Group 1 and 3 predicates indeed allow a resultative that includes their direct object, while Group 2 predicates do not.[4]

Group 1

(29) Učitel' do-dari-l-sja   knig   (do togo,   čto
      teacher DO-present-PST.SG-REFL book.GEN.PL to that.GEN that
      o-sta-l-sja   ni s   čem).
      O-remain-PST.SG-REFL not with what.INS
      'The teacher presented books until he was left with nothing.'

(30) Maša do-trebova-l-a-s'   povyšenij-a   (do togo,   čto
      Masha DO-demand-PST.SG-F-REFL promotion-GEN.SG to that.GEN that
      ee   prosto uvoli-li   s   rabot-y).
      she.GEN simply fire-PST.PL from work-GEN.SG
      'Masha demanded a promotion to the point of getting herself fired.'

---

[4]There are several important differences to note: first of all, the result state expressed by the Russian construction in question holds of the subject, rather than the direct object. While this may initially suggest that the construction cannot be used as an unaccusativity test in Russian, I maintain that it can, specifically because the subject's result state comes about by manipulating the direct object in a way specified by the verb, and this is exactly why these examples are ungrammatical with Group 2 verbs.

Group 2

(31) * Maša   do-ugošč-a-l-a-s'   podrug   (do togo,   čto vse
 Masha DO-treat-IND-PST.SG-F-REFL friend.GEN.PL to that.GEN that all
 popa-li   v reanimacij-u).
 get-PST.PL in ICU-P.F
 'Masha treated her girlfriends to the point of everyone ending up in ICU.'

(32) * Maša   do-obiž-a-l-a-s'   druz-ej   (do togo,   čto
 Masha DO-insult-IND-PST.SG-F-REFL friend-GEN.PL to that.GEN that
 o-sta-la-s'   odn-a).
 O-remain-PST.SG.F-REFL alone-SG.F
 'Masha kept insulting friends to the point that she had noone left.'

Group 3

(33) Maša   do-pisa-l-a-s'   slogan-ov   (do togo,   čto
 Masha DO-write-PST.SG-F-REFL slogan-GEN.PL to that.GEN that
 ee   stil' nača-li   uznava-t').
 she.POSS.F style begin-PST.PL recognize-INF
 'Masha wrote so many slogans that her style became recognizable.'

(34) Vanja do-za-gruž-a-l-sja   kirpič-ej   (do polu-smert'-i).
 Vania DO-ZA-load-IPFV-PST.SG.M-REFL brick-GEN.PL to half-death-GEN.F
 'Vania loaded bricks until he was half-alive.'

 Note that despite some obvious differences, the resultative construction exemplified above which I will dub "Russian Unaccusative Resultative" (RUR) bears many similarities to a construction Tatevosov (2010) refers to as a "Russian Intensive Resultative" (RIR) in (35b), which in turn is very similar to the English Reflexive Resultative (ERR) (36b).

(35) a. Turist-y   gulja-l-i.
   tourist.NOM-PL walk-PST-PL
   'The tourists walked.'
  b. Turist-y   na-gulja-l-i-s'.
   tourist.NOM-PL NA-walk-PST-PL-REFL
   'By walking, the tourists achieved a state of being satisfied.'

(36) a. The tourists walked.

  b. The tourists walked themselves tired.

The similarities between RUR and Tatevosov's RIR (as well as the ERR) are listed below. First of all, the constructions in question create telic predicates:

(37) a. Turist-y   na-gulja-l-i-s'   {za čas / *čas}.   RIR
  Tourist.NOM-PL NA-walk-PST-PL-REFL in hour / *hour
  'By walking, the tourists achieved a state of being satisfied (in an hour)'

  b. 'The tourists walked themselves tired {in an hour / *for an hour}.' ERR

(38) a. Maša do-trebov-a-la-s'   povyšenij-a   {za god /
  Masha DO-demand-IPFV-PST.SG.F-REFL promotion-GEN.SG in year /
  *god}.   RUR
  *year
  'Masha got herself a promotion in a year (by demanding it).'

  b. Vanja do-prinos-i-l-sja   [plox-ix   novost'-ej] {za
  Vania DO-bring-IPFV-PST.SG.M-REFL bad-GEN.PL news-GEN.PL in
  god / *god} (do togo,   čto ego   iz-bi-l-i).
  year / *year to that.GEN that he.ACC.M.SG IZ-beat-PST-PL
  'Vania brought so much bad news in a year that he got beaten up for it.'

  c. Vanja do-za-gruž-a-l-sja   kirpič-ej   {za čas / *čas}
  Vania DO-ZA-load-IPFV-PST.SG.M-REFL brick-GEN.PL in hour / *hour
  (do polu-smert'-i).
  to half-death-GEN.F
  'In an hour, Vania loaded bricks until he was feeling half-dead.'

Furthermore, as noted by Tatevosov, both RIR and ERR, combined with rate adverbials like 'quickly' fail to entail the truth of their non-derived counterparts modified by the same adverbial:

(39) a. John walked quickly.

  b. John walked himself tired quickly. (≠> John walked quickly.)

(40) a. Vasja bystro   beg-a-l.
          Vasia quickly run-IPFV-PST.SG.M
          'Vasja ran quickly.'

      b. Vasja bystro   na-beg-a-l-sja.
          Vasia quickly NA-run-IPFV-PST.SG.M-REFL
          'Vasja ran himself into a state of being satisfied quickly.' (≠>'Vasja ran quickly.')

Interestingly, RUR behaves in exactly the same way, with the resultative combined with rate adverbial failing to entail the truth of the non-resultative counterpart:

(41) a. Vanja bystro   za-gruž-a-l   kirpič-i
          Vania quickly ZA-load-IPFV-PST.SG.M brick-ACC.PL

      b. Vania bystro   do-za-gruž-a-l-sja   kirpič-ej   do
          Vania quickly DO-ZA-load-IPFV-PST.SG.M-REFL brick-GEN.PL to
          polu-smert'-i.   ≠> Vanja bystro   za-gruž-a-l
          half-death-GEN.F ≠> Vania quickly ZA-load-IPFV-PST.SG.M
          kirpič-i.
          brick-ACC.PL
          'Vania quickly got himself into the state of being half-dead by loading bricks.'

Tatevosov proposes that "the affixal nature of the result expression in Russian has straightforward consequences for its interpretation: in Russian, unlike in English, descriptive properties of a result state are underspecified". He demonstrates that the result state in RIRs that is obtained due to the lexical contribution of the resultative affix (na-) is a cancellable implicature:

(42) (Tatevosov 2010)
      Turist-y   na-gul'-a-l-i-s'   do iznemoženij-a.
      Tourist.NOM-PL NA-walk-IPFV-PST-PL-REFL to exhaustion-GEN
      'By walking, the tourists achieved a state of being exhausted.'

Unlike the prefix na- of RIR, which typically contributes a positive connotation, suggesting the subject enters into a pleasant state, the prefix do- of RUR typically contributes a negative connotation, suggesting the subject entered a negative state as a result of his or her actions, which is nevertheless also a cancellable implicature (cf. (43a) and (43b)):

(43) a. Maša do-trebov-a-l-a-s'   povyšenij-a   {za god /
          Masha DO-demand-IPFV-PST.SG-F-REFL promotion-GEN.SG in year /
          *god}.
          *year

      'Masha got herself a promotion in a year (by demanding it).'

      b. Maša do-trebov-a-l-a-s'   povyšenij-a   do
          Masha DO-demand-IPFV-PST.SG-F-REFL promotion-GEN.SG to

          togo,   čto ee   prosto uvoli-l-i
          that.GEN that she.ACC simply fire-PST-PL

      'Masha got herself fired by demanding a promotion too much.'

With respect to the crucial differences between RIR and RUR, it is important
to note that Tatevosov (2010) argues that both RIRs and ERRs "refer to events
in which a certain property of the participant undergoes a gradual change. This
change leads the participant to the result state whose descriptive properties are
fully specified in English and underspecified in Russian. In English, the participant undergoing change can and in Russian must be identical to the subject."
The above view naturally explains another noted property of RIRs and ERRs, discussed by Tatevosov, namely the fact that both constructions exhibit parallel lexical restrictions and "tend to be licensed for the same classes of non-derived verbs,
intransitive activity verbs or transitive activity verbs, but not for unaccusatives".
Despite all the similarities with the RIRs, RURs are crucially different semantically in that the direct object in RURs either signifies the result state obtained
through the action denoted by the verb, or crucially contributes to the result
state by being the object manipulated to a degree that a certain result state obtains (see (38c), for instance). Given their semantics, informally described above,
RIR is incompatible with a direct object while RUR is ungrammatical without
one. Interestingly, using the latter without the direct object renders the construction ungrammatical for Group 1 and 3 predicates, but dramatically improves the
grammaticality of Group 2 predicates on the resultative meaning, with such sentences being perfectly acceptable on the RIR interpretation in which the resulting
change necessarily describes the state of the subject:

(44) Group 1

      a. * Maša do-trebov-a-l-a-s'.
            Masha DO-demand-IPFV-PST.SG-F-REFL

      b. * Vania do-prinos-i-l-sja.
            Vania DO-bring-IPFV-PST.SG.M-REFL

(45)   Group 2

>   a. Maša   do-obziva-l-a-s'.
>   Masha DO-swear-PST.SG-F-REFL
>
>   b. Maša   do-obiž-a-l-a-s'.
>   Masha DO-insult-IPFV-PST.SG-F-REFL

(46)   Group 3

>   a. */?? Maša   do-pisa-l-a-s'.
>   Masha DO-write-PST.SG.F-REFL
>
>   b. * Vania do-za-gruž-a-l-sja.
>   Vania DO-ZA-load-IPFV-PST.SG.M-REFL

Thus, again, we see a clear dichotomy between Groups 1/3 and Group 2. The "direct objects" of the latter Group simply do not behave as such. Taken together, the three diagnostics discussed here provide strong evidence for the argument that Group 2 predicates do not in fact subcategorize for a direct object, as the Accusative-marked objects of such verbs do not exhibit syntactic behavior expected of direct objects. In the following section I will briefly discuss the structures I posit for the three Groups of Russian ditransitives that account for their syntactic behavior and QP scope distribution, in line with the Scope Freezing Generalization.

4 The proposed structures for the three groups of Russian ditransitives

Given that Groups 1 and 2 are essentially the mirror image of each other with respect to scope behavior, with one order of internal arguments frozen and the opposite order scopally fluid, it makes sense to approach them in a similar fashion, with the same logic applying to both Groups. Specifically, taking the Scope Freezing Generalization as our background assumption, we are committed to the conclusion that the two orders of the predicates belonging to Group 1 and Group 2, despite their differences, are derivationally related. That is, both Group 1 and Group 2 verbs will require a derivational analysis of their base-generated structures.

4.1 Possible structures for group 1 predicates

To remind the reader, Group 1 predicates are those where scope is frozen on OBL > ACC order and free on the ACC > OBL order. Logically speaking, two kinds of analyses appear to be possible, given our underlying assumptions, but we'll only consider (47a) to be a viable option here.[5] [,6]

(47) a. OBL has been overtly raised to an adjoined position.

  b. OBL has been raised to Spec,ApplP.

With respect to (47a), the only viable option is that in Figure 1, supported by the placement of agent-oriented adverbs ("deliberately", "purposefully", "willingly", etc.), which are typically assumed to adjoin high to the *v*P where the Agent role is introduced or checked, as well as the lack of verb raising to T in Russian (cf. 48a vs 48b):

Testing this prediction with a Group 1 predicate we get the following results:

(48) a. Maša special'no po-trebova-l-a   s   Ivan-a
    Masha purposefully PO-demand-PST-F from Ivan-GEN
    den'g-i.
    money.ACC-PL

    'Masha demanded money from Ivan.'

  b. * Maša po-trebova-l-a   s   Ivan-a   special'no
    Masha PO-demand-PST-F from Ivan-GEN purposefully
    den'g-i.
    money.ACC-PL

Note that the structure in Figure 1 is identical to that proposed for Russian ditransitives in Bailyn (1995, 2012) based on independent types of evidence, thus our conclusions here converge with previous research.[7]

---

[5]I assume that the frozen scope order is derived via overt movement and that in most cases ambiguous scope within the *v*P is an indicator of a base-generated order.

[6]A reviewer points out that raising into Spec, ApplP is an unjustified move since this would constitute raising into an argument position. This objection relies on assumptions that are not shared by all (see Larson 2014 for discussion). I will not develop the Raising-into-Spec,ApplP analysis here mostly due to space limitations.

[7]The conclusions regarding the base-generated order of Group 1 (and Group 3) verbs also converge with the findings reported in Titov (2017), who argues that once Information-Structural considerations licensing various derived word orders in Russian are controlled for, the "canonical" order of Russian ditransitive verbs emerges, that being the ACC > DAT order (see also

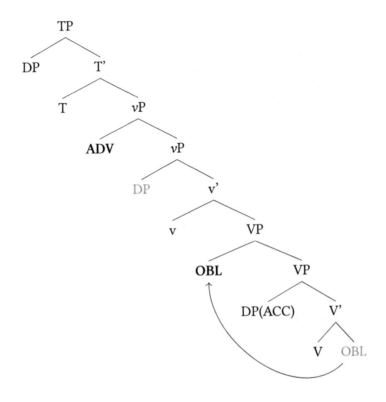

Figure 1: Derived order of a Group 1 verb.

Cépeda & Cyrino 2020 [this volume] for a similar conclusion regarding Spanish, European Portuguese and Brazilian Portuguese). Note, however, that the general results reported here contradict the conclusions of Titov (2017), as it is shown here that there is no homogeneity among Russian ditransitives, with Group 2 verbs having a different base-generated order which is reflected in significant differences in their syntactic behavior, something Titov's account has nothing to say about. Thus, one of the verbs Titov discusses, *podvergnut'*, is a typical Group 2 verb, whereas Titov argues for the same ACC » DAT base order for this and all other verbs she considers and furthermore argues that these conclusions hold quite generally for all ditransitive predicates in Russian. To the extent that the conclusions reached in this paper are correct, however, they suggest that while controlling for Information Structure licensing may be necessary, it will not be sufficient to correctly determine verbal argument structure and that QP scope distribution patterns provide a more accurate diagnostic of internal argument structure.

4.2 Possible structures for group 2 predicates

We have seen that assuming the correctness of SFG entails that the Accusative-marked object of Group 2 verbs must be generated lower than the Oblique-marked argument (see (49) below). I have proposed in Antonyuk (2015) that this is due to the fact that the low Accusative is not a true direct object, but is effectively an Oblique argument base-generated low inside a PP, with a silent P head assigning it lexical Accusative case.

(49)   V NP (ACC) NP-OBL NP (ACC)   DERIVED ORDER (frozen)

Regarding the structural possibilities themselves, as was already noted, they appear to be quite similar to those available for Group 1 verbs:

(50)   a. [PP P DP_ACC] raises over OBL and adjoin to VP
       b. [PP P DP_ACC] raises over OBL to Spec,ApplP.

In terms of the Agent-oriented adverbs, the two Groups behave alike, which means analyses requiring high adjunction with concomitant v-to-T raising are highly unlikely:

(51)   a. Maša special'no   obozva-l-a [vredn-ogo   malčik-a]
          Masha purposefully call-PST-F   capricious-ACC.M boy-ACC.M
          (nexoroš-im slov-om).
          bad-INS   word-INS
          'Masha purposefully called a capricious boy with a bad word.'
       b. * Maša obozva-l-a [vredn-ogo   malčik-a] special'no
            Masha call-PST-F   capricious-ACC.M boy-ACC.M purposefully
            (nexoroš-im slov-om).
            bad-INS   word-INS
            'Masha purposefully called a capricious boy with a bad word.'

Given these considerations, the structure of a sentence such as (52a) would seem to be something like in Figure 2, where the sentence contains two oblique complements (a DP and a PP).

(52)   a. Maša ugosti-l-a (kak-im-to   pečen'je-m) každ-ogo
          Masha treat-PST-F some-INS-IND cookie-INS   every-ACC.M
          rebenk-a.   ∃∀/∀∃
          child-ACC.M
          'Masha treated every child to some cookie.'

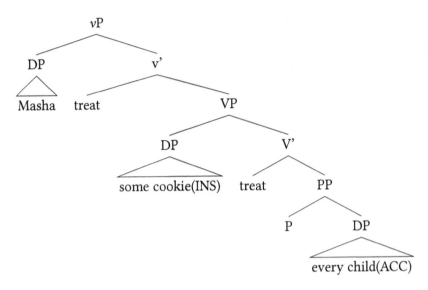

Figure 2: Base order of a Group 2 verb.

b. Maša ugosti-l-a [kako-go-to   rebenk-a] (každ-ym
   Masha treat-PST-F some-ACC.M-IND child-ACC.M every-INS.N
   pečen'je-m).   ∃∀/*∀∃
   cookie-INS.N

   'Masha treated some child to every cookie.'

The frozen order would then be derived by fronting the PP, presumably by left-adjoining it to VP as in Figure 3.[8]

Incidentally, there is further evidence for the proposal that Group 2 predicates involve two oblique phrases. Consider (53):

(53) a. Maša po-besedov-a-l-a (na kak-uju-to   tem-u)   [s
         Masha PO-talk-IPFV-PST-F on some-ACC.F-IND topic-ACC.F with
         každ-ym   drug-om].   ∃∀/∀∃
         every-INS.M friend-INS.M

         'Masha had a conversation on some topic with every friend.'

      b. Maša po-besedov-a-l-a [s   kak-im-to   drug-om] (na
         Masha PO-talk-IPFV-PST-F with some-INS.M-IND friend-INS.M on

---

[8]In Figure 3 the lower PP copy is of course taken to be silent.

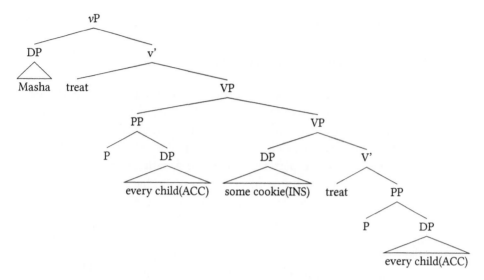

Figure 3: Derived order of a Group 2 verb.

každ-uju   tem-u).   ∃∀/*∀∃
every-ACC.F topic-ACC.F

'Masha had a conversation with some friend on every topic.

The example in (53) contains a ditransitive predicate with two overt quantificational PPs, with one of those Ps assigning Accusative case. Thus, this example is fully analogous to what I suggest for Group 2 predicates, the only difference being that the preposition assigning Accusative is overt in (53) but covert in all the other cases we've seen in this section. Finally, the strongest piece of evidence in support of the proposal that there is in fact a null P assigning Accusative case in a low position in Group 2 predicates is examples such as (54):

(54) a. Maša ot-ruga-l-a   (za ka-kuju-to   ošibk-u)
         Masha OT-scold-PST-F for some-ACC.F-IND mistake-ACC.F
         [každ-ogo   drug-a].   ∃∀/∀∃
         every-ACC.M friend-ACC.M

      'Masha scolded every friend for some mistake.'

      b. Maša ot-ruga-l-a   [kak-ogo-to   drug-a]   (za
         Masha OT-scold-PST-F every-ACC.M-IND friend-ACC.M for

každ-uju   ošibk-u).   ∃∀/*∀∃
every-ACC.F mistake-ACC.F

'Masha scolded some friend for every mistake.'

What is interesting about this example, and of utmost importance for the structural analysis advanced here, is the following: this ditransitive verb *otrugat* ('to scold') selects two Accusative-marked objects, one Oblique, occurring inside an overt Prepositional Phrase and one which looks like a regular direct object Accusative. However, the scope pattern that we find with this pair of examples, specifically the frozen scope status of (54b), suggests that (54b) is the derived order, that is, what looks like the regular direct object Accusative must have originated below the Accusative that is inside the PP. This, of course, on my assumptions suggests that the "regular" direct object Accusative in (54b) is in fact a concealed low Oblique Accusative, which originates inside a null PP and thus gets its case from a null P head. Significantly, the above "direct object" Accusative argument does not do well on the objecthood tests discussed before:

(55) a. * Maša ot-ruga-l-a   po   drug-u   za každ-uju
         Masha OT-scold-PST-F DISTR friend-DAT for every-ACC.F
         ošibk-u.   Distributive *po* test
         mistake-ACC.F

      b. ?? Maša ne   ot-ruga-l-a   podrug-i.   Genitive of Negation
            Masha NEG OT-scold-PST-F girlfriend-GEN.F

      c. * Maša do-ruga-l-a-s'   drug-a   do togo,   čto on
           Masha DO-scold-PST-F-REFL friend-ACC to that.GEN that he
           uše-l.   RUR
           leave-PST.M

         'Masha scolded her friend into leaving.' (Tatevosov 2010)

      d. Maša do-ruga-l-a-s'.   RIR
         Masha DO-scold-PST-F-REFL

         'Masha scolded her way to some negative result.'

As the above tests show, the Accusative-marked object does not behave as would be expected of a true direct object: it does not allow the distributive *po* phrase, is strongly degraded in the Genitive of Negation configuration and the Unaccusative Resultative built on it is ungrammatical while the Intensive Resultative is, as expected. The conclusion is therefore that this particular predicate does not subcategorize for a direct object but instead takes two Oblique arguments, one of which is an overt PP, with the preposition *za* marking its complement with lexical Accusative case, and another o2blique argument which is also assigned lexical Accusative case, by a silent P head. [9]

4.3 Structural possibilities for group 3 predicates

With regard to Group 3 predicates, there are two major possibilities: independent projection or a derivational relation between the two alternating orders of internal arguments. While the scope ambiguity of both orders, coupled with SFG, might suggest that the two orders are independently projected, I argue this is not the case. Consider (56):

(56) a. Job blamed [God] [for his troubles]   (Larson 1990)

     b. Job blamed [his troubles] [on God]

What makes these good candidates for independent projection is the fact that along with the change in the order of the two internal arguments, there is also clearly a change in grammatical relations, with 'God' being a DO in (56a) but an oblique in (56b). As noted by Richard Larson (p.c.), the corresponding examples with quantificational phrases are both ambiguous, as expected under my analysis:

(57) a. John blamed some employee for every mistake.   ∃∀,∀∃

     b. John blamed some mistake on every employee.   ∃∀,∀∃

Native speakers apparently also perceive an additional semantic distinction between these, as well, with (57a) being notationally related to (58a), and (57b) being related to locatives, as in (58b):

(58) a. John thanked some employee for every success.

     b. John gave/offered thanks to some employee for every success.

---

[9] While not all psychological verbs (Belletti & Rizzi 1988) allow alternating (causative) ditransitive forms, those that do necessarily form Group 2 ditransitives. Note further that while the homogeneous behavior of Group 2 verbs with respect to the unaccusativity diagnostics suggests a certain homogeneity within the Group in terms of syntactic structure, it is certainly not the case that all Group 2 verbs are psych verbs. Thus to the extent that theories arguing that the Causer argument is generated in Spec, *v*P while the Agent is generated in Spec, VoiceP, (see Kratzer 2005 and Alexiadou et al. 2006 i.a.), the verbs belonging to Group 2 are expected to differ with respect to the position of the higher internal argument (e.g., Spec, VP for non-Causers/Themes vs Spec,*v*P for Causers).

Svitlana Antonyuk

The fact that the thematic roles involved in the two alternations are different in the above cases supports the idea that they are not derivationally related. This poses a problem for the non-derivational account of Group 3 ditransitive alternations since in none of them can a parallel difference in thematic roles be detected. The only differences seem to be related to the information structural status of the two internal arguments, with their thematic roles always staying the same. Thus, it is worth considering other alternatives. With independent projection arguably ruled out and the movement of the kind implicated with Groups 1 and 2 being excluded by the fact that both orders are scopally ambiguous, I suggest that orders such as (59b) are derived via Light Predicate Raising (LPR) (following Larson 1989, 2014).

(59) a. Maša na-pisa-l-a   [kak-oj-to   slogan]   (na
          Masha NA-write-PST-F some-ACC.M-IND slogan.ACC.M on
          každ-oj   sten-e).   ∃∀/∀∃
          every-ACC.F wall-ACC.F

          'Masha wrote some slogan on every wall.'

      b. Maša na-pisa-l-a   (na kak-oj-to   sten-e)   [každ-yj
          Masha NA-write-PST-F on some-ACC.F-IND wall-ACC.F every-ACC.M
          slogan].   ∃∀/∀∃
          slogan.ACC.M

          'Masha wrote every slogan on some wall.'

Consider the derivation of (59b) in Figure 4 below:

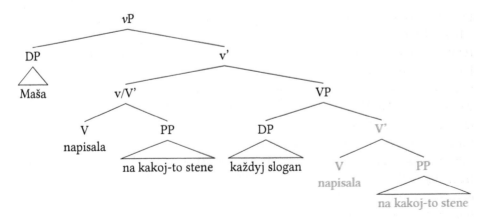

Figure 4: Derived order of a Group 3 verb.

As evident from structural relations in Figure 4, what is crucially important in relation to my analysis is that the LPR configuration does not lead to a situation where the raised PP/DP is able to c-command the other phrase, by virtue of the interfering v/V' node, thus accounting for the lack of scope freezing in these examples.

While adopting Larson's LPR analysis provides a straightforward way to account for the lack of scope freezing with Group 3 verbs, in the absence of an independent motivation for the application of such LP Raising with verbs belonging to this group, its adoption here to account for the apparent violation of the SFG with these verbs might seem too stipulative to be persuasive. However, I will argue here that Group 3 predicates are different from those in Group 2 and even from the very similar Group 1 verbs in important respects which explains their syntactic behavior. A careful examination of Group 3 verbs listed in (18) reveals that all such predicates (to the exclusion of a few verbs to be discussed shortly) share the property of taking a direct object marked with structural Accusative case and a Preposition Phrase. I argue that it is precisely the nature of the PP complement that plays the crucial role here and provides an explanation for the observed differences between Group 1 and Group 3. The limited class of PPs observed with Group 3 predicates can be characterized as sharing the property of signifying either direction (of movement) or location (*v/in, na/on, ot/from, iz/from/ k/to* or *towards*). Thus, Group 3 is crucially similar to Group 1 verbs in subcategorizing for a direct object DP marked with structural Accusative case, but unlike Group 1 verbs, Group 3 verbs take a locational/directional PP complement (whereas Group 1 verbs take a Dative case-maked DP complement or a PP which takes a relational preposition (*s/from, s/with, dlja/for*). To put this into terminology used in research on prepositional phrases, Group 3 PPs are those where the P introduces the Ground argument (see Svenonius 2003; 2007 and related research). Group 1 prepositional heads, being strictly relational, do not. Finally, another similarity between Groups 1 and 3 which at first glance might suggest that the above differentiation is unjustified, is due to the fact that some verbs classified as Group 3 are verbs like *otdat'* (to give away, to give back), which take an ACC-marked THEME and a DAT-marked GOAL argument, just like the numerous ACC/DAT verbs that belong to Group 1. *Otdat'*, in fact, is related to the verb *dat'* (give), which is a canonical Group 1 ditransitive that exhibits scope freezing on the DAT>ACC order of internal arguments (also discussed in Boneh & Nash 2017). As discussed in Antonyuk (2015), such Group 3 verbs present particular difficulties during classification attempts due to showing strong surface scope bias on DAT>ACC order, which often leads to their initial misclassification as Group 1 verbs. However, additional tests, such as the use of Constrastive Focus (Antonyuk & Larson 2016) help establish that they are in fact Group 3 verbs. Here I argue that the (lexical) prefixes verbs such as *otdat'* occur with is the very reason they behave as Group 3 verbs, unlike their unprefixed Group 1 counterparts. The prefixes taken by Group 3 verbs are crucially distinct from whatever prefixes (if any) may be found with Group 1 or Group 2 verbs in signifying direction/location, just like the PPs that occur as complements of Group 3 verbs do. The unified semantics of the class of the prepositions and prefixes that appear with Group 3 verbs suggests a natural way of explaining their behavior. If prepositions and prefixes are both elements of category P (Matushansky 2002; Biskup 2017; and esp. Svenonius 2004, 2008), then one might argue that the empirical observation that locational/directional prepositions behave in some sense as being *closer* to the verb than other prepositions (including preposition *to* in English which occurs in PP Dative constructions)[10] may be explained by the need of such prepositions (and the PPs they project) to occur at LF as syntactic units with the verb. There are two ways in which this can be achieved: either the PP raises and attaches to the verb at LF (which is arguably what happens with Group 3 verbs on their basic order), or the verb raises to its position inside the *v*P together with the PP, which is exactly what happens in cases of Light Predicate Raising. If the latter option is employed, scope freezing does not take place and the lower QP is then free to raise above the structurally higher one at LF, which then accounts for the ambiguous nature of the derived word order with Group 3 predicates, but not with Group 1 and 2. Thus, while the account sketched here needs to be fleshed out, it suggests an intuitive explanation for why Group 3 verbs pattern differently from Groups 1 and 2 as far as QP scope is concerned.

5 Conclusions

I have argued that the argument structure of ditransitives can be studied by considering their quantifier scope ambiguity and scope freezing distribution patterns. Assuming the Scope Freezing Generalization is correct and using it to probe argument structure affords us novel insights and suggests that Russian ditransitives are not a homogeneous group, but in fact subdivide into three distinct Groups, each associated with a distinct structure and a distinct set of properties. Most importantly, however, the data discussed here provide strong evidence that not all "direct objects" are in fact true direct objects with expected properties: the

---

[10] As pointed out to me by Larson (p.c.).

data presented here suggest that a whole group of such objects are in fact concealed Obliques. The derivational account of Russian ditransitives offered in this paper has a number of important consequences, with implications for argument structure, verbal alternations, the status of directional/location PPs as a natural class, the notion of ditransitivity and the status of Light Predicate Raising in the grammar that are left largely without discussion due to space limitations.[11]

Abbreviations

The abbreviations used in the glosses of this chapter follow the Leipzig Glossing Rules. Additional abbreviation: P: Prepositional case.

Acknowledgements

I gratefully acknowledge helpful feedback and suggestions for improvement I received from John F. Bailyn, Richard K. Larson, Viviane Deprez, Gillian Ramchand, Alec Marantz and Peter Hallman that led to significant improvement of this paper, as well as helpful criticisms and questions of two anonymous reviewers. This research was supported by Austrian Science Fund (FWF), Grant number: P27384-G23 awarded to Dr. Peter Hallman.

References

Alexiadou, Artemis, Elena Anagnostopoulou & Florian Schäfer. 2006. The properties of anticausatives crosslinguistically. In Mara Frascarelli (ed.), *Phases of interpretation*, 187–211. Berlin: Mouton de Gruyter.

Antonyuk, Svitlana. 2006. The scope of quantifier phrases in Russian: A QR analysis. *Linguistics in the Big Apple: Online proceedings of SUNY/CUNY/NYU/Yale Student Conference (SYNC)*.

---

[11]Note that Cépeda & Cyrino 2020 [this volume] and Cornilescu 2020 [this volume] similarly offer derivational accounts of ditransitives in Spanish, European Portuguese, Brazilian Portuguese and Romanian respectively. To the extent that these papers focus on the more prototypical ditransitives that on my account belong to Group 1 predicates where I argue ACC > DAT or DO > IO order is base-generated, our conclusions seem to converge. (Cépeda & Cyrino 2020 [this volume]) additionally argue that Spanish, European Portuguese and Brazilian Portuguese do not have a DOC, primarily based on the fact that IOs do not passivize in these languages. While passivization is not discussed in my paper, IOs in Russian (and East Slavic more generally) do passivize, thus pointing to a genuine difference in this respect between the languages under consideration.

Antonyuk, Svitlana. 2015. *Quantifier scope and scope freezing in Russian.* Stony Brook, NY: Stony Brook University. (Doctoral dissertation).

Antonyuk, Svitlana. 2017. How QP scope can weigh in on a long-time debate: The puzzle of Russian ditransitives. In Claire Halpert, Hadas Kotek & Coppe van Urk (eds.), *A pesky set: Papers for David Pesetsky.* Cambridge, MA: MIT Press. Massachusetts Institute of Technology Working Papers in Linguistics (MITWPL) special volume.

Antonyuk, Svitlana. 2018. Embracing the differences: The three classes of Russian ditransitives. In Wayles Browne, Miloje Despic, Naomi Enzinna, Simone Harmath-de Lemos, Robin Karlin & Draga Zec (eds.), *Formal Approaches to Slavic Linguistics (FASL) #25: The third Cornell meeting 2016.* Ann Arbor, MI: Michigan Slavic Publications.

Antonyuk, Svitlana. 2019. Quantifier scope in Russian. *Glossa: A Journal of General Linguistics* 4(1) (Article 54). DOI:10.5334/gjgl.562

Antonyuk, Svitlana & Richard K. Larson. 2016. *Scope freezing in PP dative constructions?* Berlin. Presentation given at Formal Description of Slavic Languages 12 (FDSL).

Antonyuk, Svitlana & Roksolana Mykhaylyk. In press. Scope freezing and object shift in Ukrainian: Does superiority matter? Remark. *Syntax.*

Bailyn, John Frederick. 1995. *A configurational approach to Russian "free" word order.* Ithaca, NY: Cornell University. (Doctoral dissertation).

Bailyn, John Frederick. 2010. What's inside VP? New (and old) evidence from Russian. In Wayles Browne (ed.), *Formal Approaches to Slavic Linguistics (FASL) #18: The Cornell meeting 2009,* 21–37. Ann Arbor, MI: Michigan Slavic Publications.

Bailyn, John Frederick. 2012. *The syntax of Russian.* Cambridge: Cambridge University Press.

Belletti, Adriana & Luigi Rizzi. 1988. Psych-verbs and θ-Theory. *Natural Language & Linguistic Theory* 6(3). 291–352. DOI:10.1007/BF00133902

Biskup, Petr. 2017. *Prepositions and verbal prefixes: The case of Slavic.* Leipzig: Universität Leipzig. (Habilitation).

Boneh, Nora & Lea Nash. 2017. The syntax and semantics of dative DPs in Russian ditransitives. *Natural Language & Linguistic Theory* 35(4). 899–953.

Bruening, Benjamin. 2001. QR obeys superiority: Frozen scope and ACD. *Linguistic Inquiry* 32(2). 233–273. DOI:10.1162/00243890152001762

Bruening, Benjamin. 2010. Double object constructions disguised as prepositional datives. *Linguistic Inquiry* 41(2). 287–305. DOI:10.1162/ling.2010.41.2.287

Cépeda, Paola & Sonia Cyrino. 2020. Putting objects in order: Asymmetrical relations in Spanish and Portuguese ditransitives. In Anna Pineda & Jaume Mateu (eds.), *Dative constructions in Romance and beyond*, 97–116. Berlin: Language Science Press. DOI:10.5281/zenodo.3776539

Cornilescu, Alexandra. 2020. Ditransitive constructions with differentially marked direct objects in Romanian. In Anna Pineda & Jaume Mateu (eds.), *Dative constructions in Romance and beyond*, 117–142. Berlin: Language Science Press. DOI:10.5281/zenodo.3776541

Dyakonova, Marina. 2005. Russian double object constructions. *Amsterdam Center for Language and Communication Working Papers* 2(1). 3–30.

Dyakonova, Marina. 2009. *A phase-based approach to Russian free word order*. Utrecht: LOT. 2007 dissertation at the University of Amsterdam.

Franks, Steven. 1995. *Parameters of Slavic morphosyntax*. New York, NY: Oxford University Press.

Greenberg, Gerald & Steven Franks. 1991. A parametric approach to dative subjects and the second dative in Slavic. *The Slavic and East European Journal* 35(1). 71–97.

Hallman, Peter. 2015. Syntactic neutralization in double object constructions. *Linguistic Inquiry* 46(3). 389–424. DOI:10.1162/LING_a_00187

Harbert, Wayne E. & Almeida J. Toribio. 1991. Nominative objects. *Cornell Working Papers in Linguistics* 9. 127–192.

Harley, Heidi. 1995. *Subjects, events and licensing*. Cambridge, MA: Massachusetts Institute of Technology. (Doctoral dissertation).

Harley, Heidi. 2002. Possession and the double object construction. *Linguistic Variation Yearbook* 2(1). 31–70.

Irvin, Patricia. 2012. *Unaccusativity at the interfaces*. New York, NY: New York University. (Doctoral dissertation).

Kratzer, Angelika. 2005. *Building resultatives*. Claudia Maienborn & Angelika Wöllstein-Leisten (eds.). Tübingen: Max Niemeyer Verlag. 177–212.

Larson, Richard K. 1988. On the double object construction. *Linguistic Inquiry* 19(3). 335–391.

Larson, Richard K. 1989. *Light predicate raising* (MIT Lexicon Project Working Papers 27).

Larson, Richard K. 1990. Double objects revisited: Reply to Jackendoff. *Linguistic Inquiry* 21(4). 589–632.

Larson, Richard K. 2014. *On shell structure*. New York, NY: Routledge.

Levin, Beth & Malka Rappaport Hovav. 1995. *Unaccusativity: At the syntax-lexical semantics interface*. Cambridge, MA: MIT Press.

Marantz, Alec. 1993. Implications of asymmetries in double object constructions. In Sam A. Mchombo (ed.), *Theoretical aspects of Bantu grammar*, 113–150. Stanford, CA: CSLI Publications.

Matushansky, Ora. 2002. On formal identity of Russian prefixes and prepositions. *MIT Working Papers in Linguistics* 42. 217–253.

Pesetsky, David. 1982. *Paths and categories.* Cambridge, MA: Massachusetts Institute of Technology. (Doctoral dissertation).

Pesetsky, David. 1995. *Zero syntax: Experiencers and cascades.* Cambridge, MA: MIT Press.

Pylkkänen, Liina. 2002. *Introducing arguments.* Massachusetts Institute of Technology. (Doctoral dissertation).

Rappaport Hovav, Malka & Beth Levin. 2001. An event structure account of English resultatives. *Language* 77(4). 766–797.

Richardson, Kylie. 2007. *Case and aspect in Slavic.* Oxford: Oxford University Press.

Svenonius, Peter. 2003. Limits on P: Filling in holes vs. Falling in holes. *Nordlyd* 31(2). 431–445. DOI:10.7557/12.13

Svenonius, Peter. 2004. Slavic prefixes and morphology. *Nordlyd* 32(2). 177–204. DOI:10.7557/12.67

Svenonius, Peter. 2007. Adpositions, particles, and the arguments they introduce. In Eric Reuland, Tanmoy Bhattacharya & Giorgos Spathas (eds.), *Argument structure*, 63–103. Amsterdam: John Benjamins.

Svenonius, Peter. 2008. Russian prefixes are phrasal. In Gerhild Zybatow, Luka Szucsich, Uwe Junghanns & Roland Meyer (eds.), *Formal description of Slavic languages*, 526–537. Frankfurt am Main: Peter Lang.

Tatevosov, Sergei. 2010. Building intensive resultatives. In Wayles Browne (ed.), *Formal Approaches to Slavic Linguistics (FASL) #18: The Cornell meeting 2009*, 289–302. Ann Arbor, MI: Michigan Slavic Publications.

Titov, Elena. 2017. The canonical order of Russian objects. *Linguistic Inquiry* 48(3). 427–457.

Chapter 3

Ditransitive constructions: What sets Brazilian Portuguese apart from other Romance languages?

Ana Regina Calindro

Federal University of Rio de Janeiro (UFRJ)

The aim of this paper is to discuss whether a particular diachronic change in the expression of indirect objects (IOs) in Brazilian Portuguese (BP) has set this language apart from other Romance languages. Since the 19th century, BP has been generalizing the use of the preposition *para* 'to' in ditransitive sentences with verbs of movement, transfer and creation. Moreover, the morphological counterpart of the dative argument in the 3rd person (the clitic *lhe(s)*) has been replaced by other strategies, while in European Portuguese (EP), IOs in the same contexts are introduced by the dummy preposition *a* and can always alternate with *lhe(s)*. According to Torres Morais (2007), these IOs in EP are dative arguments introduced by an applicative head, as also argued by Cuervo (2003) for Spanish, and Diaconescu & Rivero (2007) for Romanian. In this paper, I will propose that ditransitive sentences in BP have a different structural representation from other Romance languages, given that it cannot express dative case in the 3rd person anymore, nor via functional prepositions, nor by the clitic *lhe(s)*. Consequently, I propose that the IOs in BP should be introduced via a *p* head, based on the proposals of Svenonius (2003; 2004), Wood (2012) and the *i** single argument introducer proposal by Wood & Marantz (2017).

1 Introduction

The aim of this paper is to discuss whether a diachronic change in the expression of indirect objects (IOs) in Brazilian Portuguese (BP) has set this language apart from other Romance languages, in terms of how IOs are structured.

Since the 19th century, BP has been generalizing the use of full prepositions as *para* 'to' in ditransitive sentences with verbs of transfer and movement (cf. 1)

Ana Regina Calindro. 2020. Ditransitive constructions: What sets Brazilian Portuguese apart from other Romance languages? In Anna Pineda & Jaume Mateu (eds.), *Dative constructions in Romance and beyond*, 75–95. Berlin: Language Science Press. DOI:10.5281/zenodo.3776535

and creation (cf. 2) (cf. Freire 2005; Torres Morais & Berlinck 2006; Torres Morais & Salles 2010).

(1) Maria **enviou** uma carta para/a   o   João   / para ele.
Maria sent   a   letter $P_{para (to)/ a (to)}$ the João.OBL / to   him.3SG
'Maria sent a letter to João/to him.'

(2) Maria **preparou** o   jantar   para   o   João   / para ele.
Maria prepared the dinner $P_{para(to)}$ the João.OBL / for   him.3SG
'Maria prepared dinner for João/for him.'

In addition, the 3rd person dative argument counterpart (clitic *lhe(s)*) has been replaced in BP by other strategies, such as 3rd person pronouns preceded by *para*: *para ele(s) / ela(s)* 'to him / her / them', as we can see in the examples above.

Conversely, in the relevant context, IOs in European Portuguese (EP) are introduced by the preposition *a* and can always alternate with *lhe(s)*.

(3) A   Maria **enviou** uma carta a   o   João   / enviou-lhe   uma
The Maria sent   a   letter $P_{a (to)}$ the João.DAT / sent-3SG.DAT a
carta.
letter.
'Maria sent a letter to João/sent him a letter.'

Regarding argument structure representation, ditransitive constructions have always been a challenge for Chomsky's (1981; 1986) binary-branching model. The two first attempts to deal with the issue were Baker's (1988) incorporation hypothesis and Larson's (1988) VP shells proposal for the Prepositional Dative Construction (PDC) 'Mary gave a book to John' and the Double Object Construction (DOC) 'Mary gave John a book' in English. This phenomenon is known as the *dative alternation*.

Conversely, Marantz (1993) proposes an applicative head to introduce IOs in DOCs, building on the analysis of Bantu languages, which accounted for the absence of prepositions in DOCs (cf. Alsina & Mchombo 1993). Following this work, Pylkkänen (2002) established that there are two types of applicative constructions (low and high applicatives), which are able to explain different semantics conveyed by IOs in certain ditransitive sentences.

Based on these proposals, Cuervo (2003) and Diaconescu & Rivero (2007) show Spanish and Romanian also have the *dative alternation*. These analyses, however, differ from the ones for English ditransitives – which are based on the presence or absence of a preposition. According to the aforementioned authors, the *dative alternation* in Romance languages depends on the presence or absence of the clitic in the structure.[1] Hence, in Spanish and Romanian, the DOC is characterized by the IO being doubled by a dative clitic, which is the head of ApplP (cf. 4 and 5):

(4) a. Pablo le   **mandó** un diccionario a Gabi.
         Pablo 3SG.DAT sent   a   dictionary to Gabi.DAT
         'Pablo sent Gabi a dictionary.'

     b. [$_{VoiceP}$ *Pablo* [$_{v'}$ Voice [$_{VP}$ *mandó* [$_{ApplP}$ *a Gabi* [$_{Appl'}$ *le* [$_{DP}$ *un diccionario*]]]]]]   (Cuervo 2003: 35)

(5) a. Mihaela îi   **trimite** Mariei   o scrisoare.
         Mihaela DAT.CL sends   Mary.DAT   a letter
         'Mihaela sends Mary a letter.'

     b. [$_{VoiceP}$ *Mihaela* [$_{v'}$ Voice [$_{VP}$ *trimite* [$_{ApplP}$ *Mariei* [$_{Appl'}$ *îi* [$_{DP}$ *o scrisoare*]]]]]]   (Diaconescu & Rivero 2007: 2)

Configurations (4b) and (5b) show the dative argument in SpecApplP. The DO is licensed as its complement and ApplP is the complement of the verb. Therefore, following Pylkkänen (2002), the applicative head below the verbal root accounts for the *low applicative* – which is responsible for relating two DPs that establish a relation of direct transfer of possession. As we can see in (4b) and (5b), the clitic is the Spell-out of ApplP, as it is responsible for lexicalizing the DP person and number features in SpecApplP.

Additionally, the DOC in Spanish is characterized in terms of the IO being accompanied by a preposition (*a Gabi / a-DP*), which is a dummy element responsible for assigning dative Case to its argument. This IO is necessarily doubled by a dative clitic.

For Romanian, Diaconescu & Rivero (2007) present two DOC examples (5) and (6), the latter is similar to (4) in Spanish, as the dative IO (*la Maria*) is doubled by the dative clitic (*îi*).

(6) Mihaela îi   **trimite** la Maria   o scrisoare.
     Mihaela DAT.CL sends   to Maria.DAT a letter
     'Mihaela sends Mary a letter.'   (Diaconescu & Rivero 2007: 14)

---

[1]For an alternative perspective, cf. Cépeda & Cyrino 2020 [this volume], who assume structures with *give*-type verbs in Spanish, EP and BP are not DOCs. The authors claim dative clitics do not play any role in determining the structural position of DO and IO in these constructions.

According to the authors, sentence (6) is not part of the grammar of all speakers of Romanian. However, this example added to the assumption that when IOs are doubled by clitics in Romance languages, they are actually *a*-DP, not PP.

Pursuing the idea that clitics paired with IOs, which are actually a-DPs, is the key to understanding the *dative alternation* in Romance, Torres Morais (2007) assumes EP also presents this phenomenon. In sentences like (3), the preposition *a* in EP would also be a functional element responsible for assigning dative Case to DPs, as Cuervo (2003) proposes for Spanish (cf. 4). Consequently, the possibility of replacing the IO by a dative clitic suggests this element is the morphological expression of the dative case introduced in SpecApplP as a proper argument (cf. 7).

(7) $[_{vP}$ O João $[_{v'}$ v $[_{VP}$ enviou $[_{ApplP}$ à Maria/lhe $[_{Appl'}$ Ø $[_{DP}$ uma carta$]]]]]]$
 (Torres Morais 2007: 175)

Another important fact for the dative alternation in EP is when the IO is introduced by *para*, with pure locatives for instance, it cannot alternate with the dative clitic *lhe(s)*:

(8) A   Maria **enviou** (*lhe)   uma carta para   Lisboa.
 The Maria sent   (3SG.DAT) a   letter P$_{para(to)}$ Lisbon.OBL
 'Maria sent a letter to Lisbon.'   (Torres Morais 2007: 96)

Therefore, sentence (8) is considered a Prepositional Dative Construction (PDC) by Torres Morais (2007). Additionally, in Spanish, Cuervo (2003) considers (9) a PDC, because preposition *a* is not doubled by the dative clitic. Hence, the IO is introduced by a proper preposition that assigns oblique Case to its complement.

(9) Pablo **mandó** un diccionario a   Barcelona.
 Pablo sent   a   dictionary P$_{a(to)}$ Barcelona.OBL
 'Pablo sent a dictionary to Barcelona.'   (Cuervo 2003: 48)

If the presence of dative clitics is the main argument to support the idea that Romance languages have the *dative alternation*, it is worth noting that BP has been undergoing a diachronic change regarding its pronominal system since the 18th century. This is associated with the loss of 3rd person clitics (cf. Carvalho & Calindro 2018), as well as several changes in the prepositions used to introduce IOs, as we will discuss further in this paper. These two facts combined are the central idea for assuming BP seems to be setting different parameters from other Romance languages concerning Case assignment.

On this basis, given this pronominal system reconfiguration in BP, I assume this language is undergoing a change related to Case assignment, because dative Case cannot be assigned via a functional preposition any longer (preposition *a*), nor by its 3rd person morphological counterpart (*lhe(s)*). Consequently, BP seems to be shifting from a type of language, which had morphological case for all persons in the accusative and the dative, as EP still does, to one where Case has to be assigned via lexical prepositions.

In order to answer my main research question focusing on the differences between BP and the other Romance languages exemplified, I will analyze how BP expresses IOs both in the pronominal and prepositional phrase forms using data from previous works. First, through the analysis of the Brazilian pronominal system, which has been undergoing several changes since the 18th century (Kato et al. 2009). Next, based on Calindro (2015; 2016), I will show the prepositions that introduce IOs with transfer/movement and creation verbs in BP have a different status from the ones in Spanish, Romanian and EP. Hence, the structural representation of IOs in BP should be different from the other Romance languages analyzed, once the items involved in these structures have different status.

Bearing these facts in mind, this paper is structured as follows: §2 analyses in more details the variation and change that BP has undergone, in §2.1 regarding the pronominal system and in §2.2 regarding the prepositions that introduce IOs in BP; in §3, I propose a theoretical account of the sentences with verbs of transfer and movement in BP with a *p*P head and the universal *i** introducer (cf. Wood 2012; Wood & Marantz 2017); in §3.2, I present a similar proposal for sentences with creation verbs; and finally, in §4, conclusions are presented.

2 Diachronic change in ditransitive sentences in BP

2.1 Change in the pronominal system in BP

The pronominal system in BP has undergone modifications since the 18th century (cf. Kato et al. 2009). The table below shows the change for accusative and dative paradigms. The accusative data was adapted from Kato et al. (2009: 246), the dative paradigm was added based on Calindro (2015) and Torres Morais & Berlinck (2006) who have observed the loss of the clitic *lhe* in Portuguese from São Paulo state, as well as the work of Berlinck (1997) for Curitiba, Silveira (1999) for Freire (2005) for Rio de Janeiro.[2]

---

[2]The dative clitic *lhe* is still active in some areas of Brazil, but it was re-categorized as second person (cf. Figueiredo Silva 2007).

Table 1: 19th century clitics vs. 20th century clitics

		19th Century		20th Century	
	Nominative	Accusative	Dative	Accusative	Dative
1	eu	me	me	me	me
2	(tu)	te	te	te	te
3	ele (a)	o/a	lhe	—	—
1	nós	nos	nos	nos	nos
2	(vós)	vos	vos	—	—
3	eles (as)	os/as	lhes	—	—

According to Kato (2005), in modern BP, both 3rd person accusative and dative clitics are productive only in formal registers, suggesting they are not part of BP's core grammar anymore. Therefore, Brazilian children do not acquire them during the language acquisition process. These clitics, and also the preposition *a*, are taught at school as the prescriptive formal written and spoken Portuguese extensively based on EP register (cf. Kato et al. 2009). However, as we will see further in the text, even though in the context of transfer/movement preposition *a* is recovered through schooling, it has a different status from EP. Additionally, 3rd person accusative clitics are recovered, but 3rd person dative clitics are not (cf. 1 and 2), neither is the use of preposition *a* to introduce IOs with creation verbs (cf. 2).

Therefore, Table 1 illustrates that first and second person clitics remain in spoken and written language whereas the 3rd person clitics do not. According to Galves (2018), 1st and 2nd person clitics have dative morphology, but the dative case itself does not exist in the language any longer, so, in these contexts, their interpretation relies on a local relation with the verb. In these instances, where the clitics were lost, Case is assigned structurally via transitive prepositions (cf. Torres Morais & Salles 2010; Calindro 2015; 2016; Carvalho & Calindro 2018). Hence, BP is no longer a language which presents morphological dative case for all persons, as EP still does. Below I examine this in more detail.

As exemplified in (2), all 3rd person clitics were substituted for other strategies (lexical prepositions + full pronouns) probably because the case assigners, *v* for the accusative clitic, and Appl for the dative clitic, cannot assign case to these clitics anymore (cf. Carvalho & Calindro 2018). Thus, the loss of 3rd person clitics in BP reflects a system in which v and Appl cannot value case, so alternative structures take over, such as: zero pronouns (null objects), independent Case assigners (PPs) and default pronouns (*ele*), which have the same form for NOM/ACC. Hence, in the 20th century, sentences (10b) and (10c) below, with a null object and with an overt full pronoun respectively, became felicitous answers to the question – *Você viu o Pedro ontem?* 'Did you see Pedro yesterday?'. By contrast, the answer in (10a), with the accusative clitic, was the only legitimate one in the 19th century.

(10) a. Vi-o   na   biblioteca.   (19th century)
           (I).saw-3SG.ACC in.the library

        b. Vi-Ø   na   biblioteca.   (20th century)
           (I).saw-Ø in.the library

        c. Vi   ele   na   biblioteca.   (20th century)
           (I).saw he.3SG.NOM in.the library

           'I saw him in the library.'   (Carvalho & Calindro 2018: 94)

This variation in BP is evidence this language is taking a different path from other Romance languages concerning case assignment, i.e., BP has lost inherent Case assignment, mainly in 3rd person contexts, in favor of structural Case assignment (cf. Calindro 2015; Carvalho & Calindro 2018). So, if BP is different from other Romance languages that introduce IOs via ApplP, how does BP introduce IOs in the argument structure? In the next section, I will demonstrate that the prepositions which introduce arguments in BP are different from EP. Next, I will propose a representation for ditransitive sentences in BP.

2.2 Preposition change in BP

Several works have shown that historically, at the same time the dative clitic *lhe* disappeared, the preposition *a* was completely replaced by *para* with creation verbs in BP (cf. 3). In this context, when the preposition *a* introduces IOs, the sentences become ungrammatical for Brazilian speakers:

(11) A Maria **preparou** o   jantar a-o   João   / preparou-lhe
       the Maria prepared the dinner $P_{a\,(to)}$-the João.DAT / prepared-3SG.DAT
       o   jantar.   (EP/ *BP)
       the dinner.

       'Maria prepared dinner for João / for him.'

According to the literature, BP speakers prefer *para* in spoken language (Torres Morais & Berlinck 2007). In order to confirm this fact in written language, Calindro (2015) analyzed data collected from a book, which comprised 223 first pages from *Folha de São Paulo* – a major Brazilian newspaper – that spans the 20th century from 1920 to 2010. The author attested preposition *a* disappeared with creation verbs in the 60s. In the context of verbs of transfer and movement, however, *a* and *para* still vary throughout the century. Therefore, it was important to verify the contexts in which this variation occurs.

As mentioned before, Kato (2005) observed the preposition *a* is recovered through schooling. However, as the data show, the preposition *a* used by Brazilians is not the same in EP found in modern EP.

First of all, differently from EP, IOs introduced by *a* in BP do not alternate with all dative clitics, as discussed previously. Second of all, this preposition has spread its use to contexts where they are ungrammatical in EP.

For instance, in EP, the preposition *para* is used in two situations. Firstly, it is mandatory with a locative that cannot alternate with a dative clitic (cf. 8). Secondly, when the IO is introduced by *para* in EP, according to Torres Morais (2007), there is a semantic difference in its interpretation. In (12), differently from (3), the interpretation is that the transfer of possession is indirect, i.e., in (3) *the letter* was sent directly to *João*, while in (12), *the letter* was first sent to someone else, then to *João*, as in (13) that clearly states the transfer was done by someone else – *Pedro*. Therefore, the IO *para o João* cannot be replaced by *lhe*.[3]

(12) A Maria **enviou** (*lhe)   uma carta para   o João.
      The Maria sent   (3SG.DAT) a   letter P$_{para\,(to)}$ the João.OBL
      'Maria sent a letter to João.'   (Torres Morais 2007: 96)

(13) a. A Maria enviou uma carta para   o João   pelo Pedro.
          The Maria sent   a   letter P$_{para\,(to)}$ the João.OBL by   Pedro.

      b. A Maria enviou (*lhe)   uma carta pelo Pedro.
          The Maria sent   (3SG.DAT) a   letter by   Pedro.
          'Maria sent a letter to João via Pedro.'

Sentences (8), (12) and (13) would be examples of PDCs in EP, as part of the *dative alternation* mentioned in the introduction. The impossibility of the alternation between IOs in these examples with the 3rd person dative clitic is the main

---

[3]I would like to thank an anonymous reviewer for suggesting example (13), in order to make my discussion clearer.

evidence for Torres Morais (2007) to propose they do not bear dative case, but structural oblique Case in EP.

As for BP, IOs introduced with either *para* or *a* have the same semantic interpretation.[4] Example (11) shows the preposition *a* can also be used to introduce locatives in BP, differently from EP, where *para* has to be used to introduce locatives (cf. 8). Moreover, the ungrammaticality of *a* to introduce locatives found in EP, does not hold for BP - cf. (11) from the corpus studied by Calindro (2015: 115), in which a locative *Bosnia* is introduced by *a* in modern BP:

(14)   Atacado comboio que **levava** ajuda à   Bósnia.
       Attacked trains   that sent   aid $P_{a\,(to)}$.the Bosnia.OBL

'The trains that sent aid to Bosnia were attacked.'[5]

Therefore, the two prepositions *a* and *para* in BP share the same semantic status, indicating that *a* is no longer a dative marker as it is in EP DOCs (cf. 3 and 7). Therefore, a Brazilian child acquiring language in this context does not access this semantic difference shown in (12) for EP.

Thus, I assume that the existence of the lexical preposition *para* in EP (cf. 8, 12 and 13) enabled the reanalysis discussed above for BP which led to parametric variation between these two varieties. I hypothesize that the presence of the preposition *para* in the inventory of possibilities to introduce IOs in EP and, therefore, historical BP, coupled with the loss of dative *lhe* was the trigger for Brazilian children to generalize the use of *para* to all Locatives, Goals and Beneficiaries. Additionally, after school, Brazilians generalize the use of *a* with Locatives and Goals.[6] This fact can be viewed as an example of *Input Generalization* in Chomsky's (2005) terms. According to the author, parametric variation emerges from the interaction of an underspecified Universal Grammar, Primary Linguistic Data and the Third Factor. Biberauer & Roberts (2015) observed *Feature Economy* and *Input Generalization* are the main manifestations of the Third Factor. Hence, in the case of BP, Brazilians generalized the use of *para* to all the other contexts described previously.

Hence, in the language acquisition process in BP there is no longer the same evidence for inherent Case in the 3rd person as there is in EP (i.e. the dative clitic

---

[4]This alternation occurs in written language, as attested by Kato (2005) and Calindro (2015), after the preposition *a* is recovered through schooling. Therefore, in the language acquisition process, only *para* is available to the child. I would like to thank an anonymous reviewer of this paper, who called my attention to this fact.

[5]This example was taken from the front page of *Folha de São Paulo, published in 16/8/1992.*

[6]Preposition *a*, however, is not used in BP to introduce *beneficiaries*. For more details, cf. Calindro (2015).

lhe(s)). Morphological case has been substituted by structural Case through IOs such as *para/a ele (a)(s)* (cf. 1 and 2). The consequences of this change associated with the re-categorization of the 3rd person dative clitic *lhe(s)* as 2nd person has resulted in the loss of dative arguments introduced by an applicative head in BP.[7]

Consequently, BP is different from other Romance languages,[8] once the ApplP in BP presumably does not bear the phi-features to enter in an Agree relation with the dative clitic, so that the language has resorted to an alternative strategy, in which an independent Case assigner (*p*P) assigns Case to a DP (cf. Calindro 2015; 2016), as it will be discussed in the next section.

3 An analysis for ditransitive sentences in BP

According to what was argued in the previous section for BP, all prepositions analyzed in this paper are transitive (to use Svenonius 2004 and Cuervo 2010 terms), in the sense that they can select their complement, and also project Spec and complement positions in the argument structure.

Following Hale & Keyser (2002), Svenonius (2004) establishes prepositions are relational elements, a relation which can be captured through Figure and Ground associations (cf. Talmy 1978). In simple terms, the Figure is the moving or conceptually movable object and the Ground the reference. For instance, in the sentence 'John threw the keys on the table' *the keys* is the Figure, *the table* the Ground and the element responsible to relate them is the preposition *on*. Therefore, the Ground is the complement of the preposition. Hence, the interpretation of the Ground depends on the preposition, whereas the interpretation of the Figure does not. Thus, transitive prepositions determine selection restrictions to its complement – the Ground – but not to the Figure.

Once prepositions can project Spec and complement positions, they can be introduced in the argument structure by a *p*P projection. Wood (2012: 180) draws

---

[7]Pujalte (2010) also claims BP does not have applicative phrases. Her analysis, however, is based on a specific dialect from the state of Minas Gerais (PBM), where sentences such as *A Maria deu o livro o Pedro.* lit. 'Mary gave the book the Pedro'. My analysis and Cépeda & Cyrino's are based on a vaster register of Portuguese in order to make claims regarding the status of the ditransitive sentences in BP. For more on PBM cf. Scher (1996); Torres Morais & Salles (2010). I would like to thank an anonymous reviewer for mentioning Pujalte's work.

[8]Cépeda & Cyrino 2020 [this volume] develop a unified analysis for Spanish, EP and BP. The authors assume these languages do not have DOCs, hence, they do not have ApplP as well. Even though, in this paper I am assuming authors who defend applicative heads for Spanish and EP, my hypotheses is mainly that BP does not show the same characteristics. Therefore, my analysis can give support for Cépeda & Cyrino's proposal, at least for BP.

a parallel between the *p*P domain and the *v*P domain, insofar as the prepositional structure involves a "light preposition" *p* and a P as categories *v* and V in the verbal domain.

(15) [VoiceP Agent [Voice' [Voice [*v*P [*v* [Theme]]]]]]
      [*p*   P   Figure [*p'*   [*p* [PP [P   [Ground]]]]]]

Therefore, following the concepts of Figure and Ground, in ditransitive constructions the DO would be the Figure introduced in Spec*p*P. The complement of the *p* head is a Ground argument (the IO) accompanied by a transitive preposition introduced by a PP head (cf. 16). As mentioned before, the transitive preposition is placed under PP because it establishes a relation with the Ground not the Figure, since it applies selection restrictions to the IO, not the DO. For instance, with verbs of transfer and movement, the preposition *para* can only select complements that have *goal* or *beneficiary* theta-roles.

(16)

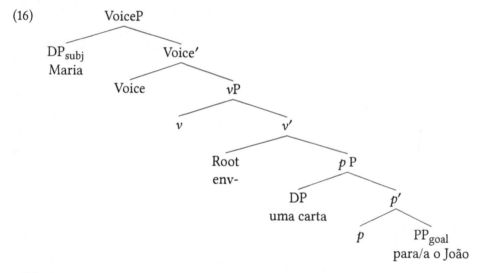

The transitive preposition as relational element can be responsible for holding a thematic relation between the DO and the IO. As such, this crucially confirms Cuervo's (2010) proposal according to which ditransitive verbs do not require two separate arguments, but select a *relation* between DO and the IO. For Cuervo (2010), this relation can be introduced in the argument structure by an applicative head, a small clause or a prepositional phrase.

As argued before, BP does not have applicative heads in its argument structure, as it cannot express morphologically dative case anymore, as EP does. Additionally, I am assuming IOs in the relevant structures are introduced by transitive prepositions. Consequently, the oblique complement is introduced via a *p*P in the argument structure. Therefore, the EP applicative construction (7) was reanalyzed in BP as (16).

3.1 The *i**-single argument introducer proposal

In this section, I adopt Wood & Marantz's (2017) proposal of a single argument to account for the representation of ditransitive structures with transfer, movement and creation verbs in BP. Importantly, this proposal allows us to explain the two different semantic readings conveyed by the preposition *para* in sentences with creation verbs, as we will see in §3.2. However, to understand the characteristics of this single argument introducer, I will first analyze ditransitive sentences with transfer and movement verbs which have just been discussed in the previous section.

Wood & Marantz (2017) propose the main heads which add participants to the event (*Voice, low applicative, little p, prepositions (P), high applicative*) can be reduced to one *i** single argument introducer. In these terms, three of the basic heads are defined in (17), depending on the syntactic contexts they occur:

(17) a. Little *p* (figures): Bare *i** that merges with a PP.

  b. Voice (agents): Bare *i** that merges with a *v*P.

  c. Low appl (possessors): Bare *i** that merges with a DP. (Wood & Marantz 2017: 258)

The introducer *i** is a categorically unspecified head that does not start the derivation with a categorical feature, its categorial feature is valued by the categorial feature of the first constituent it merges with as result of a combination of an unvalued category (CAT) which may or may not trigger Merge with a constituent of category D, such as: {[CAT: __], [S: D]}. The underscore indicates an unvalued CAT feature and *i** would be the notation for this feature bundle. The selectional features are annotated in brackets, $P_{[S:\ D]}$, for instance, is a head of category P that selects (S) for a constituent of category D (Wood & Marantz 2017: 257). Hence, the main purpose of *i** is to close off the extended projection of the first constituent with which it merges (cf. 18).

For instance, when PP merges with *i**, its categorical feature of *i** is valued as P, and the semantic interpretation of the preposition depends on the root. The preposition *in* is different from *on*, because the root √IN has the semantics of *container* while √ON of *surface*. Hence, the authors' proposal for a sentence as '*the car on the road*' is as follows:

(18)

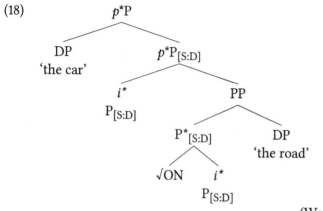

(Wood & Marantz 2017: 259)

The difference between this analysis and the one represented in (16) is the way the preposition is treated in relation to the argument it introduces. In the previous account, the preposition was only related to the Ground, not the Figure (cf. 16). Under this new view, the preposition is a root that merges with i^* to establish different semantic conditions for its complement, so it is possible to represent the different semantics prepositions may convey. The lower i^*, when merged with √ON, for example, assigns the DP *the road* the θ-role associated with it, so that the DP is interpreted as a *surface*. Finally, in (18), the highest i^* is merged with the *p*P and then with the DP, assigning to it the idea of Figure, associated to the element in Spec*p*P.

In BP, in the structures of verbs of transfer and movement, the default semantics of the prepositions *a* and *para* is of Goal/Recipient.[9] I assume the representation of these constructions can also be realized via i^*. Hence, the derivation of sentence (1), represented in (19), is the following: the categorial preposition *para* merges with i^* and then adjoins to the DP *o João* projecting a PP. Assuming that the DO-theme *uma carta* is analogous to the DP-Figure *the road* presented in (18) merged in Spec*p*P, *p* introduces a DO in its specifier. Additionally, PP is capable of denoting a transfer of possession between DO and IO - *o João*. Next, if the verb denotes an event which implies an agent, *v* introduces such a DP – *Maria*. Hence, *v*P consists of an i^* attached to *v*P and then *p* is attached to i^* merged with *p*P, forming *p*P.

---

[9] *Para* can also be Beneficiary whereas *a* cannot, for more details cf. Calindro (2015).

(19)

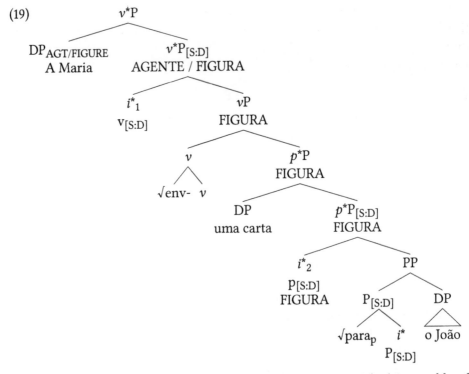

In the next section, we will see that the representation with *i** is capable of maintaining the two beneficiary interpretations that can be instantiated by *para* with creation verbs in BP.

3.2 An analysis for ditransitive sentences with creation verbs

In an attempt to propose a representation that can account for creation verbs as well as movement and transfer verbs, Marantz (2009; 2013) proposes that the DOs of creation verbs can be interpreted as eventualities, as they represent the object resulting from an action. In sentence (20), the author suggests the cake is an event itself, as it was once a group of ingredients and then becomes a final product after the action of someone making it.

The IO can be interpreted as benefitting from this change of state event that the DO has gone through (Marantz 2013: 156). Hence, in (20), there is a possession relation between the DO – *John* – and the IO – *a cake*, as there would be between the DO and the IO in a DOC in English or in the sentence represented in (11) from BP. Besides, the DO is also the beneficiary of *Mary's baking*:

(20)   Mary baked John a cake.

Therefore, sentence (2) in BP can project a similar structure to (16), given in (21). Because, following Marantz's view, creation verbs can also be interpreted as dynamic events are. Hence, creation verbs can be represented in the same way movement and transfer verbs are (cf. 21):

(21)

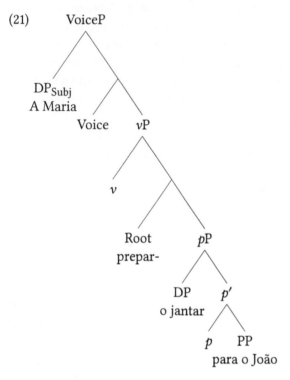

This representation, however, does not account for the two semantic readings conveyed to the DP *o João*: *beneficiary of the theme* – 'dinner', which would be the low applicative reading; or *beneficiary of the event* of *Maria* having prepared dinner, which would be the high applicative.

Wood & Marantz (2017) distinguish *little p, Voice,* and *low applicatives* from *PP* and *high applicatives* because the latter convey semantics of their own, independently from the element they attach to. Therefore, *PP* and *high applicatives* are *i** heads with which lexical roots are merged. Hence, the high applicatives function as a root-adjoined *i**, since the θ-role it assigns to the DP in its specifier is not implied by the *v*P semantics. Therefore, the θ-roles related to the high applicative are the same introduced by prepositions - Beneficiary and Locative.

This is particularly interesting for creation verbs whose IOs have semantics of *beneficiary*. In essence, a high applicative projection is like a *v*P because it also closes off the projection of the root, and not of the applicative head it creates. In addition, all elements that can select a *v*P can also select a high applicative. Therefore, when the IO is the Beneficiary of the event, its semantics is of a high applicative.

As argued previously, BP does not have applicatives, so the IOs are introduced through a prepositional phrase. Since *i** is able to adjoin to a p, also following the idea that creation verbs are dynamic events as well, as discussed before. Additionally, it must be established that, according to Acedo-Matellán (2010), prepositions function as any other lexical categories that have a neutral root and a category that determines the functional head. Hence, prepositions can be prepositional roots with categorial features that will adjoin to an *i** and generate a PP (cf. 22).

In (22), the categorial preposition *para* merges with *i** and then adjoins to the DP *João* projecting a PP. Next, *i** merges with *v*P, valuing its categorial feature as *v*, projecting *v** [S, D]. Finally, the DP *Maria* is merged, closing off the *v**P. Consequently, the interpretation of *João* as the Beneficiary of the theme is conveyed, i.e., he is the one who dinner was prepared for.

(22)

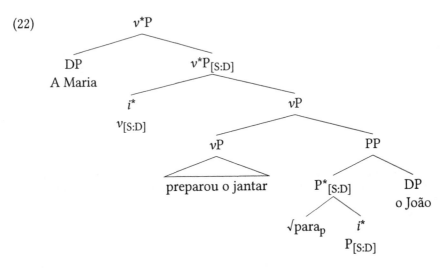

In the second interpretation (cf. 23) – dinner may be appreciated by people other than *João*, which is why *João* is the *beneficiary of the event*, i.e., *João* is the beneficiary of the event of *Maria* preparing dinner, and will not necessarily eat it. For example, *João* should prepare dinner, but he is sick, so *Maria* will do it for him.[10]

---

[10]I would like to thank an anonymous reviewer who suggested these semantic readings should be made clearer for those not familiar with BP.

(23)

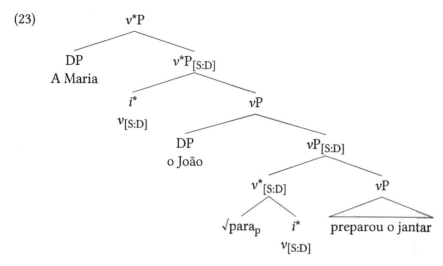

The prepositional root in (23) is a neutral category. Thus, if i^* merges the prepositional root with a neutral feature, it generates v^*, not P^*, which, when merged with vP, values the categorical feature of v by projecting $vP_{[S:\ D]}$. Subsequently, the categorial feature of D is checked by merging $vP_{[S:\ D]}$ with the DP *João*. Similarly, the external argument *Maria* is added to the structure. Therefore, this representation captures the interpretation of a *high applicative*, since the argument *o João* is related to the event, which is the second possible interpretation for sentence (2).

4 Final Remarks

In this paper, I analyzed a change in progress in the introduction of IOs in ditransitive sentences in BP. With dynamic verbs of transfer and movement, the preposition *a* is substituted by transitive preposition *para* in spoken varieties of BP, however in written register they co-occur in modern BP. Hence the preposition *a* and *para* have the same status of a transitive prepositions, which are relational elements. This change coupled with the loss of the 3rd person dative clitics *lhe(s)* accounts for a change in the representation of ditransitive sentences, when BP is compared to other Romance languages and, in particular, to EP.

On this basis, I proposed that the argument structure of ditransitive sentences in BP does not entail applicative heads, as other Romance languages do. Hence, in this language, the relation between the DO and the IO selected by the verbal root is introduced in the argument structure by a *p*P.

This representation, however, does not capture the two semantic readings that the IO introduced by *para* with creation verbs can have. As such, the representation of creation verbs should necessarily involve the single argument introducer *i**, with which it is possible to provide a more accurate account for both interpretations conveyed by the preposition *para* in these contexts.

Abbreviations

The abbreviations used in the glosses of this chapter follow the Leipzig Glossing Rules. Additional abbreviation: CL clitic.

Acknowledgements

I would like to express my gratitude to Alice Corr, who proofread this paper.

References

Acedo-Matellán, Víctor. 2010. *Argument structure and the syntax-morphology interface: A case study in Latin and other languages.* Barcelona: Universitat de Barcelona. (Doctoral dissertation).

Alsina, Àlex & Sam A. Mchombo. 1993. Objects asymmetries and the Chichewa applicative construction. In Sam A. Mchombo (ed.), *Theoretical aspects of Bantu grammar*, 50–93. Stanford, CA: CSLI Publications.

Baker, Mark C. 1988. *Incorporation: A theory of grammatical function changing.* Chicago, IL: Chicago University Press.

Berlinck, Rosane. 1997. *Sobre a realização do objeto indireto no português do Brasil.* Florianópolis: PUC-RS.

Biberauer, Theresa & Ian Roberts. 2015. Rethinking formal hierarchies: A proposed unification. *Cambridge Occasional Papers in Linguistics* 7. 1–31.

Calindro, Ana Regina. 2015. *Introduzindo argumentos: Uma proposta para as sentenças ditransitivas do português brasileiro [Introducing arguments: The case of ditransitives in Brazilian Portuguese].* São Paulo: University of São Paulo. (Doctoral dissertation).

Calindro, Ana Regina. 2016. Introducing indirect arguments: The locus of a diachronic change. *Rivista di Grammatica Generativa* 38. 35–44.

Carvalho, Janayna & Ana Regina Calindro. 2018. A unified account for the loss of third person clitics in Brazilian Portuguese. In Danniel Carvalho & Dorothy Brito (eds.), *Pronomes: Morfossintaxe e semântica*, 91–110. Salvador: Edufba.

Cépeda, Paola & Sonia Cyrino. 2020. Putting objects in order: Asymmetrical relations in Spanish and Portuguese ditransitives. In Anna Pineda & Jaume Mateu (eds.), *Dative constructions in Romance and beyond*, 97–116. Berlin: Language Science Press. DOI:10.5281/zenodo.3776539

Chomsky, Noam. 1981. *Lectures on government and binding.* Dordrecht: Foris Publications.

Chomsky, Noam. 1986. *Knowledge of language.* New York, NY: Praeger.

Chomsky, Noam. 2005. Three factors in language design. *Linguistic Inquiry* 36(1). 1–22.

Cuervo, María Cristina. 2003. *Datives at large.* Cambridge, MA: Massachusetts Institute of Technology. (Doctoral dissertation). https://dspace.mit.edu/handle/1721.1/7991.

Cuervo, María Cristina. 2010. Against ditransitivity. *Probus* 22(2). 151–180.

Diaconescu, Rodica & María Luisa Rivero. 2007. An applicative analysis of double object constructions in Romanian. *Probus* 19(2). 209–233.

Figueiredo Silva, Maria Cristina. 2007. A perda do marcador dativo e algumas das suas consequências [The loss of the dative marker and some consequences]. In Ataliba Castilho, Maria Aparecida Torres Morais, Ruth Lopes & Sonia Cyrino (eds.), *Descrição, história e aquisição do português brasileiro*, 85–110. São Paulo: FAPESP.

Freire, Gilson. 2005. *A realização do acusativo e do dativo anafórico de 3ª: Pessoa na escrita brasileira e lusitana [Third person anaphoric accusative and dative in Brazilian and European writing].* Rio de Janeiro: UFRJ. (Doctoral dissertation).

Galves, Charlotte. 2018. *Ainda sobre os pronomes do português brasileiro [Still on Brazilian Portuguese pronouns].* Alessandro Boechat Medeiros & Andrew Nevins (eds.). Campinas: Pontes.

Hale, Ken & Samuel Keyser. 2002. *Prolegomenon to a theory of argument structure.* Cambridge: MIT Press.

Kato, Mary. 2005. Gramática do letrado: Questões para a teoria gramatical. In Maria Marques & Erwin Koller (eds.), *Ciências da linguagem: Trinta anos de investigação e ensino*, 131–145. Braga: CEHUM.

Kato, Mary, Sonia Cyrino & Vilma Corrêa. 2009. Brazilian Portuguese and the recovery of lost clitics through schooling. In Acrisio Pires & Jason Rothman (eds.), *Minimalist inquiries into child and adult language acquisition*, 245–272. Berlin: Mouton de Gruyter.

Larson, Richard K. 1988. On the double object construction. *Linguistic Inquiry* 19(3). 335–391.

Marantz, Alec. 1993. Implications of asymmetries in double object constructions. In Sam A. Mchombo (ed.), *Theoretical aspects of Bantu grammar*, 113–150. Stanford, CA: CSLI Publications.

Marantz, Alec. 2009. *Resultatives and re-resultatives: Direct objects may construct events by themselves.* Paper presented at Penn Linguistics Colloquium.

Marantz, Alec. 2013. Verbal argument structure: Events and participants. *Lingua* 130. 152–168. DOI:10.1016/j.lingua.2012.10.012

Pujalte, Mercedes. 2010. *Construcciones com y cin aplicativos em el español del rio da la plata y el português brasileño.* ms. Universidad Nacional del Comahue.

Pylkkänen, Liina. 2002. *Introducing arguments.* Massachusetts Institute of Technology. (Doctoral dissertation).

Scher, Ana Paula. 1996. *As construções com dois complementos no Inglês e no Português do Brasil [Constructions with two complements in English and Brazilian Portuguese].* Campinas: Unicamp. (MA thesis).

Silveira, Gessilene. 1999. *A realização variável do objeto indireto (dativo) na fala de Florianópolis.* Florianópolis: UFSC. (Doctoral dissertation).

Svenonius, Peter. 2003. Limits on P: Filling in holes vs. Falling in holes. *Nordlyd* 31(2). 431–445. DOI:10.7557/12.13

Svenonius, Peter. 2004. Adpositions, particles and the arguments they introduce. In Eric Reuland, Tammoy Bhattacharya & Giorgos Spathas (eds.), *Argument structure*, 63–103. Philadelphia, PA: John Benjamins.

Talmy, Leonard. 1978. Figure and ground in complex sentences. In Joseph Greenberg (ed.), *Universals in human language*, 625–649. Stanford, CA: Stanford University Press.

Torres Morais, Maria Aparecida. 2007. *Dativos [datives].* University of São Paulo. (professorship thesis).

Torres Morais, Maria Aparecida & Rosane Berlinck. 2006. A caracterização do objeto indireto no português: Aspectos sincrônicos e diacrônicos [The characterization of the indirect object in Portuguese: Synchronic and diachronic aspects]. In Tania Lobo, Ilza Ribeiro, Zenaide Carneiro & Norma Almeida (eds.), *Novos dados, novas análises*, 73–106. Salvador: EDUFBA.

Torres Morais, Maria Aparecida & Rosane Berlinck. 2007. 'eu disse pra ele' ou 'disse-lhe a ele': A expressão do dativo nas variedades brasileira e europeia do português. ['Eu disse para ele' or 'disse-lhe a ele': The dative expression in Brazilian and European Portuguese varieties]. In Ataliba Castilho, Maria Aparecida Torres Morais, Ruth Lopes & Sônia Cyrino (eds.), *Descrição, história e aquisição do português brasileiro.* São Paulo: Pontes.

Torres Morais, Maria Aparecida & Heloísa Salles. 2010. Parametric change in the grammatical encoding of indirect objects in Brazilian Portuguese. *Probus* 22(2). 181–209.

Wood, Jim. 2012. *Icelandic morphosyntax and argument structure.* New York, NY: New York University. (Doctoral dissertation).

Wood, Jim & Alec Marantz. 2017. The interpretation of external arguments. In Roberta D'Alessandro, Irene Franco & Ángel J. Gallego (eds.), *The verbal domain*, 255–278. Oxford: Oxford University Press. DOI:10.1093/oso/9780198767886.001.0001

Chapter 4

Putting objects in order: Asymmetrical relations in Spanish and Portuguese ditransitives

Paola Cépeda
Stony Brook University

Sonia Cyrino
University of Campinas

Spanish, European Portuguese, and Brazilian Portuguese allow two possible linear orders for the direct object (DO) and indirect object (IO) in ditransitives: DO>IO and IO>DO. The goal of this paper is twofold. First, we show that the arguments supporting a Double Object Construction (DOC) in these languages are inconclusive on both semantic and structural grounds. Accordingly, we claim that there is no DOC in these three languages. Second, we provide evidence that DO>IO and IO>DO are derivationally related. We show that DO>IO is the base order and that IO>DO is the result of an information structure operation, the latter order being possible only when IO conveys given information in the discourse and occupies the specifier of a low-periphery TopP. We offer a unified analysis that contributes to a comparative understanding of ditransitives in Romance.

1 Introduction

Spanish, European Portuguese (EP), and Brazilian Portuguese (BP) allow two possible linear orders for the direct object (DO) and indirect object (IO) in ditransitive constructions: DO may precede or follow IO; that is, both DO>IO and IO>DO are possible. Examples are offered in (1) for Spanish and (2) for EP and BP (with the preposition *a* and *para*, respectively):

Paola Cépeda & Sonia Cyrino. 2020. Putting objects in order: Asymmetrical relations in Spanish and Portuguese ditransitives. In Anna Pineda & Jaume Mateu (eds.), *Dative constructions in Romance and beyond*, 97–116. Berlin: Language Science Press. DOI:10.5281/zenodo.3776539

(1)　a.　Spanish DO>IO

　　　　Olga (le)　　dio　[$_{DO}$ una manzana] [$_{IO}$ a　Mario].

　　　　Olga 3SG.DAT gave　　an　apple　　　　to Mario

　　　　'Olga gave an apple to Mario.'

　　b.　Spanish IO>DO

　　　　Olga (le)　　dio　[$_{IO}$ a　Mario] [$_{DO}$ una manzana].

　　　　Olga 3SG.DAT gave　to Mario　　　an　apple

　　　　'Olga gave an apple to Mario.'

(2)　a.　EP/BP DO>IO[1]

　　　　A　Olga deu　[$_{DO}$ uma maçã] [$_{IO}$ a/para o　Mario].

　　　　the Olga gave　　an　apple　　to　　the Mario

　　　　'Olga gave an apple to Mario.'

　　b.　EP/BP IO>DO

　　　　A　Olga deu　[$_{IO}$ a/para o　Mario] [$_{DO}$ uma maçã].

　　　　the Olga gave　to　　the Mario　　　an　apple

　　　　'Olga gave an apple to Mario.'

For these three languages, there is a debate in the literature on the availability of a Double Object Construction (DOC), similar to the configuration found in English. Larson (1988; 2014) argues that English ditransitive verbs such as *give* allow both a Prepositional Phrase dative configuration (PP-dative), as in (3a), and a DOC configuration, as in (3b), and that these two configurations are derivationally related.[2]

(3)　a.　English PP-dative

　　　　Olga gave [$_{DP}$ an apple] [$_{PP}$ to Mario].

　　b.　English DOC

　　　　Olga gave [$_{DP}$ Mario] [$_{DP}$ an apple].

Demonte (1995), Bleam (2003), Cuervo (2003), Cuervo (2010), a.o., have claimed that, when the IO-doubling clitic appears in Spanish sentences such as those in (1),

---

[1]BP, unlike EP and Spanish, does not use the preposition *a* in dative constructions. On the loss of the preposition *a* and the syntax of *para* in BP, see Calindro (2020 [this volume]).

[2]Other derivational accounts for the relationship between (3a) and (3b) in English have been presented in the literature. For an interesting review of arguments, see Rappaport Hovav & Levin (2008) and Hallman (2015). It is worth noting that the generalizations we arrive at in this paper hold independently of these theoretical positions, since we argue that there is no construction such as (3b) in Spanish or Portuguese.

the sentences resemble the English DOC. In contrast, the clitic-less ditransitive corresponds, in their view, to a PP-dative. It has also been claimed that the basic order in this kind of constructions is IO>DO. For Portuguese sentences such as those in (2), Torres Morais & Salles (2010) have claimed that the order IO>DO is equivalent to the English DOC.

In this paper, we investigate whether *give*-type verbs in Spanish and Portuguese exhibit the kind of derivational relation they show in English. After analyzing the arguments that have been used to support the existence of DOC in these languages, we claim that there is no DOC in either Spanish, EP, or BP, and that the different linear orders for DO and IO are derivationally related. Our unified analysis aims to contribute to a better understanding of ditransitives in Romance, a topic that has been scarcely analyzed comparatively (except for Pineda 2016).

The paper is structured as follows. In §2, we analyze the arguments used to support a DOC approach for Spanish, EP, and BP, and propose that there is no conclusive evidence in favor of a DOC in these languages. In §3, we argue that the IO>DO order is strictly related to information structure. We offer our conclusions in the last section.

2 The asymmetry of DO and IO in Spanish and Portuguese

In this section, we examine the syntactic and semantic arguments supporting a DOC approach for Spanish, BP and EP (as defended by Demonte 1995; Cuervo 2003; Torres Morais & Salles 2010, a.o.). We claim that these arguments are not conclusive, as DO and IO have asymmetrical properties regardless of their linear order.

2.1 DO>IO and IO>DO are derivationally related

For English, Harley (1995) proposed decomposing verbal units into a CAUSE and another abstract element, either LOC(ATION) or HAVE. The order DO>IO corresponds to CAUSE + LOC, whereas IO>DO corresponds to CAUSE + HAVE. Therefore, these two orders correlate with two independent structures. Examples in (4) and (5) are adapted from Harley (1995).

(4) a. DO>IO (= CAUSE + LOC)
         Olga gave an apple to Mario.

b.

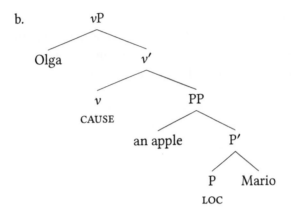

(5)   a.   IO>DO (= CAUSE + HAVE)
Olga gave Mario an apple.

b.

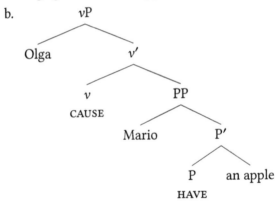

Harley's independent structures have been applied to the analysis of Romance ditransitives (Bleam 2003; Costa 2009; Brito 2014; 2015). The central argument used has been based on the non-compositionality of idiomatic expressions. Let us consider Brito's (2014; 2015) analysis as an example of this approach.

When discussing EP ditransitives, Brito (2014; 2015) concludes that there is no English-like DOC in EP and the DO>IO and IO>DO orders correspond to the different underlying structures in (6).

(6)   a. DO>IO

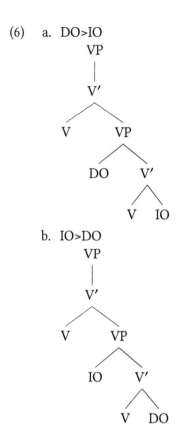

b. IO>DO

Using idiomatic expressions to support her claim, Brito (2014) argues that certain idioms have a necessarily strict order since the idiomatic meaning is lost when the order is reversed. Thus, the idiomatic reading in (7a), *dar pérolas aos porcos* 'give something valuable to someone who does not appreciate it' usually appears as DO>IO (6a), while the idiomatic reading in (8a), *dar a Deus o que o diabo não quis* 'pass as a good person after a sinful life' is related to IO>DO (6b).

(7)   a. EP idiomatic DO>IO
         A   Olga deu   [DO pérolas] [IO aos   porcos].
         the Olga gave   pearls   to.the pigs
         'Olga cast pearls before swine.'

      b. EP non-idiomatic IO>DO
         A   Olga deu   [IO aos   porcos] [DO pérolas].
         the Olga gave   to.the pigs   pearls
         'Olga gave pearls to the pigs.'

(8)   a.   EP idiomatic IO>DO
Dar [IO a Deus] [DO o   que   o   diabo não quis].
give   to God   the what the devil not wanted
'To pass as virtuous despite an immoral past.'

b.   EP non-idiomatic DO>IO
Dar [DO o   que   o   diabo não quis]   [IO a Deus].
give   the what the devil not wanted   to God
'To give God what the Devil did not want.'

In the three languages, some idioms seem to have the form V+DO, with IO in sentence-final position (as in (7a) for EP) and many times as an empty slot to be filled. For example, Spanish *dar lata a alguien* 'give someone a hard time' and BP *dar canja a alguém* 'make things easy for someone' have IO slots filled by *a/para Olga*, respectively, in (9).

(9)   a.   Spanish
Mario (le)   está dando lata   a Olga.
Mario 3SG.DAT is   giving tin.can to Olga
'Mario is giving Olga a hard time.'

b.   BP
O   Mario está dando canja   para a   Olga.
the Mario is   giving chicken.broth to   the Olga
'Mario is making things easy for Olga.'

Sentences like (9) have been used as an argument to claim that V+DO must form a constituent and, therefore, IO must be generated higher than DO (Bleam 2003). However, Larson (2014; 2017) argues convincingly that idiomatic expressions are not a conclusive argument for the existence of two independent structures, let alone for DOC.

First, the so-called *idiomatic reading* is in fact compositional: the objects always receive specific meanings. Larson (2017) shows that speakers can interpret the alleged idiomatic reading in a phrase even in isolation. He finds support for this in the dictionary entries. For instance, the English sentence *Olga gave Mario a kick* can be interpreted as 'Olga gave Mario some feeling of excitement'. But this meaning is exactly what Larson finds in the dictionary entry for *kick*:

(10)   **kick** n... 5 *Slang* a feeling of pleasurable stimulation. (*AHDEL*)

(Larson 2017: 406)

The same analysis can be applied to Spanish and Portuguese. The examples in (11) suggest that the Spanish and Portuguese sentences in (9) are really non-idiomatic since *lata* and *canja* can be interpreted as 'bothersome situation' (11a) and 'easy situation' (11b), respectively, even without the presence of the verb.

(11)　a.　Spanish
　　　　　¡Esto es una lata!
　　　　　 this is an　annoyance
　　　　　'This is annoying!'

　　　b.　BP
　　　　　Isto é　uma canja!
　　　　　this is an　　ease
　　　　　'This is easy!'

This shows that the so-called idiomatic expressions appear to be fully compositional. Therefore, in ditransitive structures, DO and the verb do not necessarily form a constituent that excludes IO. Even if we are persuaded that DO>IO and IO>DO are not derivationally related, idiomatic expressions cannot be used as a core argument for that claim. But are DO>IO and IO>DO really not related? In what follows, we argue that they are.

May (1977) shows that quantifier scope ambiguities offer relevant information about sentence structure. For instance, the sentences in (12) and (13) both contain two quantifiers: the universal *every* (represented as ∀) and the existential *a* (represented as ∃). For each sentence, we show the surface scope (the reading in which the scope of the quantifiers follows the superficial order of the constituents) and the inverse scope (the reading that results from inverting the linear order of the quantifiers):

(12)　Every ambassador visited a country.

　　　a.　Surface scope: ∀ > ∃
　　　　　For every ambassador, there is a (potentially different) country that she/he visited.

　　　b.　Inverse scope: ∃ > ∀
　　　　　There is one country that every ambassador visited.

(13)　An ambassador visited every country.

　　　a.　Surface scope: ∃ > ∀
　　　　　There is one ambassador that visited every country.

    b. Inverse scope: $\forall > \exists$
        For every country, there is a (potentially different) ambassador that
        visited it.

We focus on linear $\exists > \forall$ sentences like (13) to test inverse scope (see Larson
2014). English is a fluid scope language since it typically allows quantified arguments in simple sentences to be read with varying scopes. However, in some
constructions, scope seems *frozen* in its surface order (i.e., the inverse scope is not
possible). For instance, whereas (14a) is scopally ambiguous, (14b) is not because
the scope has frozen.

(14)   a. English $\exists > \forall, \forall > \exists$
        The President assigned [a country] [to every ambassador].

    b. English $\exists > \forall, {}^*\forall > \exists$
        The President assigned [an ambassador] [every country].

We find the same asymmetries in Spanish and Portuguese ditransitives with
give-type verbs. When DO contains an existential quantifier ($DO_\exists$), IO contains
a universal quantifier ($IO_\forall$), and the order is $DO_\exists > IO_\forall$, the sentence is scopally
ambiguous: it has both a surface and an inverse scope reading. In contrast, when
DO contains a universal quantifier ($DO_\forall$), IO contains an existential quantifier
($IO_\exists$), and the order is $IO_\exists > DO_\forall$, the scope in the sentence is frozen: no inverse
scope reading is allowed. BP examples are provided in (15).

(15)   a. BP $DO_\exists\ IO_\forall$: $\exists > \forall, \forall > \exists$
        A Olga deu [DO um presente] [IO para todos os alunos].
        the Olga gave   a   gift   to   every the students
        'Olga gave a gift to every student.'

    b. BP $IO_\exists\ DO_\forall$: $\exists > \forall, {}^*\forall > \exists$
        A Olga deu [IO para um aluno] [DO todos os presentes].
        the Olga gave   to a   student   every the gifts
        'Olga gave a student every gift.'

Sentence (15a), $DO_\exists\ IO_\forall$, has two possible readings. Its surface scope reading
is that there is one gift that Olga gave to every student. Its inverse scope reading
is that, for every student, there is a (potentially different) gift that Olga gave to
them. In contrast, sentence (15b), $IO_\exists\ DO_\forall$, can only be interpreted with a surface
scope reading: there is one student to whom Olga gave every present. The inverse
scope is not possible, which means that it has frozen.

Antonyuk (2015; 2020 [this volume]) proposes a theory of scope freezing based on overt movement. Scope freezing occurs when a quantifier raises over another to a c-commanding position as a result of a single instance of movement. We use scope freezing as a diagnostic tool for observing the argument structure of ditransitives. Whereas sentences with no instances of object movement must be scopally ambiguous, sentences in which one object has moved over the other must be interpreted in scope freezing terms.

The interpretation of the sentences in (15) suggests that they have different structures. Based on the possible scope ambiguity for DO>IO, we claim that there has been no object movement in (15a). Conversely, in (15b), based on the frozen scope of IO>DO, IO must have moved from a lower position to a higher one crossing over DO. The same scope asymmetry is also found in EP and Spanish. In the latter, the presence/absence of a dative clitic does not play any role in altering the scope relations between two co-occurring quantifiers. We return to the dative clitic's role in §2.2.

This scope asymmetry strongly indicates that DO>IO and IO>DO must be related and that the base order is DO>IO, as proposed by Larson (1988; 2014). IO>DO must be derived by movement.[3]

2.2 There is no DOC in Spanish or Portuguese

As already mentioned, scholars such as Demonte (1995), Bleam (2003), Cuervo (2003), Cuervo (2010), a.o., claim that the presence of the dative clitic in Spanish indicates a DOC. In this section, we show that the presence of the clitic does not support a DOC analysis for Spanish, EP, and BP. Although we refer to examples by Demonte (1995), our discussion also applies to other scholars' work, as they use Demonte (1995) as the base of their proposals. In addition, we show that the impossibility of passivization suggests against a DOC analysis for these three languages.

Demonte (1995) argues that only with the presence of the clitic can an anaphoric or possessive DO appear higher than an IO. To support her claim, she finds a contrast between (16a)/(17a), without a clitic, and (16b)/(17b), with a clitic, respectively (examples based on Demonte):

---

[3]Comparable freezing facts and sensitivity to the different orders of DO and IO have been used to argue for an IO>DO base order in Germanic languages, DO>IO being the result of scrambling (see Abraham 1986; Choi 1996; Bacovcin 2017, a.o.). For reasons of space, we leave a discussion of this proposal for future work.

(16) Spanish

    a. El tratamiento devolvió [$_{DO}$ a sí misma] [$_{IO}$ a Olga].
       the therapy gave-back to her self to Olga
       Intended: 'The therapy helped Olga to be herself again.'

    b. El tratamiento **le** devolvió [$_{DO}$ la estima de sí misma] [$_{IO}$
       the therapy 3SG.DAT gave-back the esteem of her self
       a Olga].
       to Olga
       'The therapy gave Olga her self-esteem.'

(17) Spanish

    a. La profesora entregó [$_{DO}$ su$_i$ dibujo] [$_{IO}$ a cada niño$_i$].
       the teacher gave-back his/her drawing to each child
       'The teacher gave each child their drawing.'
       (* for Demonte)

    b. La profesora **le** entregó [$_{DO}$ su$_i$ dibujo] [$_{IO}$ a cada
       the teacher 3SG.DAT gave-back his/her drawing to each
       niño$_i$].
       child
       'The teacher gave each child their drawing.'

However, the grammaticality differences offered by Demonte are not informative of the underlying structure of ditransitive constructions. First, the grammaticality difference of the sentences in (16) is not an effect of the presence of the dative clitic, as the same difference arises when adding the clitic to (16a) or removing it from (16b) (also noted by Pineda 2013; 2020). Rather, the contrast arises from the different internal structure of the DO DPs: [$_{DO}$ a sí misma] 'herself' in (16a), and [$_{DO}$ la estima de sí misma] 'her self-esteem' in (16b). The grammaticality of (16b) is due to the deeper structural position of the anaphor.

Second, against Demonte's (1995) judgment, we consider (17a) unquestionably grammatical (so does Pineda 2013; 2020). Thus, there are no real grammaticality differences between (17a) and (17b). The grammaticality effects remain the same regardless of the presence or absence of the dative clitic for both sentences. We conclude that the dative clitic in Spanish does not play any role in determining the structural position of DO or IO.

But does the presence of a clitic inform about a DOC? When analyzing English ditransitives, Oehrle (1976) claimed that DO>IO sentences such as (18a) and

IO>DO sentences such as (18b) have a different interpretation in terms of *possession entailment*. Oehrle says that the English DOC entails that there is a successful transfer or change of possession, either literally or symbolically. Therefore, by uttering (18a), the speaker does not have any commitment to whether Mario actually learned Quechua. In contrast, only in (18b) is there a possession entailment: Mario was transferred knowledge and, therefore, he did in fact learn Quechua.

(18) English
  a. Olga taught Quechua to Mario.
  b. Olga taught Mario Quechua.

Demonte (1995) assumes Oehrle's analysis for English to be directly applicable to Spanish sentences depending on the absence or presence of a clitic. She differentiates between sentences with and without a clitic and argues that the presence of the clitic assures a possession entailment. To test this claim, we analyze the sentences in (19a) and (19b) (adapted from Demonte). We think that these sentences are ideal to test whether the presence of the clitic plays a role in conveying a transfer of possession, because they do not contain a *give*-type verb in the main clause. If the transfer of possession is a property of the clitic, then the sentence containing a clitic must entail a transfer of possession. However, as we show, the presence of the clitic does not generate a possession entailment.

Sentence (19a) contains no clitic in the main clause and includes a *para*-phrase ('for'). The fact that the main clause can be continued by *que luego le dio a Mario* 'which she later gave to Mario' is interpreted by Demonte as a suggestion that there is no transfer of possession because there is no clitic supporting that interpretation. Sentence (19b) contains the clitic *le* in the main clause and an *a*-phrase ('to'). Demonte adds a double question mark to the continuation *que luego le dio a Mario* under the assumption that the presence of the clitic conveys a clear transfer of possession. In other words, she assumes that in (19b) the cake is now in the possession of Olga, so it cannot be further transferred to Mario.

(19) Spanish
  a. Hizo [una torta] [**para** Olga] (que luego le   dio a Mario).
      made a   cake for Olga that later 3SG.DAT gave to Mario
      'She made a cake for Olga (which she later gave to Mario).'
  b. **Le**   hizo [una torta] [a Olga] (que luego le   dio a
      3SG.DAT made a   cake to Olga that later 3SG.DAT gave to

Mario).
Mario
'She made a cake for Olga (which she later gave to Mario).'
(?? for Demonte)

However, the semantics proposed by Demonte for these sentences is not accurate. In both (19a) and (19b), the transfer of possession is not an *entailment*, but an *implicature*. An implicature is an inference that may not hold in the context of other information and, thus, can be canceled. Entailments cannot be canceled. *Hacerle una torta a Olga* 'making a cake for Olga' does not entail that Olga is in the possession of the cake, which suggests that the clitic is not playing any role in conveying transfer of possession. Rather, the continuation *que luego le dio a Mario* in both (19a) and (19b) cancels the inference that Olga is in the possession of the cake, which makes this inference an implicature. Note that (19b) is not judged ungrammatical by Demonte. Since the presence of the clitic does not generate a possession entailment, its presence or absence does not change the meaning of the sentence. The presence of the clitic does not support a DOC analysis.

A further argument against a DOC analysis is passivization. English DOCs are able to passivize the argument generated in the IO position. Larson (1988) explains that passivization and the PP-dative/DOC alternation are related processes, since passives advance an object to a subject position, while DOCs advance an indirect object to a direct object position. IO passivization is shown in (20), where *Mario* was generated as an IO, even though it appears occupying the subject position after spell-out.

(20)   English
       Mario was given an apple.

However, IO passivization is simply not allowed in Spanish, EP, or BP. The examples in (21) show the impossibility of the counterparts of (20) in these three languages. Note that the presence of the dative clitic in Spanish does not improve the grammaticality of the sentence (21b).

(21)   a. EP/BP
          *O   Mario foi   dado uma maçã.
           the Mario was given an   apple
          Intended: 'Mario was given an apple.'

b. Spanish
    *Mario (le)   fue dado una manzana.
    Mario 3SG.DAT was given an apple
    Intended: 'Mario was given an apple.'

The absence of IO passivization in Spanish, EP, and BP has been largely overlooked as if it did not offer any insights for these languages. But, if IO passivization is not possible, then we need to assume that IO in IO>DO is not occupying any object position (Larson 2014), even though its linear order may suggest differently. We return to this issue in §3. For now, it is safe to say that, if IO is not occupying an object position when it precedes DO, then it is not accurate to claim that IO>DO is a DOC.

We conclude that the claim that there is DOC in Spanish, EP, and BP does not have support in the data, and there is no solid semantic or structural evidence for a DOC in these three languages.

3 The order of objects and information structure

We have claimed that there is no DOC in Spanish, EP, or BP and that the base structure is DO>IO in these three languages. In this section, we propose that information structure shapes the IO>DO configuration in these languages.

3.1 The distribution of DO>IO and IO>DO

In Romance languages, given information (i.e., information assumed or already supplied in the context) appears early in the sentence and does not carry sentential stress, whereas new information (i.e., information introduced for the first time in an interchange) typically occurs sentence-finally and receives a special intonation (Zubizarreta 1998). When the whole sentence conveys new information, its linear order follows the default, unmarked structure.

The informationally unmarked order for ditransitives is DO>IO. This is the default order for answering a general question with no topic-comment structure, such as 'what happened?'. Observe the BP example in (22), which is an answer to the question *O que aconteceu?* 'What happened?'

(22)   A Olga deu [$_{DO}$ uma maçã] [$_{IO}$ para o Mario].
       the Olga gave   an   apple   to   the Mario
       'Olga gave an apple to Mario.'

In (22), the whole sentence conveys new information in the discourse. DO>IO is the only appropriate order to answer the question, which offers support to the claim that this is the base structure for ditransitives. The same generalization applies to both EP and Spanish.

Besides, following the general pattern for Romance, DO>IO is also the unique answer to the question 'to whom?', which asks for IO. Since IO encodes new information in the answer to such a question, it appears in final position. These effects are found in Spanish, EP, and BP. Therefore, the sentence in (22) can also be the answer to the question *A quem deu a Olga uma maçã?* 'Who did Olga give an apple to?'. As we discuss in the next subsection, although the answers to 'what happened?' and 'to whom?' are linearly identical, they certainly differ structurally.

So DO>IO is the default order when the whole sentence is the new information and when IO conveys new information. In contrast, the IO>DO order is more constrained. First, IO>DO appears when DO encodes new information, as the answer to the question 'what?' and, as is regular in Romance, occurs in final position. An example appears in (23) in BP, which is the answer to the question *O que a Olga deu para o Mario?* 'What did Olga give to Mario?'

(23)   A   Olga deu [$_{IO}$ para o   Mario] [$_{DO}$ uma maçã].
       the Olga gave   to   the Mario   an   apple
       'Olga gave an apple to Mario.'

Second, IO>DO also appears when DO is heavy, that is, when it is either a long or complex constituent. Previous corpus and theoretical studies in Romance (Beavers & Nishida 2010 for Spanish, Brito 2014 for EP, Mioto 2003 for BP) show that it is expected to find a heavy DO in final position.[4] Examples in (24) show a contrast for EP.

(24)   a. ?/#A Olga deu [$_{DO}$ três razões para não aceitar o   trabalho] [$_{IO}$
          the Olga gave   three reasons to   not accept the job

---

[4]IO>DO is also found in non-Romance languages with a heavy DO. In the following English examples (adapted from Larson 2014), (i.b) is not a DOC as IO contains the preposition 'to':

(i)   English IO>DO
      a. ?/#Olga gave [$_{DO}$ a reason not to accept the job] [$_{IO}$ to Mario].
      b.   Olga gave [$_{IO}$ to Mario] [$_{DO}$ a reason not to accept the job].

ao   Mario].
to.the Mario

Intended: 'Olga gave Mario three reasons not to accept the job.'

b. A Olga deu [_{IO} ao   Mario] [_{DO} três razões para não aceitar
    the Olga gave   to.the Mario   three reasons to   not accept
    o   trabalho].
    the job

'Olga gave Mario three reasons not to accept the job.'

For cases like (23) and (24), IO>DO is the most natural order. IO>DO is, there-fore, the result of a discourse-related configuration that affects the basic order of the arguments of ditransitives. From these facts, we conclude that the IO>DO order should be explained in terms of information structure.

3.2 A low left periphery

Belletti (2004) argues that the verb phrase is endowed with a fully-fledged periph-ery of discourse-related structural positions, in parallel with the high left periph-ery. Her seminal work has been successfully developed in the recent literature (Mioto 2003; Quarezemin 2005; Jiménez-Fernández 2009, a.o.) and is relevant for us to explain the IO>DO order in Spanish, EP, and BP. We propose a low left periphery that minimally contains a Topic Phrase (TopP), a Focus Phrase (FocP), and the verbal domain (*v*P), as shown in (25). TopP and FocP are motivated by the discursive processes that change the order of sentence constituents.

(25) [TopP [FocP [*v*P]]]

We propose that IO>DO is possible when IO occupies TopP and DO occupies FocP. Consider again the BP IO>DO answer in (23), repeated below as (26).

(26) A Olga deu [_{IO} para o Mario] [_{DO} uma maçã].
      the Olga gave   to the Mario   an   apple
      'Olga gave an apple to Mario.'

As argued in §2.1, the DO *uma maçã* 'an apple' in (26) is generated higher than the IO *para o Mario* 'to Mario'. This base order is altered by two movement operations, which are motivated by information structure properties in the low left periphery. First, since DO encodes new information by offering the exact answer to the question 'what?', it moves from its verb-internal position to the low FocP. This movement is not surprising as answers to questions are associated with focus (Rooth 1992). Second, since IO offers given information, it moves from its initial position to the low TopP, crossing over both DO's base position and its landing site. Additionally, the complex V+*v* has moved to Tense, as is the general case in Romance. A structure for (26) is shown in (27). The arrows mark the movements towards the low left periphery.

(27)

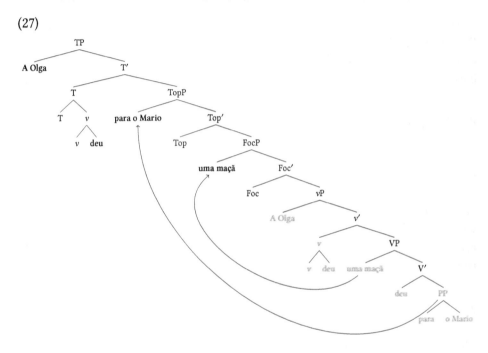

As for the DO>IO order in sentences such as (22), repeated below as (28), the syntactic structure depends on the kind of discourse-related information it conveys. When the whole sentence is the new information, the low left periphery does not host any constituent and we could safely say that both DO and IO remain in situ, as in (28a). In contrast, when only IO conveys the new information, both DO and IO move to the specifier of TopP and FocP in the low left periphery, respectively, as shown in (28b).

(28) A Olga deu [DO uma maçã] [IO para o Mario].
      the Olga gave   an apple   to   the Mario
      'Olga gave an apple to Mario.'

a. [$_{TP}$ A Olga T+v+deu [$_{vP}$ <A Olga> <v+deu> [$_{VP}$ [uma maçã] <deu> [para o Mario]]]]

b. [$_{TP}$ A Olga T+v+deu [$_{TopP}$ [uma maçã] Top [$_{FocP}$ [para o Mario] Foc [$_{vP}$ <A Olga> <v+deu> [$_{VP}$ <uma maçã> <deu> <para o Mario>]]]]]

The analyses we have proposed for IO>DO and DO>IO apply equally to BP, EP, and Spanish. Our proposal can account for the fact that it is possible to find an IO>DO order in Spanish and Portuguese, which is derivationally related to the basic order DO>IO, without assuming a DOC construction for these languages.[5]

4 Conclusions

In this paper, we have dismissed the arguments supporting a DOC approach for Spanish and Portuguese while showing that there are no DOCs in these languages. We have proposed that the internal argument structure of ditransitives is based on a DO>IO order. The IO>DO order is a derived configuration, which we have explained in terms of movement to a low left periphery with discourse-related positions available. Our comparative approach unifies the analysis of ditransitives in Spanish, EP and BP.

Abbreviations

The abbreviations used in the glosses of this chapter follow the Leipzig Glossing Rules.

Acknowledgements

Both authors thank Richard Larson, the participants at the Syntax Seminar at Stony Brook University (Fall 2015), the audiences at the International Workshop on Dative Structures in Barcelona (Spring 2017), at the 47th Linguistic Symposium on Romance Languages at the University of Delaware (Spring 2017), and at the Department of Linguistics at Stony Brook University (Spring 2017), as well as two anonymous reviewers. Both authors also express their gratitude to Russell Tanenbaum, who proofread the document. The first author thanks the support

---

[5]For a formal proposal on the role of information structure features, see Cépeda & Cyrino (2017).

of the American Council of Learned Societies (Mellon/ACLS Dissertation Completion Fellowship 2017–2018). The second author thanks the support of CNPq–Conselho Nacional de Desenvolvimento Científico e Tecnológico, Brazil (Grant 303742/2013-5), FAPESP- Fundação de Amparo à Pesquisa do Estado de São Paulo, Brazil (Grants 2012/06078-9 and 2014/17477-7), and Ministerio de Economía y Competitividad, España (FFI2014/52015-P).

References

Abraham, Werner. 1986. Word order in the middle field of the German sentence. In Werner Abraham & Sjaak de Meij (eds.), *Topic, focus and configurationality: Papers from the 6th Groningen Grammar Talks*, 15–38. Amsterdam: John Benjamins.

Antonyuk, Svitlana. 2015. *Quantifier scope and scope freezing in Russian*. Stony Brook, NY: Stony Brook University. (Doctoral dissertation).

Antonyuk, Svitlana. 2020. The puzzle of Russian ditransitives. In Anna Pineda & Jaume Mateu (eds.), *Dative constructions in Romance and beyond*, 43–74. Berlin: Language Science Press. DOI:10.5281/zenodo.3776533

Bacovcin, Hezekiah Akiva. 2017. *Parameterising Germanic ditransitive variation: A historical-comparative study*. Philadelphia, PA: University of Pennsylvania. (Doctoral dissertation).

Beavers, John & Chiyo Nishida. 2010. The Spanish dative alternation revisited. In Sonia Colina, Antxon Olarrea & Ana Maria Carvalho (eds.), *Romance linguistics 2009: Selected papers from the 39th Linguistic Symposium on Romance Languages (LSRL)*, 217–230. Amsterdam: John Benjamins.

Belletti, Adriana. 2004. Aspects of the low IP area. In Luigi Rizzi (ed.), *The structure of CP and IP: The cartography of syntactic structures,* 16–51. Oxford: Oxford University Press.

Bleam, Tonia. 2003. Properties of double object construction in Spanish. In Rafael Núñez-Cedeño, Luis López & Richard Cameron (eds.), *A Romance perspective on language knowledge and use: Selected papers from the 31st Linguistic Symposium on Romance Languages (LSRL)*, 233–252. Amsterdam: John Benjamins.

Brito, Ana Maria. 2014. As construções ditransitivas revisitadas: Alternância dativa em Português Europeu? In António Moreno, Fátima Silva, Isabel Falé, Isabel Pereira & João Veloso (eds.), *Textos selecionados do XXIX Encontro Nacional da Associação Portuguesa de Linguística*, 103–119. Coimbra: Associação Portuguesa de Linguística.

Brito, Ana Maria. 2015. Two base generated structures for ditransitives in European Portuguese. *Oslo Studies in Language* 7(1). 337–357.

Calindro, Ana Regina. 2020. Ditransitive constructions: What sets Brazilian Portuguese apart from other Romance languages? In Anna Pineda & Jaume Mateu (eds.), *Dative constructions in Romance and beyond*, 75–95. Berlin: Language Science Press. DOI:10.5281/zenodo.3776535

Cépeda, Paola & Sonia Cyrino. 2017. *A point of order: Object asymmetries in Spanish and Portuguese ditransitives.* Manuscript.

Choi, Hye-Won. 1996. *Optimizing structure in context: Scrambling and information structure.* New Brunswick, NJ: Rutgers University. (Doctoral dissertation).

Costa, João. 2009. A focus-binding conspiracy: Left-to-right merge, scrambling and binary structure in European Portuguese. In Jeroen van Craenenbroeck (ed.), *Alternatives to cartography*, 87–108. Berlin: De Gruyter Mouton.

Cuervo, María Cristina. 2003. *Datives at large.* Cambridge, MA: Massachusetts Institute of Technology. (Doctoral dissertation). https://dspace.mit.edu/handle/1721.1/7991.

Cuervo, María Cristina. 2010. Two types of (apparently) ditransitive light verb constructions. In Karlos Arregi, Zsuzsanna Fagyal, Silvina A. Montrul & Annie Tremblay (eds.), *Romance linguistics 2008: Interactions in Romance. Selected papers from the 38th Linguistic Symposium on Romance Languages (LRSL)*, 139–155. Amsterdam: John Benjamins.

Demonte, Violeta. 1995. Dative alternation in Spanish. *Probus* 7(1). 5–30. DOI:10.1515/prbs.1995.7.1.5

Hallman, Peter. 2015. Syntactic neutralization in double object constructions. *Linguistic Inquiry* 46(3). 389–424. DOI:10.1162/LING_a_00187

Harley, Heidi. 1995. If you have, you can give. In *Proceedings of the 15th West Coast Conference on Formal Linguistics (WCCFL)*, 193–207. Stanford, CA: CSLI.

Jiménez-Fernández, Ángel. 2009. The low periphery of double object constructions in English and Spanish. *Philologia Hispalensis* 23. 179–200.

Larson, Richard K. 1988. On the double object construction. *Linguistic Inquiry* 19(3). 335–391.

Larson, Richard K. 2014. *On shell structure.* New York, NY: Routledge.

Larson, Richard K. 2017. On "dative idioms" in English. *Linguistic Inquiry* 48(3). 389–426.

May, Robert. 1977. *The grammar of quantification.* Cambridge, MA: Massachusetts Institute of Technology. (Doctoral dissertation).

Mioto, Carlos. 2003. Focalização e quantificação. *Revista Letras* 61. 169–189.

Oehrle, Richard. 1976. *The grammatical status of the English dative alternation.* Cambridge, MA: Massachusetts Institute of Technology. (Doctoral dissertation).

Pineda, Anna. 2013. Double object constructions and dative/accusative alternations in Spanish and Catalan: A unified account. *Borealis: An International Journal of Hispanic Linguistics* 2. 57–115.

Pineda, Anna. 2016. *Les fronteres de la (in)transitivitat: Estudi dels aplicatius en llengües romàniques i basc.* Barcelona: Institut d'Estudis Món Juïc. Published and revised version of the doctoral dissertation.

Pineda, Anna. 2020. Double object constructions in Romance: The common denominator. *Syntax.*

Quarezemin, Sandra. 2005. *A focalização do sujeito no PB.* Florianópolis: Universidade Federal de Santa Catarina. (MA thesis).

Rappaport Hovav, Malka & Beth Levin. 2008. The English dative alternation: The case for verb sensitivity. *Journal of Linguistics* 44. 129–167. DOI:10.1017/S00222267070049

Rooth, Mats. 1992. A theory of focus interpretation. *Natural Language Semantics* 1. 75–116.

Torres Morais, Maria Aparecida & Heloísa Salles. 2010. Parametric change in the grammatical encoding of indirect objects in Brazilian Portuguese. *Probus* 22(2). 181–209.

Zubizarreta, Maria Luisa. 1998. *Prosody, focus, and word order.* Cambridge, MA: MIT Press.

Chapter 5

Ditransitive constructions with differentially marked direct objects in Romanian

Alexandra Cornilescu
University of Bucharest

The paper discusses Romanian data that had gone unnoticed so far and investigates the differences of grammaticality triggered by differentially marked direct objects in ditransitive constructions, in binding configurations. Specifically, while a bare direct object (DO) may bind a possessor contained in the indirect object (IO), whether or not the IO is clitic doubled, a differentially marked DO may bind into an undoubled IO, but cannot bind into an IO if the latter is clitic doubled. Grammaticality is restored if the DO is clitic doubled in its turn. The focus of the paper is to offer a derivational account of ditransitive constructions, which accounts for these differences. The claim is that the grammaticality contrasts mentioned above result from the different feature structures of bare DOs compared with differentially marked ones, as well as from the fact that differentially marked DOs and IO have common features. Differentially marked DOs interfere with IOs since both are sensitive to the animacy hierarchy, and include a syntactic [Person] feature in their featural make-up. The derivational valuation of this feature by both objects may create locality problems.

1 Problem and aim

In this paper, I turn to data not discussed for Romanian so far and consider the differences of grammaticality triggered by differentially marked direct objects (i.e. DOs with Differential Object Marking, from now one, DOM-ed DOs) in ditransitive constructions, in *binding* configurations.

Alexandra Cornilescu. 2020. Ditransitive constructions with differentially marked direct objects in Romanian. In Anna Pineda & Jaume Mateu (eds.), *Dative constructions in Romance and beyond*, 117–142. Berlin: Language Science Press. DOI:10.5281/zenodo.3776541

Specifically,[1] bare DOs easily bind a possessor contained in a dative IO, whether the latter is clitic doubled (from now on, CD-ed) or not, as in (1) - (2). The picture changes when the DO is DOM-ed. It is still possible for a DOM-ed DO to bind into an undoubled IO (3), but if the IO is doubled, the sentence is ungrammatical (4). While co-occurrence of the DOM-ed DO with a dative clitic results in ungrammaticality, if the DOM-ed DO is doubled, sentences are grammatical, again irrespective of the presence/absence of the dative clitic, as in examples (5) and (6).

(1) $DP_{theme} > DP_{goal}$
Banca   a   retrocedat multe case$_i$ proprietarilor   lor$_i$ de drept.
bank.DEF has returned   many houses ownersDEF.DAT their of right
'The bank returned the houses to their rightful owners.' (Cornilescu et al. 2017a: 162)

(2) $DP_{theme} > $ **cl-DP** $_{goal}$
Banca   **le$_j$=a**   retrocedat multe case$_i$ proprietarilor$_j$ lor$_i$ de
bank.DEF 3PL.DAT=has returned   many houses owners.DEF.DAT their of

drept.
right
'The bank returned many houses to their rightful owners.' (Cornilescu et al. 2017a: 162)

(3)   DOM-ed $DP_{theme} > DP$ $_{goal}$
Comisia   a   repartizat pe   mai   mulți medici$_i$ rezidenți unor
board.DEF has assigned   DOM more many medical residents some.DAT
foști   profesori   de-ai lor$_i$.
former professors of   theirs
'The board assigned several medical residents to some former professors of theirs.'

---

[1]Judgments on possessor binding in Romanian ditransitive constructions and some of the examples come from an experiment described in detail in Cornilescu et al. (2017b). Unless otherwise specified, examples and acceptability judgments belong to the author.

(4)   *DOM-ed DP$_{theme}$ > cl-DP$_{goal}$
      *Comisia   **le**=a   repartizat pe   mai   mulți medici$_i$ rezidenți
      board.DEF 3PL.DAT=has assigned   DOM more many medical residents
      unor   foști   profesori   de-ai lor$_i$.
      some.DAT former professors of   theirs
      'The board assigned several medical residents to some former professors
      of theirs.'

(5)   **cl-DOM-ed DP$_{theme}$** > DP$_{goal}$
      Comisia   **i**=a   repartizat pe   mai   mulți medici$_i$ rezidenți
      board.DEF 3PL.ACC=has assigned   DOM more many medical residents
      unor   foști   profesori   de-ai lor$_i$.
      some.DAT former professors of   theirs
      'The board assigned several medical residents to some former professors
      of theirs.'

(6)   **cl- DOM-ed DP $_{theme}$>cl-DP $_{goal}$**
      Comisia   **i=l=a**=repartizat   pe   fiecare medic   rezident
      board.DEF 3SG.F.DAT=3SG.M.ACC=assigned DOM each   medical resident
      unei   foste   profesoare   a   lui.
      some.DAT former professor.F.DAT GEN his
      'The board assigned each resident doctor to a former professor of his.'

Critical is the difference between (2) and (4), and also between (4) and (5)-(6) where the DO is doubled.

The aim of the chapter is to offer a derivational account of ditransitive constructions, which accommodates these differences. I claim that the grammaticality contrasts above result from the different feature structure of bare DOs compared with DOM-ed ones, and from the fact that DOM-ed DOs and IOs need to check the same [Person] feature against the same functional head.

2 On Romanian dative DPs

2.1 Inflectional datives and the animacy hierarchy

In Romanian nouns have *inflectional dative morphology* and, additionally, exhibit *prepositional marking*, employing the locative preposition *la* 'at'/'to'. An essential property of inflectional datives (=Inf-DAT) is that they are highly sensitive to the animacy hierarchy and have a higher cut-off point than *la*-datives, as seen in (8).

(7) human > animate > inanimate

(8) a. Am   turnat vin   la musafiri/musafirilor.
         have.1SG poured wine at guests/guests.DEF.DAT
         'I poured wine to the guests.'
     b. Am   dat   apă   la cai/?cailor.
         have.1SG given   water at horses/?horses.DEF.DAT
         'I poured water to the horses.'
     c. Am   turnat apă   la flori/*?florilor.
         have.1SG poured water at flowers/*?flowers.DEF.DAT
         'I poured water to the flowers.'

One theoretical difficulty that immediately arises is that of incorporating scalar concepts like the animacy hierarchy or the definiteness hierarchy into the discrete binary system of a minimalist grammar. Richards (2008) argues that the animacy hierarchy and the definiteness hierarchy are semantic and pragmatic in nature and should be viewed as *syntax-semantics interface phenomena*. Crucially, he proposes that nouns which are sensitive to these hierarchies should be lexically specified for a binary grammatical [Person] feature (Rodríguez-Mondoñedo 2007 for Spanish). It is this [Person] feature which triggers the interpretation of a given NP along the two hierarchies, checking its position on the two scales. Nouns which accept the Inf-DAT enter the derivation lexically marked as [+Person]. Since this is a syntactic feature, it must be checked during the derivation.

2.2 On the internal structure of *la*-datives

The preposition *la* 'at'/'to' is not only a *functional dative marker*, but it is also the core *lexical preposition* of the location and movement frames. The lexical preposition *la* assigns accusative case to its object. This accusative cannot be replaced by a dative, and, as correctly pointed out by both reviewers, accusative *la*-phrases do not co-occur with dative clitics. All movement and location verbs may combine with lexical accusative *la*-phrases, rejecting, however, dative *la*-phrases. An example is the verb *merge* 'go', which is compatible only with lexical *la*, but not with functional dative *la*. Substitution of the *la*-phrase with a dative DP is impossible (9a), and a dative clitic is equally ungrammatical (9b).

(9) a. Ion a   mers la Maria/**Mariei.
     Ion has gone at Maria.ACC/Maria.DAT
     'Ion went to Maria.'

   b. * Ion îi=merge   (Mariei).
     Ion 3SG.F.DAT=goes Maria.DAT
     'Ion is going to Maria.'

One specification is required at this point. Even for unaccusative verbs like
plăcea 'like', which always select a dative Experiencer, either inflectional or prepositional, co-occurrence of a dative *la*-phrase with a clitic is possible only in the
third person. In the first and in the second person, the clitic may co-occur only
with an inflectional dative strong pronoun, never with a prepositional dative, as
apparent in (10b) below:

(10) a. Ciocolata   le=place   copiilor   /la copii.
        chocolate.DEF 3PL.DAT=like.3SG children.DEF.DAT /at children
        'Children like chocolate.'

    b. Ciocolata   îmi=place   şi   mie/*şi   la mine.
        chocolate.DEF 1SG.DAT=like.3SG also I.DAT/also at me
        'I also like chocolate.'

Verbs in the movement frame do not behave uniformly regarding the realization of their Goal argument. While some never select a dative (e.g. *merge* 'go'),
others (e.g. *ajunge* 'arrive' or *veni* 'come') may select a dative on condition that
the Goal DP is [+Person]; the dative Goal is realized as a clitic, doubled by a
strong pronoun or by a dative *la*-phrase, provided that the clitic is third person,
as already shown in (10). Thus, in (11a) the *la*-phrase is lexical; in (11b), the Goal
is a dative phrase realized as a clitic. The first person dative clitic can only be
doubled by a dative strong pronoun, while the *la*-phrase is out (11c). The relevant example is however (11d), an example attested in Google, where the Goal is
a dative, and the dative clitic is doubled by a dative *la*- phrase. As the comparison of (11a) and (11d) shows, the *la*-phrase is interpreted as a dative only when it
co-occurs with a dative clitic.

(11) a. Pachetul a   ajuns **la mine/la Londra** ieri.
        parcel.DEF has arrived at 1SG.ACC/at London yesterday
        'The parcel got to me/to London yesterday.'

    b. Pachetul **mi=a**   ajuns şi   mie   ieri.
        parcel.DEF **1SG.DAT**=has arrived also 1SG.DAT yesterday

  c. Pachetul **mi**=a   ajuns   (***la mine**)   şi   mie   ieri.

    parcel.DEF **1SG.DAT**=has arrived (at   1SG.ACC) also 1SG.DAT yesterday

    'The parcel got to me too yesterday.'

  d. Acum le=au   venit **la mulţi**   deciziile de recalculare

    now   3PL.DAT=have come at. many.ACC decisions of recalculation

    a   pensiilor.

    GEN.ART pensions.DEF.GEN

    'Now many have got their decisions for recalculation of their

    pensions.'

In the rest of this section I examine the internal structure of the *la*-phrase when it is a dative, i.e. when it is clitic-doubled. As a dative-marker *la* is puzzling, since it is described as a "dative preposition", but, as seen above in (9a), it clearly assigns accusative case to its complement (Figure 1). On the other hand, *la*-phrases may take dative clitics (11c), and, as well-known, clitics and their associates always agree in Case. This suggests that, as a dative marker, *la* simply assigns Case to a DP *subcomponent* of the dative phrase, while the whole *la*-phrase has *an uninterpretable valued dative feature* (Figure 2), which agrees with the clitic's Case feature. The marker *la* has become an *internal constituent* which extends the dative phrase (Figure 2), i.e. a K(ase) marker like the marker of DOM (López 2012). An additional role of this morpheme is that of a category shifter, which reanalyzes the PP into a KP, therefore, an extended DP.

The categorial change from P to K may be viewed as an instance of *downward re-analysis* (Roberts & Roussou 2003), likely to have occurred out of the need to improve the correspondence between syntactic features and their PF representation.

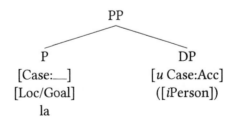

Figure 1: Lexical *la* assigns accusative Case

In time, there gradually emerged two different changes in the function of the Locative PP in Figure 1. One has been the extension of *la* from verbs that have Goals or Possessor-Goals in their a-structure (verbs of giving and throwing) to

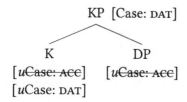

Figure 2: K assigns accusative to DP, while the KP has an uninterpretable dative feature.

verbs that select Beneficiaries (e.g. verbs of creation, like *face* 'make, do', *coace* 'bake', etc.), and even verbs that select Maleficiary or Source, i.e. the opposite of Goal, (e.g. *fura* 'steal'). Thus the preposition *la* widens its thematic sphere, but it is partly desemanticized, since the thematic content of the *la*-phrase almost completely follows from the descriptive content of the selecting verb. Secondly, while any kind of DP may assume the Location/Goal θ-role, these extended interpretations (e.g. Beneficiary, Maleficiary) are compatible only with nouns high in the animacy hierarchy. As explained, such nouns grammaticalize their inherent human feature as a syntactic [Person] feature (Richards 2008).

(12) Possessor-Goal
      Mama   (le)=a   dat   prăjituri copiilor   /la copii.
      mother.DEF 3PL.DAT=has given cakes   children.DEF.DAT /at children
      'Mother gave cakes to the children.'

(13) Beneficiary
      Mama   (le)=a   copt   prăjituri copiilor   /la copii.
      mother.DEF 3PL.DAT=has baked cakes   children.DEF.DAT /at children
      'Mother baked cakes for the children.'

(14) Maleficiary/Source
      Nişte vagabonzi le=au   furat   copiilor   /la copii
      some tramps   3PL.DAT-have stolen children.DEF.DAT /at children
      jucăriile.
      toys.DEF
      'Some tramps stole the toys from the children.'

At this point, there was an imperfect match between features and their exponents, since *la* had partly lost its thematic content, and an obligatory syntactic

[+Person] feature in the nominal matrix had no PF realization (Figure 1). This tension led to the re-analysis of *la* as a PF exponent of the [Person] feature of the noun. As such *la* becomes a higher K part of the nominal expression, where K is a spell-out of [*i*Person]. Syntactically, K is a Probe that values an uninterpretable [*u*Person:___] feature of the DP through agreement (Figure 3).

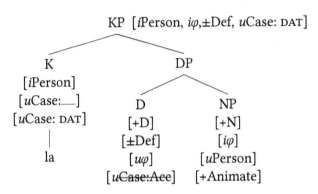

Figure 3: K is a spell-out of the [Person] feature.

Compared to Figure 1, the representation in Figure 3 is "simpler", since the grammatical feature [*i*Person], synchretically realized by N in Figure 1 is realized as a separate lexical item in Figure 3.

Like Inf-DAT, *la*-DAT is sensitive to the animacy hierarchy, but the selectional properties of *la* are not identical to those of the dative inflection. For instance, both types of datives are compatible with names of corporate bodies (15), but only Inf-DAT is also felicitous with *abstract* nouns (16).

(15) (Le)=a   împărțit   banii   la niște asociații
     (3PL.DAT)=has handed_out money.DEF at some associations
     caritabile/unor   asociații   caritabile.
     charitable/some.DAT associations charitable
     'He handed out the money to some charities.'

(16) A supus   proiectul *la atenția   bordului/atenției
     has submitted project.DEF *at attention board.DEF.GEN/attention.DEF.DAT
     bordului.
     board.DEF.GEN
     'He submitted the project to the board's attention.'

Conclusions so far:

1. Nouns may come from the lexicon with an unvalued [*u*Person] feature.

2. Dative *la* is a K component which spells-out an [*i*Person] feature, historically resulting through downward re-analysis of the homonymous [Location] preposition. K selects DPs which are [*u*Person] and values their [*u*Person] feature.

3. A KP nominal expression is complex, since it contains a smaller DP. The K-head case-licenses the smaller DP. K also contains an *uninterpretable valued* dative feature checked during the derivation.

2.3 Why a clitic is sometimes required

In theory, like any functional head, the clitic should be a response to some internal need of the *la*-phrase. It is plausible that dative *la*, an [*i*Person] spell-out, further eroded semantically, becoming an uninterpretable [*u*Person], at least sometimes.[2] The KP continues to have all the features in (17), except that [Person] is uninterpretable (17).

(17) KP [*u*Person, +D, ±Def, *i*φ, *u*Case: DAT]

Given this feature structure a pronominal clitic is required to derivationally supply an [*i*Person] feature. Clitics are known to be sensitive to features like [+D, +Def, ...] and cannot combine with nominal projections smaller than DP. They may, however, combine with projections larger than DPs, i.e. KPs, where these features are specified, since they percolate from the D-head.

Concluding, *la*+DP constituents are KPs, where K is a dative head. With verbs of movement and location, including ditransitive ones, *la* + DP are also still analyzable as PPs expressing Goal/Location.

2.4 The internal structure of the inflectional dative phrase

The analysis of [*la*$_K$] above suggests a parallel treatment for the dative morphology, K$_{dative}$, which I will also consider a Person exponent. Nouns inflected for the dative are endowed with [*u*Person__], given their sensitivity to the animacy hierarchy. This feature is valued KP-internally, when K$_{dative}$ has an interpretable

---

[2]An important empirical generalization (Cornilescu 2017) regarding Romanian dative clitics is that they are obligatory for non-core datives, but optional for core datives. In the analysis proposed here, this means that the [Person] feature on dative KPs is uninterpretable by default and can be interpretable only for *core datives*, which have the property of being s-selected by the verb.

Person feature, i.e. K is [*i*Person, Case-Dative___]. Alternatively, if K's semantic feature is bleached, then K_{dative} is [*u*Person] and simply realizes Case. In such situations, CD is obligatory and [*u*Person] is checked KP-externally, using a clitic derivation.

Importantly, like *la*-DAT, Inf-DAT are ambiguous between a KP and a PP categorization. The PP analysis is, for example, required for adjectives that select Inf-DAT complements (e.g. *util* 'useful', *folositor* 'useful', *necesar* 'necessary'). Since adjectives are not case-assigners, the Dative is licensed by a null preposition which finally incorporates into the adjective.

Inside *v*P, when the Inf-DAT is clitic doubled or, at least, may have been clitic doubled, the Inf-DAT is analyzable as a KP. However, when doubling is impossible, the Inf-DAT must be projected as a PP, since otherwise it cannot check either Case or Person. One example is that of sentences containing two Inf- DAT phrases, of which the higher must be CD-ed and the lower cannot be CD-ed (since they compete for the same *v*P internal position at some point).

(18) Ion și=a   vândut casa   unor   rude   /la niște
      Ion 3SG.M.REFL.DAT=has sold   house.DEF some.DAT relatives /at some
      rude.
      relatives
      'Ion sold his house to some relatives.'

Some results:

1. Datives inside *v*P –whether *la*- DAT or Inf- DAT - are uniformly either KPs or PPs.

2. *La*- and K_{dative} are exponents of Person which encode sensitivity to the animacy hierarchy.

3. When K is [*i*Person], the Person feature of datives is checked KP-internally, while the Case feature is checked derivationally. The clitic is unnecessary and thus impossible.

4. When K is [*u*Person], the ultimate exponent of Person is the clitic, whose presence is mandatory.

A consequence:

- Given the feature structure of datives [*u/i* Person, *u* Case: Dative], the applicative verb that licenses them should be endowed with the following features: V_{appl}[*u*Person, *u*Case:___].

3 Briefly on the syntax of Romanian DOM

3.1 Background

The obligatory marker of Romanian DOM is the spatial preposition *pe* 'on'/'towards'/'against', similar to Spanish *a*. Unlike *a*, however, *pe* assigns accusative case to its object. Therefore, Romanian is not among the many languages where DOM-ed DOs and IOs share the same dative/oblique case, sameness of case representing an explicit connection between the two (Manzini & Franco 2016).

One of the reviewers stresses that DOM *pe* derives from the *directional* uses of the Old Romanian preposition *p(r)e*, which was often used with directional/-Goal verbs (e.g. *striga* 'call', *asculta* 'listen to', *întreba* 'ask'), as well as with verbs which entailed the presence of an opponent (e.g. *lupta* 'fight'), as in the following example:

(19)   Old Romanian (Hill & Mardale 2017: 395)
Au   ascultat **pre mine**.
have listened DOM me
'They have listened to me.'

Significant research on the history of DOM has demonstrated that in Old Romanian the presence of the functional preposition *p(r)e* was a means of upgrading the object, signaling a *contrastive topic* interpretation (Hill 2013; Hill & Mardale 2017). Furthermore, in Old Romanian , *p(r)e* was not restricted to animate nouns, as shown in (20) below:

(20)   Old Romanian (Hill & Mardale 2017: 396)
Şi   deaderă lui   Iacov **pre bozii**   cei striini.
and gave   DAT Jakob DOM weeds.DEF the foreign
'And they gave to Jakob the foreign weeds.'

In Modern Romanian, the noun classes compatible with DOM have been reduced to animate, predominantly [+human] nouns. This restriction is in line with the change in the discourse function of DOM, "from a marker of Contrastive Topic [...] to a *backgrounding device* for the [+human] noun in the discourse (Hill 2013: 147)". Thus in Modern Romanian, the most frequent discourse role of DOM-ed objects is that of *familarity topic*, a role which is strengthened by the frequent association of DOM with clitic doubling (Hill & Mardale 2017).

Reinterpreting these important results in the framework of our analysis, it follows that although they do not share Case, DOM-ed DOs and IOs share other properties in Romanian, too. Thus, DOM is sensitive to the animacy hierarchy, which means that both DOM-ed DOs and IOs grammaticalize [Person].

Similarly, the DOM marker *pe* 'on'/'to(wards)' can easily be analyzed as a K head (López 2012; Hill & Mardale 2017), a spell-out of Person, behaving in all respects like dative *la*, except that *pe*-phrases check an accusative feature. Tentatively, the feature structure of *pe*-KPs is as follows: [*u/i*Person, *u*Case:Acc]. When *pe* selects the [*u*Person] option, a clitic extends the KP, forming a chain that ultimately values the [*u*Person] feature.

In harmony with its familiar topic discourse role, DOM is also sensitive to the definiteness hierarchy (21), which arranges nominal expression by order of their referential stability. Thus, DOM is obligatory for personal pronouns and proper names, which are always referentially stable, it is felicitous but optional with definite and indefinite DPs, and it is impossible with determinerless nouns.

(21)   personal pronouns > proper names > definite phrases > indefinite specific > indefinite non-specific > bare plurals > bare singular

In its turn, CD is *possible* and *optional* for all accusative KPs, while being *obligatory* only for personal pronouns. Finally CD is not possible for bare DOs, i.e. it operates on KPs, not DPs, presumably because only KPs are marked for [Person].

3.2 The syntax of DOM

As for the syntax of DOM, I have provisionally adapted to Romanian the analysis in López (2012). López maintains the classical view that accusative case originates in *v*. In DOM languages there are two strategies of checking the accusative. Some objects remain *in situ* and satisfy their Case requirement by incorporation into the lexical verb V, which finally incorporates into *v*. DOM-ed objects scramble to the specifier of an αP located between the little *v* and the lexical VP, a position where they are directly probed by little *v*, as in Figure 4.

The background assumption is that the grammar operates with nominals of different sizes (22), which may have different syntactic and semantic properties.

(22)   KP > DP > NumP > NP

In Romanian the cut-off point between objects that scramble and objects that remain *in situ* is the NumP: i.e. NumP and NPs remain *in situ*, DPs may scramble, KPs *must scramble*. On the semantic side, *in situ* objects are interpreted as predicates, objects that scramble are interpreted as arguments.

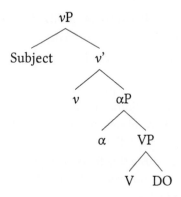

Figure 4: Structure of vP proposed by (López 2012)

4 Dative clitics and CD-Theory

4.1 On clitics

As already shown, with CD, both dative and accusative clitics select KPs [*u*Person], showing sensitivity to the animacy hierarchy. Accusative clitics also observe the definiteness hierarchy. For instance they exclude bare quantifiers; in contrast, dative doubling is possible for any nominal provided that it has an overt determiner (Cornilescu 2017).

For the current analysis what matters most is that CD-ed DOs and IOs exit the *v*P, passing through a *v*P-periphery position which allows them to bind and outscope the subject in Spec, *v*P (Dobrovie-Sorin 1994; Cornilescu et al. 2017a; Tigau 2011). Binding of the subject is impossible for undoubled objects. Thus in (23), the CD-ed dative *fiecărui profesor* 'every.DAT professor' binds and outscopes the preverbal subject *câte doi studenţi* 'some two students'. Similarly, in (24), the post-verbal doubled DO may bind a possessive in the preverbal subject, but this is not possible for the undoubled DO.

(23) Câte doi studenţi i=au   ajutat fiecărui profesor.
      some two students 3SG.M.DAT=have helped each.DAT professor
      'Each professor was helped by two students.'

(24) a. Muzica   lor$_i$ îi   =plictiseşte pe mulţi$_{i/j}$.
         music.DEF their 3PL.ACC bores   DOM many
         'Their own music bores many people.'

b. Muzica   lor*$_{i/j}$ plictiseşte pe mulţi$_i$.
   music.DEF their*$_{i/j}$ bores   on many$_i$
   'Their music bores many people.'

The identity of the *v*P periphery projection through which clitics pass on the way to T is still under debate. Some researchers (e.g. Ciucivara 2009) propose that this is a projection where clitics check Case, while others argue that it is a PersonP at the *v*P periphery (Belletti 2004; Stegovec 2015), in whose specifier any [*u*Person] nominal can value this feature (Figure 5). In line with the analysis above, I have adopted the second proposal. Since Person is an agreement feature, rather than an operator one, Spec, PersonP is an *argumental position*. In conclusion, before going to the Person field above T (Ciucivara 2009), the clitic phrase reaches a *Person P*, at the *v*P periphery, above the subject constituent Figure 5.

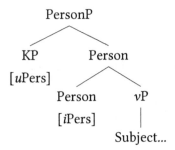

PersonP

KP   Person
[*u*Pers]

Person   *v*P
[*i*Pers]

Subject...

Figure 5: Configuration of Person checking at the *v*P periphery

4.2 A suitable clitic theory: Preminger 2019

Of the many available theories of CD, I have selected Preminger (2019), which is theoretically more motivated and also simpler. For instance, it does not require a big DP. Rather the starting point is a standard DP/KP. In Preminger's interpretation, CD is an instance of *long D-head movement*, as in Figure 6. The D moves from its DP position and adjoins to little *v*, skipping the V head (which is why this is an instance of long head movement).

What is specific to the CD chain is that both copies of D are pronounced, the higher one is the clitic, the lower one is (part of) the associate DP. Pronunciation of two copies of a chain is allowed only if a phasal boundary is crossed (the DP boundary in Figure 6). The two copies are often phonologically distinct.

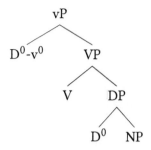

Figure 6: Configuration of cliticization proposed by (Preminger 2019)

5 On the syntax of ditransitives

5.1 Previous results

My analysis of ditransitives assumes the syntax of DOM above. For reasons presented in detail elsewhere (Cornilescu et al. 2017a), I have adopted a *classical derivational analysis* of the dative alternation (Harada & Larson 2009; Ormazabal & Romero 2017). Previous research on Romanian ditransitives (Diaconescu & Rivero 2007; Cornilescu et al. 2017a) has brought to light several properties relevant for ditransitive binding configurations.

a. Binding evidence points to the fact that in Romanian ditransitives the internal arguments show a Theme-over-Goal structure. Thus, as sentences (1) and (2) above indicate, the bare DO can bind, not only into an undoubled dative, but also into a doubled one. A Theme-over-Goal base configuration has also been argued for other Romance languages (see, for instance, Cépeda & Cyrino 2020 [this volume] on Portuguese).

b. In ditransitive constructions, the DO and IO show *symmetric binding potential*, so that there is often an ambiguity between direct and inverse binding for the same pattern. The preferred reading is the one where the surface order corresponds to the direction of binding. For lack of space I will ignore these ambiguities in the analysis below.

c. There is no difference between the CD-ed and the clitic-less constructions, as far as c-command configurational properties are concerned (Cornilescu et al. 2017a), i.e. the DO and the IO have symmetric binding abilities irrespective of the presence of the clitic.

I claim that Romanian possesses a genuine alternation between a Prepositional Dative construction, similar to the *to*-construction in English, and a pattern similar to the Double Object Construction, where the dative is analyzed as a KP. In the Prepositional Dative construction, the P is null and has the usual role of case-licensing its KP complement. If the null P incorporates, the dative is licensed by an applicative head with the features V_{appl} [uPerson, uCase:___], for reasons explained in §2.4 above.

The focus of the analysis that follows is to understand why some otherwise available binding configurations become degraded when the DO is DOM-ed.

In order to bring out the contribution of DOM in ditransitive constructions, we compare derivations where the DO is a DP, not a KP, in which case it is not marked for [Person], with derivations in which the DO is DOM-ed, and has [Person] marking. The IO is also successively a PP, a KP, a cl+KP.

5.2 The DO is a DP (i.e. it is not DOM-ed)

In the basic ditransitive configuration the dative is a PP. This configuration, which corresponds to example (1) above unambiguously expresses a Theme > Goal interpretation (well-attested). The null P checks Case, and K is [iPerson], irrespective of whether the IO is an Inf-DAT or a la-DAT.

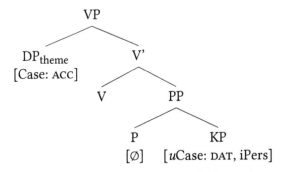

Figure 7: Case checking when the IO is a PP

When null P incorporates, as in Figure 8, V_{appl} [uPers, uCase:__] is projected. In Figure 8, both nominals in the domain of V_{appl} could value the Case feature of V_{appl}, but only the Goal can value its [uPers__] feature, since the Theme is a DP not marked for [Person]. Suppose a derivation is intended where the IO binds and precedes the DO, as in example (25) below. In this case, the DO need not move, while the IO should raise past it to Spec, Appl. This derivation is straightforward. V_{appl} is allowed to case-license the Theme first, since V_{appl} encounters the DO first, when it probes its domain. Next, adopting the locality theory in Dogget (2004) in order to maintain the standard direction of Agree, the Goal moves to an outer Spec,VP, above the Theme. In this position it can be probed by V_{appl}, which thus values its own [uPers] feature. At the following step, the Goal KP moves further up to Spec, V_{appl}P where it checks Case by Agree with little v.

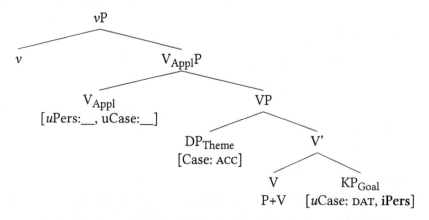

Figure 8: Applicative configuration where the IO is a KP which values the Person feature of Appl

(25) IO before DO; IO > DO
      Recepţionerul arătă **fiecărui turist**$_i$ camera **lui**$_i$.
      receptionist.DEF showed each.DAT tourist room.DEF his
      'The receptionist showed each tourist his room.' (Cornilescu et al. 2017a)

Cliticization is unnecessary, since the Goal is s-selected, and its Person feature is interpretable. Symmetric binding is predicted to be available, since in the initial structure, Theme c-commands Goal, and in the derived structure(s), Goal c-commands Theme. Next we consider (26), where a CD-ed IO binds and precedes a bare DO.

(26) Statul **le=a** estituit **foştilor** **proprietari** casele
      state.DEF 3PL.DAT=has returned former.DEF.DAT owners houses.DEF
      naţionalizate.
      nationalized
      'The state returned the nationalized houses to their former owners.'

The presence of the clitic shows that the dative KP is [uPers], as in Figure 9. For the sake of simplicity I will again consider a derivation where the DO does not scramble and V_{appl} checks its Case feature through Agree. At this point, both of the Goal's features are unchecked, and V_{appl} still has an unvalued [*u*Person] feature.

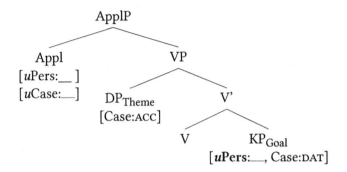

Figure 9: Applicative configuration where the IO KP cannot value the Person feature of Appl

The Goal moves to a position (an outer specifier of VP) where it is accessible to V_{appl} and there is Agree between V_{appl} and the dative, which now shares a [*u*Person] feature, but neither feature is deleted, since both occurrences of the features are unvalued and uninterpretable. The two features are related by agreement and count as instances of the same feature (Pesetsky & Torrego 2007). As in the preceding derivation, the Goal raises to Spec, Appl and checks Case with little *v*, but its [*u*Person] feature is still unvalued. This is what forces movement to the PersonP, at the *v*P-periphery, as in Figure 10. When all the features of the Goal have been valued, the goal undergoes cliticization.

CD was obligatory because the Goal's Person feature could not be checked inside *v*P.

5.3 When DOM-ed themes and dative goals combine

Sentences with DOM and datives create locality problems, since both objects are KPs marked for the same [*i/u* Person] feature and both may value the [*u*Person] feature of V_{appl}. The empirical facts are summed up in (27):

(27)   a.   A *pe*-marked DO binds an undoubled IO without problems (sentence (3) above)

      b.   A *pe*-marked DO cannot bind a CD-ed IO (sentence (4) above).

      c.   A CD-ed *pe*-marked Object can bind an IO, irrespective of CD (sentences (5)-(6) above).

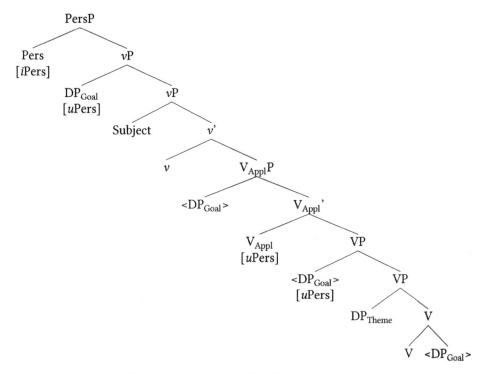

Figure 10: DP Goal raises to the vP periphery to check its uninterpretable Person feature

These facts follow from the analysis. A natural explanation for why a *pe*-marked object can bind an IO (= (27a)) is that, in this case the IO stays low and may be (re)analyzed as a PP, thus not competing with the DO.

The *pe*-marked DO in Figure 11 scrambles, and it is only for this reason that a landing site is projected between little *v* and VP, as in López's analysis. The DO is [*i*Person] and does not need to move beyond its case checking position (Spec, *α*P). Let me turn to situations (27b)-(27c) now. When the IO is CD-ed and there is DOM, the result is ungrammatical, as in sentence (4) above. A CD-ed *pe*-object restores grammaticality, as in (5) above. Since CD-ed DOM-ed objects are unproblematic, it could be suggested that sentence (4) is ungrammatical because, at the current stage in the evolution of Romanian, *pe*-DOs are well-formed only if they are also CD-ed. The following Google example shows however, that CD is not obligatory for *pe*-DOs, except for personal pronouns.

Alexandra Cornilescu

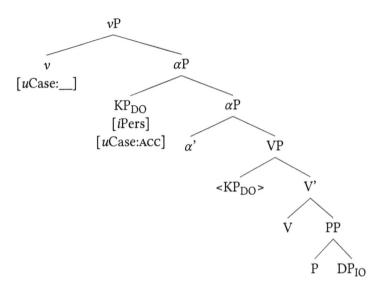

Figure 11: Configuration of accusative Case checking for DOM-ed DO

(28) Zavaidoc a   tocmit **pe** **un asasin** care a   injunghiat=o
      Zavaidoc has hired   DOM an assassin who has stabbed=3SG.F.ACC
      mortal   pe   Zaraza.
      mortally DOM Zaraza
      'Zavaidoc hired an assassin who stabbed Zaraza to death.' (presentation
      of the Zaraza restaurant on Google)

Therefore, the marginality of (4) cannot be attributed to the absence of the
clitic, but to some kind of "interference" between the *pe*-DOs and CD-ed IOs.
I suggest that the problem concerns the locality of Agree, interfering with the
feature structure of the two objects.

Consider the following intermediate stage (Figure 12) in the derivation of sentences like (4). If the IO is CD-ed, then its Person feature is uninterpretable and
the dative KP must check both Person and Case against appropriate functional
heads. On the other hand the DOM-ed DO is [*i*Pers] (since it does not need a
clitic) and must only value its Case.

When V_{Appl} probes its c-command domain, the DOM-ed object is the first that
it encounters, so V_{Appl} agrees with the closer goal and values its own Person and
Case features and it further attracts the KP-DO to its Specifier, since, by assumption, DOM-ed DOs scramble (López 2012). The IO is trapped in its merge position,
and cannot check Case and Person anymore, so that the derivation crashes.

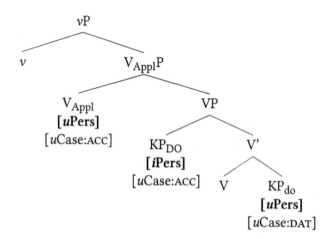

Figure 12: The DOM-ed DO checks both features of the applicative head.

The problem disappears if the DO is CD-ed, as in sentences (5) and (6) above. For simplicity's sake I will examine sentences where the CD-ed *pe*-DO binds an undoubled IO. In this case, the *pe*-DP is endowed with an uninterpretable Person feature, which will be checked in the *v*P periphery PersonP, just as with datives.

The accusative clitic's role is syntactic: intuitively "it moves the Theme out of the Goal's way" (Anagnostopoulou 2006), as in Figure 13. The DO moves to Spec, V_{Appl}, a position where it can be probed by little *v* which checks its accusative Case. Next it targets the PersP at the *v*P periphery, where it Agrees with the [*i*Pers] head and values [*u*Pers]. When all the DO's features have been checked, cliticization is mandatory. The features of V_{Appl} have not been valued yet and the IO is free to move to the outer Spec, VP, where the IO is probed by V_{appl} checking its case. The IO, whose person feature is interpretable, values the Person feature of V_{appl} and needs to raise no further. Resort to the Accusative clitic is a repair strategy: while the *DOM-ED DP $_{theme}$ >cl- DP $_{goal}$ pattern is severely degraded, the pattern cl- DOM-ED DP $_{theme}$ >cl-DP $_{goal}$, which differs from the preceding only through the presence of the accusative clitic, is fully grammatical.

6 Some theoretical implications of the analysis

Summing up the data we started with in (1) – (6) above and considering the categorial status of the arguments, as well as their (non)-clitic status, we obtain the patterns in (29).

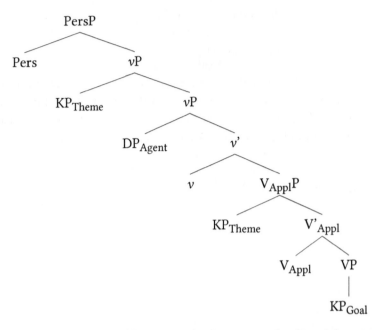

Figure 13: A clitic doubled DOM-ed DO moves to the vP periphery to check Person.

(29)   a. KP-DO   *KP-IO/PP-IO
       b. Cl-KP   KP-IO
       c. Cl-KP   Cl-KP-IO
       d. *K-DO   Cl-DP IO
       e. DP-DO   Cl-KP-IO

The critical property of the patterns is the need to check the [*u*Pers] against the Appl head. Sentences of type (29e), where the DO is a bare DP, which does not need to check Person, are fine irrespective of whether the IO is doubled or undoubled. In contrast, patterns (29a)-(29d) contain two nominals (KPs) that check Person, the DOM-ed direct object and the IO. These types of sentences rely on the configuration in (30), where the same Appl head should Agree with two arguments, a configuration familiar from the analysis of PCC effects (see Sheehan 2020 [this volume] and the references therein).

(30) Appl[*u*Person]   DOM DO [*i*/*u*Person]   IO [*i*/*u*Person]

What differentiates between (29e) and (29a)-(29d) is that in (29a)- (29d), but not in (29e), not only the IO, but also the DO agrees with Appl. Recall that according to Preminger (2019), PCC effects are likely to occur whenever the relevant DO agrees with *v* or Appl. Indeed the distribution of the asterisks in (29a)- (29d) may be restated as a form of PCC, as also suggested for Spanish ditranstives with DOM by Ormazabal & Romero (2013).

(31)   PCC-like effects in Romanian ditransitives
        In a combination of DOM-ed DO and IO, the IO can be doubled (or a
        clitic) only if the DO is also doubled (or a clitic).

The admissible patterns in (29a)-(29d) fall in line with this generalization. Pattern (29a), where neither argument is provided with a clitic would be ungrammatical if the dative had been a KP[*u*Person]. This ungrammaticality is not detected, since the dative is a second, locative argument and can be analyzed as a PP which checks the Case and Person feature of the DP, PP internally, as shown in the discussion of Figure 11 above. Projection as a PP in Figure 11 functions as a repair strategy. In the ungrammatical (29d), the undoubled DO blocks the lower clitic-doubled dative, preventing it from checking Person (and Case) and producing a PCC-like effect. Patterns (29b)-(29c) are fine since the DO and IO arguments check Person against different heads (Person P, ApplP, respectively), avoiding the problem of multiple arguments agreeing with the same head.

Finally, the data analyzed in this paper provide further evidence for Sheehan's (this volume) insight that PCC-like phenomena do not depend on (non)clitic status of the arguments, but on the emergence of a configuration of type (30). In the ungrammatical pattern (4)/(29d), the DO, in the intervener role, is not a clitic, only the IO is.

7 Conclusions

- DOM-ed DOs interfere with IOs since both are sensitive to animacy hierarchy, codified as Person.

- The interaction of DOM-ed DO and IOs in Romanian is a classical locality problem based on the fact that the same applicative head matches two nominals in its c-command domain, regarding Person. The head agrees with the closer object, i.e. the DO. In such configurations, the IO must be a PP, i.e. it cannot be doubled.

- When the DO object is CD-ed, the IO may be a KP and may access V_{appl} and it may even be CD-ed.

Abbreviations

The abbreviations used in the glosses of this chapter follow the Leipzig Glossing Rules.

Acknowledgements

I would like to express my gratitude for the wonderful help I got from the reviewers and the editors in finalizing the paper. Remaining errors are all mine.

References

Anagnostopoulou, Elena. 2006. Clitic doubling. In Martin Everaert & Henk van Riemsdijk (eds.), *The Blackwell companion to syntax*, 519–581. Malden, MA: Blackwell.

Belletti, Adriana. 2004. Extended doubling and the VP periphery. *Probus* 17(1). 1–36.

Cépeda, Paola & Sonia Cyrino. 2020. Putting objects in order: Asymmetrical relations in Spanish and Portuguese ditransitives. In Anna Pineda & Jaume Mateu (eds.), *Dative constructions in Romance and beyond*, 97–116. Berlin: Language Science Press. DOI:10.5281/zenodo.3776539

Ciucivara, Oana. 2009. *A syntactic analysis of pronominal clitic clusters in Romance*. New York, NY: New York University. (Doctoral dissertation).

Cornilescu, Alexandra. 2017. Dative clitics and obligatory clitic doubling in Romanian. In Adina Dragomirescu, Alexandru Nicolae, Camelia Stan & Rodica Zafiu (eds.), *Sintaxa ca mod de a fi. Omagiu Gabrielei Pană Dindelegan la aniversare*, 131–148. Bucureşti: Editura Universităţii din Bucureşti.

Cornilescu, Alexandra, Anca Dinu & Alina Tigău. 2017a. Experimental data on Romanian double object constructions. *Revue Roumaine de Linguistique* 62(2). 157–177.

Cornilescu, Alexandra, Anca Dinu & Alina Tigău. 2017b. Romanian dative configurations: Ditransitive verbs, a tentative analysis. *Revue Roumaine de Linguistique* 62(2). 179–206.

Diaconescu, Rodica & María Luisa Rivero. 2007. An applicative analysis of double object constructions in Romanian. *Probus* 19(2). 209–233.

Dobrovie-Sorin, Carmen. 1994. *The syntax of Romanian.* Berlin: Mouton de Gruyter.

Dogget, Teal. 2004. *All things being unequal: Locality in movement.* Cambridge, MA: Massachusetts Institute of Technology. (Doctoral dissertation).

Harada, Naomi & Richard K. Larson. 2009. Datives in Japanese. In Ryosuke Shibagaki & Reiko Vermeulen (eds.), *Proceedings of the 5th Workshop on Altaic Formal Linguistics (WAFL)*, 109–120. Cambridge, MA: MIT Press.

Hill, Virginia. 2013. The direct object marker in Romanian: A historical perspective. *Journal of Australian Linguistics* 33(2). 140–151.

Hill, Virginia & Alexandru Mardale. 2017. On the interaction of differential object marking and clitic doubling in Romanian. *Revue Roumaine de Linguistique* 62(4). 393–409.

López, Luis. 2012. *Indefinite objects: Scrambling, choice functions, and differential marking.* Cambridge, MA: MIT Press.

Manzini, M. Rita & Ludovico Franco. 2016. Goal and DOM datives. *Natural Language and Linguistic Theory* 34. 197–240.

Ormazabal, Javier & Juan Romero. 2013. Differential object marking, case and agreement. *Borealis: An International Journal of Hispanic Linguistics* 2(2). 221–239.

Ormazabal, Javier & Juan Romero. 2017. Historical changes in Basque dative alternations: Evidence for a P-based (neo) derivational analysis. *Glossa: A Journal of General Linguistics* 2(1). 78. DOI:10.5334/gjgl.103

Pesetsky, David & Esther Torrego. 2007. The syntax of valuation and the interpretability of features. In Simin Karimi, Vida Samiian & Wendy K. Wilkins (eds.), *Phrasal and clausal architecture: Syntactic derivation and interpretation*, 262–294. Amsterdam: John Benjamins.

Preminger, Omer. 2019. What the PCC tells us about "abstract" agreement, head movement and locality. *Glossa: A Journal of General Linguistics* 4. DOI:10.5334/gjgl.315

Richards, Mark. 2008. Defective Agree, case alternation, and the prominence of person. *Linguistische Arbeitsberichte* 86. 137–161.

Roberts, Ian & Anna Roussou. 2003. *Syntactic change: A minimalist approach to grammaticalization.* Cambridge: Cambridge University Press.

Rodríguez-Mondoñedo, Miguel. 2007. *The syntax of objects: Agree and differential object marking.* Storrs, CT: University of Connecticut. (Doctoral dissertation).

Sheehan, Michelle. 2020. The Romance Person Case Constraint is not about clitic clusters. In Anna Pineda & Jaume Mateu (eds.), *Dative constructions in Romance and beyond*, 143–171. Berlin: Language Science Press. DOI:10.5281/zenodo.3776543

Stegovec, Adrian. 2015. It's not Case, it's person! Reassessing the PCC and clitic restrictions in O'odham and Warlpiri. In Pocholo Umbal (ed.), *Proceedings of the poster session of the 33rd West Coast Conference on Formal Linguistics (WC-CFL)*, 131–140. Vancouver: Simon Fraser University Working Papers in Linguistics.

Tigau, Alina Mihaela. 2011. *Syntax and semantics of the direct object in Romance and Germanic languages.* Bucharest: Bucharest University Press.

Chapter 6

The Romance Person Case Constraint is not about clitic clusters

Michelle Sheehan
Anglia Ruskin University

This chapter provides further evidence that the Person Case Constraint (PCC) in Romance is not limited to clitic clusters. Previously, this has been shown for Spanish (Ormazabal & Romero 2013), but I show that, in Italian, French, and Catalan causatives, a $1^{st}/2^{nd}$ person direct object is incompatible not only with dative clitics but also with full dative arguments (see also Postal 1989; Bonet 1991). This is different from the manifestation of the PCC in ditransitive contexts where only dative clitics are ruled out. The difference follows, I argue, if ditransitives in these languages have two underlying structures so that a DP introduced by a/à can be either dative or locative, in line with broader cross-linguistic patterns (see Harley 2002; Demonte 1995; Cuervo 2003 on Spanish; Anagnostopoulou 2003; Fournier 2010 on French; Holmberg et al. 2019 on Italian, and the discussion in the introduction to this volume). For this reason, indirect object DPs marked with a/à must trigger PCC effects in causatives but not in ditransitives, as only in the former are they unambiguously dative. Further support for this claim comes from Spanish, a language which morphologically distinguishes locative vs. dative phrases in ditransitives via clitic doubling (Cuervo 2003) and which shows PCC effects with all animate direct objects (Ormazabal & Romero 2007, 2013). I show that these facts are compatible with approaches to the PCC based on intervention (Anagnostopoulou 2003, 2005 amongst others), but raise challenges for those which rely crucially on the weak/clitic status of datives (Bianchi 2006; Stegovec 2017).

Michelle Sheehan. 2020. The Romance Person Case Constraint is not about clitic clusters. In Anna Pineda & Jaume Mateu (eds.), *Dative constructions in Romance and beyond*, 143–171. Berlin: Language Science Press. DOI:10.5281/zenodo.3776543

1 The Person Case Constraint

Like many languages, French, Spanish, Catalan and Italian are subject to the Person Case Constraint (PCC), originally called the *me lui constraint* by Perlmutter (1971):[1]

(1) Strong Person Case Constraint (based on Bonet 1991: 181–182)

    a. In a combination of a direct object and an indirect object, the direct object has to be third person

    b. where both the indirect object and the direct object are phonologically weak.

In Romance languages, this strong version of the constraint rules out the possibility of a $1^{st}/2^{nd}$ person direct object clitic (glossed here as ACC) in the presence of a dative clitic, for example, the following combination of 1st person accusative and 3rd person dative clitics (see Perlmutter 1971; Kayne 1975; Postal 1981 on the PCC in French):

(2) French (Kayne 1975: 173)
    *Paul me   lui   présentera.
    Paul 1SG.ACC= him.DAT= present.3SG.FUT
    Intended: 'Paul will introduce me to him.'

The presence of (1b) is seemingly crucial to the definition of the PCC because the effect disappears, in ditransitives, where the indirect object is a non-clitic (Kayne 1975; Rezac 2008). The meaning intended to be conveyed by (2) can easily be conveyed using an unfocussed tonic pronoun introduced by *à*, which is exceptionally allowed in such contexts:[2]

(3) French (Kayne 1975: 174)
    Paul me   présentera   à lui.
    Paul 1SG.ACC= present.3SG.FUT to 3SG
    'Paul will introduce me to him.'

---

[1]Though the PCC was first discovered as the *me-lui constraint* and investigated in Romance (Perlmutter 1971), it has been found to hold in a wide range of unrelated languages (see Bonet 1991; Albizu 1997; Rezac 2008; Haspelmath 2004; Adger & Harbour 2010). In fact, one of the key contributions of Bonet (1991) was to unify the Romance constraint with a parallel effect observed in rich agreement systems. I thank an anonymous reviewer for asking me to clarify this. See also Bonet (2007) for an overview.

[2]I gloss *a/à* as 'to' throughout for expositional purposes, but one of the main claims of this paper is that sometimes this morpheme is a realisation of dative case marking and at other times it is a locative preposition.

At least for some speakers, Italian, Spanish and Catalan seem to be subject to a weaker form of the PCC, as described by Bonet (1991), again building on Perlmutter (1971):[3]

(4) Weak Person Case Constraint (based on Bonet 1991: 181–182):

    a. In a combination of a direct object and an indirect object, if there is a third person, it has to be the direct object

    b. where both the indirect object and the direct object are phonologically weak.

In the Romance context, this weaker version of the PCC allows for the possibility of a $1^{st}/2^{nd}$ person accusative clitic as long as the dative is also $1^{st}/2^{nd}$ person, with many speakers preferring a reading whereby the 2nd person clitic functions as the direct object in such cases (see Bonet 1991: 180, fn 5 citing a personal communication from Alex Alsina on Catalan; Ormazabal & Romero 2010: 332 on Spanish, but see also the discussion in Bonet 2007):

(5) Italian (Bianchi 2006: 2027)[4]
    %Mi ti   ha affidato.
    1SG= 2SG= has entrusted
    'He entrusted you to me/me to you.'

(6) Catalan (Bonet 1991: 179)
    %Te' m   van recomanar per la feina.
    2SG= 1SG= PST recommend for the job
    'They recommended me to you/you to me for the job.'

(7) Spanish (Perlmutter 1971: 61)
    %Te me   recomendaron.
    2SG= 1SG= recommended.3PL
    'They recommended me to you/you to me.'

---

[3] There are other subtle differences between the languages too, which require an explanation, notably order in the clitic cluster. A more substantive difference is that Italian, like Spanish and Catalan and unlike French, allows $1^{st}/2^{nd}$ person reflexive direct objects to combine with dative clitics (see Kayne 1975; Bianchi 2006). We abstract away from this difference here for reasons of space.

[4] Note that Bianchi actually gives this example to be ungrammatical but then discusses at length the fact that some speakers accept such examples. I represent this with %.

French is usually reported to disallow this clitic combination altogether (Kayne 1975; Quicoli 1984) and certainly combinations of 1st and 2nd person objects seem to be more restricted in French than in the other three languages. However, Bonet (1991: 180) cites Simpson & Withgott (1986) who report that some speakers nonetheless allow them.

Ormazabal & Romero (2007) discuss the weak/strong distinction in Romance and note that there is substantial sensitivity to individual verbs and variability across speakers regarding the acceptability of examples such as (5)-(7). For this reason, they conclude that there is no clear-cut distinction between strong and weak PCC "languages". Actually, the fact that in combinations of 1st and 2nd person objects, it is almost always the 2nd person clitic which must be the direct object suggests rather that there is merely variation regarding the extent to which person features are decomposed in PCC contexts (see also Anagnostopoulou 2005 for an account along these lines). This can also be seen in Spanish *leísta* dialects in which 3rd person animate direct objects also trigger PCC effects (Ormazabal & Romero 2007, 2010, 2013):[5]

(8) Spanish (Ormazabal & Romero 2007: 321)
     Te   lo/*le   di.
     2SG.DAT= 3SG.M.ACC=/him.ACC= gave
     'I gave it/him to you.'

In these *leísta* dialects, animate 3rd person singular masculine direct objects are marked with the clitic *le*, rather than *lo*, which is usually reserved for inanimate 3rd person singular masculine direct objects. According to Ormazabal & Romero, the animate direct object clitic *le* is ruled out in (8) in the presence of a dative clitic, as a PCC effect. In such contexts, the inanimate masculine 3rd person singular direct object clitic *lo* is possible and can exceptionally be interpreted as either animate or inanimate. The implication is that the PCC can apply differently in different languages, depending on which features are syntactically active. In Spanish, animacy is marked also on 3rd person clitics and so animate 3rd person direct objects also trigger PCC effects. In French, Italian and Catalan, animacy is not syntactically active in 3rd person contexts, and so animate arguments do not trigger PCC effects unless 1st/2nd person. Likewise, for most French

---

[5] The observant reader will notice that I have not specified that only animate 3rd person singular masculine *clitics* induce PCC effects. As we shall see below, this is because animate full DP direct objects marked with personal *a* also trigger PCC effects in Spanish (see Ormazabal & Romero 2013).

speakers, [person] is not decomposed into [speaker] and [addressee], and so we see only the strong PCC.

In what follows, I will not address low level variation across varieties (and speakers) regarding which precise person features are sensitive to the PCC. Instead, I will focus mainly on "strong PCC contexts", in which a $1^{st}/2^{nd}$ person direct object is combined with a 3rd person dative as this combination is robustly ruled out in all the Romance languages under discussion.[6] This is because my focus here is to show that the Romance PCC is not limited to clitic clusters, contrary to the commonly held view, and to discuss the theoretical implications of this fact. I will, however, return at several points to Spanish and 3rd person animate objects, as these are particularly revealing regarding the true nature of the PCC.

2 Some core properties of the PCC

Substantial cross-linguistic work on the PCC has identified that it has a number of core characteristics. Firstly, note that Bonet's definition of the PCC alludes to the necessarily weak status of both arguments. This is because, as she showed, the PCC holds both in languages with rich agreement such as Basque, in (a subset of) contexts where the verb shows agreement with both internal arguments, and also in Romance ditransitives, in contexts where both internal arguments are clitics. It would appear, then, if we consider only ditransitives, that the PCC is sensitive to the weak status of datives (Bonet 1991; Anagnostopoulou 2005; Bianchi 2006; Stegovec 2017). As noted above for French, making the indirect object into a full pronoun mitigates the PCC. In Italian, the same is true, and making the direct object into a strong pronoun has the same effect. In (9a), the dative is a full pronoun, whereas in (9b) the accusative direct object is. In both cases, no PCC effect is observed (Bianchi 2006):

(9) Italian (Bianchi 2006: 2041)

    a. Mi   presenteranno   a lui.
        1SG.ACC= introduce.3PL.FUT to him

    b. Gli   presenteranno   me.
        them.DAT= introduce.3PL.FUT 1SG.ACC

        'They will introduce me to him.'

---

[6]It would, of course, be very interesting to look into what determines micro-parametric variation of this kind but doing so is beyond the scope of the current chapter.

This sensitivity to the weak status of *both* internal arguments is something which is also often reported in broader cross-linguistic studies (see Stegovec 2017, but cf. Ormazabal & Romero 2007). In languages such as Basque, the PCC has been shown to hold only where both arguments agree with the verbal complex (Laka 1996). In non-finite contexts, where there is no agreement, the PCC fails to hold and 1st/2nd person direct objects are freely available, for example (Laka 1996; Preminger 2019):

(10) Basque (Preminger 2019: 7, citing Laka 1996: 98)
Gaizki irudi-tzen Ø-zai-Ø-t   [zuk   ni
wrong look-IPFV 3SG-be-SG.ABS-1SG.DAT 2SG.ERG 1SG.ABS
harakin-ari   sal-tze-a].
butcher-ART.SG.DAT sell-NMLZ-ART.SG.ABS
'It seems wrong to me [for you to sell me to the butcher.]'

Unsurprisingly, then, some analyses of the PCC rely crucially on *both* internal arguments being weak pronouns/clitics/agreement morphemes (Bianchi 2006, Stegovec 2017).

Data from Spanish ditransitives challenge the claim that clitichood of both arguments is crucial to the Romance PCC, however. As Ormazabal & Romero (2013) note, animate direct objects marked with personal *a* (so-called differential object marking – DOM) are ruled out in Spanish wherever an associated dative is clitic-doubled. Consider the paradigm in (11):

(11) Spanish (Ormazabal & Romero 2013: 224)
    a. Enviaron *(a)   todos los enfermos a la doctora Aranzabal.
        sent.3PL   DOM all   the.PL sick.PL   to the doctor Aranzabal
        'They sent all the sick people to doctor Aranzabal.'
    b. Enviaron *(a)   Mateo/tu   hijo a los doctores.
        sent.3PL   DOM Mateo/your son to the doctors
        'They sent Mateo/your son to the doctors.'
    c. Le   enviaron (*a)   todos los enfermos a la doctora
        3SG.ACC= sent.3PL   DOM all   the sick.PL   to the doctor
        Aranzabal.
        Aranzabal
        'They sent doctor Aranzabal all the sick people.'

d. *Les   enviaron (a)   Mateo/tu hijo a los doctores.
   3PL.DAT= sent.3PL   DOM Mateo/your son to the doctors
   Intended: 'They sent the doctors Mateo.'

These examples show that where the indirect object is not doubled by a dative clitic, a DOM-marked direct object is fully grammatical (11a–b). However, where the indirect object gets clitic-doubled, either the direct object must occur without DOM, as in (11c), or the example is simply ungrammatical (11d). Animate direct objects occurring without DOM are "deanimised", they claim, and this is highly semantically constrained.

The reason why animate full DP direct objects can trigger PCC effects in Spanish, according to Ormazabal and Romero is because they are marked with DOM, and this is a morphological reflex of Agree with *v*. More generally, it has been claimed that the PCC holds wherever the relevant kind of direct object overtly agrees with *v* and not otherwise (see Preminger 2019). There is a parametric difference between Spanish and the other languages with respect to the syntactic behaviour of animate full DPs: only in Spanish do they agree with *v*.

A possible interpretation of these data is that the PCC holds only where both internal arguments agree with the same functional head, with clitic doubling being the realisation of dative agreement in Spanish. In other words, these data show that the clitichood of the direct object is not essential to the Romance PCC, but they also seem to suggest that the clitichood of the *indirect* object *is* crucial. If clitic doubling is a form of agreement, then it is in precisely those contexts where the indirect object fails to "agree" that the PCC also fails to hold (11a–b).

There is an alternative interpretation of these facts, however, which is more likely to be correct. Demonte (1995) and Cuervo (2003) use a number of tests to show that examples like (11a–b) without clitic doubling of the indirect object are instances of the prepositional dative construction. Examples (11c–d), on the other hand, are instances of the double object construction (DOC), as diagnosed by the presence of clitic doubling of the dative.[7] In fact, according to Cuervo (2003) clitic doubling *le* is not the reflex of agreement, but rather the spellout of the Appl head itself. In other words, the second "a DP" in the two sets of examples has a different syntactic status: in (11a–b), it is a locative, base-generated below the direct object (12a), and, in (11b–c), it is a dative, introduced by an Applicative

---

[7]Pineda (2013; 2020) challenges the details of this claim with data suggesting that clitic doubling is not obligatory in the DOC. What is crucial for our purposes is that where there is clitic doubling, this implies the DOC and in the absence of clitic doubling indirect objects have the possibility of functioning as locative PPs.

(Appl) head above the direct object (12b) (see Harley 2002; Harley & Miyagawa 2017, building on the initial insights of Oehrle 1976):[8]

(12) Structures for the double object construction (a) and the prepositional dative (b)

a.

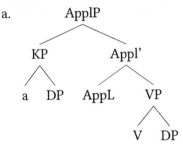

b.

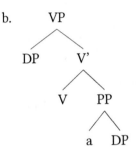

On these (well-motivated) assumptions, there is an alternative reason that the PCC holds only in the presence of a dative clitic: because this element serves to indicate the presence of an Applicative head. The presence of the clitic in (11c–d) therefore indicates a radically different underlying structure, which is not morphologically disambiguated in Italian, French and Catalan.[9] In order to ascertain whether the PCC is sensitive only to this structural difference or to the presence of the dative clitic itself, we need a context in which an indirect object marked with *a/à* is not clitic-doubled but cannot function as a locative. If the PCC holds in such contexts then we will know that the weak status of the

---

[8] There is disagreement in the literature regarding the position of this low Applicative below or above V. I remain agnostic on this point here as either way an indirect object introduced by Appl will function as an intervener between *v* and the direct object.

[9] Ormazabal & Romero (2013) offer a different competition-based account of this pattern whereby the two a-marked DPs compete for the same Case position in spec *v*P. Space precludes a full discussion, but, while attractive, it seems that their account cannot be extended to the causative data to be discussed below, where the PCC holds with full DPs even in the absence of clitic doubling.

indirect object is not crucial to the PCC. In the following section I show that the *faire-infinitif* causative is such a context, and that in such cases the PCC can be observed to hold for all datives, not just clitics.

3 The PCC in causatives

A consideration of causatives shows that the PCC data for French, Italian and Catalan in ditransitive contexts are actually misleading. As Bonet (1991) and others have noted, the PCC (somewhat unsurprisingly) also holds with dative clitic causees in the *faire-infinitif* (Postal 1981; Quicoli 1984; Rezac 2008):[10]

(13) French (Rezac 2008: 66, citing Postal 1981; Quicoli 1984)
      *Je vous   lui   laisserai   voir.
      I 2SG.ACC= her.DAT= let.3PL.FUT see
      Intended: 'I will let her see you.'

As Bonet further notes, however, following Postal (1989), full DP datives are also banned in the presence of first/second person direct objects in this context in French:

(14) French (Postal 1989: 2)

      a. *Marcel vous   a   fait   épouser au   médecin.
          Marcel 2PL.ACC= has made marry to.the doctor
          Intended: 'Marcel had the doctor marry you.'

      b. *On nous   a   fait choisir à Jacques.
          one us.ACC= has made choose to Jacques
          Intended: 'One/we had Jacques choose us.'

      c. *On vous   laissera   connaître à Louise.
          one 2PL.ACC= let.3SG.FUT know   to Louise
          'We will let Louise meet you.'

These kinds of examples contrast minimally with examples involving a 3rd person direct object (even an animate one), which are fully grammatical, as Postal notes:

---

[10]I use the term *faire-infinitif* here to denote a particular kind of Romance causative, following Kayne (1975). Its crucial properties include: (i) dative on transitive causees, (ii) VS order for the caused event, (iii) causees which are agentive and (iv) causers which are not. Space precludes a discussion of minor differences between languages and I merely adopt the most uncontroversial account here, for expository reasons.

(15) French (Postal 1989: 2)

    a. Marcel l'   a   fait épouser au   médecin.
       Marcel her.ACC= has made marry to.the doctor
       'Marcel had the doctor marry her.'

    b. On les   a   fait choisir à Jacques.
       one them.ACC= has made choose to Jacques
       'We had Jacques choose them.'

Postal calls this the "Fancy Constraint" and perhaps for this reason it is not usually discussed in connection with the PCC. It is, however, essentially a simpler version of the PCC, which we will call the "Simpler PCC":

(16) Simpler PCC (first version)

    a. In a combination of a direct object and dative in a causative construction, the direct object has to be third person.
    b. If the direct object is phonologically weak.

I call (16) "simpler" because it imposes no requirement on the status of the indirect object. This is the version of the PCC which holds also in Catalan and Italian causatives (the Catalan example is from Bonet and the Italian example from my own informants).

(17) Catalan (Bonet 1991: 195)

    *Em   van   fer   escollir a la Teresa.
     1SG.ACC= go.3PL make choose to the Teresa
     'They made Teresa choose me.'

(18) Italian

    *Ti   ho   fatto picchiare a mio fratello.
     2SG.ACC= have.1SG made beat   to my brother
     Intended: 'I made my brother beat you.'

The same effect can be observed in Spanish (both Peninsular and Rioplatense), though it is more difficult to observe because of the additional availability of an ECM construction with these verbs (see Strozer 1976; Torrego 2010). Because of these complications, I discuss Spanish in a separate section below.

As Postal also notes, the Fancy Constraint holds only where the causee is dative, and not where it is introduced by a preposition like *par/de* or where the causee is not overtly expressed:

(19)   French (Postal 1989: 3)

    a. Marcel vous   a   fait épouser par le médecin.
       Marcel 2PL.ACC= has made marry by the doctor
       'Marcel had the doctor marry you.'

    b. On nous   a   fait   choisir.
       One us.ACC= has made choose
       'They had us chosen/We had ourselves chosen.'

This is further potential evidence that we are dealing with the PCC. Though the structure of the *faire-par* construction remains contested, there is widespread recognition that the 'by phrase' in examples like (19a) has adjunct-like properties and is not even projected in (19b) (see Guasti 1996; Folli & Harley 2007; Sheehan & Cyrino 2016 for recent discussion). In any case, evidence from binding shows that a *by*-phrase causee does not c-command the accusative object in the *faire-par* construction, whereas a dative causee in the *faire-infinitif* does, as Burzio (1986) shows:

(20)   Italian (Burzio 1986)

    Ho   fatto riparare la propria$_i$ macchina a Gianni$_i$ / *da Gianni$_i$.
    have.1SG made repair the own   car   to Gianni / by Gianni
    'I made Gianni repair his own car.'

In fact, there is evidence that in the *faire-par* construction, c-command relations are reversed, with the accusative object binding into the *by*-phrase causee (Sheehan & Cyrino 2016):

(21)   Italian (Sheehan & Cyrino 2016: 286)

    a. Ho   fatto leggere [ogni libro]$_i$ dal   suo$_i$ autore.
       have.1SG made read   each book by.the its author
       'I had each book read by its author.'

    b. *Ho   fatto leggere il   suo$_i$ libro da [ogni autore]$_i$.
       have.1SG made read   the his book by each author

It seems reasonable to assume, then, that the lack of PCC effects in such contexts can be attributed to the fact that the *by*-phrase does not intervene (in c-command terms) between *v* and the accusative argument.

The dative causee in the *faire-infinitif*, however, is argument-like, obligatory and merged in a position which c-commands the accusative internal argument. This is reflected by the anaphor binding pattern in (20). Folli & Harley (2007) propose that dative causees are merged in a righthand specifier of a lower *v*P, a proposal which I adopt here for ease of exposition, though other options are possible. In Italian and French, at least, all accusative and dative clitics must cliticise onto the causative verb (Kayne 1975; Burzio 1986; Guasti 1993). If cliticisation is mediated by Agree, as Preminger (2019) claims, then a defective intervention configuration clearly arises as the FARE verb which I take to be an instance of a higher *v*, is clearly higher than the causee. The direct object clitic *lo* is therefore c-commanded by *v* and 'a Gianni,' and 'a Gianni' is c-commanded by the higher FARE *v*, despite the unmarked word order:

(22) Basic structure of *faire-infinitif*

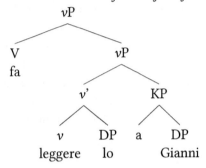

Postal proposes that, while the Fancy Constraint is widespread in French, it is not observed where the verbal complement of *faire* is headed by *connaître/reconnaître* or *voir*, providing the following data:

(23) French (Postal 1989: 4)

    a. On vous   fera   connaître à Louise.
        one 2PL.ACC= make.3SG.FUT know   to Louise
        'We made Louise meet you.'

    b. Jacques nous   a   fait   voir à ses chefs.
        Jacques us.ACC= has made see to his bosses
        'Jacques made his bosses see us.'

This is a potentially important distinction, which might shed important light on the nature of the PCC, if robust. Judgments on such examples are varied, however, and, although the effect might be less categorical than with other verbs, experimental results suggest that at least with *voir*, the PCC still holds in its simpler form.

Given the sensitivity of judgments of this kind, 14 such examples were included as fillers (with a parallel context) in a large online survey, taken by 42 people. Questions were presented in randomised order and rated on an 8-point scale from 0 to 7. Mean scores are given across participants. The results show a clear contrast: examples with 3rd person direct objects were clearly grammatical, receiving an average of acceptability of just under 5, regardless of the features of the indirect object (24a). Examples with two clitics received a slightly lower average mean (24b), probably for processing reasons. All examples were presented along with a context (given in French) set in a busy classroom at the beginning of the school year:

(24) French non-PCC contexts of *faire-voir* 'show'

    a. La professeure **te/lui/me**   fait   voir **Jean**, qui se
        the teacher   2SG.DAT/her.DAT/1SG.DAT= makes see Jean, who SE
        sent nerveux.
        feels nervous
        'The teacher shows you/her/me Jean, who is feeling nervous.'
                                  [mean rating: **4.98/4.86/4.62**]

    b. La professeure **me**   le   fait   voir.
        the teacher   1SG.DAT= him.ACC= makes see
        'The teacher shows me him.'   [mean rating: **4.45**]

This is as expected as these are non-PCC contexts in French because the direct object in all cases is 3rd person.

There is a clear contrast when we consider examples with 1st/2nd person direct object and a 3rd person causee, the 'strong PCC' context. These were most unacceptable with dative clitics (25a), but were also rated very low with full DP datives (an average of around 2 on the 8-point scale) (25b):

(25) French PCC contexts of *faire-voir* 'show'

    a. *Le professeur **me/te**   **lui**   fait voir.
        the teacher   1SG.ACC/2SG.ACC= him.DAT= make see
        Intended: 'The teacher shows me/you to him.'
                             [mean ratings: **0.49/0.50**]

    b. *?La professeure **me/te**   fait   voir à Marie, qui se
        the teacher   1SG.ACC/2SG.ACC= makes see to Marie, who SE
        sent à l' aise.
        feels at the ease
        Intended: 'The teacher shows me/you to Marie, who is feeling at ease.'
        [mean ratings: **1.79/2.05**]

While further empirical investigation of the kinds of contrasts noted by Postal with individual verbs is clearly warranted, these initial experimental data suggest that the simpler PCC also holds with full dative DPs even where the embedded verb is *voir*.

The implication of the Catalan, Italian and French causative patterns is that the PCC in Romance languages is *not* limited to contexts where the indirect object is a clitic or an element triggering morphological agreement. The languages in question fail to have clitic doubling of datives and yet the PCC still holds even where the dative is a full DP. In this way, the data show that the PCC holds wherever (i) the direct object has the relevant (language-specific) person/animacy feature; (ii) *v* establishes a detectable Agree relation with this direct object; and (iii) an indirect object of any kind intervenes in that Agree relation. This can lead either to ungrammaticality (strong PCC) or interaction between phi-features (weak PCC).

There is evidence that Postal's Fancy Constraint is just the PCC from the kinds of repairs which are available in this context. Recall that in ditransitive contexts, changing a dative clitic into a tonic pronoun marked with *a/à* serves to repair the PCC. In causative contexts, PCC violations can only be repaired by making the *direct* object into a tonic pronoun:

(26) French
      Je n'   ai   fait frapper que toi à Jean.
      I NEG have made hit   but 2SG to Jean
      'I only made Jean hit YOU.'

(27) Italian
      Ho   fatto picchiare TE a mio fratello.
      have.1SG made beat   2SG to my brother
      'I made my brother beat YOU.'

But, unlike in ditransitive contexts, changing the status of the dative does not help here: tonic pronouns are also banned in the presence of 1st/2nd person direct object clitics, just as full dative DPs are:

(28) Italian[11]
      *Ti   ho   fatto picchiare a lui/LUI.
       2SG.ACC= have made beat   to him/HIM
      Intended: 'I made him/HIM beat you.'

In sum, we have seen that a "simpler PCC" applies to causatives such that a $1^{st}/2^{nd}$ person direct object clitic is ruled out in the presence of any kind of dative in French, Italian and Catalan. Why do the data pattern differently in causative vs. ditransitive contexts? In ditransitive contexts we saw that, with the exception of Spanish (which has clitic doubling), no PCC effect was observed with full DP datives. In §5, I propose that this is because ditransitives are structurally ambiguous in French, Italian and Catalan, just as they are in Spanish. As we saw for Spanish ditransitives, then, the PCC holds only where a DP is dative and not where it is locative. Before presenting this proposal, however, I discuss the behaviour of Spanish in causative contexts, as these data present additional complications, but essentially serve to reinforce the point being made.

4 Spanish causatives

According to Torrego (2010), clitic doubling of datives in the *faire-infinitif* is optional, at least for some Spanish speakers (see also Pineda 2013; 2020 regarding ditransitives). I take the VS order in (29) to indicate that this is an instance of the *faire-infinitif* nonetheless:

(29)   Spanish (Torrego 2010: 448)
       La entrenadora (le)   hizo repetir el ejercicio a la atleta.
       the trainer   (her.DAT=) made repeat the exercise to the athlete
       'The trainer made the athlete repeat the exercise.'

In a PCC context then, a $1^{st}/2^{nd}$ person clitic is unsurprisingly ruled out in the presence of a clitic-doubled dative. Note that this a spurious 'se' context in Spanish:

---

[11]Another possible repair for some Italian speakers is to make the causee accusative, giving rise to an ECM-type complement without clitic climbing (Schifano & Sheehan 2017):

(i)   %Lo/*gli   fece   picchiar=mi.
      3SG.ACC/3SG.DAT= made beat.INF=1SG.ACC
      'She made him beat me.'

ECM is not usually possible with Italian FARE (but see Burzio 1986; Schifano & Sheehan 2017 for discussion). This repair is not possible with full DP causees, for unclear reasons, making it only partially parallel to what is described for Spanish below.

(30) Spanish
　　　*Marcelo se　　　　te　　　　hizo saludar al　　invitado.
　　　Marcelo him.DAT= 2SG.ACC= made greet　to.the guest
　　　Intended: 'Marcelo made the guest greet you.'

What is more interesting, from our perspective, is what happens where the dative clitic is absent. Examples such as (31a–b) should be potentially ambiguous with either the clitic or the full DP functioning as the causee. This is because, as in the other Romance languages, 1st and 2nd person clitics are not morphologically distinguished for accusative and dative case and because, due to DOM, all animate internal arguments in Spanish are introduced by *a*. In both cases, however, the 1st/2nd person clitic can only be construed as a dative causee:

(31) Spanish

　　a. Marcelo te　　　　　　　hizo ver al　　médico.
　　　　Marcelo 2SG.ACC=.*ACC/DAT= made see to.the doctor
　　　　(i) 'Marcelo made you see the doctor.'
　　　　(ii) *'Marcelo made the doctor see you.'

　　b. Nos　　　　dejará　ver a　Luisa.
　　　　us.*ACC/DAT= let.FUT see to Luisa
　　　　(i) 'He made us see Luisa.'
　　　　(ii) *'He made Luisa see us.'

This is essentially the same effect described for Italian, French and Spanish: it is not possible to have a 1st/2nd person direct object in the presence of a dative argument. The only difference is that the presence of DOM means that the example is not ungrammatical, as the alternative reading in (i) is available. There is much more to be said about Spanish causatives, however.

In addition to the *faire-infinitif*, many varieties of Spanish appear to permit ECM complements of *hacer* 'make'. For our purposes, the relevant properties of this type of complement is that: (i) transitive causees can be realised as accusative clitics; (ii) SV order is observed in the caused event; (iii) clitic climbing is not possible (Strozer 1976; Treviño 1992, 1993; Torrego 2010; Tubino 2011). Consider the following examples by way of illustration of these properties in Mexican Spanish:

(32) Mexican Spanish (Treviño 1992: 311, 169)

    a. Juan lo   hizo leer estos libros.
       Juan him.ACC= made read these books
       'Juan made him read these books.'

    b. Él hizo [a Sadat exportar=las   desde Francia].
       He made to Sadat export.INF=them.ACC from France

    c. *Él las   hizo [a Sadat exportar desde Francia].
       he them.ACC= made to Sadat export.INF from France

Once we accept that in Spanish, unlike in French, Italian and (for the most part) Catalan, an ECM-type of complement is available under the FARE cognate verb, some apparently quirky properties of Spanish causatives can be attributed to the PCC.[12]

First, consider the curious fact that animate direct object clitics cannot climb onto the causative verb in Spanish causatives (Rivas 1977; Bordelois 1988; Torrego 2010):

(33) Spanish (Torrego 2010: 463)

    a. *El me   lo   hizo saludar.
       he 1SG.DAT= him.ACC= made greet
       'He made me greet him.'

    b. El me   hizo saludar=lo.
       he 1SG.DAT= made greet=him.ACC

In the current context, and bearing in mind the fact that Spanish displays PCC effects with animate 3rd person direct objects, (33a) looks like a PCC effect. If this is the case, then it is not the clitic cluster that is a problem, nor the dative 1st person clitic, but rather the animate direct object which attempts to Agree with *hacer* 'make' past the dative causee.[13] Example (33b) is grammatical, however, because it involves a more biclausal ECM construction in which the accusative clitic does not form an Agree dependency with the matrix little v, but rather with a little v in the embedded clause. As the causee asymmetrically c-commands this lexical verb, it does not function as an intervener in (33b).

---

[12] Actually a minority of Catalan speakers do seem to permit ECM under *fer*, but this is certainly not a majority pattern (see Pineda et al. 2018).

[13] As noted above, a similar effect is attested with the 3rd person masculine singular animate clitic *le* in *leísta* dialects of Spanish. I am not sure to what extent animate direct object clitics in non-*leísta* dialects also trigger PCC effects in ditransitives.

As this ECM causative is "biclausal" in the relevant sense, it also fails to be subject to more standard PCC effects. Speakers of Latin American varieties of Spanish and many Peninsular varieties readily accept examples such as the following:

(34) Spanish

    a. (?)Marcelo hizo al   invitado saludar=te.
        Marcelo made to.the guest   greet=2SG.ACC
       'Marcelo made the guest greet you.'

    b. (?)Dejará a Luisa ver=nos.
        let.FUT to Luisa see=us.ACC
       'They will let Luisa see us.'

These examples clearly have an interpretation whereby the $1^{st}/2^{nd}$ person clitic is construed as a direct object, as indicated in the gloss, and so there is no PCC effect in evidence. Again, this is because the direct object clitic does not agree with the matrix little v. In this way, PCC effects in Spanish causatives are more nuanced than in the other Romance languages under discussion.

Now consider examples involving an animate direct object with DOM. As discussed above, these kinds of direct objects trigger PCC effects in Spanish ditransitives in the presence of clitic doubling. With causatives, the pattern is slightly different:

(35) Spanish

    a. *Ana hizo saludar a su marido al   invitado.
        Ana made greet   to her husband to.the guest

    b. *Ana le   hizo saludar a su marido al   invitado.
        Ana him.DAT= made greet   to her husband to.the guest

    c. Ana hizo al   invitado saludar a su   marido.
        Ana made to.the guest   greet   to her husband

    d. %Ana le   hizo al   invitado saludar a su   marido.
        Ana him.DAT= made to.the guest   greet   to her husband
       'Ana made the guest greet her husband.'

If we take the basic position of the causee to indicate the difference between the *faire-infinitif* and ECM causatives, then these data show that PCC holds with DOM-marked full DP direct objects in the *faire-infinitive* regardless of whether the indirect object is clitic-doubled. In (35a–b), the VS order in the caused event indicates that this is an instance of the *faire-infinitive*, with clause union. For this reason, a DOM-marked direct object is not possible, by hypothesis, because the dative blocks agreement with the causative verb. Crucially, this is true not only in (35b), where we see clitic doubling of the dative parallel to what we saw with ditransitives, but also in (31a), where there is no dative clitic. This follows if, as noted above, clitic doubling is optional in the Spanish *faire-infinitive* (see also Pineda 2013; 2020, who claims this is true also in Spanish ditransitives). Regardless of clitic doubling, then, the presence of a dative causee will trigger a PCC effect. As described in (12) above, in ditransitive constructions, a non-doubled indirect object has the option of being interpreted as a locative, and it is this fact which makes the presence of a clitic crucial to the PCC in this context. The same is not true in the *faire-infinitif*, where DPs introduced by *a/à* always have the status of datives, base-generated between the direct object and the causative *v*.

Now consider (35c–d), which have SV order in the caused event and so can be taken to be instances of ECM causatives. All speakers accept (35c), and this is as expected if this is a biclausal ECM context. Additionally, however, speakers from Argentina and certain parts of Spain also allow (35d). In fact, these speakers also allow, even prefer, clitic doubling of the ECM causee with clitic direct objects, even in "strong PCC" contexts, with $1^{st}/2^{nd}$ person direct objects:

(36) Spanish

    a. %Marcelo le   hizo al   invitado saludar=te.
       Marcelo him.DAT= made to.the guest   greet=2SG.ACC
       'Marcelo made the guest greet you.'

    b. %Clara le   hizo al   invitado saludar=lo.
       Clara him.DAT= made to.the guest   greet=him.ACC
       'Clara made the guest greet him.'

I leave open the status of the matrix dative clitic in such examples. The fact that such examples are not subject to the PCC suggests that they cannot be instances of the *faire-infinitif* with a fronted causee. Ormazabal & Romero (2013) analyse them as instances of raising to object. It still remains unclear to me, however, how a dative clitic doubles an accusative causee (see also Ordóñez & Saab 2017 for one proposal). What is clear from these data, however, despite the open questions, is that Spanish also displays PCC effects with both clitic and full DP datives, in parallel with the other Romance languages under discussion, once we control for the availability of ECM (or raising to object) complements.

5 Theoretical implications

Early approaches to the PCC characterised it as a morphological constraint (see Bonet 1991, for example). More recently, however, significant challenges have been raised for this position (see Preminger 2019 for an overview), and the facts discussed here can be seen as further evidence that the PCC is not about morphology. In fact, the main aim of this chapter has been to show that the relevance of the PCC is *not* limited to clitic clusters in Romance. As we have seen, when we consider Spanish DOM-marked direct objects and *faire-infinitif* causatives, the PCC can be shown not to care about the weak/strong status of the indirect object. All that matters is the syntactic structure and the agreeing status of the direct object.

While there have been many syntactic analyses of the PCC, most recent approaches reduce to the idea that it arises where "two arguments are in the domain of a single probing head" (Nevins 2007: 290). A line of research stemming from Anagnostopoulou (2003, 2005) formalises this in terms of defective intervention, whereby a probe attempts to agree with a goal with person features over a dative intervener (see Anagnostopoulou 2003, 2005; Nevins 2007; Rezac 2008; Preminger 2019). A distinct, but related approach, by Adger & Harbour (2010) attributes the PCC to the fact that a single head with one set of person features cannot both agree with an animate [+participant] Theme and introduce an animate [+participant] argument in its specifier as these functions both require a distinct person feature. Note that, in their system, 3$^\text{rd}$ person Themes are always [-participant], whereas animate recipients/benefactives are [+participant] even if they are 3$^\text{rd}$ person. Both kinds of approaches rely crucially on the fact that the direct object must Agree with a functional head. In the defective intervention approach, this is a head higher than the dative, such as *v*. In Adger & Harbour's alternative account, it is Appl, the same head which introduces the applied argument.

Bianchi (2006) and Stegovec (2017), on the other hand, provide analyses which aim to capture the fact that (in ditransitives) the PCC holds only if both internal arguments are weak elements. In Stegovec's (2017) approach, for example, weak arguments enter the derivation without a person feature and must receive one via agreement with a phase head. As the indirect object generally intervenes between the direct object and the phase head *v*, this leads to an intervention problem wherever both are weak 1$^\text{st}$/2$^\text{nd}$ person pronouns. The Spanish data in ditransitives are already problematic for these latter kinds of accounts, as are the Romanian facts presented by Cornilescu (2020 [this volume]) [§6], and the causative patterns show quite clearly that, in Romance at least, this kind of approach makes the wrong predictions.

Mainstream accounts can, however, easily accommodate the Simpler PCC defended here. In the defective intervention approach, based on Anagnostopoulou (2003, 2005); Béjar & Rezac (2003) and Rezac (2008), the PCC arises because a dative argument intervenes between a probe (v) and its [+person] goal, the accusative direct object:

(37) $v_{[\text{phi:}\,]} > \text{DP}_{\text{DAT}} > \text{DP}_{[+\text{person}]}$

On this kind of approach, it is actually mysterious why the PCC would only apply to dative clitics. For the defective intervention account to extend to causatives, it has to be the case that the internal argument of the embedded predicate agrees with *fare* (if *fare* is an instance of little v, or with the v dominating it, otherwise), with the causee acting as an intervener:

(38) $\text{fare}_{[\text{phi:}\,]} > \text{DP}_{\text{DAT}} > \text{DP}_{[+\text{person}]}$

Given that internal arguments obligatorily cliticise onto *fare/faire* in both Italian and French, this kind of analysis seems promising.

On Adger & Harbour's (2010) approach, as noted above, the basic prediction is also that there would be no sensitivity to the clitic/non-clitic distinction, just as there is no sensitivity to the case-marking of the higher argument. For them, the PCC arises where a single head must both agree with the internal [+participant] direct object and introduce an animate [+participant] specifier:

(39) $^{*}[_{\text{ApplP}} \text{DP}_{[+\text{participant}]} \text{Appl} \ldots \text{DP}_{[+\text{participant}]}]$

This leads to ungrammaticality because a given head can only enter into an Agree relation with the same feature once, and the spec-head relation is conceived of as Agree-based. Whichever head introduces the causee in the *faire-infinitif*: Appl (Ippolito 2000; Ordóñez 2008; Torrego 2010; Pitteroff & Campanini 2014) or v (Folli & Harley 2007), this head will be prevented from agreeing with a [+participant] Theme.[14]

So why, then, does it appear to be the case that the PCC holds only where the dative is a clitic in ditransitive contexts in Romance? The answer, I propose,

---

[14]Note that it is more controversial to claim that the lowest direct object is Case-licensed by *fare/-faire*. Belletti & Rizzi (2012) argue that it is, against Folli & Harley's (2007) position. The controversy relates partly to the status of passivisation of the *faire-infinitif* in Italian and French. As Preminger (2019) shows, it is, in any case, possible, and perhaps necessary, to restate this kind of account without the need for abstract Case as long as cliticisation involves Agree.

comes from the two potential structures for ditransitives and the fundamental ambiguity of *a/à* as a dative/locative marker, discussed above in relation to Spanish. Following Holmberg et al. (2019) and Fournier (2010), we propose that (like Spanish) Catalan, Italian and French have two distinct structures for ditransitives (see Demonte 1995; Cuervo 2003; Harley 2002; Harley & Miyagawa 2017). These are as illustrated above by (12), repeated here as (40):

(40)   Structures for the double object construction (a) and the prepositional dative (b)

a.

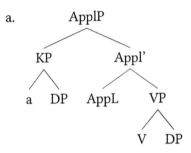

b.

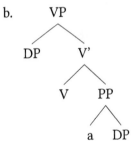

In the extensive literature on the topic, it has been argued that many unrelated languages permit both kinds of structures, regardless of surface case morphology (see Marantz 1993; Pesetsky 1995; Cuervo 2003; Anagnostopoulou 2003; Pylkkänen 2002, 2008; Miyagawa & Tsujioka 2004; Bruening 2010; Harley & Miyagawa 2017). The issue remains contentious, however, as several of the other papers in this volume show; see, especially: Calindro (2020 [this volume]) and Cépeda & Cyrino (2020 [this volume]) on Brazilian Portuguese, Cornilescu (2020 [this volume]) on Romanian, and Antonyuk (2020 [this volume]) on Russian. If the Romance languages under discussion have two structures for distransitives, as outlined above, then PCC effects are predicted to hold only in structures like (40a) and not in those like (40b) (see Rezac 2008 on parallel contrasts in Basque). It is only in configurations like (40a) that the indirect object will function as an intervener. Where *a/à* is the head of a locative PP which is base-generated below the accusative direct object, no intervention effect will arise.

In other words, it is this structural ambiguity in ditransitives which gives rise to the false impression that the PCC only holds with dative clitics. Full DPs introduced by *a/à* which occur with ditransitive verbs can be either dative or locative, having either the structure in (40a) or that in (40b), whereas dative clitics are unambiguously dative, and so must have a structure akin to that in (40a).[15] Consider, by way of illustration, the French examples in (2)-(3) above, repeated here as (41a–b):

(41)   French (Kayne 1975: 173–174)

    a. *Paul me   lui   présentera.
        Paul 1SG.ACC= him.DAT= present.3SG.FUT
        Intended: 'Paul will introduce me to him.'

    b. Paul me   présentera   à lui.
        Paul 1SG.ACC= present.3SG.FUT to him
        'Paul will introduce me to him.'

Example (41a) is ungrammatical because it must have the structure in (40a), whereby the dative intervenes between *v* and the direct object (in its base position). Example (41b), however, is grammatical because it can be constructed with the structure in (40b). I assume that, with the structure in (40a), it is also ungrammatical, in parallel with (41a), and so only (40b) is possible (see also Anagnostopoulou 2003; Rezac 2008 for similar proposals).

Further support for this view comes from the fact that, in French and Catalan, the indirect object can be (exceptionally) realised as a locative clitic as a PCC repair strategy (see Postal 1990; Rezac 2008 on French; Bonet 1991, 2007 on Catalan):

(42)   French
    %Paul m'   y   présentera.
    Paul 1SG.ACC= there= present.3SG.FUT
    'Paul will introduce me to him.'

What is usual about such examples is that the locative clitics cannot unusually index animate arguments. Presumably, this is exceptionally permitted in such contexts to avoid ungrammaticality.

---

[15]For concreteness, I assume that clitics originate in argument positions, but there are other possibilities.

More generally, this proposal sheds new light on one of the main kinds of PCC repairs: they simply involve the prepositional dative construction not a PF repair. This explains immediately why there is no quantifier stranding in such contexts (Kayne 1975; Rezac 2008):

(43) French (Rezac 2008: 98)

    a. Elle la   leur   a   **tous** présentée.
        she her.ACC= them.DAT= has all   introduced

        'She has introduced her to all of them.'

    b. Elle m'   a   (*tous) présentée à eux.
        she 1SG.ACC= has all   introduced to them

        'She has introduced me to (*all of) them.'

Example (43a) shows that cliticisation permits quantifier float. The fact that this is not possible in (43b) follows if this repair involves a different base-generated structure, rather than a PF repair.

In causative contexts, *a/à* always indicates dative so these repairs are not possible, as noted above. This is because causees cannot be introduced as locatives headed by *a/à*, presumably for semantic reasons. Note that they can be introduced as adjunct PPs, however (in the *faire-par* construction), and this too is not subject to the PCC for parallel reasons: because the PP adjunct fails to intervene between the probe and the direct object.

6 Conclusions

In this short article, I have argued that the PCC is simpler than previously thought. It blocks a 1st/2nd person direct object in the presence of any kind of intervening dative argument. The reason we observe PCC only with clitics in ditransitives is that *a/à* is fundamentally ambiguous between being a locative and a dative marker and so only clitics are unambiguously dative.[16] We have seen, furthermore, this is actually what is predicted by many, though not all, existing analyses of the PCC: any kind of dative will act as a defective intervener. In order for this to be the case, we must accept that there are two distinct structures for Romance ditransitives. While this has long been proposed for Spanish (Demonte

---

[16] A reviewer asks why the PCC does not hold optionally with full DPs even in ditransitive contexts. My claim is that it does but that this is not detectable as the locative repair is, in such cases, homophonous with the PCC-violating structure. In Spanish, where they are not homophonous, differences arise, as shown in (11) above.

1995; Cuervo 2003), it remains more controversial for Italian, French and Catalan. Nonetheless, recent research has proposed, on a completely independent basis, that there are also two underlying structures for ditransitives in these languages.

Abbreviations

The abbreviations used in the glosses of this chapter follow the Leipzig Glossing Rules.

Acknowledgements

This research was partly funded by the British Academy. A version of this work was presented at Going Romance (2017) at University of Bucharest. Many thanks to everyone who offered feedback and critique. The usual disclaimers apply.

References

Adger, David & Daniel Harbour. 2010. Syntax and syncretisms of the Person Case Constraint. *Syntax* 10(1). 2–37.

Albizu, Pablo. 1997. *The syntax of person agreement.* Los Angeles, CA: University of Southern California. (Doctoral dissertation).

Anagnostopoulou, Elena. 2003. *The syntax of ditransitives: Evidence from clitics.* Berlin: Walter de Gruyter.

Anagnostopoulou, Elena. 2005. Strong and weak person restrictions: A feature checking analysis. In Lorie Heggie & Francisco Ordóñez (eds.), *Clitic and affix combinations: Theoretical perspectives*, 199–235. Amsterdam: John Benjamins.

Antonyuk, Svitlana. 2020. The puzzle of Russian ditransitives. In Anna Pineda & Jaume Mateu (eds.), *Dative constructions in Romance and beyond*, 43–74. Berlin: Language Science Press.   DOI:10.5281/zenodo.3776533

Béjar, Susana & Milan Rezac. 2003. Person licensing and the derivation of PCC effects. In Ana-Teresa Pérez-Leroux & Yves Roberge (eds.), *Romance linguistics: Theory and acquisition*, 49–62. Amsterdam: John Benjamins.

Belletti, Adriana & Luigi Rizzi. 2012. Moving verbal chunks in the low functional field. In Laura Brugè, Anna Cardinaletti, Giuliana Giusti, Nicola Munaro & Cecilia Poletto (eds.), *Cartography of syntactic structures 7*, 129–137. New York, NY: Oxford University Press.

Bianchi, Valentina. 2006. On the syntax of person arguments. *Lingua* 116(12). 2023–2067. DOI:10.1016/j.lingua.2005.05.002

Bonet, Eulàlia. 1991. *Morphology after syntax: Pronominal clitics in Romance.* Cambridge, MA: MIT. (Doctoral dissertation).

Bonet, Eulàlia. 2007. The Person Case Constraint and repair strategies. In Roberta D'Alessandro, Susann Fischer & Gunnar Hrafn Hrafnbjargarson (eds.), *Person restrictions*, 103–128. Berlin: Mouton de Gruyter.

Bordelois, Ivonne. 1988. Causatives: From lexicon to syntax. *Natural Language & Linguistic Theory* 6(1). 57–93. DOI:10.1007/BF01791592

Bruening, Benjamin. 2010. Double object constructions disguised as prepositional datives. *Linguistic Inquiry* 41(2). 287–305. DOI:10.1162/ling.2010.41.2.287

Burzio, Luigi. 1986. *Italian syntax: A Government-Binding approach.* Dordrecht: Reidel.

Calindro, Ana Regina. 2020. Ditransitive constructions: What sets Brazilian Portuguese apart from other Romance languages? In Anna Pineda & Jaume Mateu (eds.), *Dative constructions in Romance and beyond*, 75–95. Berlin: Language Science Press. DOI:10.5281/zenodo.3776535

Cépeda, Paola & Sonia Cyrino. 2020. Putting objects in order: Asymmetrical relations in Spanish and Portuguese ditransitives. In Anna Pineda & Jaume Mateu (eds.), *Dative constructions in Romance and beyond*, 97–116. Berlin: Language Science Press. DOI:10.5281/zenodo.3776539

Cornilescu, Alexandra. 2020. Ditransitive constructions with differentially marked direct objects in Romanian. In Anna Pineda & Jaume Mateu (eds.), *Dative constructions in Romance and beyond*, 117–142. Berlin: Language Science Press. DOI:10.5281/zenodo.3776541

Cuervo, María Cristina. 2003. *Datives at large.* Cambridge, MA: Massachusetts Institute of Technology. (Doctoral dissertation). https://dspace.mit.edu/handle/1721.1/7991.

Demonte, Violeta. 1995. Dative alternation in Spanish. *Probus* 7(1). 5–30. DOI:10.1515/prbs.1995.7.1.5

Folli, Raffaella & Heidi Harley. 2007. Causation, obligation, and argument structure: On the nature of little v. *Linguistic Inquiry* 38(2). 197–238. DOI:10.1162/ling.2007.38.2.197

Fournier, David. 2010. *La structure du prédicat verbal: Une étude de la construction à double objet en français.* University of Toronto. (Doctoral dissertation).

Guasti, Maria Teresa. 1993. *Causative and perception verbs: A comparative study.* Torino: Rosenberg & Sellier.

Guasti, Maria Teresa. 1996. Semantic restrictions in Romance causatives and the incorporation approach. *Linguistic Inquiry* 27(2). 294–313.

Harley, Heidi. 2002. Possession and the double object construction. *Linguistic Variation Yearbook* 2(1). 31–70.

Harley, Heidi & Shigeru Miyagawa. 2017. Syntax of ditransitives. In Mark Aronoff (ed.), *Oxford research encyclopedia of linguistics.* Oxford: Oxford University Press. DOI:10.1093/acrefore/9780199384655.013.186

Haspelmath, Martin. 2004. Explaining the ditransitive Person-Role Constraint: A usage-based approach. *Constructions* 2. https://journals.linguisticsociety.org/elanguage/constructions/article/view/3073.html.

Holmberg, Anders, Michelle Sheehan & Jenneke van der Wal. 2019. Movement from the double object construction is not fully symmetrical. *Linguistic Inquiry* 50(4). 677–722. DOI:10.1162/ling_a_00322

Ippolito, Michela. 2000. *Remarks on the argument structure of Romance causatives.* Manuscript.

Kayne, Richard S. 1975. *French syntax: The transformational cycle.* Cambridge, MA: MIT Press.

Laka, Itziar. 1996. *A brief grammar of Euskara, the Basque language.* Vitoria-Gasteiz: Euskal Herriko Unibertsitatea [University of the Basque Country]. http://www.ehu.eus/en/web/eins/basque-grammar.

Marantz, Alec. 1993. Implications of asymmetries in double object constructions. In Sam A. Mchombo (ed.), *Theoretical aspects of Bantu grammar*, 113–150. Stanford, CA: CSLI Publications.

Miyagawa, Shigeru & Takae Tsujioka. 2004. Argument structure and ditransitive verbs in Japanese. *Journal of East Asian Linguistics* 13. 1–38.

Nevins, Andrew. 2007. The representation of third person and its consequences for person-case effects. *Natural Language and Linguistic Theory* 25(2). 273–313. DOI:10.1007/s11049-006-9017-2

Oehrle, Richard. 1976. *The grammatical status of the English dative alternation.* Cambridge, MA: Massachusetts Institute of Technology. (Doctoral dissertation).

Ordóñez, Francisco. 2008. *Causativas y la distribución del sujeto causado en español: Evidencia para un núcleo aplicativo.* Hermosillo Sonora. Paper presented at X Encuentro Internacional de Lingüística del Noroeste.

Ordóñez, Francisco & Andrés Saab. 2017. Sobre la distribución de los sujetos causados en dos dialectos del español [On the distribution of causee subjects in two Spanish dialects]. *Estudos Linguísticos e Literários* 58. 186–209. DOI:10.9771/ell.v0i58.26811

Ormazabal, Javier & Juan Romero. 2007. The object agreement constraint. *Natural Language and Linguistic Theory* 25(2). 315–347. DOI:10.1007/s11049-006-9010-9

Ormazabal, Javier & Juan Romero. 2010. The derivation of dative alternations. In Maia Duguine, Susana Huidobro & Nerea Madariaga (eds.), *Argument structure and syntactic relations from a crosslinguistic perspective*, 203–232. Amsterdam: John Benjamins.

Ormazabal, Javier & Juan Romero. 2013. Differential object marking, case and agreement. *Borealis: An International Journal of Hispanic Linguistics* 2(2). 221–239.

Perlmutter, David M. 1971. *Deep and surface structure constraints in syntax*. New York, NY: Holt Rinehart & Winston.

Pesetsky, David. 1995. *Zero syntax: Experiencers and cascades*. Cambridge, MA: MIT Press.

Pineda, Anna. 2013. Double object constructions and dative/accusative alternations in Spanish and Catalan: A unified account. *Borealis: An International Journal of Hispanic Linguistics* 2. 57–115.

Pineda, Anna. 2020. Double object constructions in Romance: The common denominator. *Syntax*.

Pineda, Anna, Norma Schifano & Michelle Sheehan. 2018. *Transitivity in Catalan and Italian: Evidence from causatives*. Olomouc. Paper presented at Olinco.

Pitteroff, Marcel & Cinzia Campanini. 2014. Variation in analytic causative constructions: A view on German and Romance. *The Journal of Comparative Germanic Linguistics* 16(2–3). 209–230. DOI:10.1007/s10828-014-9059-5

Postal, Paul M. 1981. A failed analysis of the French cohesive infinitive construction. *Linguistic Analysis* 8(3). 281–323.

Postal, Paul M. 1989. *Masked inversion in French*. Chicago, IL: University of Chicago Press.

Postal, Paul M. 1990. French indirect object demotion. In Paul Postal & Brian Joseph (eds.), *Studies in Relational Grammar 3*, 104–200. Chicago, IL: University of Chicago Press.

Preminger, Omer. 2019. What the PCC tells us about "abstract" agreement, head movement and locality. *Glossa: A Journal of General Linguistics* 4. DOI:10.5334/gjgl.315

Pylkkänen, Liina. 2002. *Introducing arguments*. Massachusetts Institute of Technology. (Doctoral dissertation).

Pylkkänen, Liina. 2008. *Introducing arguments* (Linguistic Inquiry Monographs 49). Cambridge, MA: MIT Press.

Quicoli, A. Carlos. 1984. Remarks on French clitic systems. *Linguistic Analysis* 14(1). 55–95.

Rezac, Milan. 2008. The syntax of eccentric agreement: The Person Case Constraint and absolutive displacement in Basque. *Natural Language and Linguistic Theory* 26(1). 61–106. DOI:10.1007/s11049-008-9032-6

Rivas, Alberto M. 1977. *A theory of clitics.* Cambridge, MA: Massachusetts Institute of Technology. (Doctoral dissertation).

Schifano, Norma & Michelle Sheehan. 2017. Italian *faire*-infinitives: The special case of *volere.* In Mirko Grimaldi, Rosangela Lai, Ludovico Franco & Benedetta Baldi (eds.), *Structuring variation in Romance linguistics and beyond: In honour of Leonardo M. Savoia,* 161–175. Amsterdam: John Benjamins.

Sheehan, Michelle & Sonia Cyrino. 2016. Variation and change in the faire-par causative. In Ernestina Carrilho, Alexandra Fieis, Maria Lobo & Sandra Pereira (eds.), *Romance languages & linguistic theory,* 279–304. Amsterdam: John Benjamins.

Simpson, Jane & Meg Withgott. 1986. Pronominal clitic clusters and templates. In Hagit Borer (ed.), *The syntax of pronominal clitics,* 149–174. Orlando, FL: Academic Press.

Stegovec, Adrian. 2017. Between you and me: Two cross-linguistic generalizations on person restrictions. In Aaron Kaplan, Abby Kaplan, Miranda K. McCarvel & Edward J. Rubin (eds.), *Proceedings of the 34th West Coast Conference on Formal Linguistics (WCCFL),* 498–508. Somerville, MA: Cascadilla Proceedings Project.

Strozer, Judith R. 1976. *Clitics in Spanish.* Los Angeles, CA: UCLA. (Doctoral dissertation).

Torrego, Esther. 2010. Variability in the case patterns of causative formation in Romance and its implications. *Linguistic Inquiry* 41(3). 445–470.

Treviño, Esthela. 1992. Subjects in Spanish causative constructions. In Paul Hirschbüler & E. F. K. Koerner (eds.), *Romance languages and modern linguistic theory: Selected papers from the XX Linguistic Symposium on Romance Languages University of Ottawa, April 10–14, 1990,* 309–324. Amsterdam: John Benjamins. DOI:10.1075/cilt.91

Treviño, Esthela. 1993. *Las causativas del español con complemento infinitivo.* México: El Colegio de México.

Tubino, Mercedes. 2011. *Causatives in Minimalism.* Amsterdam: John Benjamins.

Part II

Possessor datives, experiencer datives and related structures

Chapter 7

Aspectual datives (and instrumentals)

Ludovico Franco
Università di Firenze

Paolo Lorusso
Istituto Universitario Studi Superiori (IUSS) Pavia

Dative adpositions instantiate part-whole/inclusion (⊆) relations that hold between the goal and the direct object in the thematic grids of ditransitives. We assume that the same primitive part-whole relation is found: i) when the dative adposition is used in locative contexts; ii) with genitive adpositions, as shown by the widespread genitive/dative syncretism across natural languages. Instrumental inflections/adpositions are also an instantiation of the same primitive part-whole relation, but they denote the reverse with respect to genitives/datives (⊇). We describe progressive aspectual constructions involving adpositions, crosslinguistically. We propose that the dative adpositions found in progressive periphrases are the lexicalization of the same basic 'part-whole/inclusion' content: the part-whole relation does not hold between argumental/thematic material but between two events, one event being the time of reference which is 'part of' the time-frame of a second embedded event/set of events. The variation in the adpositions found with the Italian aspectual periphrases is accounted for in the terms of the 'direction' (⊆) vs. (⊇) of the inclusion primitive predicate that implies different interpretations: progressive vs. prospective aspect, respectively.

1 Introduction: background and aims

In recent work, Manzini & Savoia (2011); Manzini & Franco (2016); Franco & Manzini (2017a,b) propose that dative morphemes are part-whole/inclusion predicates (cf. Belvin & den Dikken 1997), notated (⊆), whose basic context of occurrence can be illustrated for English *to* in (1).

Ludovico Franco & Paolo Lorusso. 2020. Aspectual datives (and instrumentals). In Anna Pineda & Jaume Mateu (eds.), *Dative constructions in Romance and beyond*, 175–194. Berlin: Language Science Press.
DOI:10.5281/zenodo.3776545

(1)   a.   I gave the books **to** Peter.

b.   [$_{VP}$ *gave* [$_{PredP}$ *the books* [[$_⊆$ **to**] *Peter*]]]]

Following Kayne (1984); Pesetsky (1995); Beck & Johnson (2004); Harley (2002), among others, we can assume that in (1) a possession/part-whole/inclusion relation holds between the dative (*Peter*) and the theme of the ditransitive verb (*the books*).

Manzini & Savoia (2011); Manzini & Franco (2016) and Franco & Manzini (2017a) ascribe the same ($⊆$) content to genitives. Consider English in (2a). The *of* preposition (or the *'s* genitive ending) introduces a possession relation between the argument it selects, namely *the woman* (the possessor), and the head of the DP, namely (*the*) *children* (the possessum). The content of the *'s* case or the *of* preposition is the same part/whole elementary predicate $⊆$ assumed for datives. Thus, in (2b) ($⊆$) takes as its internal argument the sister DP (the possessor) and as its external argument the head N/D (the possessum) – saying that 'the children' is in the domain of inclusion of 'the woman'.

(2)   a.   The woman's children/the children **of** the woman

b.   [$_{DP}$ *the children* [$_{PP⊆}$ **of** *the woman*]]

Manzini & Savoia (2011) argue that the widespread genitive/dative syncretism (e.g. in Romanian as in (3)) precisely corresponds to such a common lexicalization. This approach is not incompatible with languages like English with two separate lexicalizations for 'to' (dative) and 'of' (genitive). Simply genitive 'of' is specialized for DP-embedding of ($⊆$) and dative 'to' for sentential embedding of ($⊆$).[1]

(3)   a.   (I)-l   am   dat   băieț-i-l-**or**   / fet-e-l-**or**.
him.it I.have given boy-M.PL-DEF-OBL / girl-fpl-DEF-OBL
'I gave it to the boys/ girls.'

---

[1]The part-whole ($⊆$) proposal for genitives and datives has been further articulated in Manzini & Franco (2016); Franco & Manzini (2017a) in order to account for the fact that formally identical genitive/dative DPs display different interpretive behaviours – as well as for the fact that cross-linguistically, syntactico-semantic differences may result in different lexicalization pattern. For instance, while with goal datives the ($⊆$) relator establishes a relation between two arguments (namely the goal and the theme), with experience datives the ($⊆$) relator introduces a relation between an argument (experiencer) and an event (the VP) (cf. Manzini & Franco 2016: 230–231). This is in line with the Applicative literature (cf. Pylkkänen 2008, which assumes that the same Appl head (externalized by dative/oblique) can be attached to different points in the syntactic tree (High Appl vs. Low Appl heads).

b. pahar-ul   băiet-i-l-**or**   / fet-e-l-**or**
    glass-msg.DEF boy-M.PL-DEF-OBL / girl-fpl-DEF-OBL
    'the glass of the boys/ girls'

Franco & Manzini (2017b) extend the part-whole proposal to the other oblique item, most likely to occur as a case inflection in natural languages (Caha 2009), namely the instrumental; in English the core lexicalization of the instrumental is by the adposition *with*. We employ here the cover term 'instrumental' for all the semantic values that can be rendered with *with*-like morpheme (cf. Stolz et al. 2006). Our starting point is the observation made by Levinson (2011) that possession relations may be realized by *with*, as illustrated in (4). The relation in (4) is reversed with respect to that in (1)–(2), since the preposition *with* embeds the possessum, while the possessor is the head of the DP.

(4) The woman with the children

Franco & Manzini (2017b) show that instrumental inflections/adpositions precisely denote the reverse relation with respect to genitives/datives, by which the possessum, rather than the possessor is in the oblique case. For instrumentals they therefore adopt the ($\supseteq$) content and label, as illustrated in (5). What (5) basically says is that the complement of *with* ('the children') is the possessum (a part) of the possessor (the whole) 'the woman'.

(5) $[_{DP}$ *the woman* $[_{PP(\supseteq)}$ *with the children*$]]$

Franco & Manzini further claim that *with*-type morphemes provide very elementary means of attaching (i.e. including) extra participants (themes, initiators, etc.) (in)to events (VP or vP predicates, cf. fn. 1) – with specialized interpretations derived by pragmatic enrichment (contextual, encyclopaedic) at the C-I interface, and extend the proposal to account for the observation that the instrumentals can be employed cross-linguistically in triadic verb constructions alternating with datives,[2] as illustrated in (6)–(7) respectively with English and Persian examples.

(6) a. He presented his pictures **to** the museum.   [dative]

     b. He presented the museum **with** his pictures.   [instrumental]

---

[2]Franco & Manzini (2017b) also account for dative/instrumental syncretism (eventually including DOM objects), arguing that the inclusion predicate ($\subseteq$) corresponding to 'to' or dative case and its reverse ($\supseteq$), corresponding to 'with' or instrumental case, may reduce to an even more primitive content capable of conveying inclusion in either direction (cf. §3).

(7) Persian
    a. Pesar sang-ro **be** sag zad.   [dative]
        boy stone-DOM to dog hit.PST.3SG
        'The boy hit the dog with the stone.'

    b. Pesar sag-ro **ba** sang zad.   [instrumental]
        boy dog-DOM with stone hit.PST.3SG
        'The boy hit the dog with the stone.'

In this paper, we focus on the adpositional morphemes surfacing in aspectual periphrases in Italian and beyond. We precisely concentrate on imperfective/progressive periphrases. Our main claim is that the 'dative' morpheme in (8), which happens to be involved in the encoding of progressive aspect in many Romance varieties (Manzini et al. 2017) and beyond (e.g. Jóhannsdóttir 2011 for Icelandic) lexicalizes the same basic 'part-whole/inclusion' content illustrated above. Notice that also dative morphemes introducing modal periphrases have been analysed as inclusion/part-whole relational devices in the recent literature (cf. Bjorkman & Cowper 2016; Tsedryk 2020 [this volume]).

Following Berwick & Chomsky (2011), we take the lexicon to be the locus of externalization, pairing syntactico-semantic and phonological content: we assume a steady ($\subseteq$) signature for all the occurrences of the 'dative' *a* (to, at) adposition of Italian. In (8), basically, we might say that a ($\subseteq$) part/whole relation hold of event pairs, saying that one event is 'part of' (or *a stage of*, cf. Landman 1992) of a second event – or rather a set of events/an event type. Specifically, we may say that the event which is introduced within the matrix (finite) verb phrase is anchored to the time of reference (or viewpoint, cf. Comrie 1976, or the utterance time, cf. Higginbotham 2009) and is 'part of' the embedded event introduced by the ($\subseteq$) relator.

(8) a. Gianni sta/è   a studiare.
      Gianni stay.PRS.3SG/be.PRS.3SG P study.INF
      'Gianni is studying.'

    b. [$_{\text{IP/TP}}$ *Gianni è* [($\subseteq$) *a* [$_{\text{VP}}$ *studiare*]]]

This study is not aimed at providing any sort of formal semantic characterization of progressive aspect: rather, it is limited to a morphosyntactic account of the occurrences of ($\subseteq$) relators in aspectual periphrases. However, we must note that the idea of a part-whole rendering for progressives is far from being new. Comrie (1976: 16) argues that: "perfectivity indicates the view of a situation as a single whole (...) while the imperfective pays essential attention to the internal struc-ture of the situation". Comrie's approach pays attention to the internal temporal structure of the event, proposing that, in a sense, the perfective–imperfective contrast can be accounted for in terms of a whole vs. structured time-frame of the event which in our terms, can be described as an whole vs. part–whole con-trast. Bach (1986) further argues that a progressive operator in the verbal domain is the counterpart of the partitive operator in the nominal domain, both instanti-ating a part-whole/sub-set relation. Filip (1999) is even more radical in claiming that: 'the semantic core of many, possibly all, aspectual systems can be charac-terized in terms of the basic mereological notions 'part' and 'whole'' (Filip 1999: 158). Given this, we think that translating a part-whole relational content for (progressive) aspect into morphosyntax is a welcome result.

This quite trivial claim has at least two non-trivial consequences. First, the idea of a part-whole syntax for progressives stands against the widespread idea (both within the typological and theoretical literature) that progressives are cross-lin-guistically realized in the form of a locative predication (Mateu & Amadas 1999; Bybee et al. 1994; Demirdache & Uribe-Etxebarria 1997). Second, the idea of an aspectual ($\subseteq$) relator seems *prima facie* to be inadequate to consistently repre-sent progressives in Romance. There are, in fact, Romance languages where no locative/dative preposition is found and the most common morphosyntactic 'pro-gressive' device is the 'BE PLUS gerund' periphrasis, as illustrated in (9) for Italian and Spanish.

(9)   a. Italian
         Gianni sta   studiando.
         Gianni stay.PRS.3SG study.GER
         'Gianni is studying.'

      b. Spanish
         Juan está   estudiando.
         Juan stay.PRS.3SG study.GER
         'Juan is studying.'

We aim to show that the encoding of progressive aspectual relations by means of adpositional devices does not rely on a primitive locative content of the seman-tics they express (and of their mapping into syntax). Rather, we will show that adposition-based aspectual periphrases share a primitive relation of 'inclusion' (the same relation which is at work with dative/genitives) of an event within a set of events or between the reference time and the time-frame of an event/set of events. We will substantiate this claim with a set of cross-linguistic examples in which the expression of progressive meaning relies on *with*-like adpositions and HAVE predicates, which – contra previous assumptions (Freeze 1992; den Dikken 1998) – seem to have a *bona fide* non-locative value, as demonstrated in Levinson (2011). We will then provide a morphosyntactic analysis of Italian progressive periphrases, assuming that gerunds encode a covert (⊆) operator which is compatible with a prepositional value (Gallego 2010; Franco 2015). We will further show that the (⊆)/(⊇) divide in the oblique case systems of natural languages put forward by Franco & Manzini (2017b) for the encoding of argumental/thematic material is relevant also within the aspectual domain.

2 Non-locative progressives periphrases (with datives and beyond)

Cross-linguistically, the same material can be recruited from the lexicon to encode argumental and aspectual relation among syntactic constituents. A case in point is the dative adposition *a* in a full set of Romance varieties, which, for instance, happens to have a role also in the encoding of progressives, as illustrated in (10), with Italian examples.

(10)   Italian

    a. Gianni ha dato un libro **a** Maria.   [dative]
       Gianni has given a   book P Maria

       'Gianni has given a book to Maria.'

    b. Gianni è **a** lavorare.   [progressive]
       Gianni is P work.INF

       'Gianni is working.'

In a number of typological and theoretical studies progressive aspect has been linked to locative constructions (Bybee et al. 1994; Mateu & Amadas 1999; Demirdache & Uribe-Etxebarria 1997). This is *prima facie* a reasonable characterization also for Italian, given that, for instance, the goal of motion is commonly expressed by the same *a* preposition, as in (11).

(11) Gianni va   **a** casa.
      Gianni goes P home
      'Gianni goes (to) home.'

Bybee et al. (1994: 129–130) write: "The majority of progressive forms in our database derive from expressions involving locative elements (...). The locative notion may be expressed either in the verbal auxiliary employed or in the use of postpositions or prepositions indicating location —'at', 'in', or 'on'. The verbal auxiliary may derive from a specific postural verb (...), or it may express the notion of being in a location without reference to a specific posture but meaning only 'be at', 'stay', or, more specifically, 'live' or 'reside'".

Actually, this characterization for progressives appears to be too restrictive. A more general part-whole characterization devoid of locative endowments (at least for adpositions) seems more appropriate, once we consider a wider set of cross-linguistic data. Indeed, *with*-like morphemes, which happen to encode possession but not location (cf. Levinson 2011) and HAVE predicates[3] (which are not listed among the 'locative' auxiliaries in Bybee et al.'s sample), are recruited to encode progressives in various natural languages. In our term, such evidence shows that not only dative-like ($\subseteq$) morphemes, as illustrated in (10), but also instrumental-like ($\supseteq$) relators can be employed to convey a progressive interpretation. We discuss this issue in some details in §3, specifically devoted to Romance aspectual periphrases.

Here, we concentrate on cross-linguistic data, relying on the exhaustive typological survey provided in Cinque (2017) (who lists up to twenty different strategies unrelated to locatives employed to encode progressives among natural languages), illustrating a set of aspectual periphrases not involving locative constructions.

For instance, there are many languages which employ a 'be with' strategy to encode progressive meaning. The *with* adposition introduces an infinitive form of the lexical verb. This progressive periphrasis is widespread among African languages (cf. Cinque 2017:556). Such periphrasis is actually similar to the Romance one illustrated in (8) and (10), except for the relator selected from the lexicon (*to* vs. *with*).

---

[3]Levinson (2011), arguing against locative approaches to possession, convincingly shows that a non-locative approach to HAVE is superior to locative accounts in explaining possession in Germanic languages and accounting for the variation in preposition incorporation (cf. Kayne 1993; Harley 2002) within Germanic (and beyond)).

(12) Wó tɛ   na jo dandù.
     3PL with INF eat honey
     'They are eating honey.' (Baka, Kilian-Hatz 1992: 29)

(13) Tu li l'   oku-lya.
     we be with INF-eat
     'We are eating.' (Umbundu, Heine & Kuteva 2002: 83)

(14) Ní.dí. na.kuzà.ta.
     I.am with.work.INF
     'I am working.' (Lunda, Bantu, Kawasha 2003: 194)

In a number of Iranian languages, progressive aspect is encoded through a HAVE + lexical verb periphrasis (Cinque 2017: 556), as illustrated in (15) for Persian. Note that both verbs are inflected and agree with the external argument. This pattern is reminiscent of the one illustrated in Manzini et al. (2017) for Southern Italian varieties, in which the 'dative' *a* introduces finite complements, as illustrated in (16) for Conversano (Apulia). Actually, the adpositional relator does not surface in all Southern Italian varieties, as shown in (17) for Monteparano (Apulia). We may posit a silent adpositional relator (Kayne 2003) both for Persian and the Monteparano dialect. As we have seen, HAVE verbs are characterized with a general 'inclusion' content (cf. fn. 3), that Manzini & Franco (2016) assume to be analogous to *with*-like ($\supseteq$) morphemes.

(15) Persian
     Ali dare mikhore / (Man) daram   mikhoram.
     Ali has eat.3sg / (I)   have.1SG eat.1SG
     'Ali is eating'/'I'm eating.'

(16) Conversano
     U   stek   a ffattsə /u ste a   ffeʃə.
     it.CL stay.1SG to do.1SG / it.CL stay.3SG to   do.3SG
     'I am doing it'/'He/she is doing it.'

(17) Monteparano
Lu   ʃtɔ   ccamu.
him.CL stay.1SG call.1SG
'I am calling him.'

Quite interestingly, a pattern involving a HAVE/HOLD verb periphrasis for progressive is present also in Italo-Romance, as illustrated in (18)–(19) for Abruzzi-Molise dialects (Cinque 2017: 555). Again the (dative) relator may be overt (18) or not (19) (this time with infinitive lexical verbs, showing that the finiteness of the embedded lexical verb is actually independent from the overt presence of the relator).

(18) Abruzzese
Təném a mmagná.
we.hold to eat.INF
'We are eating.' (Rohlfs 1969: 133)

(19) Abruzzese
Té   ppjjove.
it.holds rain.INF
'It is raining.' (Ledgeway 2016: 266)

Thus, in spite of the fact that many languages adopt 'locative metaphors' to encode the progressive, the data introduced above suggest that a more general (⊆)/(⊇) inclusion/part-whole content instantiates the relation between events and event properties that a part of the formal semantics literature, briefly reviewed in §1, identifies with progressive aspect. What holds of examples like (16) and (18) including an overt relator, also holds of 'bare' finite embeddings – for instance with the Apulian variety of Monteparano in (17) or Persian (15) – or bare infinitive embedding as in (19), if the content of the progressive (i.e. part/whole) is given in virtue of the selection of an abstract preposition à la Kayne.

Following Manzini & Savoia (2011); Franco & Manzini (2017a,b), we see no reason why spatial meanings should be primitive with respect to meanings connected to relations between events or between events and their participants, suggesting that it is in fact spatial relations that may be conceived as specialization of all-purpose relations ('contains'/'is part of') when a location is involved.

The *with* adposition introduced in (12)–(14) has the interesting property of expressing no spatial relation at all (Levinson 2011) – as does the genitive preposition *of* considered in §1, assumed to express the same (⊆) content of datives.[4]

The Italian preposition *da*, which does also have locative meaning, makes an interesting case study, illustrated in some details in Franco & Manzini (2017a; 2017b). In Romance, the lexicalization of (spatial) adpositions seems to vary according to whether their object, i.e. the Ground in a Figure-Ground configuration (Svenonius 2006), is a high-ranked or low-ranked referent (Fábregas 2015 on Spanish). In Italian, with inanimate referents, state and motion-to are lexicalized by *a* 'at, to' or *in*, as in (20a), and motion-from is lexicalized by *da*, as in (20b). However in (20c) it can be seen that state, motion-to and motion-from with human referents are all lexicalized by the *da* preposition.

(20) a. Sono/vado **in/a** casa.
         I.am/I.go   in/to home
         'I am at home/in the house'/'I go home/into the house.'

      b. Vengo **da**   casa.
         I.come from home
         'I come from home.'

      c. Sono/vado/esco **dal**   parrucchiere.
         I.am/I.go/I.exit from.the hairdresser
         'I am at/I go to/I come from the hairdresser.'

---

[4]The locative semantics found with progressives is an instantiation of a more general part-whole relation, which is also called zonal inclusion by Belvin & den Dikken (1997: 170), meaning that all locative relations can be reduced to a primitive part-whole relation with the figure/locatum as the part and the ground/location as the whole. The non primitive status of locative can be accounted for by the fact that while locative adpositions alternate with non-locative ones, the non-locative adpositions such as *of* are not found in alternation with locative adpositions. For example in English the instrumental adposition *with* alternates with locative prepositions (*on /against*) (i)–(iii) or with the dative/locative *to* (iv).

   (i)   a. John sprayed the paint on the wall.
          b. John sprayed the wall with paint.

   (ii)   a. John embroidered peonies on the jacket.
          b. John embroidered the jacket with peonies.

   (iii) a. John hit the fence with a stick.
          b. John hit a stick against the fence.

   (iv)   a. He presented the museum with his pictures.
          b. He presented his pictures to the museum.

Crucially, directionality and other specifications of location that are spatially salient are missing from *da*'s core denotation – or its compatibility with the different locative predicates in (20c) could not be explained. Given the ability for *da* to play any locative role with human referents, the natural conclusion is that locative meaning derives neither from the intrinsic content of *da*, nor of course from that of its complement (a human referent) – but from the locative nature of the stative/directional predicate. A reasonable characterization for the oblique morpheme *da* in Italian is again that of a general relator involving a part-whole predicate, devoid of any intrinsic locative content.

3 Datives (and instrumentals) in Italian progressive/prospective periphrases

At this point, we want to show that also intra-linguistically we may have variation concerning the relator(s) recruited from the lexicon to encode aspectual (progressive) periphrases. We will take Italian as a case study. We have seen in §1 that, in Italian, a progressive interpretation can be rendered either with a 'be/stay + dative preposition + infinitive' schema (8a) or a 'stay + gerund' (9a) schema (cf. Bertinetto 2000).

Interestingly, the gerund periphrasis in Italian is able to encode not only a progressive meaning, but also a prospective one. Indeed, the progressive interpretation is somewhat conditioned by the Aktionsart of the verbal item. Following Vendler's (1967) canonical typology, we may say that (at least usually) the progressive interpretation is available with activities (e.g. 'John is working') and accomplishments (e.g. 'John is drawing a square'), while it is not readily available with states (e.g. '#John is knowing the answer'). With achievements things are less clear-cut. Indeed, as noted in Cinque (2017: 538) with achievements that have preparatory stages (e.g. 'the plane is landing', 'John is leaving', etc.): "Progressive aspect appears to apply to the stages that precede the final achievement thus resulting in a Prospective aspect interpretation". In Italian, the prospective aspect interpretation triggered by achievement verbs can be rendered with the same (progressive) 'stay+gerund' periphrasis, as illustrated in (21).

(21) Prospective aspect (achievements)

    a. L' aereo sta atterando.
        the airplane stay.PRS.3SG landing
        'The plane is landing.'

b. Il bambino sta   nascendo.
    the baby   stay.PRS.3SG being.born
    'The baby is being born.'

Nevertheless, the 'be/stay + (dative) preposition + infinitive' verb periphrasis, readily available for 'progressive' activities and accomplishments, is not able to encode prospective aspect. Indeed, Italian resorts to a different relator, the adposition *per*, to render prospectives, as illustrated in (22), matching the examples in (21).

(22)   a. L' aereo   sta   **per/*ad** atterrare.
           the airplane stay.PRS.3SG for/to   land.INF
           'The plane is landing.'

       b. Il bambino sta   **per/*a** nascere.
           the baby   stay.PRS.3SG for/to being.born.INF
           'The baby is about to be born.'

Franco & Manzini (2017b) ascribe to the Italian adposition *per* the same 'instrumental' ($\supseteq$) content expressed by the *con* ('with') morpheme, based (among others) on the evidence that *con* and *per* are both able to lexicalize causers, as in (23). Following their insight, it is possible to assume that the ($\supseteq$) relation between the *con/per* phrase and the VP event in (23) yields inclusion in an event/-concomitance with it. In a sense, (23) is paraphrasable as something like: "The government raised taxes and the crisis was part of its acting to raise them." (cf. Franco & Manzini 2017b: 8–9).

(23)   Il pericolo di conflitto aumentò **con/per** il   golpe.
       the danger   of conflict   increased with/for the coup
       'The danger of a confrontation increased with/for the coup.'

Actually, the same general relation (causation, in this case), may have more than one lexicalization in a given language. Though Italian *con* can express cause, there is no doubt that causation is also expressed, by a different preposition, namely *per*. The closest rendering of *per* in English is *for*, which expresses both purpose ('they do it for financial gain') and causation ('he died for the want of food'), as Italian *per* does. It seems that *per* relates two events through the same basic ($\supseteq$) operator that we have postulated for *with* morphemes (see Franco & Manzini 2017b: 26–27 for further evidence connecting *for* and *with* in Romance).

In order to conceptually account for the ($\subseteq$)/($\supseteq$) split in the encoding of Progressive vs. Prospective aspect, we may start from Jespersen's (1924:277) insight that Progressive aspect is "a temporal frame encompassing some reference time". Progressive aspect indeed seems to refer to an event which takes place at a certain time point (or interval) which is related to the reference/utterance time and at the same time is 'contained within' the natural unfolding/time-frame of a more general event (cf. Dowty 1979; Higginbotham 2004; among others).[5]

With achievement verbs the temporal frame encompassing the event is very narrow (i.e. punctual), so that they can be perceived as (partially) 'included' by the (more extended) time of reference, giving rise to a prospective interpretation. With activities or accomplishments, the event includes the time of reference (interpreted as a point in time) as its part. In other words, achievements are somewhat 'momentaneous' and cannot have subintervals, so that the progressive cannot pick up a (point in) time within the event.[6]

In present terms, we may assume that the time of reference/utterance is a superset ($\supseteq$) of the temporal frame of the event when we render prospective aspect, while it is a subset ($\subseteq$) of the temporal frame of the event whenever we render a progressive interpretation.

From a morphosyntactic viewpoint, when we consider the Italian 'be/stay + 'oblique' adposition + infinitive verb' periphrasis, there is no difference in the encoding of prospective vs. progressive aspect, except for the different relator ($\subseteq$) vs. ($\supseteq$) selected from the lexicon.[7]

---

[5]This semantics of progressive is obtained through the analysis of Higginbotham (2009); Parsons (1989); Landman (1992) among others, which proposes that a progressive sentence requires for its truth that the event in question holds, not that it culminates. The event holds at the utterance/reference time. In the case of progressives in the past, the past auxiliary expresses a time which is previous to the utterance time (Higginbotham 2009). That is, *Mary is eating an apple* is true if the actual event realizes sufficiently (holds) much of the type of event (temporal frame) of Mary's eating an apple: so the actual event is a subset of the type event of Mary eating an apple since Mary may not have finished to eat the apple. For a more detailed analysis of the semantic of progressives for this type of constructions see Manzini et al. (2017).

[6]As suggested by Rothstein (2004), if the achievement is coerced to being an accomplishment, it is possible to assume that the progressive picks up a time immediately preceding the culmination of the event.

[7]Languages vary in the lexical tools (e.g. aspectual periphrases) they employ to convey (different) aspectual flavours. French and Romanian employ axial parts/relational nouns (Svenonius 2006) to encode progressive meaning (e.g. French *être en train de*+infinite, Romanian *a fi în curs de a*+infinite); Italian can also encode prospective meaning in a similar vein (e.g. *essere sul punto di*+infinite). In Icelandic the progressive periphrasis can be employed to convey a terminative/cessative value (e.g. *Ég var að borða*, both: 'I was eating/I just finished eating', cf. Jóhannsdóttir 2011). In Japanese the same aspectual marker -*te i*- can refer to either progressive or resultative meaning (Shirai 1998). It is a likely scenario that these various interpretations (both intra and cross-linguistically) based on a given morphosyntactic template are derived by pragmatic enrichment at the C-I interface. The same can be said of the ($\supseteq$) based African periphrases illustrated in (12)–(14).

Standardly assuming that the auxiliary moves to fill the Inflectional projection (Manzini et al. 2017 and references cited there), we can provide the rough representation in (24) and (25), respectively for the examples in (8a)and (22a). (24) basically says that the reference time (as represented in the tensed matrix clause) is 'part of' the time frame of the (embedded) event, where the operator (⊆) 'sub-set' is instantiated by the dative adposition *a*, while (25) says that the reference time spans (i.e. include) the (punctual) time frame depicted by the event, where the operator (⊇) 'super-set' is lexicalized by the *per* adposition.

(24)

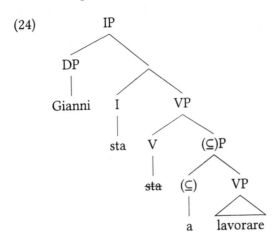

(25)

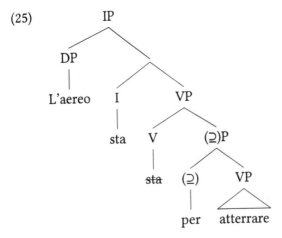

At this point, we still have to explain why the 'stay + gerund periphrasis' is able to encode both progressive and prospective aspect, and how such device can be related, from a morphosyntactic viewpoint, to our 'part-whole' model of aspectual periphrases.

We follow Gallego (2010, cf. Mateu 2002; Franco 2015) in assuming that Romance gerunds incorporate an adposition, namely the *−ndo* morpheme is an inflectional counterpart of the prepositions which embed infinitive complements in the examples above. Consider the minimal pair below, involving a ($\subseteq$) relator (cf. also Casalicchio 2013, from which the example (26) is taken).

(26) a. **A** ben guardare si   nota   la differenza.
      P well watch.INF CL.ARB note.PRS.3SG the difference

   b. Guarda**ndo** bene si   nota   la differenza.
      watching   well CL.ARB note.PRS.3SG the difference
      both: 'If one looks well, one notices the difference'.

Quite interestingly, gerunds often happen to express the ($\supseteq$) content that we have ascribed to *with* and *for* morpheme.[8] Consider the minimal pairs below, with an 'instrument' (27) and a 'purpose' (28) flavour.

(27) a. Il   dottore ha curato il paziente somministrando un antibiotico.
      the doctor has cured the patient administering   an antibiotic
      'The doctor cured the patient administering an antibiotic.'

   b. Il   dottore ha curato il paziente **con** la somministrazione di un
      the doctor has cured the patient with the administration   of an
      antibiotico.
      antibiotic
      'The doctor cured the patient with the administration of an antibiotic.'

(28) a. Gianni lo   dice scherzando.
      Gianni CL.ACC says joking

   b. Gianni lo   dice **per** scherzo.
      Gianni CL.ACC says for joke
      'Gianni says that as a joke.'

Given this evidence, we can assume that the gerund inflection in Italian is able to encode both ($\subseteq$) and ($\supseteq$) contents. More specifically, we hypothesize that the *−ndo* inflection does not differentiate between the two specular 'inclusion'

---

[8]Note that according to Franco & Manzini 2017b the ($\supseteq$) relation between a *with/for* phrase and a *v*P/VP event precisely yields inclusion in an event/concomitance with it.

relations, instantiating an all-purpose oblique, spanning from datives to instrumentals (cf. Franco & Manzini 2017b: 24–28, for relevant data from Kristang and
Southern Italian dialects). This explains why the 'stay + gerund' periphrasis is
able to encode both progressive and prospective aspect, always bearing in mind
that the aspectual interpretations depends on the aktionsart of the verbs that
enter in the aspectual constructions (i.e. achievements vs accomplishments, see
21–22). We roughly schematize our proposal in structures (29)–(30), for (9a) and
(21a), respectively. These structures crucially prospect a lexical entry for −*ndo*,
where this element is associated with both (⊆) and (⊇) content.

(29)

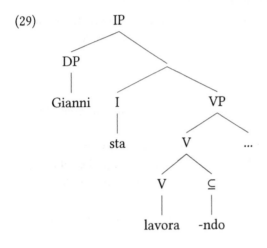

(30)

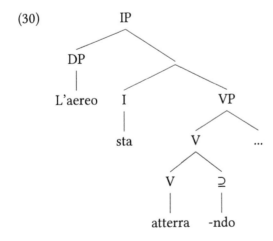

4 Conclusion

In this paper, we have addressed the morphosyntactic status of the adpositional morphemes surfacing in aspectual periphrases in Italian and beyond. We have shown that adposition-based aspectual periphrases share a primitive relation of 'part-whole/inclusion' (the same ($\subseteq$) relation which is at work with datives/genitives) of an event within a set of events or, alternatively, between the reference time and the time-frame of an event/set of events. We have supported this claim with a series of cross-linguistic examples in which the expression of progressive meaning relies on *with*-like adpositions and HAVE predicates, which seem to have a clear non-locative value (Levinson 2011). We have provided a morphosyntactic analysis of Italian progressive periphrases, assuming that gerunds encode an inflectional 'inclusion' relator which is compatible with a prepositional value. We have finally argued that the ($\subseteq$)/($\supseteq$) distinction advanced by Franco & Manzini (2017b) for the encoding of argumental/thematic material, happens to be relevant also in the realm of aspectual periphrases.

Abbreviations

The abbreviations used in the glosses of this chapter follow the Leipzig Glossing Rules. Additional abbreviations: ARB arbitrary; CL clitic; GER gerund.

Acknowledgements

We thank two anonymous reviewers for their comments and criticism. We also thank Greta Mazzaggio and Michelangelo Zaccarello for the proofreading of the Chapter. The usual disclaimers apply. The authors contribute equally to this work. Ludovico Franco takes responsibility for §2 and §3 and Paolo Lorusso for §1.

References

Bach, Emmon. 1986. The algebra of events. *Linguistics and Philosophy* 9. 5–16.
Beck, Sigrid & Kyle Johnson. 2004. Double objects again. *Linguistic Inquiry* 35(1). 97–124.
Belvin, Robert & Marcel den Dikken. 1997. There, happens, to, be, have. *Lingua* 101(3–4). 151–183.

Bertinetto, Pier Marco. 2000. The progressive in Romance, as compared with English. In Östen Dahl (ed.), *Tense and aspect in the languages of Europe*, 559–604. Berlin: Mouton de Gruyter.

Berwick, Robert & Noam Chomsky. 2011. The biolinguistic program: The current state of its evolution and development. In Anna Maria Di Sciullo & Cedric Boeckx (eds.), *The biolinguistic enterprise*, 19–41. Oxford: Oxford University Press.

Bjorkman, Bronwyn & Elizabeth Cowper. 2016. Possession and necessity: From individuals to worlds. *Lingua* 182. 30–48.

Bybee, Joan, Revere Perkins & William Pagliuca. 1994. *The evolution of grammar*. Chicago: University of Chicago Press.

Caha, Pavel. 2009. *The nanosyntax of case*. University of Tromsø. (Doctoral dissertation).

Casalicchio, Jan. 2013. *Pseudorelative, gerundi e infiniti nelle varietà romanze: affintà (solo) superficiali e corrispondenze strutturali.* Università di Padova. (Doctoral dissertation).

Cinque, Guglielmo. 2017. On the status of functional categories (heads and phrases). *Language and Linguistics* 18. 521–576.

Comrie, Bernard. 1976. *Aspect*. Cambridge: Cambridge University Press.

Demirdache, Hamida & Miriam Uribe-Etxebarria. 1997. The primitives of temporal relations. In David Martin, Roger Michaels & Juan Uriagereka (eds.), *Step by step: Essays on Minimalist Syntax in honor of Howard Lasnik*, 157–186. Cambridge, MA: MIT Press.

den Dikken, Marcel. 1998. Predicate inversion in DP. In Artemis Alexiadou & Chris Wilder (eds.), *Possessors, predicates and movement in the determiner phrase*, 177–214. Amsterdam: Benjamins.

Dowty, David. 1979. *Word meaning and Montague Grammar*. Dordrecht: Reidel.

Fábregas, Antonio. 2015. Direccionales con *con* y Marcado Diferencial de Objeto. *Revue Romane* 50. 163–190.

Filip, Hana. 1999. *Aspect, situation types and noun phrase semantics*. New York: Garland.

Franco, Ludovico. 2015. The morphosyntax of adverbs of the carpone/i type in (old and modern) Italian. *Probus* 27. 271–306.

Franco, Ludovico & M. Rita Manzini. 2017a. Genitive/'of' arguments in DOM contexts.

Franco, Ludovico & M. Rita Manzini. 2017b. Instrumental prepositions and case: Contexts of occurrence and alternations with datives. *Glossa: A Journal of General Linguistics* 2(1) (Article 8). 1–47. DOI:10.5334/gjgl.111

Freeze, Ray. 1992. Existentials and other locatives. *Language* 68(3). 553–595. DOI:10.2307/415794

Gallego, Ángel. 2010. On the prepositional nature of non-finite verbs. *Catalan Journal of Linguistics* 9. 79–102.

Harley, Heidi. 2002. Possession and the double object construction. *Linguistic Variation Yearbook* 2(1). 31–70.

Heine, Bernd & Tania Kuteva. 2002. *World lexicon of grammaticalization.* Cambridge: Cambridge University Press.

Higginbotham, James. 2004. The English progressive. In Jacqueline Guéron & Jacqueline Lecarme (eds.), *The syntax of time*, 329–358. Cambridge, MA: MIT Press.

Higginbotham, James. 2009. *Tense, aspect, and indexicality* (Oxford Studies in Theoretical Linguistics). Oxford: Oxford University Press.

Jespersen, Otto. 1924. *The philosophy of grammar.* London: Allen & Unwin Ltd.

Jóhannsdóttir, Kristín. 2011. *Aspects of the progressive in English and Icelandic.* University of British Columbia. (Doctoral dissertation).

Kawasha, Boniface Kaumba. 2003. *Lunda grammar.* University of Oregon. (Doctoral dissertation).

Kayne, Richard S. 1984. *Connectedness and binary branching.* Dordrecht: Foris.

Kayne, Richard S. 1993. Towards a modular theory of auxiliary selection. *Studia Linguistica* 47(1). 3–31. DOI:10.1111/j.1467-9582.1993.tb00837.x

Kayne, Richard S. 2003. Silent years, silent hours. In Lars-Olof Delsing, Cecilia Falk, Gunlög Josefsson & Halldór Á. Sigurðsson (eds.), *Grammar in focus: Festschrift for Christer Platzack*, vol. II, 209–226. Lund: Wallin & Dalholm.

Kilian-Hatz, Christa. 1992. *Der Komitativ im Baka: Eine Fallstudie zur Grammatikalisierung.* Universität zu Köln. (MA thesis).

Landman, Fred. 1992. The progressive. *Natural Language Semantics* 1. 1–32.

Ledgeway, Adam. 2016. The dialects of southern Italy. In Adam Ledgeway & Martin Maiden (eds.), *The Oxford guide to Romance languages*, 246–269. Oxford: Oxford University Press.

Levinson, Lisa. 2011. Possessive *with* in Germanic: Have and the role of P. *Syntax* 14. 355–393.

Manzini, M. Rita & Ludovico Franco. 2016. Goal and DOM datives. *Natural Language and Linguistic Theory* 34. 197–240.

Manzini, M. Rita, Paolo Lorusso & Leonardo M. Savoia. 2017. A/bare finite complements in Southern Italian varieties: Mono-clausal or bi-clausal syntax. *QULSO* 3. 11–59.

Manzini, M. Rita & Leonardo M. Savoia. 2011. Reducing 'case' to denotational primitives. *Linguistic Variation* 11. 76–120.

Mateu, Jaume. 2002. *Argument structure: Relational construal at the Syntax-Semantic Interface.* Universitat Autònoma de Barcelona. (Doctoral dissertation).

Mateu, Jaume & Laia Amadas. 1999. Extended argument structure: Progressive as unaccusative. *Catalan Working Papers in Linguistics* 7. 159–174.

Parsons, Terence. 1989. The progressive in English: Events, states and processes. *Linguistics and Philosophy* 12(2). 213–241.

Pesetsky, David. 1995. *Zero syntax: Experiencers and cascades.* Cambridge, MA: MIT Press.

Pylkkänen, Liina. 2008. *Introducing arguments* (Linguistic Inquiry Monographs 49). Cambridge, MA: MIT Press.

Rohlfs, Gerhard. 1969. *Grammatica storica della lingua italiana e dei suoi dialetti.* Vol. 3, Sintassi e formazione delle parole. Torino: Einaudi.

Rothstein, Susan. 2004. *Structuring events.* Oxford: Blackwell.

Shirai, Yasuhiro. 1998. Where the progressive and resultative meet: Imperfective aspect in Japanese, Korean, Chinese, and English. *Studies in Language* 22. 661–692.

Stolz, Thomas, Cornelia Stroh & Aina Urdze. 2006. *On comitatives and related categories.* Berlin: De Gruyter.

Svenonius, Peter. 2006. The emergence of axial parts. *Nordlyd* 33. 1–22.

Tsedryk, Egor. 2020. The modal side of the dative: From predicative possession to possessive modality. In Anna Pineda & Jaume Mateu (eds.), *Dative constructions in Romance and beyond*, 195–219. Berlin: Language Science Press. DOI:10.5281/zenodo.3776547

Vendler, Zeno. 1967. *Linguistics in philosophy.* Ithaca, NY: Cornell University.

Chapter 8

The modal side of the dative: From predicative possession to possessive modality

Egor Tsedryk

Saint Mary's University

This chapter examines predicative possession (e.g., I have a book) in relation to possessive modality (e.g., I have to buy a book) (Bhatt 1997; Bjorkman & Cowper 2016). Bjorkman & Cowper (2016) report that in Hindi-Urdu and Bengali (BE-languages), possessive modality consistently correlates with the dative case, whereas predicative possession allows other obliques, namely genitive. They propose that both predicative possession and possessive modality are reducible to an interpretable feature encoding inclusion, [INCL], and suggest that the dative case is a morphosyntactic realization of [INCL] combined with a modal operator within a single syntactic head via featural composition. Focusing on Russian – another BE-language – I show that there are problems with this analysis. Russian data indicates that possessive modality in this language is to be derived from directional (vector-like) semantics of the head that introduces the dative. I offer a unified account of the dative used with an NP and the one used with a TP, assuming a single argument-introducing head, i^* (Wood & Marantz 2017).

1 Background

The BE + OBLIQUE pattern in BE-possession languages, or BE-languages (Isačenko 1974) has been taken as evidence to support a unified analysis of possession and necessity, as in (1), an example from Bengali (Bjorkman & Cowper 2016: 43). Bjorkman & Cowper (2016: 31) use the term "possessive modality" to refer to constructions like (1b), which express modal necessity and have a morphosyntactic resemblance to predicative possession.

Egor Tsedryk. 2020. The modal side of the dative: From predicative possession to possessive modality. In Anna Pineda & Jaume Mateu (eds.), *Dative constructions in Romance and beyond*, 195–219. Berlin: Language Science Press. DOI:10.5281/zenodo.3776547

(1) a. **Amar bondhu-r** akʈa boi aatʃhe.
my   friend-GEN one book be.PRS
'My friend has a book.'

  b. **Amar bondhu-ke** je-te   ho-be.
my   friend-DAT go-INF be-FUT
'My friend has to leave.'

Note that there is a discrepancy in the case marking of the bolded DPs in (1a) and (1b). Interestingly, possessive modality consistently correlates with the dative case.[1] As Bhatt (1997: section 8.1) suggests, the dative could be related to a lack of control over a situation, but he does not develop this idea any further.[2]

Bhatt (1997) offers an account of possessive modality, relying on the idea that HAVE is a result of incorporating a "prepositional determiner" (D/P) into the underlying verb BE (following Freeze 1992 and Kayne 1993). Along the lines of Kayne's analysis, a sentence like *I have a book* has the structure in (2a) (several technical details being put aside). The possessor (Subj) is base-generated with the possessee (within an agreement phrase), and it has to move for case reasons. In BE-languages, the specifier position of D/P is a case position, but in HAVE-languages, it is not. Thus, Subj is forced to move further. Spec,DP is assumed to be an A'-position and, in order to avoid improper movement, D/P has to incorporate into BE (I am not going to expand on this idiosyncrasy of Kayne's analysis; see Myler 2016: 320–328 for an overview and a critical assessment). A sentence like *I have to buy a book*, on the other hand, has the structure in (2b), which is very similar to (2a). The only difference is in the type of D/P's complement: in (2b), it is a proposition with a modal operator (Mod).

(2) a. [Subj$_i$ BE [$_{DP}$ t'$_i$ D/P [$_{AgrP}$ t$_i$ *a book*]]]
  b. [Subj$_i$ BE [$_{DP}$ t'$_i$ D/P [$_{ModP}$ Mod [*to* [t$_i$ *buy a book*]]]]]

According to this analysis, possessive modality expresses a relation between an individual and a proposition containing a modal operator: *I have (an obligation) to buy a book.*

Bjorkman & Cowper (2016) on the other hand, argue against a modal operator in the propositional component of possessive modality. They analyze possession

---

[1]Bhatt (1997: example 7) reports a case of possessive modality in Bengali with a genitive subject. However, Bjorkman & Cowper (2016: 46) report that the dative case is the preferred option in their informant's dialect.

[2]The same idea is also recurrent in the literature dealing with so-called "involuntary state constructions" in Slavic (Rivero 2009: 154; Rivero & Arregui 2012: 312).

and necessity in terms of inclusion. The latter is not formally defined, but the basic idea is expressed in the following lines:

> Though *inclusion* or *part-whole* seems to be a reasonable relation to postu-late in the domain of inalienable possession, [... a] potentially more inter-esting possibility is that abstract possession relations, such as alienable pos-session and kinship relations, can also be usefully seen as involving some kind of inclusion or containment. [...] A clear statement of this type of intu-ition can be found, for example, in the following lines from Boneh & Sichel (2010):
>
>> "We take Part-Whole to be broader than inalienable possession and to include also social relations and inanimate Part-Whole" (pp. 2–3)
>>
>> "[T]he complement of the applicative head [= a subset of possessees] can be understood as **falling within the sphere** of the applied argu-ment." (p. 28, emphasis ours)
>
> The idea of containment within a sphere of influence, expressed in the sec-ond of these quotes, suggests a possible link between inclusion and the no-tion of *control*, discussed in the context of typological work on possession by authors such as Heine (1997) and Stassen (2009). (Bjorkman & Cowper 2016: 33–34)

Bjorkman & Cowper propose to formalize inclusion as a morphosemantic fea-ture, [INCL], specifying a functional verbal/applicative-like head, labeled as little v (cf. $\subseteq$ and $\supseteq$ in Franco & Lorusso 2020 [this volume]). According to Bjorkman & Cowper, [INCL] is responsible for the projection of an asymmetric structure, in which the possessor ("the applied argument" in the passage above) asymmet-rically c-commands the complement of the head bearing this feature.

The link between predicative possession and possessive modality (modal ne-cessity) is captured as follows. In the case of predicative possession, [INCL] re-lates individuals, or arguments of type e (possessor and possessee). There are two options for v[INCL] in (3): it can assign case to its complement (in HAVE-languages) or it can introduce an oblique argument in the specifier of v[INCL] (in BE-languages).

(3)

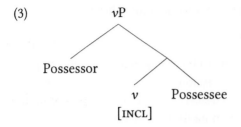

In the case of possessive modality, the arguments related by [INCL] are sets of worlds, or arguments of type $\langle s, t \rangle$: (i) a set of accessible worlds of the modal base and (ii) a set of worlds in which a given proposition is true (the first set is a subset of the second). According to Bjorkman & Cowper, whenever inclusion is extended from individuals to sets of worlds, the syntactic realization of these arguments changes as well. More precisely, the argument associated with accessible worlds is realized as a modal feature on the head that bears [INCL]: either [ROOT] or [EPIST] (epistemic). That is, the semantic co-argument of the proposition is not merged in the specifier position of v (v is an intransitive head in this case); the latter hosts the subject raising out of the proposition.

(4)

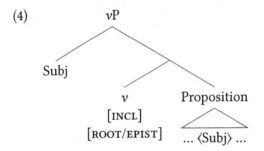

Finally, different combinations of features result in different realizations in morphology. In English – and hypothetically other HAVE-languages – v[INCL] is realized as *have* irrespectively of whether or not there is an additional modal feature. In Bengali – and hypothetically other BE-languages – [INCL] is realized in the specifier position, based on the following rules (Bjorkman & Cowper 2016: 46).

(5)　　a.　v[INCL][ROOT/EPIST] $\rightarrow$ DAT

　　　　b.　v[INCL] $\rightarrow$ GEN

In other words, languages are expected to vary with regard to the degree of feature specification in morphology and the locus of the morphosyntactic realization of [INCL] and other features it is paired with (specifier or head + complement).

Generally, I agree with Bjorkman & Cowper's analysis of HAVE in both predicative possession and possessive modality, but I disagree with their treatment of the dative case in BE-languages, at least in a subset of such languages. Their analysis might be a good fit for Hindi/Bengali, but I will show that it faces problems when applied to a BE-language like Russian. These problems are discussed in §2. As we will see, Russian has predicative possession with both a locative (actual) possessor and a dative (possible/prospective) possessor. The former is indeed the bearer of feature [INCL], but the latter has a purely directional meaning ('towards'). It is the latter that I propose to link to possessive modality, not the former. Following Tsedryk (2020), I use Wood & Marantz's (2017) single argument-introducing head in my analysis of both possessors. §3 elaborates on such notions as "sphere" and "control", mentioned in the excerpt from Bjorkman & Cowper (2016), preceding (3) above. In §4, I use the same argument introducer in my analysis of possessive modality in Russian. Finally, §5 concludes.

2 Focus on Russian

2.1 Overview

In (6), I provide a Russian equivalent of a pair like the one in (1), presenting predicative possession in (6a) and possessive modality in (6b). The latter example illustrates a so-called "dative infinitive" construction expressing modal necessity, which – according to Bjorkman & Cowper – is a prerequisite of possessive modality.[3]

---

[3]Bjorkman & Cowper (footnote 18) briefly mention Russian, but the only example they provide is a *wh*-question in (i) (from Jung 2011: 105). As shown in Tsedryk (2018) (see also Fortuin 2007), Russian dative infinitive constructions may have different modal flavours (necessity, ability and deontic flavours), depending on the morphosyntactic makeup of the clause (see §4).

   (i) Začem mne   bylo   tam ostavat'sja?
      why   me.DAT be.PST.N.SG there stay.INF
      'Why was I supposed to stay there?'

   Moreover, Bhatt (2006: ch. 4) has shown that infinitival questions in English exhibit a variable modal behaviour (*could*, *would* or *should*), depending on the context and the embedding verb (e.g., *Ásta knows where to get gas, Ásta decided where to get gas, Ásta told Hafdís where to get gas*; see Bhatt 2006: 124). In other words, infinitival questions are not a perfect testing ground for modal necessity or possessive modality, as defined by Bjorkman & Cowper.

(6) a. **U menja** est'   kniga.
         at me.GEN be.EXIST book.NOM
         'I have a book.'

     b. **Mne**   zavtra   rano vstavat'.
         me.DAT tomorrow early get.up.IPFV.INF
         'I have to get up early tomorrow.'   (Tsedryk 2018: ex. (20a))

To apply Bjorkman & Cowper's analysis, we would have to assume that the existential light verb (v_{exist}) in (6a) bears feature [INCL], which is responsible for the merger of the locative PP in Spec,vP, as shown in (7a). As for (6b), it would have the structure in (7b), where [INCL] is clustered with feature [ROOT], responsible for the dative case assigned to the subject raised to Spec,vP.

(7) a.

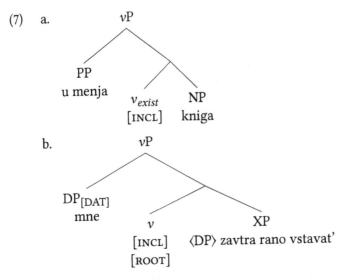

     b.

Even though this analysis seems to unify predicative possession with possessive modality, it faces a number of problems when put under the scrutiny of a careful examination. The goal in §2.2 is a more detailed analysis of predicative possession in Russian. I start with the locative possessor. Possessive modality in Russian will be left for §4.

2.2 Where is [INCL]?

One of the complications that we face with Russian is that it overtly marks its possessors with a locative preposition *u* 'at' assigning the genitive case, as in (8). It means that v[INCL] in (7a) has nothing to do with the genitive case marking, and the rule in (5b) cannot be applied. The fact that Russian has a prepositional element *u* 'at' raises a question about the relevance of [INCL] in *v*: it is plausible that [INCL] is encoded by *u* 'at' and, as far as morphosyntactic rules are concerned, we only need to replace the category in (5b), replacing *v* by P, as in (8b).

(8) a.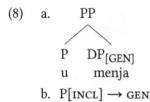

b. P[INCL] → GEN

Moreover, the structure in (7a) – with feature [INCL] in *v* – makes a wrong prediction about the set-theoretic relationship between the specifier and the complement of *v*. In Tsedryk (2020), I show that the complement of the existential light verb *est'* 'be' in predicative possession denotes a set of individuals with a characteristic function. That is, it has to be of type ⟨e, t⟩, not of type ⟨e⟩ (individual). Even if we have a DP like *eta kniga* in (9) we still have type ⟨e, t⟩ (this kind of book). In other words, expressions like *est' kniga* in (6a) or *est' eta kniga* below are generalized quantifiers of type ⟨⟨e, t⟩, t⟩ (see Tsedryk 2020 for more data and further discussion).

(9) U menja est'   eta kniga.
     at me.GEN be.EXIST [this book].NOM
     'I have this (kind of) book.'

Now, assuming that the locative/possessive *u*-PP is also of type ⟨e, t⟩ (following Heim & Kratzer 1998: 65), we predict with feature [INCL] in (7a) that we should have a set-subset relation between *u*-PP and the NP/DP. Crucially, we do not have the reading of possession of a set of books – that is, the interpretation is not of a set of books contained/included in a larger set of the objects belonging to the speaker. From a set-theoretic point of view, we have an intersection (not containment) between a set of books and a set of individuals that are in speaker's domain/sphere. The meaning of the existential expression *est' kniga* from (6a) is given in (11a).[4] Denotation of *u menja* is given in (11b), where 'within'(*d*(speaker'))(x)' is to be read as "x is within the domain/sphere of the speaker" (cf. "sphere" in the excerpt from Bjorkman & Cowper, above (3)).[5] Note

---

[4] I use Heim & Kratzer's (1998) λ-notation.
[5] For now, just assume that domain/sphere is synonymous of ownership. A more general definition will be provided in §3. Composition of 'within'(*d*(speaker'))(x)' will be covered in §2.3.

that inclusion is part of the denotation in (11b), not that in (11a) (where the predicate/head is *est'*). In (11c), we have a result of Functional Application between (11a) and (11b). (12) shows the calculation of a truth value in a syntactic tree.[6]

(10)   *Functional Application:* "If α is a branching node, {β, γ} is the set of α's daughters, and $[\![β]\!]$ is a function whose domain contains $[\![γ]\!]$, then $[\![α]\!]$ = $[\![β]\!]([\![γ]\!])$."   (Heim & Kratzer 1998: 44)

(11)   a. $[\![\text{est' kniga}]\!] = λf∈ D_{\langle e,\ t\rangle} . ∃x∈ D_e,\ \text{book'}(x) ∧ f(x)$
      b. $[\![\text{u menja}]\!] = λx∈ D_e . \text{within'}(d(\text{speaker'}))(x)$
      c. $[\![\text{est' kniga}]\!] ([\![\text{u menja}]\!]) = ∃x∈ D_e,\ \text{book'}(x) ∧ \text{within'}(d(\text{speaker'}))(x)$

(12)

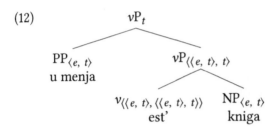

In short, if we assume a feature like [INCL] in Russian predicative possession, it should be part of the possessive *u*-PP (i.e., it is formally encoded by *u* 'at', not the verb).[7] Assuming this feature in the existential light verb *est'*, as in (7a), is problematic for two reasons: (i) it is redundant, and (ii) it makes a false prediction about the inclusion relation between the specifier (set) and the complement (subset) of *v*. I conclude that predicative possession in a BE-language like Russian does not support a structure like (3)/(7a) where [INCL] is supposed to relate the specifier to the complement. In addition to a set-subset relation, we also have to take into account intersection of two sets, as it is the case in (12): set one, denoted by PP *u menja* 'at me', intersects with set two, denoted by NP *kniga* 'book'.

---

[6]The structure in (12) is a simplified version of the structure proposed in Tsedryk (2020), where I analyze the existential BE as a composition of a category-defining head *v* (dummy copula) and Q_{exist} that forms a small clause, as in (i) (the truth value is obtained in QP, and then *v* is added to verbalize the structure): (i) [$_{vP}$ v[$_{QP}$ PP [$_{QP}$ *est'* [$_{NP}$ *kniga*]]]]

[7]The adposition/preposition *u* 'at' would correspond to ⊇ in (Franco & Lorusso 2020 [this volume]), if we had to find a common set-theoretic denominator among P-heads, abstracting away from their thematic differences (locative, instrumental, etc.). However, the distinction between ⊆ and ⊇ is not useful in the logical form. In fact, the right side of the formula in (11c) could be rewritten as either ∃x ∈ D_e, d(speaker') ⊇ book'(x) or ∃x ∈ D_e, book'(x) ⊆ d(speaker'). At this point, it is not clear to me how the use of these set-theoretic symbols would fit compositional rules assumed in this chapter.

If Russian does not have evidence of a *v*-head bearing [INCL] that would introduce a possessor, it weakens considerably the hypothesis that the dative in (6b) has anything to do with such a head (+ a modal feature). This state of affairs is complicated even further by the possibility of using a dative with the existential *est'* in Russian.

2.3 Predicative possession with a dative

A curious fact about Russian predicative possession is that it also allows using a dative DP, as in (13a). This dative is interpreted as a prospective/possible possessor, not the actual one, as in (6a). The sentence in (13a) means that there is a presupposed set of books (implied by *tože* 'also') and one of the members of this set is a potential candidate for Vanja's possession. As shown in (13b), this dative can co-occur with the actual possessor.

(13) a. **Vane**   tože est'   kniga.
          Vanja.DAT also be.EXIST book.NOM
          'There is also a book for Vanja.'

      b. **U menja** tože est'   **Vane**   kniga.
          at me.GEN also be.EXIST Vanja.DAT book.NOM
          'I also have a book for Vanja.'

What is important for the current discussion is that the dative in (13) cannot be analyzed along the lines of inclusion, as it is not an actual possessor. That is, we do not have feature [INCL] in (13a), and in (13b) we have [INCL], but this feature is part of *u*-PP, as suggested in §2.2. We cannot claim that the dative in (13) involves [INCL] + a modal feature either, since *kniga* 'book' is arguably not a proposition. At the same time, the availability of this dative makes me wonder if it is to be linked to the dative in (6b). In other words, it is not the locative with feature [INCL] that is relevant for possessive modality in (6b), but the dative denoting a possible possessor. And, by transitivity, if this dative is not specified for [INCL], we have to reconsider Bjorkman & Cowper's claim that the dative in possessive modality cases should be attributed to [INCL] + [ROOT] features, as stipulated in (5b). Note that we would still have to establish a link between predicative possession and possessive modality, but this link is to be established between the dative in (13) and the modal dative (6b), not between the possessor in (6a) and the modal dative in (6b).[8]

---

[8]I do not know if datives like the one in (13) exist in Hindi or Bengali. However, their absence would not be an argument in favour of Bjorkman & Cowper's analysis and an argument against my proposal that the dative in modal contexts has a primarily directional meaning.

In Tsedryk (2020), I use Wood & Marantz's (2017) argument introducer (i^*) to derive both the locative and the dative in (13). Let me show how these derivations proceed, as they serve as a step towards my analysis of the modal dative in (6b), which will be presented in §4. I start with a brief outline of the assumptions about i^* (see also Calindro 2020 [this volume]). Assumptions about argument-introducing heads are independently motivated. Whether or not one assumes a single argument-introducing head (as I do here) or a set of distinctive applicative heads (Pylkkänen 2008; Cuervo 2003; Markman 2009) is a matter of methodological choice. My proposal can be implemented in either way. However, the main advantage of Wood & Marantz's framework is that it provides an additional insight into the category of applied arguments, restricting the proliferation of possible applicative structures (see discussion of (27)).

The main function of i^* is to extend an XP by adding a DP to it and to "close off" that XP (Wood & Marantz 2017: 258). Whenever an existing XP is extended by i^*, the asterisk is projected to mark this extension, as shown in (14) ("*" is a notational convention that captures the basic function of i^*).

(14)

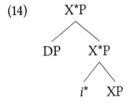

In (14), we have a bare i^*, but the relevant structure for us is the one in (15), where a lexical root merges with i^* before the latter merges with an XP. In (16), I list the assumptions pertaining to the feature specification of i^* (see Tsedryk 2020 for a discussion of (16d); Wood & Marantz assume that $\sqrt{}$ is responsible for the thematic role assigned to DP).

(15)

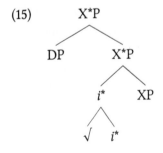

(16) a. *i** has a set of two features: (i) a selectional feature, [s:D] (it selects for a DP) and (ii) an unvalued categorial feature, [cat:__] ([s:D] does not have to be checked/saturated immediately).

   b. XP values [cat:__].

   c. If XP is a DP, [cat:__] is valued as P (i.e., [s:D] is checked before [cat:__] is valued).

   d. The inherent case assigned to DP is determined by √.

In Tsedryk (2020), I assume two lexical roots, √at and √to. The first one bears the inherent genitive case, √at[GEN], and encodes inclusion ('within'). The second one bears the inherent dative case, √to[DAT], and encodes directionality ('towards'). If there is a feature like [INCL], this feature is a property of the first lexical root, which assigns the genitive case. This assumption captures the intuition behind the rule in (8b). The only proviso is that the root is not categorial: category P is derived; the relevant structure is shown in (17), which is an *i**-version of (8a). The derivation in (17) proceeds as follows: √at[GEN] merges with *i** (the root does not project; only its grammatical feature (case) is projected to the resulting branching node). DP checks [s:D] before [cat: __] is valued, and [cat:__] receives value P under (16c).[9] Case is assigned to the category that checks [s:D] (under sisterhood). The form *u* spells out the root in the context of P.

(17)

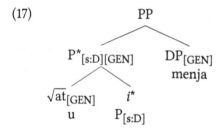

As for the dative in (13), it is derived from the root √to[DAT] that merges with *i** and the latter "closes off" an NP, as shown in (18).[10] In this case, [cat:__] receives value N before [s:D] is checked. The dative case is assigned to the DP that checks [s:D] upon the final merger in (18). The root does not have an overt exponent in this context (without P).[11]

---

[9]Wood & Marantz (2017) do not put the asterisk in PP. My understanding of this *-less labeling is that PPs by definition do not extend an already existing XP.

[10]I use N instead of the category-defining head n, but it is just a notational choice.

[11]Russian does have an overt preposition, *k* 'towards', which encodes direction and assigns the dative case.

(18)

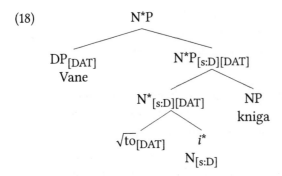

Finally, let me add a couple of remarks related to the semantic composition in these structures. This part of the analysis (not presented in Tsedryk 2020) is my own extension of the ideas related to the semantic side of i^*. Wood & Marantz (2017) take i^* as a semantically open function $\lambda x.x$ whose construal (namely the thematic role assigned to the argument it introduces) is determined by the root and the XP it merges with (Agent, Beneficiary, Figure, etc.). In the context of the discussion involving such notions as inclusion and domain/sphere, I would like to make a slight refinement, suggesting that i^* is a function that introduces a domain/sphere (d) of an individual, as in (19).

(19) $[\![i^*]\!] = \lambda x \in D_e \, . \, d(x)$

The goal behind (19) is to tie i^*'s features, [s:D] and [cat:__], with its semantic content. That is, the DP that i^* selects is supposed to denote an individual and the XP that values i^*'s categorial feature "falls within the sphere" of that individual (as put in the quote from Bjorkman & Cowper above (3); see the bolded part). At the same time, we should keep in mind that the XP and the selected DP may coincide in a PP structure like (17), but we still want to capture the same intuition that there is a domain involved, even if we do not have an X*P. To achieve this goal, I define both spatial roots as functions that can semantically compose with i^*, as in (20). When merging these roots with i^*, we compute the corresponding branching nodes, which are functions of type $\langle e, \langle e, t \rangle \rangle$, as shown in (21). The next compositional step for the uppermost node in (17) is Functional Application between the DP (*menja* 'me.GEN') and (21a), which results in (22), repeating (11b).

(20) a. $[\![\sqrt{at}]\!] = \lambda f \in D_{\langle e, \, t \rangle} \, . \, [\lambda y \in D_e \, . \, [\lambda x \in D_e \, . \, \text{within'}(f(y))(x)]]$
      b. $[\![\sqrt{to}]\!] = \lambda f \in D_{\langle e, \, t \rangle} \, . \, [\lambda y \in D_e \, . \, [\lambda x \in D_e \, . \, \text{towards'}(f(y))(x)]]$

(21)   a. $[\![P^* \text{ in (17)}]\!] = \lambda y \in D_e . [\lambda x \in D_e . \text{within'}(d(y))(x)]$

   b. $[\![N^* \text{ in (18)}]\!] = \lambda y \in D_e . [\lambda x \in D_e . \text{towards'}(d(y))(x)]$

(22) $[\![PP \text{ in (17)}]\!] = [\![u \text{ menja}]\!] = \lambda x \in D_e . \text{within'}(d(\text{speaker'}))(x)$

As for the composition of the lower N*P node in (18), we have to combine the function in (21b) with the one in (23). Functional Application would not work, but N* and NP nodes can compose by Predicate Conjunction (24).

(23) $[\![NP \text{ in (18)}]\!] = [\![\text{kniga}]\!] = \lambda x \in D_e . \text{book'}(x)$

(24)   *Predicate Conjunction:* "If α is a branching node, {β, γ} is the set of α's daughters, and $[\![\beta]\!]$ and $[\![\gamma]\!]$ are both in D_f, f a semantic type which takes n arguments, then $[\![\alpha]\!] = \lambda(a_1, ..., a_n) . [\![\beta]\!](a_1, ..., a_n) \wedge [\![\gamma]\!](a_1, ..., a_n)$." (Myler 2016: 41).

As Myler (2016) notes, following Wood (2015), this rule is similar to Kratzer's (1996: 122) Event Identification. The latter takes a function of type $\langle e, \langle s, t \rangle \rangle$ and conjoins it with a function $\langle s, t \rangle$, returning a function of the first type (where s is an eventuality). In our case, there are no event variables; we conjoin a function of type $\langle e, \langle e, t \rangle \rangle$ in (21b) with the one of type $\langle e, t \rangle$ in (23), obtaining again a function of type $\langle e, \langle e, t \rangle \rangle$, as in (25a). This function in its turn composes with the DP *Vane*, resulting in (25b).

(25)   a. $[\![\text{lower N*P in (18)}]\!] = \lambda y \in D_e . [\lambda x \in D_e . \text{towards'}(d(y))(x) \wedge \text{book'}(x)]$

   b. $[\![\text{upper N*P in (18)}]\!] = [\![\text{Vane kniga}]\!] = \lambda x \in D_e . \text{towards'}(d(\text{vanja'}))(x) \wedge \text{book'}(x)$

That is, the N*P *Vane kniga* is of the same type as the NP *kniga*, which makes it compatible for further composition with *est'*, as shown in (26b), which is the structure of (13b). In (26a), I provide the logical form of (13b) (abstracting away from the adverbial *tože*); (26a) reads as follows: there is some x, of type *e*, such that x is directed towards the domain/sphere of Vanja (= prospective possession) and x is within the domain/sphere of the speaker (= actual possession).[12]

---

[12] If there were no *u*-PP, as in (13a), the structure would still have an implicit argument of type $\langle e, t \rangle$ that would compose with the lower vP node. This implicit argument would correspond to a presupposed set of books.

(26) a. $[\![(13b)]\!] = [\![\text{u menja est' Vane kniga}]\!] = \exists x \in D_e,\ \text{book'}(x) \wedge$
        $\text{towards'}(d(\text{vanja'}))(x) \wedge \text{within'}(d(\text{speaker'}))(x)$

   b.

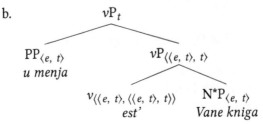

In conclusion, if we assume Wood & Marantz's *i**, which encompasses both prepositions and applicatives, we predict that a PP can never be introduced in an applicative structure of the type in (18), since *i** does not have the right feature to select for a PP. In other words, we cannot have a structure like (27) with a lexical root encoding inclusion and a PP as a sister of X*P. Assuming that [INCL] is closely tied to the genitive case, this feature would further percolate to the branching *i** node and establish an inclusion relation between PP (possessor) and XP (possessee). However, this implementation of Bjorkman & Cowper's original idea is incompatible with *i**, unless we make additional assumptions in order to accommodate PP selection. This is another reason (in addition to redundancy and wrong set-theoretic predictions mentioned in §2.2) to exclude Bjorkman & Cowper's proposal for languages like Russian, which overtly mark their possessors as PPs.[13]

(27)

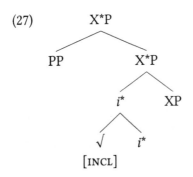

Since Russian allows datives in the context of predicative possession, I hypothesize that these datives (involving directionality), not the locative PPs (encoding

---

[13]Note that we can have a structure like (27) but with a DP instead of a PP. This would be the case of a genitive DP without a P context. That is, we potentially can have genitive applied arguments. Russian does not have them, but they might exist in other languages. These languages (a subset of BE-languages) would fit Bjorkman & Cowper's analysis.

inclusion), are also used in modal contexts when there is an XP of propositional type. I will illustrate an implementation of this idea in §4. Before moving to this part of my analysis, I will elaborate on the notion of domain/sphere, as well as the spatial relations it underlies. I will show that inclusion ('within') and directionality ('towards'), used in the analysis of predicative possession in this section, are paradigmatically related at a conceptual level.

3 Possession and control

In cognitive grammar, possession is represented as an abstract image schema that has a "reference point" (= possessor), a "target" (= possessee) and a "dominion", which is "[a] conceptual region (or the set of entities) to which a particular reference point affords direct access (i.e., the class of potential targets)" (Langacker 1993: 6; see also Langacker 2009: 82). Langacker's "dominion" corresponds to what I was previously referring to as "domain/sphere" (d). If we follow Bjorkman & Cowper's suggestion to analyze possession in terms of inclusion, it seems natural to conceptualize the latter as a spatial relationship between the domain/sphere of a reference point, $d(R)$, and a target point (T), as in Figure 1a, which is a simplified version of Langacker's schemas (e.g., it does not show a conceptualizer).

As we can see in Figure 1a and Figure 1b, there are two self-excluding logical possibilities: either $d(R)$ includes T or $d(R)$ excludes T. However, exclusion does not rule out a possibility of including T within $d(R)$ if we add a vector, as in Figure 1c. Assuming inertia, if T continuously moves towards $d(R)$, we can infer from the vector in Figure 1c that T will cross the inclusion boundary at some point. That is, even though T is not included in $d(R)$ in the actual world, inclusion is still possible in an "inertia world" (Dowty 1979: 148).[14] It is thus plausible to differentiate between inclusion in the actual world and the one in an inertia (possible) world, as in Figure 1d. Crucially, motion and the end-point are inferred from the directional vector, but they are not part of the dative meaning itself (see Fábregas & Marín 2020 [this volume]).

Possession (as a meta category) can thus be conceptualized as a feature-geometric system in (28), where the sisters are mutually excluding privative features

---

[14]Dowty (1979) uses an inertia function in his definition of the progressive operator, assuming a branching time model. My use of the term, applied to a conceptual metaphor, is rather informal a this point. Interestingly, the dative does correlate with the imperfective operator in dative infinitive constructions (§4), but a detailed account of this correlation in the aspectual domain is beyond the scope of this paper.

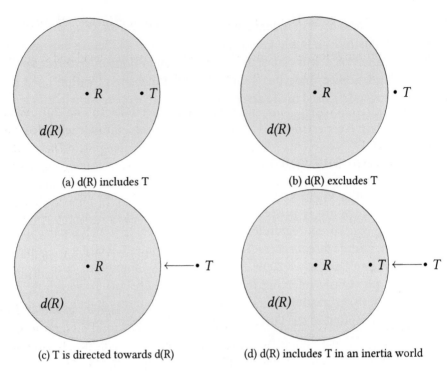

(a) d(R) includes T   (b) d(R) excludes T

(c) T is directed towards d(R)   (d) d(R) includes T in an inertia world

Figure 1: Spatial relationships between the domain/sphere of a reference point, $d(R)$, and a target point (T)

and dominance corresponds to implication. The terminal nodes are the lexical roots (and their grammatical case features) assumed in §2.3.[15]

(28)

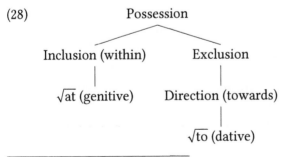

---

[15]My analysis does not contradict (Franco & Lorusso 2020 [this volume]), who observe that dative morphology can mark inclusion in world languages. It is expected that languages vary at the morphological level (the dative being more or less polysemous). My point is that the dative is not reducible to inclusion universally. Russian makes a clear morphological distinction between locational and directional meanings. For example, Russian cannot mark actual possession using the dative like French (e.g., *ce livre est à moi* 'this book is mine'; cf. (13)).

Finally, in order to bridge the above features with the modal uses of the dative, let me touch upon the notion of control, mentioned in §1 (see the excerpt from Bjorkman & Cowper above (3)). I shall start with a slight detour and provide further details on $d(R)$ and its content. What class of potential targets can we have? As a conceptual region (in Langacker's terms), $d(R)$ includes first of all R's physical body and, depending on R's animacy and human attributes, $d(R)$ can also include R's living space, personal belongings, social relations and, ultimately, controlled situations. The list of things that can be included in $d(R)$ seems to be heterogeneous, but all these elements (we may call them "particulars") can be sorted into two main types, individuals and situations. In situation semantics (Kratzer 1989, 2002, 2019), $d(R)$ can be thought of as a "thick particular", as opposed to a "thin particular". In Kratzer's own words:

> We may consider particulars with all their 'properties'. This gives us the notion of a 'thick' particular. Alternatively, we may have a conception of a 'thin' particular. A thin particular is a particular with all its 'properties' stripped off (the 'residue' in more traditional terminology). When we say that a state of affairs is a particular's having a 'property' or two or more particulars standing in some 'relation', the notion of a thin particular is involved. Thick particulars are themselves states of affairs (but not every state of affairs is a thick particular, of course). (Kratzer 1989: 613)

As a thick particular, $d(R)$ is a set of thin particulars (cf. "entities" in Langacker's definition). Thin particulars, in their turn, are conceptualized as either individuals (e) or situations (s). That is, T can be of type s as well as of type e. This distinction will be relevant for us in §4, where I will use the same functions and compositional rules as in §2.3, but incorporating situations. Exclusion of a situation from $d(R)$ implies a lack of control over that situation in the actual world. However, adding a vector, as in Figure 1c, we infer that a situation is under control in an inertia world. This is what makes the dative – terminal node $\sqrt{\text{to}}$ in (28) – a good fit for a modal use. This last point finally brings us to my analysis of possessive modality in Russian.

4 Possessive modality in Russian

As I have already mentioned in footnote 3, not all dative infinitive constructions in Russian have possessive modality, which is restricted to declarative imperfective clauses, as in (29a). In (29b), I show that the verb cannot be perfective.

The perfective aspect becomes possible if we add negation, as in (30a), or use a *wh*-phrase, as in (30b), but the modal flavour is not the same (see Fortuin 2007; Tsedryk 2018).

(29) a. Vane   zavtra   rano vsta-va-t'.
         Vanja.DAT tomorrow early get.up-IPFV-INF
         'Vanja has to get up early tomorrow.'

      b. *Vane   zavtra   rano vsta-t'.
         Vanja.DAT tomorrow early get.up.PRF-INF
         [the same as in (29a)]

(30) a. Vane   zavtra   rano ne vsta-t'.
         Vanja.DAT tomorrow early NEG get.up.PRF-INF
         'Vanja will not be able to get up early tomorrow.'

      b. Vo skol'ko   Vane   zavtra   vsta-t'?
         at what.time Vanja.DAT tomorrow get.up.PRF-INF
         'At what time should Vanja get up tomorrow?'

In what follows, I will focus on possessive modality and will not attempt an analysis of the modal flavours in (30), as this endeavour would take me too far afield. However, the syntactic derivation that I propose below can be applied to all dative infinitive constructions.

In a nutshell, my main idea is that i^* can create a dative applicative structure on the top of a TP, just like it creates such a structure on the top of an NP; compare (31) with (18).[16]

(31)

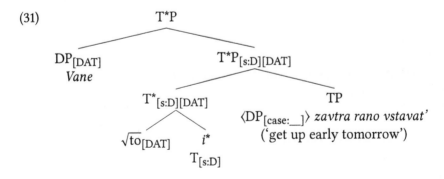

---

[16] A high applicative structure on the top of a TP is not new. It has already been proposed by Rivero (2009) and Rivero & Arregui (2012) for involuntary state constructions in Slavic.

Apart from the categorial difference, (31) is different from (18) by its derivational history: it is a raising structure (DP has a copy within TP). This peculiarity of (31) is derived from Chomsky's (2013) labeling algorithm, which resolves labeling ambiguity in cases like (32a): two maximal projections are merged and do not share any features. In order to label α, we have to merge an extra head H (which projects an HP) and move either XP or YP. Suppose it is XP that has to move, as in (32b). This movement creates a "discontinuous element" (Chomsky 2013: 44), whose lower copy becomes irrelevant for labeling, and α is labeled as YP.

(32) a. $[_\alpha$ XP YP]

b. $[_\beta$ XP $[_{HP}$ H $[_{YP}$ ⟨XP⟩ YP]]]

We have the same situation in (33a), where the subject raises from its thematic position (Spec, vP) and merges with a TP. Since we have an infinitival TP (without agreement features), there are two consequences: (i) DP cannot be case-marked and (ii) α cannot be labeled. We have to merge a case-assigning head. This is where i^* comes into play. However, it cannot be a bare i^* (which does not have its own case feature to assign); it has to be i^* with a case assigning root.

(33) a. $[_\alpha$ DP TP]

b. $[_\beta$ $i^*_{[DAT]}$ $[_\alpha$ DP TP]]

c. $[_{T^*P}$ DP$_{[DAT]}$ $[_{T^*P}$ T$^*_{[DAT]}$ $[_{TP}$ ⟨DP⟩ TP]]]

For simplicity's sake, I identify it as $i^*_{[DAT]}$ in (33b). Note that $i^*_{[DAT]}$ does not have a categorial value at this point, since α is not yet labeled in (33b). When DP moves (for case reasons), α is labeled as TP, i^* receives its categorial value (T*), β becomes T*P, DP receives the dative case (checking [s:D]), and we obtain the structure in (33c). The tree in (31) is the final state of this derivation.

Interpretation of the nodes in (31) is provided in (34). The main difference between (31) and (18) is that the category expanded by i^* in (31) is a proposition (p). As defined in (34d), it is a function of type ⟨s, t⟩, compared to the NP of type ⟨e, t⟩ in (23). Correspondingly, T* in (31) is of type ⟨$e,$ ⟨s, t⟩⟩ (see (34c)), compared to type ⟨$e,$ ⟨e, t⟩⟩ of N* in (18) (see (21b)). Just like with the NP, the semantic composition in (34) proceeds by Functional Application in all cases except (34e), which is derived by Predicate Conjunction. We end up with a T*P, as in (34f), which has the same semantic type as the TP in (34d), but with a directional semantics of the dative.

(34)   a. $[\![i^*]\!] = \lambda x \in D_e . d(x)$

   b. $[\![\sqrt{\text{to}}]\!] = \lambda f \in D_{\langle s,\ t\rangle} . [\lambda y \in D_e . [\lambda x \in D_s . \text{towards'}(f(y))(x)]]$

   c. $[\![T^* \text{ in (31)}]\!] = \lambda y \in D_e . [\lambda x \in D_s . \text{towards'}(d(y))(x)]$

   d. $[\![TP \text{ in (31)}]\!] = \lambda x \in D_s . p(x)$

   e. $[\![\text{lower } T^*P \text{ in (31)}]\!] = \lambda y \in D_e . [\lambda x \in D_s . \text{towards'}(d(y))(x) \wedge p(x)]$

   f. $[\![\text{upper } T^*P \text{ in (31)}]\!] = \lambda x \in D_s . \text{towards'}(d(\text{vanja'}))(x) \wedge p(x)$

According to (34f), situations (in which *p* is true) are directed towards Vanja's domain/sphere, but Vanja is not their controller, planner, or "director" (in the sense of Copley 2008: 272). There is a potentially infinite number of possible situations that could be excluded from Vanja's domain/sphere. Thus, the remaining step in the computation is to provide the modal base that would restrict all possible situations to those that are relevant in a given context (*c*).[17] The modal base (MB), as defined in (35a), consists of all (contextually salient) preparatory situations (*Prep*) applied to a function of type $\langle s, t \rangle$ (cf. "preparatory process" in Cipria & Roberts 2000: 328–331, following Moens & Steedman 1988).[18] Functional Application between (35a) and (34f) results in (35b), which is read as follows: for all x, such as x is a preparatory situation, it is true that x is directed towards Vanja's domain/sphere, and *p* holds. The tree in (36) shows this last step of the derivation in syntax (a merger between C, which provides the modal base, and T*P).

(35)   a. $[\![\text{MBPrep}]\!]^c = \lambda f \in D_{\langle s,\ t\rangle} . \forall x \in D_s, Prep(x) \rightarrow f(x)$

   b. $[\![\text{MBPrep}]\!]^c ([\![\text{upper } T^*P \text{ in (31)}]\!]) = \forall x \in D_s, Prep(x) \rightarrow$
       $[\text{towards'}(d(\text{vanja'}))(x) \wedge p(x)]$

---

[17] I abstract away from the accessibility relation here. An articulated account is yet to be developed.

[18] Sentences like (29a) imply a topic situation, as in (i) (in brackets). Preparation for the main event (Vanja's early rising tomorrow) is an alternative to the topic situation (Vanja's sitting for long time).

   (i)   Vane   zavtra   rano   vsta-va-t'   (on ne   možet s   vami dolgo   sidet').
        Vanja.DAT   tomorrow   early get.up-IPFV-INF   he NEG can   with you long.time to.sit
        'Vanja has to get up early tomorrow (he can't sit with you for long time).'

(36)

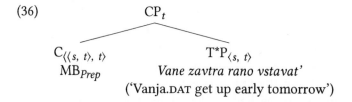

$$\text{CP}_t$$

$$\text{C}_{\langle\langle s,\, t\rangle,\, t\rangle} \qquad \text{T*P}_{\langle s,\, t\rangle}$$
$$\text{MB}_{Prep} \qquad \textit{Vane zavtra rano vstavat'}$$
$$\text{('Vanja.\textsc{dat} get up early tomorrow')}$$

The imperfective entails that every preparatory situation is interpreted as an inertia situation (without interruptions), which inevitably reaches Vanja's domain/sphere in a corresponding inertia world (cf. "preparatory inertia" in Rivero & Arregui 2012: 324 and Arregui et al. 2014: 327).[19]

To summarize, possessive modality in Russian is represented by a subset of dative infinitive constructions, declarative and imperfective. My goal in this section was to show that there is a parallel between the datives introduced above NP and those introduced above TP. In the latter case, the dative entails that a situation is not under control in the actual world, but can be brought under control in an inertia world. This possibility is derived from the directional semantics of the dative argument introducer in the context of inertia situations entailed by the imperfective.

5 Conclusion

Predicative possession and possessive modality show a striking similarity, but they also differ with respect to case marking in BE-languages. Possessive modality correlates with the dative case. Bjorkman & Cowper (2016) propose to capture the attested similarity, using a morpho-semantic feature, [INCL], which encodes inclusion within an abstract domain/sphere. As for the dative case, they suggest

---

[19]Rivero & Arregui (2012: 325) claim that the imperfective in Russian (and West Slavic) does not have access to preparatory inertia, as it cannot have intentional readings. This claim is partly true. Indeed, the imperfective in Russian cannot have intentional readings in the past tense, as shown in (i).

(i) *Vanja   vsta-va-l   v pjat' utra   poka ne otmenili   trenirovku.
     Vanja.NOM get.up-IPFV-PST at five of.morning until NEG canceled.3PL practice
     Intended: 'Vanja was planning to get up at 5 am until the practice was canceled.'

However, Rivero & Arregui do not consider Russian dative infinitive constructions, as in (29a), which do have an intentional reading (e.g., the intention is to get up early tomorrow). There is some "clash" between the imperfective and the past tense in Russian, preventing intentional readings in cases like (i), but otherwise the claim that preparatory inertia is not available for the imperfective in Russian is too strong.

that it is a spell-out of [INCL] bundled with a modal feature, [ROOT] or [EPIST]. I have shown that this analysis, when applied to Russian, has a number of limitations. First, it makes false predictions with respect to locative (actual) possessors. Second, it has little to say about the predicative possession with dative (prospective) possessors. I suggested that the link between predicative possession and possessive modality should be established via directional semantics of the head introducing this dative in two syntactic contexts, NP (sets of individuals) and TP (sets of situations). In my analysis, I used Wood & Marantz's (2017) argument introducer and two spatial roots, $\sqrt{at}$ and $\sqrt{to}$. Possessive modality is derived from the directional semantics of the second root and inertia situations entailed by the imperfective. My analysis leads to a hypothesis that possessive modality in other BE-languages could also be linked to directional semantics (even if a language does not use the same datives as Russian). The dative case used in possessive modality structures is not a trivial matter of language-specific spell-out rules; it calls for a careful crosslinguistic investigation.

Abbreviations

The abbreviations used in the glosses of this chapter follow the Leipzig Glossing Rules.

Acknowledgements

I would like to thank two anonymous reviewers for their detailed comments on the earlier draft.

References

Arregui, Ana, María Luisa Rivero & Andrés Salanova. 2014. Cross-linguistic variability in imperfectivity. *Natural Language & Linguistic Theory* 32(2). 307–362. DOI:10.1007/s11049-013-9226-4

Bhatt, Rajesh. 1997. Obligation and possession. In Heidi Harley (ed.), *Papers from the UPenn/MIT Roundtable on Argument Structure and Aspect* (MIT Working Papers in Linguistics 32). Cambridge, MA: MIT Press.

Bhatt, Rajesh. 2006. *Covert modality in non-finite contexts*. New York, NY: Mouton de Gruyter.

Bjorkman, Bronwyn & Elizabeth Cowper. 2016. Possession and necessity: From individuals to worlds. *Lingua* 182. 30–48.

Boneh, Nora & Ivy Sichel. 2010. Deconstructing possession. *Natural Language & Linguistic Theory* 28. 1–40.

Calindro, Ana Regina. 2020. Ditransitive constructions: What sets Brazilian Portuguese apart from other Romance languages? In Anna Pineda & Jaume Mateu (eds.), *Dative constructions in Romance and beyond,* 75–95. Berlin: Language Science Press. DOI:10.5281/zenodo.3776535

Chomsky, Noam. 2013. Problems of projection. *Lingua* 130. 33–49.

Cipria, Alicia & Craige Roberts. 2000. Spanish imperfecto and pretérito: Truth conditions and aktionsart effects in a situation semantics. *Natural Language Semantics* 8(4). 297–347. DOI:10.1023/A:1011202000582

Copley, Bridget. 2008. The plan's the thing: Deconstructing futurate meanings. *Linguistic Inquiry* 39(2). 261–274. DOI:10.1162/ling.2008.39.2.261

Cuervo, María Cristina. 2003. *Datives at large.* Cambridge, MA: Massachusetts Institute of Technology. (Doctoral dissertation). https://dspace.mit.edu/handle/1721.1/7991.

Dowty, David. 1979. *Word meaning and Montague Grammar.* Dordrecht: Reidel.

Fábregas, Antonio & Rafael Marín. 2020. Datives and stativity in psych predicates. In Anna Pineda & Jaume Mateu (eds.), *Dative constructions in Romance and beyond,* 221–238. Berlin: Language Science Press. DOI:10.5281/zenodo.3776549

Fortuin, Egbert. 2007. Modality and aspect: Interaction of constructional meaning and aspectual meaning in the dative-infinitive construction in Russian. *Russian Linguistics* 13. 201–230. DOI:10.1007/s11185-007-9015-y

Franco, Ludovico & Paolo Lorusso. 2020. Aspectual datives (and instrumentals). In Anna Pineda & Jaume Mateu (eds.), *Dative constructions in Romance and beyond,* 175–194. Berlin: Language Science Press. DOI:10.5281/zenodo.3776545

Freeze, Ray. 1992. Existentials and other locatives. *Language* 68(3). 553–595. DOI:10.2307/415794

Heim, Irene & Angelika Kratzer. 1998. *Semantics in generative grammar.* Oxford: Blackwell.

Heine, Bernd. 1997. *Possession.* Cambridge: Cambridge University Press.

Isačenko, Alexander V. 1974. On have and be languages: A typological sketch. In Michael Flier (ed.), *Slavic forum: Essays in linguistics and literature,* 43–77. The Hague: Mouton.

Jung, Hakyung. 2011. *The syntax of the BE-possessive: Parametric variation and surface diversities.* Amsterdam: John Benjamins.

Kayne, Richard S. 1993. Towards a modular theory of auxiliary selection. *Studia Linguistica* 47(1). 3–31.   DOI:10.1111/j.1467-9582.1993.tb00837.x

Kratzer, Angelika. 1989. An investigation of the lumps of thought. *Linguistics and Philosophy* 12(5). 607–653.   DOI:10.1007/BF00627775

Kratzer, Angelika. 1996. Severing the external argument from its verb. In Johan Rooryck & Laurie Zaring (eds.), *Phrase structure and the lexicon*, 109–137. Dordrecht: Kluwer.

Kratzer, Angelika. 2002. Facts: Particulars of information units? *Linguistics and Philosophy* 25(5–6). 655–670.   DOI:10.1023/A:1020807615085

Kratzer, Angelika. 2019. Situations in natural language semantics. In Edward N. Zalta (ed.), *Stanford encyclopedia of philosophy*. Stanford: Metaphysics Research Lab, Stanford University. https://plato.stanford.edu/archives/sum2019/entries/situations-semantics/. Summer 2019 edn. First published Mon Feb 12, 2007; substantive revision Wed Feb 6, 2019.

Langacker, Ronald. 1993. Reference-point constructions. *Cognitive Linguistics* 4(1). 1–38.   DOI:10.1515/cogl.1993.4.1.1

Langacker, Ronald. 2009. *Investigations in Cognitive Grammar*. Berlin: Mouton De Gruyter.

Markman, Vita. 2009. Applicatives TO, FROM, and AT: On dative and locative possessors in Russian. In Anisa Schardl, Martin Walkow & Muhammad Abdurrahman (eds.), *Proceedings of North East Linguistic Society (NELS) 38*, vol. 2, 123–134. Amherst, MA: GLSA Publications.

Moens, Marc & Mark Steedman. 1988. Temporal ontology and temporal reference. *Computational Linguistics* 14(2). 15–28.

Myler, Neil. 2016. *Building and interpreting possessive sentences*. Cambridge: MIT Press.

Pylkkänen, Liina. 2008. *Introducing arguments* (Linguistic Inquiry Monographs 49). Cambridge, MA: MIT Press.

Rivero, María Luisa. 2009. Intensionality, high applicatives, and aspect: Involuntary state constructions in Bulgarian and Slovenian. *Natural Language and Linguistic Theory* 27(1). 151–196.   DOI:10.1007/s11049-008-9059-8

Rivero, María Luisa & Ana Arregui. 2012. Building involuntary states in Slavic. In Violeta Demonte & Louise McNally (eds.), *Telicity, change, and state: A crosscategorial view of event structure*, 300–332. New York, NY: Oxford University Press.

Stassen, Leon. 2009. *Predicative possession*. Oxford: Oxford University Press.

Tsedryk, Egor. 2018. Dative-infinitive constructions in Russian: Are they really biclausal? In Wayles Browne, Miloje Despic, Naomi Enzinna, Simone Harmath-de Lemos, Robin Karlin & Draga Zec (eds.), *Formal Approaches to Slavic Linguistics (FASL) #25: The third Cornell meeting 2016*, 298–317. Ann Arbor, MI: Michigan Slavic Publications.

Tsedryk, Egor. 2020. Introducing possessors in Russian: A new perspective based on the single argument introducer. In Tania Ionin & Jonathan MacDonald (eds.), *Formal Approaches to Slavic Linguistics (FASL) #26: The first Urbana-Champaign meeting 2017*, 398–416. Ann Arbor, MI: Michigan Slavic Publications.

Wood, Jim. 2015. *Icelandic morphosyntax and argument structure*. Dordrecht: Springer.

Wood, Jim & Alec Marantz. 2017. The interpretation of external arguments. In Roberta D'Alessandro, Irene Franco & Ángel J. Gallego (eds.), *The verbal domain*, 255–278. Oxford: Oxford University Press. DOI:10.1093/oso/9780198767886.001.0001

Chapter 9

Datives and stativity in psych predicates

Antonio Fábregas
UiT-Norway's Arctic University

Rafael Marín
CNRS (UMR 8163) & Université de Lille

This article discusses the question of how the meaning contribution of a dative
is obtained. Despite the different formal instantiations that a dative can take, its
semantics is typically very stable cross-linguistically. In particular, datives typically express goals of motion and experiencers; importantly, in experiencer contexts they are associated with a stative reading of the predicate, which in principle
clashes with the goal semantics. In this chapter we argue that datives are semantically defined as initial boundaries, but specifically, when interpreted as experiencers, they are introduced by a prepositional layer that prevents the boundary
semantics from extending to the whole predicate.

1 A correlation between datives and stativity

As noted by many, dative-experiencer psych verbs are systematically stative,
while reflexively-marked ones involve some form of dynamicity (cf. Belletti &
Rizzi 1988; Marín & McNally 2011). The contrast can be shown through several
tests: dative marked verbs reject speed adverbials (1), and *parar de* 'stop' (3),
which select dynamic predicates. Reflexively-marked psych predicates are compatible with all of these (2), (4).

(1)   a.   A Juan le   agrada París (*rápidamente).   DAT
            to Juan him.DAT pleases Paris (*quickly)
            Intended: 'Juan quickly starts liking Paris.'

 Antonio Fábregas & Rafael Marín. 2020. Datives and stativity in psych
predicates. In Anna Pineda & Jaume Mateu (eds.), *Dative constructions in Romance and beyond*, 221–238. Berlin: Language Science Press.
DOI:10.5281/zenodo.3776549

b. A Juan le   gusta Sandra (*rápidamente).   DAT
to Juan him.DAT likes Sandra (*quickly)
Intended: 'Juan quickly starts liking Sandra.'

c. A Juan le   duele la cabeza (*rápidamente).   DAT
to Juan him.DAT hurts the head   (*quickly)
Intended: 'Juan quickly starts getting a headache.'

(2)   a. Juan se olvida de todo (rápidamente).   REFL
Juan SE forgets of all   (quickly)
'Juan quickly forgets everything.'

b. Juan se acuerda   de todo (rápidamente).   REFL
Juan SE remembers of all   (quickly)
'Juan quickly remembers everything.'

c. Juan se desentiende   de todo (rápidamente).   REFL
Juan SE pretends.not.to.know of all   (quickly)
'Juan quickly pretends not to know anything.'

(3)   a. *A Juan paró   de agradarle París.   DAT
to Juan stopped of loving   Paris
Intended: 'Juan does not like Paris anymore.'

b. *A Juan paró   de gustarle María.   DAT
to Juan stopped of liking   María
Intended: 'Juan does not like María anymore.'

c. *A Juan paró   de dolerle la cabeza.   DAT
to Juan stopped of hurting the head
Intended: 'Juan's head does not hurt anymore.'

(4)   a. Juan paró   de olvidarse de pagar las facturas.   REFL
Juan stopped of forgetting of paying the bills
'Juan does not forget to pay bills anymore.'

b. Juan paró   de acordarse   de todos los cumpleaños.   REFL
Juan stopped of remembering of all   the birthdays
'Juan does not remember all birthdays anymore.'

c. Juan paró   de desentenderse   de sus hijos.   REFL
Juan stopped of pretending.not.to.know of his children
'Juan does not ignore his children anymore.'

This is not a lexical accident, but a real property of datives: several predicates compatible with both reflexive and dative marking show that the dative version is systematically stative according to the same tests.

(5)   a. A Juan le   preocupan las cosas (*rápidamente). DAT   DAT
        to Juan him.DAT worry   the things (*quickly)
        Intended: 'Juan gets quickly worried about things.'

    b. Juan se preocupa por las cosas (rápidamente).   REFL
        Juan SE worries   for the things (quickly)
        'Juan gets quickly worried about things.'

(6)   a. *A Juan pararon de preocupar=le las cosas.   DAT
         to Juan stopped of worry=him   the things
        Intended: 'Juan does not worry about things anymore.'

    b. Juan paró   de preocupar=se siempre por sus hijos.   REFL
        Juan stopped of worry=SE   always for his children
        'Juan does not worry about his children anymore.'

Importantly for our purposes, the reflexive pronoun has been analysed as a remnant of the accusative case (Medová 2009). The question is, then, whether the dative- vs. reflexive-marking contrast can be understood as a specific instance of the more general dative- vs. accusative-marking contrast in psych predicates (Fernández Ordóñez 1999; Landau 2010; Cifuentes Honrubia 2015; Fábregas et al. 2017), among many others. As is well-known for Spanish, the accusative construal is dynamic, and the dative one is static.

(7)   a. A María sus hermanas la   asustan (rápidamente).   ACC
        to María her sisters   her.ACC frighten (quickly)
        'María's sisters get her scared quickly.'

    b. A María la   oscuridad le   asusta   (*rápidamente).   DAT
        to María the darkness her.DAT frightens (*quickly)
        Intended: 'Darkness gets María scared quickly.'

(8) a. A María paró   de asustar=la   su hermano.   ACC
         to María stopped of scare=her.ACC her brother

         'María's brother does not scare her anymore.'

     b. * A María paró   de asustar=le   la economía.   DAT
         to María stopped of scare=her.DAT the economy

         Intended: 'Economy does not scare María anymore.'

The generalisation is robust, at the very least for Spanish: with psychological verbs, dative marking imposes a stative reading.[1] Accusative marking – and reflexive marking, which we take to be an instance of the accusative – is related to a dynamic construal.

So far so good. The problem, however, emerges when we ask ourselves what the contribution of a dative is in the light of examples like (9), which are also attested in the same languages.

(9) A Juan le   entregué el paquete.
     to Juan him.DAT gave   the package

     'I gave Juan the package.'

In (9), the dative argument is interpreted dynamically. In particular, it is taken to be a path of transference through which the package travels. It is not only that the dative marking is not associated with stativity in such cases: the dynamicity of the predicate involves an alleged path that is apparently introduced by dative marking.

The problem then is how one can make cases like (9) compatible in terms of the semantic contribution of the dative with examples like (1) or (3). We seem to need a path reading that dynamises the predicate in (9), but just the opposite in the other cases.[2]

---

[1] See, however, Fábregas & Marín (2015) for the observation that accusative-marking psych verbs such as *amar* 'love' or *odiar* 'hate' are also stative, but display slightly different aspectual properties. Note that we do not claim that there is a bi-univocal relation between stativity and dativisation, but rather that it is unexpected for datives to appear within truly stative predicates.

[2] One anonymous reviewer proposes that this should not be so problematic given that predicates have some independence with respect to their arguments in terms of aspectual definition (eg., a predicate can be dynamic even if it combines with a stative preposition). Note, however, that here we have the opposite problem. On the assumption that stativity is obtained by lack of dynamicity and other aspectual properties (Jaque Hidalgo 2014), the situation here reduces to how some dynamic object provided by an argument fails to compose with the predicate to produce a non-stative construal. Remember that in current theoretical assumptions, structures add information, but cannot remove previously added information or substitute it.

We take it as the default option in linguistic analysis to expect that the same formal marking carries the same semantic interpretation (that is, we do not think that the Distributed Morphology view of case as dummy morphological marking without interpretation should be blindly assumed). Once we adopt the stronger option that dative marking should make the same contribution across structures, this alternation is a serious puzzle for the semantics of a dative, and note that if we remove the semantic criterion to identify a dative, we are left with very little in order to characterise datives as a cross-linguistic class (see Cabré & Fábregas 2020 [this volume]). The formal instantiation of datives varies across languages, but their semantics are fairly stable. Cross-linguistic accounts of the prototypical semantic values of datives (such as Næss 2009) mention that the main values are recipients, goals and benefactives, but also experiencers. The first two values are dynamic, or at least strongly suggest a transference scenario where there is dynamic event, while the last one is clearly stative, given the facts we saw. All these values are expressed (among others) by the Spanish dative:

(10) a. A María le dieron el premio.   recipient
           to María her gave the prize
           'They gave the prize to María.'

      b. A María no se le acercó   nadie.   goal of motion
           to María not SE her approached nobody
           'Nobody approached María.'

      c. A María le preparamos un pastel.   benefactive
           to María her prepared   a pie
           'We made a pie for María.'

      d. A María le gusta Jorge.   experiencer
           to María her likes Jorge
           'María likes Jorge.'

One possible way out of the puzzle would be to say that in the dynamic cases, it is actually the accusative argument that defines dynamicity. There is some initial plausibility to the claim. With psychological predicates that have both a form of accusative and a dative, the accusative overrides the dative's association to stativity, as (11) shows.

(11) A Juan se le   olvidan las cosas (rápidamente).   DAT+REFL
      to Juan SE him.DAT forget the things (quickly)
      'Juan forgets things quickly.'

This approach would not be enough, though. Stativity is not imposed by default on verbs whose only (overt) argument (Pineda 2016; 2020) is marked as dative.

(12) a. A María le   estuve gritando en mi despacho.
          to María her.DAT was   shouting in my office
          'I was shouting at María in my office.'

      b. A Juan le   estuvieron pegando en la   calle.
          to Juan him.dat were   hitting   in the street
          'Someone was hitting Juan in the street.'

This pattern of data is, then, quite complex. Here are the main generalisations: (i) outside psychological predicates, datives can be associated with dynamic interpretations; (ii) inside psychological predicates, arguments with a dative and no form of accusative are systematically stative.

The main question is then what kind of unified interpretation of datives in semantic terms can account for this apparently conflicting behaviour. The next section is devoted to this problem, specifically what kind of semantic contribution a dative makes so that both stative and non-stative readings are allowed. In the course of this section we will see that there is a reduced number of non-psychological predicates that can appear with dative marking, but we will also show that their behaviour is less prototypically stative than dative-marked psych predicates. Section §3, then, will analyse the specific case of psych predicates with dative arguments, and will argue that the semantic contribution of the dative is made opaque in such contexts by the presence of a locative silent preposition that introduces them, à la Landau (2010). Section §4 presents the consequences and conclusions of the approach.

2 The analysis, step one: The denotation of a dative

We believe that one crucial aspect of the theory needed to approach this phenomenon is that it should contain a set of primitives that can be shared by different grammatical categories, as we believe this is the most direct way of explaining how the information contained in one argument can be read by the predicate to define its aspectual information. We therefore start the analysis from the assumption that an ontology of semantic primitives codifying aspect as a form of boundedness that can also be present in nouns contains the following objects, defined in Piñón (1997):

(13) a. Bodies: ——

      b. Boundaries: |

In Piñón (1997) the boundary and the body differ in that the latter lacks any extension. Only the body has some particular 'length', which in the temporoaspectual domain is translated as denoting a time interval. The boundary itself is a point in a geometric sense, that is, it lacks any extension and an addition of several boundaries does not add up to a body.

When the body is instantiated in verbal categories, and therefore translates into aspectual information, two types of body are differentiated: stative bodies, which do not involve any form of dynamicity, and dynamic bodies.

Boundaries come in two flavours: left boundaries (14a), which can be translated as an initiation subevent in the aspectual domain, and right boundaries (14b), which can be translated as the termination, inside the same domain. Importantly, these two flavours are not necessarily derived configurationally from their relative position with respect to a body. The ontology allows boundaries, left or right, to appear independently of bodies, so that the denotation of some predicates can involve a pure boundary denotation (Marín & McNally 2011).[3] (15) gives just some of the potential configurations that can be obtained with this system.

(14) a. [

      b.]

(15) a. [——]

      b. [——

      c.]——

      d. []

      e.]

Within this system, if the dative semantics was really associated with a transference semantics, it would display the combination in (16a) – if the starting point were included in its denotation – or (16b) – if only the path and the goal of the transference were denoted. Either way, containing a final boundary we would expect that combined with a predicate it will give rise to a telic interpretation.

---

[3]To be precise, Piñón (1997) assumes that boundaries must be relational elements and therefore treats them as only existing when adjacent to bodies. We here follow Marín & McNally's (2011) proposal, where the two ontological types are independent of each other and individual predicates might correspond only to boundaries, or only to bodies.

(16)   a. [——]
       b. ——]

Instead, we will argue that datives are associated with a single left boundary (17). This boundary contains three ingredients that contextually give meaning to dative-interpretations beyond prototypical goal cases: (i) it does not impose telicity, because the boundary is the initial one and it does not entail movement or arrival to a goal; (ii) it involves an orientation, because the left boundary forces a transition towards a goal; (iii) by combination of the previous two properties, it can denote extended contact with an external entity, because the oriented transition is directed towards an entity and it does not arrive at its location, but approaches its margins.

(17)   [

Let us start the analysis by presenting our evidence for this.

One first point of evidence comes from non-psychological verbs that select a dative. In them, although with differences with respect to psychological predicates that we will discuss later, stative readings are also possible. If the denotation of the dative is anything like (16), there should be a mismatch. The alternative would be to arbitrarily decide that datives never count for the aspectual denotation of the predicate with which they combine, something that we will see cannot be true in §3.1.

Consider the reasoning step by step. Incremental theme verbs (Tenny 1987; Krifka 1989, among others) illustrate the situation where a denotation built with the primitives in (16) triggers a telic interpretation involving development in time. In a predicate like *to eat an apple*, the only internal argument is a bounded entity with extension, and as such it corresponds to the representation in (18a), trivially meaning that an apple is an entity that occupies space beyond a point, and has a beginning and an end. Correspondingly, the predicate (18b) composed by a combination of this internal argument and the verb has the equivalent internal structure by object-event isomorphism (Ramchand 2008): *to eat an apple* is an eventuality that has temporal extension (beyond a point), a beginning and an end – which correspond to the beginning and the end of the apple that is consumed.[4]

---

[4]An anonymous reviewer suggests that the solution to the puzzle could be to accept that specifiers do not intervene in the aspectual definition of a predicate (assumption that is also made in Ramchand 2008). We will not adopt it here because we want to treat specifiers as second complements of heads, and in this sense specifiers should not be ontologically different from objects with respect to semantics.

(18) a. una manzana = [——]
          an apple

    b. comer una manzana = [——]
          to.eat an apple

Consider now (19). This predicate is not stative in the same sense that *gustar* or other dative-marked psych verbs are (cf. §3.1.), but clearly the predicate is not telic (19b), as one should expect if the denotation of the dative (20) were (16). We are thus faced with only two options: either we impose (arbitrarily) that datives do not interact at all with their predicates in terms of aspect, or the denotation of the dative is not (16).

(19) a. Le   falta una silla.
          him.DAT lack one chair
          'He lacks one chair.'

    b. *Le   faltó   una silla en diez minutos.
          him.DAT lacked one chair in ten minutes
          Intended: 'It took him ten minutes to lack one chair.'

(20) a. le = [——]

    b. faltarle una silla = [——] (counterfactually)

Instead, if the denotation of datives were just contact, and specifically contact as a left boundary ('[') not imposing any form of telicity, (19) would follow. The dative would just mean that there is some kind of contact between the dative-marked element and the verb, but no transfer would be entailed.

Our second piece of evidence that '[' is indeed the denotation of the dative comes from its marking in Spanish. It is well-known that the preposition used for datives (21a) is the same one that one sees to mark spatial goals (21b) – among other functions.

(21) a. Le   envié   un libro a María.
          her.DAT sent.1SG a   book to María
          'I sent a book to María.'

    b. Envié   un libro a Berlín.
          sent.1SG a   book to Berlin
          'I sent a book to Berlin.'

This could be interpreted as an argument that datives are paths of transfer, but Fábregas (2007) shows that for Spanish, that preposition acts as a place P. It can combine with stative predicates, and in such cases the interpretation associated with it is contact – as opposed to inclusion within a region. The use of *a* in stative contexts is favoured with DPs that express limits, boundaries and points inside scales.

(22) a. Juan está a la orilla.
          Juan is   at the shore

      b. Juan está al   borde.
          Juan is   at.the edge

      c. El pan   está a cuatro euros.
          the bread is   at four   euros
          'The bread costs four euros.'

      d. El pollo   está a cuatro grados.
          the chicken is   at four   degrees
          'The chicken is at a temperature of four degrees.'

In other words, (22) shows that *a* is more similar to English *at* than *to*. The semantics of contact without implying telicity (Marín & McNally 2011), as in (22), force a reading where the contribution of the element marked as *a* is '[' and not any of the representations in (16).

Let us go now to the third piece of evidence. Different works, but significantly Romero (1997), have argued that Spanish datives – at least those that involve clitic doubling – codify a form of telicity whereby the intended transfer has been completed. Pineda (2016), however, has shown that even with clitic doubling there is no real distinction in terms of telicity with datives. Here we will just concentrate on showing that under no circumstances does the dative marked argument entail full transfer. Consider (23), which are completely natural instances where one explicitly denies that there was full transfer and cause no contradiction.

(23) a. Le   escribí un poema a alguien que nunca lo recibirá.
          him.DAT wrote a poema to someone that never it will.receive
          'I wrote a poem to someone that will never receive it.'

      b. Le   preparé una tarta a Pilar, pero nunca llegó   a verla
          her.DAT prepared a   cake to Pilar, but never arrived to see.it

porque murió.
because died
'I made Pilar a cake, but she never saw it because she died.'

At best, given (23), the full transfer has to be understood as a cancellable implicature. What the datives in (23) express, given that full transfer is not included here, is that there is an intention to transfer it, or to put it in slightly more technical terms, that the actions are conceived as oriented towards an entity, marked with the dative. However, this result is obtained if datives denote left boundaries '[' that entail that there is the initiation of a movement oriented with respect to a goal. In this case – where the verbs do involve some path – the only entailment is that there is an intended goal, but without any claim about whether there is an entity that arrives at that goal.

Consider now our fourth piece of evidence. This account allows for an elegant unification between the many uses of datives in a language like Spanish (RAE/ASALE 2009). There are at least five different cases beyond dative experiencers, which we leave for §3:

(24) a. A María le   dieron el   premio.
         at María her gave   the prize
         'They gave the prize to María.'

      b. A María no se le   acercó   nadie.
         at María not SE her approached nobody
         'Nobody approached María.'

      c. A María le   preparamos un pastel.
         at María her prepared   a   pie
         'We made a pie for María.'

      d. Le   faltan sillas.
         her lacks chairs
         'She lacks chairs.'

      e. Le es fiel.
         him is faithful
         'She is faithful to him.'

(24a) is a predicate of transfer. (24b) is one instance of a locative dative, where the dative-marked argument is interpreted as a position towards which something moves. (24c) is a benefactive. (24d) shows one case of a dative with a stative predicate unable to express telicity. (24e) is one instance of a dative within a copular structure, associated to the property expressed by the adjective *faithful*.

The notion of transfer is evidently not fit to account, at least, for the last two cases. In these cases, instead, the abstract contact reading with '[', where the eventuality is denoted as being intended or directed towards the dative-marked argument, intuitively captures the meaning of the predicate. (24e) trivially means that the infidelity was directed towards him, while (24d) means that the lack of chairs is not absolute, but oriented to the needs or expectations of the dative-marked argument. Similarly, the benefactive is the entity towards which the event is directed (24c); the movement in (24b) is directed towards the dative-marked argument, and the transfer – which might take place or not – is directed towards the same entity in (24a). Of relevance also is the fact that in at least three cases there is no need to define a path: (24c) is compatible with a scenario where neither the cake nor María move from their positions, and there is no need to transfer in either of the last two types of verbs.

In other words, associating the dative to a transfer denotation as in (16) simply does not allow for a unified account of all these uses of the dative in Spanish, does not explain the use of the preposition that marks it in Spanish, and makes the wrong predictions in terms of aspectual impact and composition. Treating it as meaning contact and orientation directly captures the intuitions and the spirit of the applicative analysis (Cuervo 2003), with the possibility that the two related entities are defined configurationally depending on the height at which the applicative is introduced and the nature of the complement of the applicative.

3 The analysis, step two: What makes experiencers special

However, this is not enough for dative-marked experiencers. In this section we will show that with dative-marked psych predicates, not even the left boundary is transferred to the whole predicate. We will show first that even in a stative verb like *faltar* 'lack', this left boundary has an impact on its aspectual definition (§3.1), something that further argues against arbitrarily deciding that datives do not contribute to the aspectual make-up of their predicates. Second, we will focus on psych predicates and discuss why even the boundary is excluded from the predicate as a whole (§3.2). We will propose that Landau (2010) is right in the claim that experiencers are introduced by Ps, and we will argue that it is this P that isolates the dative from the predicate, making its aspectual contribution invisible to the verb.

3.1 *Faltar* vs. *gustar*

Even though they are both stative (25), García Fernández et al. 2006, *faltar* 'lack' displays some properties of behaviour that suggest that it should be considered at least a stage-level stative verb. This verb expresses an eventuality that can be located in space (26) and it can restrict a temporal-aspectual operator, producing a reading where the eventuality expressed by the verb holds only at some time periods between the same two entities x and y, both specific (Kratzer 1995: cf. 27),[5] things that are impossible with the dative-marked psych predicates.

(25)   *A Juan pararon de {faltarle / gustarle} las sillas.
        at Juan stopped of lack-him / like-him the chairs
        Intended: 'Juan does not lack / like chairs anymore.'

(26)   A Juan le   faltan   sillas en el despacho.
       at Juan him lack.3PL chairs in the office
       'Juan lacks chairs in the office.'

(27)   a. Cada vez que le   falta   su ayudante, Juan usa al   mío.
          each time that him lack.sg his assistant, Juan uses the mine
          'Whenever Juan assistant isn't there, he uses mine.'
       b. *Cada vez que le   gusta que venga, Juan me da   un beso.
          each time that him likes that I.come, Juan me gives a   kiss
          Intended: 'Whenever he is pleased that I come, Juan kisses me.'

Our claim is that *faltar*, and other verbs like it (*sobrar* 'to have too many', *quedarle bien algo* 'to have something fit someone well'), are not pure individual-level states because of the boundary contribution of the dative, which at least provides some information in addition to the stative body that the verb denotes. For explicitness, assume a structure like (28) for such verbs, with Init(iation)P as the stative head that relates the two entities. The dative-marked argument contributes the boundary and Init contributes the stative body.

---

[5]Note that here we avoid indefinite or non-specific arguments so as not to have them be taken as variables to license quantification over situations. In other words: *Whenever he likes a movie, she recommends it* does not quantify over time periods where the liking relation holds between one specific x and one specific y, but over situations where different y's (movies) produce different situations with respect to x.

(28)   InitP = [———

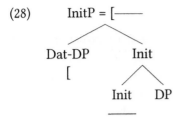

This means, then, that with a verb like *gustar*, where the dative is an experiencer, the boundary cannot be accessible for the verbal predicate. How do we obtain this result? The next section explains how.

3.2 Experiencers as covert P-locatives

Landau (2010) has argued that dative experiencers have more structure than it seems at first sight. Specifically, he has argued that they are introduced by a silent P. The initial evidence comes from a set of facts pointed out by Landau where experiencers behave differently from other internal arguments that should in principle be identical to them. (29) illustrates one such case: an apparently plain accusative argument cannot be anaphoric to the c-commanding subject if it is an experiencer.

(29)   a. John and Mary resemble each other.   non-experiencer
       b. *John and Mary concern each other.   experiencer

Experiencers are, in a sense, more isolated from their syntactic context than equivalent non-experiencer arguments. The following contrast, which to the best of our knowledge was first noticed by Alejo Alcaraz (p.c.), is an instance of the same general situation. With a verb like *venir* 'come', a dative can trigger a PCC violation in interaction with the subject (30a). However, the effect disappears if the verb is interpreted as a psych predicate (30b).[6]

(30)   a. *Nos   vinisteis tarde.
             us.DAT came.2PL late
           'You came late (and that affected us).'

---

[6]We are grateful to a second anonymous reviewer who pointed out to us that the choice of constructions we had at an initial stage could make the constraint be misinterpreted as an effect of possessive datives. Note that the structures with *venir* 'come' and *caer* 'fall' do not contain constituents which could be taken to be possessed by the dative argument.

b. Nos   vinisteis bien.
   us.DAT came.2PL well
   'You produced a positive effect on us.'

Similarly, compare *(Os) nos caísteis por las escaleras ('You fell down the stairs, and that affected us') with *Nos caísteis bien* ('You became dear to us'), or *Nos llegasteis tarde* 'You arrived late on us' with *Nos llegasteis al alma* 'You became dear to us'. The generalisation is that experiencer internal arguments are 'protected' by something that prevents them from checking features with the outside environment, something that at the same time avoids the PCC effect in (30) and blocks the anaphora in (29). Landau (2010) analyses internal argument experiencers as arguments of a silent P.

Thus, in contrast with (28), the structure of a dative-marked psych verb would be the one in (31), where the P makes the boundary denotation of the dative inaccessible. Thus, just the stative body (----) contributed by Init is relevant.

(31)   InitP = ——

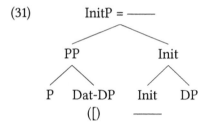

Even though datives denote boundaries, when they are projected as experiencers they are contained within a PP that isolates the aspectual contribution of the dative from the rest of the predicate. Stativity, then, is an epiphenomenon in which the experiencer structure prevents the dative from introducing primitives beyond what Init defines.

Similarly, we correctly expect that if there is a second internal argument beyond the dative – as was the case with dative + reflexive predicates – the result is not stative, because that second argument can add further aspectual information. It is just the dative that is unable to do so in experiencer contexts because it is contained within the prepositional structure.

What happens with accusative marked experiencers, such as the dynamic structures presented in §1? Crucially, Landau (2010) shows that these predicates are not psychological in the grammatical sense – they denote psych-eventualities conceptually, but their grammatical behaviour is identical to any other change of state verb in terms of aspectual contribution, binding, passivisation, etc. In other words, the argument conceptually interpreted as experiencer is an affected argument in such cases, and it is not introduced by a P layer because it is not an experiencer in grammatical or structural terms. It then receives whatever case the verb assigns to it, and makes the aspectual contribution expected from that case marking in the relevant syntactic position (cf. Royo 2020 [this volume] for an alternative view).

Finally, is it a matter of chance that the dative in our analysis appears only in the context of P in psychological verbs, or is there a more principled reason for this? In theory, any other case would have been treated in the same way under P, and would have been interpreted statively because of the role of P, so the deep connection cannot be in this sense. One property of datives vs. accusatives, however, makes it plausible that the dative would be the case that emerges when the argument is dissociated from the verb by a PP layer. In contrast to accusative, Spanish datives act as inherent case – for instance, in rejecting conversion to nominative in passive structures, so we expect that it will be the one to emerge compulsorily in cases where the verb does not establish a direct licensing relation with the argument, as it is with PP-embedded experiencer arguments.

Abbreviations

The abbreviations used in the glosses of this chapter follow the Leipzig Glossing Rules.

4 Conclusions

In this chapter we have argued that the right denotation for a dative is not a whole transfer or even the end-point of an intended transfer process, but rather the opposite: the initial orientation towards a goal, expressed through a left boundary [. We have shown that this denotation is more compatible with the marking facts in Spanish and the various uses of the dative in this language. We have furthermore argued that this boundary makes an aspectual contribution to the whole predicate, except for the case of psych predicates, which are purely stative. In such cases, we have argued that Landau (2010) is right in the claim that experiencers are protected by PP layers. This, we argued, explains the close relation between stativity and dative-marking in psych predicates.

References

Belletti, Adriana & Luigi Rizzi. 1988. Psych-verbs and θ-Theory. *Natural Language & Linguistic Theory* 6(3). 291–352. DOI:10.1007/BF00133902

Cabré, Teresa & Antonio Fábregas. 2020. Ways of being a dative across Romance varieties. In Anna Pineda & Jaume Mateu (eds.), *Dative constructions in Romance and beyond*, 395–411. Berlin: Language Science Press. DOI:10.5281/zenodo.3776565

Cifuentes Honrubia, José Luis. 2015. Causativity and psychological verbs in Spanish. In Elisa Barrajón López, José Luis Cifuentes Honrubia & Susana Rodríguez Rosique (eds.), *Verb classes and aspect*, 110–131. Amsterdam: John Benjamins.

Cuervo, María Cristina. 2003. *Datives at large*. Cambridge, MA: Massachusetts Institute of Technology. (Doctoral dissertation). https://dspace.mit.edu/handle/1721.1/7991.

Fábregas, Antonio. 2007. The Exhaustive Lexicalisation Principle. *Nordlyd* 34(2). 165–199. DOI:10.7557/12.110

Fábregas, Antonio & Rafael Marín. 2015. Deriving individual-level and stage-level psych verbs in Spanish. *The Linguistic Review* 32(2). 167–215. DOI:10.1515/tlr-2014-0022

Fábregas, Antonio, Ángel L. Jiménez Fernández & Mercedes Tubino. 2017. What's up with dative experiencers. In Ruth E. V. Lopes, Juanito Ornelas de Avelar & Sonia M. L. Cyrino (eds.), *Romance Languages and Linguistic Theory 12: Selected papers from the 45th Linguistic Symposium on Romance Languages (LSRL), Campinas, Brazil*, 29–48. Amsterdam & Philadelphia: John Benjamins.

Fernández Ordóñez, Inés. 1999. Leísmo, laísmo y loísmo. In Ignacio Bosque & Violeta Demonte (eds.), *Gramática descriptiva de la lengua española*, 1317–1398. Madrid: Esposa.

García Fernández, Luis, Ángeles Carrasco Gutiérrez, Bruno Camus Bergareche & María Martínez-Atienza. 2006. *Diccionario de perífrasis verbales*. Madrid: Gredos.

Jaque Hidalgo, Matías. 2014. *Causatividad y estatividad: Algunos ejemplos del español*. Madrid: Universidad Autónoma de Madrid. (Doctoral dissertation).

Kratzer, Angelika. 1995. Stage-level and individual-level predicates. In Gregory N. Carlson & Francis Jeffry Pelletier (eds.), *The generic book*, 125–175. Chicago, IL: University of Chicago Press.

Krifka, Manfred. 1989. Nominal reference, temporal constitution and quantification in event semantics. In Renate Bartsch, Johan van Benthem & Peter van Emde-Boas (eds.), *Semantics and contextual expressions*, 75–115. Dordrecht: Foris.

Landau, Idan. 2010. *The locative syntax of experiencers.* Cambridge, MA: MIT Press.

Marín, Rafael & Louise McNally. 2011. Inchoativity, change of state and telicity. *Natural Language and Linguistic Theory* 29. 467–502.

Medová, Lucie. 2009. *Reflexive clitics in the Slavic and Romance languages: A comparative view from an antipassive perspective.* Princeton, NJ: Princeton University. (Doctoral dissertation).

Næss, Åshild. 2009. Varieties of dative. In Andrej L. Malchukov & Andrew Spencer (eds.), *The Oxford handbook of case*, 572–581. Oxford: Oxford University Press.

Pineda, Anna. 2016. *Les fronteres de la (in)transitivitat: Estudi dels aplicatius en llengües romàniques i basc.* Barcelona: Institut d'Estudis Món Juïc. Published and revised version of the doctoral dissertation.

Pineda, Anna. 2020. From dative to accusative: An ongoing syntactic change in Romance. *Probus: International Journal of Romance Linguistics* 32(1). 129–173.

Piñón, Christopher. 1997. Achievements in an event semantics. In Aaron Lawson (ed.), *Proceedings of Semantics and Linguistic Theory (SALT) VII*, 276–293. Ithaca, NY: CLC Publications.

Ramchand, Gillian. 2008. *Verb meaning and the lexicon: A first phase syntax.* Cambridge: Cambridge University Press.

Real Academia de la Lengua Española (RAE & Asociación de Academias de la Lengua Española (ASALE). 2009. *Nueva gramática de la lengua española.* Madrid: Espasa.

Romero, Juan. 1997. *Construcciones de doble objeto y gramática universal.* Madrid: Universidad Autónoma de Madrid. (Doctoral dissertation).

Royo, Carles. 2020. The accusative/dative alternation in Catalan verbs with experiencer object. In Anna Pineda & Jaume Mateu (eds.), *Dative constructions in Romance and beyond*, 371–393. Berlin: Language Science Press. DOI:10.5281/zenodo.3776563

Tenny, Carol L. 1987. *Grammaticalizing aspect and affectedness.* Cambridge, MA: Massachusetts Institute of Technology. (Doctoral dissertation).

Part III

Applicatives

Chapter 10

The lexical underspecification of Bantu causatives and applicatives

Mattie Wechsler

This paper presents original evidence for an additional merge location and semantic interpretation of Bantu applicatives, drawing on complex multiply applicativized and causativized constructions for empirical support. The paper also identifies and discusses challenging data from Bantu causatives. Previous analyses of causative and applicative constructions in the world's languages have enumerated different kinds of causative and applicative heads, stored separately in the lexicon, each with their own particular selectional requirements.

As the number of attested structural positions, potential complements, and semantic interpretations for these heads grow in the literature, however, the model bloats and becomes less compelling. I ultimately adopt a recent analysis from Wood & Marantz (2017) and assert that a single underspecified argument introducer is sufficient to account for the Bantu data I present. In order to accommodate the new theory of argument introduction, I also propose a new, more semantically-oriented, model of causative complement selection.

1 Introduction

For my analysis, I assume that even in languages without explicit applicative morphology, applicative argument-introducing heads are responsible for the additional arguments in dative/ditransitive/double-object constructions. Therefore, while this paper occurs in the applicative section of a volume on dative structures, my analysis will not make use of, or rely on, this distinction.

In this paper I argue that evidence from Bantu supports a model with fewer argument introducers available in the lexicon than previous accounts (most prominently, Pylkkänen 2008) have suggested. My analysis makes heavy use of Wood

Mattie Wechsler. 2020. The lexical underspecification of Bantu causatives and applicatives. In Anna Pineda & Jaume Mateu (eds.), *Dative constructions in Romance and beyond*, 241–271. Berlin: Language Science Press.
DOI:10.5281/zenodo.3776551

& Marantz's (2017) work, which argues similarly for a radically reduced inventory of argument-introducing heads.

In §2, I present challenging data from Bantu causatives. Ultimately, I argue that causatives are underspecified for categorial complement selection, and I propose an original treatment of cross-linguistic variation in causative constructions.

In §3, I structure my analysis around the assumption that all applicatives are underlyingly the same as one another, as well as all other non-core argument introducers. I demonstrate that the same applicative surface structure often corresponds to multiple underlying structures, and I also present original evidence for an additional applicative merge-location in Shona.

In §4, I acknowledge a few sticking points in the analysis, speculate about some unanswered questions, and identify fruitful areas for further research on the topics and issues plumbed in this paper.

2 Causatives

2.1 Data from Bantu

Consider the following:

(1) Shona

    a. Tinotenda a-nyur-a.
        1.Tinotenda sm1-drown-FV
        'Tinotenda drowned.'

    b. * Tinotenda a-nyur-a   ne-kuda.
          1.Tinotenda sm1-drown-FV with-love
         'Tinotenda drowned intentionally.'

    c. Tinotenda a-nyur-is-a   Tatenda ne-kuda.
        1.Tinotenda sm1-drown-CAUS-FV 1.Tatenda with-love
        'Tinotenda drowned Tatenda intentionally.'

(2) Shona

    a. Tinotenda a-ka-yimb-a   ne-kuda.
        1.Tinotenda sm1-PST-sing-FV with-love
        'Tinotenda sang intentionally.'

b. Tinotenda a-ka-yimb-is-a   Tatenda ne-kuda.
   1.Tinotenda sm1-pst-sing-caus-fv 1.Tatenda with-love
   i.'Tinotenda intentionally made Tatenda sing.'
   ii. *'Tinotenda made Tatenda intentionally sing.'

In (1) causativization appears to "add" an Agent to a structure without one.[1] Superficially, (2) looks the same. In (2), however, only the Causer is an Agent, which would imply that causativization in one case entails the "addition" of an Agent and in another, both the "addition" and "subtraction" of an Agent.

It is difficult to ascribe a single syntactic function to Shona causatives, because the differences exhibited between causative constructions and their non-causative counterparts are not consistent. Pylkkänen (2008) grapples with the same conundrum, but cross-linguistically. Her typological proposal distinguishes two variables, merge height and a property she calls VOICE-BUNDLING. Causatives either select as their complement VoiceP (PHASE-SELECTING), vP (VERB-SELEC-TING), or the verb root √ (ROOT-SELECTING). Additionally, causatives are either of the Voice-bundling type, meaning that they merge with Voice to create a single Agent-introducing head, or they are of the Non-Voice-bundling type, meaning that they merge as a free head in the structure and are not syntactically bound to Voice.

For Pylkkänen (and for my analysis), causatives are not argument introducers. They introduce a causative meaning and a syntactic relationship between an Agent (introduced by Voice) and the event conveyed by the verb phrase. Pylkkänen makes this distinction because some languages allow causative constructions without an overt Causer role. In languages with the Voice-bundling type of causative, however, this split is all but irrelevant because Voice-bundled causatives constitute a single Causer-introducing head.

Because verb-selecting causatives merge below Voice, and Voice is the only head that introduces Agents, the subject is the only agentive argument. Phase-selecting causatives are merged above Voice and allow for two agentive arguments. Agent-oriented modification of the Causee diagnoses the merge loca-

---

[1]In describing causative alternations, it is easy to lean on metaphor that conflates theory. Within the theoretical framework of this paper, it is not considered to be the case that causative constructions are formed by applying a transformational causative process to an already generated non-causative sentence. When I discuss what a causative head "adds to" or "subtracts from" a structure, I'm not referring to the cognitive process of causativization as it occurs in a speaker's mind when their native grammar generates a causative construction, but to the comparison of two already generated sentences in an alternation. For literal descriptions of grammatical processes, I use words like "introduce" or "merge".

tion of the causative. The possible interpretations in (2) show that Shona causative constructions have only one agentive argument and therefore do not merge above Voice. In this respect, Shona is unlike Venda, which according to Pylkkänen has phase-selecting causatives:

(3) Venda (Pylkkänen 2008: 83)
     Muuhambadz o-reng-is-a   Katonga modoro nga dzangalelo.
     1.salesman SM1-buy-CAUS-FV 1.Katonga 9.car   with 10.enthusiasm
     i. 'The salesman eagerly made Katonga buy the car.'
     ii. 'The salesman made Katonga eagerly buy the car.'

In (3) 'eagerly' can modify either 'the salesman' or 'Katonga', therefore indicating that in Venda causatives merge above Voice.

Pylkkänen's typology offers an explanation for the difference between (2) and (3), but it leaves an important question unanswered: what head introduces the non-agentive Causee when Voice introduces Agents exclusively? Causative constructions with non-agentive Causees are cross-linguistically common (Kulikov 2001; Kittilä 2013), so this gap in the theory is not insignificant. Pylkkänen acknowledges this shortfall but does not seek to address it in her analysis (2008:107). I do seek to address it, and I propose a solution in §2.2

While this structural puzzle does not apply to languages with phase-selecting causatives, like Venda, such languages do pose a related problem:

(4) Venda Pylkkänen (2008: 2)

     a. Mahada o-nok-a.
         6.snow SM1-melt-FV
         'The snow melted.'

     b. Mukasa o-nok-is-a   mahada.
         1.Mukasa SM1-melt-CAUS-FV 6.snow
         'Mukasa melted the snow.'

Venda's phase-selecting causative supposedly needs to merge with Voice, but Voice is not present in the Agent-lacking unaccusative construction in (4).

The data in (3)-(4) shows that in both Venda and Shona causatives merge with more than one kind of complement. Furthermore, flexible selectional requirements do not appear to be atypical of Bantu causatives:

(5) Bemba (Givón 1969, 329: 18 via Pylkkänen 2008: 115)
Naa-mu-fu-und-ishya   uku-laanda iciBemba ku-mufulo.
SM1-PST-OM1-learn-CAUS-FV INF-speak 4.Bemba on-purpose
i. 'I, on purpose, made him learn to speak Bemba.'
ii. *'I made him on purpose learn to speak Bemba.'

(6) Bemba (Givón 1969: 155)

a. Aba-Bemba ba-ali-ful-a.
all-2.Bemba SM2-PROG-multiply-FV
'The Bemba people multiplied.'

b. Leesa a-a-fu-shy-a   aba-Bemba.
1.God SM1-PST-multiply-CAUS-FV all-2.Bemba
'God multiplied the Bemba people.'

Bemba demonstrates the same variation in causative complement selection as Shona, embedding unaccusative structures, as well as non-agentive external arguments in unergative and transitive verb phrases.

Kim (2011) argues that in causativized transitive and unergative structures, non-agentive Causees are introduced by unpronounced high applicative heads (see §3 for a detailed explanation of low and high APPL). This proposal is economical in that high applicative heads are available in the lexicon of Bantu languages (and Korean, from which Kim draws her evidence for the solution), they merge in between Voice and the verb, and they are associated with non-agentive arguments. Furthermore, though it is irrelevant to the Bantu data, Korean Causees are dative arguments, that is, they pattern with the distribution and morphological marking of applied/indirect objects, such as Benefactives and Recipients (Kim 2011).[2]

In Pylkkänen's model of argument introduction, however, these various causative heads are all separate lexical items, specified each for a particular selec-

---

[2]Although Bantu does not have any morphological case marking, I want to take this opportunity to clarify this paper's stance on abstract Case in Bantu. I do not adopt the recent analysis from Diercks (2012), who argues that Bantu languages parametrically opt out of abstract Case-licensing en masse. I assume that the arguments in my Bantu data require abstract Case-licensing (see van der Wal 2015; Sheehan & van der Wal 2016; Halpert 2012, and Wechsler 2014; 2016 for evidence of Case features in Bantu). I am unable to devote the analysis in this paper towards identifying a licensing head for each argument, but I consider further research into i^*'s role in Case-licensing to be an important next step in assessing the utility and feasibility of this analysis.

tional requirement, and acquired by any given language from a universal inventory. Kim's proposal adds another head (two, if it also comes in Voice-bundling and Non-Voice-bundling varieties), an applicative-selecting causative, to both Pylkkänen's universal inventory, and to any given language with causative diversity similar to that of Shona and Bemba. The resulting system is congested, and I assert that the causative data in (1)-(6) provide an opportunity to simplify both the lexicons of the individual languages as well as the universal inventory.

Rather than an inventory of 6–8 distinct causative heads, from which many languages would have to select multiple items to account for their range of causative diversity, I argue that causative heads specified for a maximum complement size offer a better solution. This proposal captures the fact that causativized unnaccusative structures occur both in languages with Voice-selecting and verb/applicative-selecting causatives, despite unaccusatives apparently contradicting selectional requirements for larger complements. The notion that causatives have an upper-limit, rather than one categorial mandate is intuitive, and my analysis is reminiscent of a similar proposal, made by Haspelmath (2016) involving his concept of the "spontaneity scale".

Section §2.2 focuses on clarifying this paper's treatment of argument introducers, drawing heavily on Wood & Marantz (2017). Their proposal has serious implications for the mechanics involved in causative complement selection, but by building on the notion of "complement size" and formulating a more specific definition of that concept, I am able to better accommodate both the new theory and the data. I also use Wood & Marantz's analysis to make a proposal about the identity of the head responsible for introducing non-agentive Causees in constructions like those in (2) and (6).

2.2 Wood & Marantz's i^*

Wood & Marantz (2017) assert that all non-core arguments in any language are introduced by the same underspecified head, "i^*". They provide a distinct syntactic structure for Voice, low and high applicative heads, and prepositional heads, little p and big P, arguing that if syntax can account for the difference between these semantically varying instances of argument introduction, then it is redundant to have the lexicon store categorially separate heads.

Voice is simply the product of i^* merging with the verbalizing head little v and allowing for the introduction of an external agentive argument. Figure 1, adapted from their work (2017: 261), demonstrates this structure.

While i^* **can** introduce an Agent following its merge with little v, it can also have an expletive interpretation and introduce non-agentive external arguments.

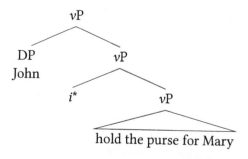

Figure 1: Wood & Marantz's *i** introducing an Agent

The meaning of *i** can be computed in one of two ways at the syntax-semantics interface. Either *i** can imbue a relation implied by the semantics of its complement between the argument it introduces and that complement (non-expletive), or alternatively it can provide only a means for structural insertion, contributing no semantic "glue" to assist in integrating the argument it introduces (expletive).

The expletive interpretation is only available when an alternative strategy of semantic integration exists. The Japanese adversity causative, reproduced from Wood & Marantz in (7), demonstrates this point.

(7) Japanese (Wood & Marantz 2017: 274)
      Taroo-ga musuko-o si-ase-ta.
      Taro-NOM son-ACC die-CAUS-PST
      i. 'Taro caused his son to die.'
      ii. 'Taro's son died on him.'

The second possible meaning in (7), where *Taro* is negatively affected by his son's death (but crucially does not play any role in bringing it about), is the adversity causative interpretation. The event of Taro's son's death does not necessitate an agentive participant, so *i** need not necessarily (though it may, as in the first interpretation of (7)) relate an Agent to that event. As a non-agentive affectee, the DP *Taroo-ga* must be semantically integrated into the structure by some mechanism. Wood & Marantz argue that, in a structure similar to possessor-raising, *Taroo* is introduced by expletive *i**, but integrated by saturating a possessor role generated lower down in the DP *musuko-o*. This structure, adapted from a similar rendering in Wood & Marantz (2017: 274), is approximated in (8).

(8) [*Taroo* [*i** [$_{vP}$ *die*-CAUS [$_{DP}$ POSSESSOR *son*]]]]

The arrow in (8) represents the relationship between the possessor role and the argument *Taroo* that saturates it. This relationship is mandatory in the adversity causative interpretation. If *musuko* is implied to be another person's son, then *Taroo* has no semantic integration strategy besides merging as an agentive Causer role.

With *i** as the only introducer of non-core arguments, the answer to the previous question about the identity of the introducer responsible for non-agentive Causees is quite straightforward: *i** introduces all Causees, and I assume that when Causees are non-agentive, *i** manifests its expletive interpretation. However, the question remains: why are Causees obligatorily non-agentive in languages like Shona and Bemba to begin with? Pylkkänen's typology no longer represents a viable explanation, because collapsing the entire canonical argument-introducing infrastructure into a single functional head removes much of the machinery used to describe causative diversity in previous analyses: Agents, high applicative arguments, and non-agentive Causees are rendered categorially equivalent in terms of complement selection. This challenge is exemplified by the nearly identical structures for the Shona construction in (2) and the Venda construction in (3), provided sans adjunct in Figure 2.

The only difference between the structures in Figure 2 (besides the presence of a DO) is that the lower *i** in the Venda sentence, which introduces the Agent, *Katonga*, is non-expletive, and the lower *i** in the Shona sentence, which introduces the non-Agent, *Tatenda*, is expletive.

2.3 Thematic weight

In §2.1, I argued that causatives have a maximum "complement size" restriction, rather than a specific categorial mandate. I propose now that the "size" of a complement is determined by what I call THEMATIC WEIGHT. Thematic weight is the sum of the thematic value of every (non-prepositional) nominal argument in a given constituent. I quantify the thematic value of an argument based on its semantic role, with Agents having the highest value and Themes (or Patients) having the lowest. Thematic hierarchies have been proposed by many authors (Jackendoff 1972, Belletti & Rizzi 1988, and Grimshaw 1990, to name a few) and while these proposals differ in a number of ways, I follow the general consensus and assume the broad ordering in (9) is sufficient.

(9) Agent>Experiencer/Goal>Theme/Patient

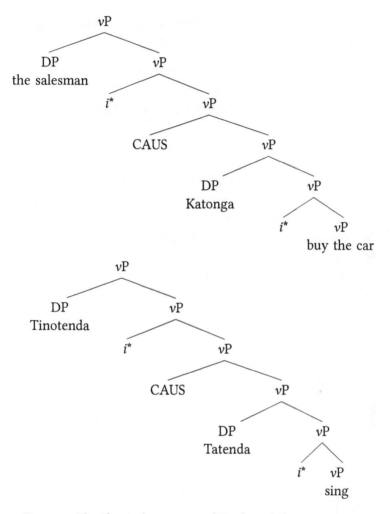

Figure 2: The identical structures of Venda and Shona causatives

In §2.1 I demonstrated that Causees can occur in any of the three thematic tiers in (9). In the Venda sentence in (3) the Causee is an Agent, in the Shona sentence in (2) the Causee is an Experiencer,[3] and in the Bemba sentence in (6) the Causee

---

[3]The traditional definition of "Experiencer" is not a perfect fit for non-agentive Causees of this variety, but because I want to avoid getting bogged down in the profligate lists of thematic relations available in the literature, and also because, for my analysis, the hierarchical tier is more important than the role itself, I consider the imprecision of this and other thematic labels to be acceptable compromises at the present.

is a Patient. For the purposes of calculating thematic weight, I assign numerical values to each of the thematic tiers from (9) in Table 1.

Table 1: Numerical values of thematic roles

Agent	Experiencer/Goal/Benefactive	Theme/Patient
3	1	0

Note that these values are stipulative. Multiple authors, Wunderlich (1997) and Mylne (1999) among them, have proposed feature-based decompositions of thematic roles, and more targeted research of this sort could provide a path towards an improved formalization of thematic weight. Furthermore, it is quite possible that the relative weightiness of these roles, as well as which properties and features are grammaticalized as weighty, represents a source of parametric variation. Therefore, the values in Table 1 are merely a starting point.

I propose that Shona causative heads take complements with a maximum thematic weight of 2, and that Venda causatives take complements with a maximum thematic weight of 4 (or potentially more[4]). Therefore, any complement with an Agent is too thematically heavy for a Shona causative to embed. When i^* introduces non-agentive Causees in unergative and transitive constructions in Shona, it has an expletive interpretation because otherwise it would introduce an Agent, which would render the complement incompatible with the weight limit of Shona causatives. I also assume that the causative head introduces a Causee and Causer role, and that the Causee role provides the semantic pretense necessary for the expletively-introduced non-Agentive Causee to be integrated into the construction.

My thematic weight proposal is far more semantically motivated than previous treatments of complement selection in causative constructions. The Shona sentences in (10) help justify this departure.

---

[4]I propose the maximum thematic weight of 3 for complements of Shona causatives based partially on Wechsler (2014), which explores limitations on the total number of arguments Shona verbs are able to sustain. Without data on the extent to which Venda allows co-occurring causative and applicative heads, I am unable to make an equally precise claim about its causative complement selection.

(10) Shona

    a. Tinotenda   a-ka-donh-es-es-a   Tatenda poto ye-mvura.
       1.Tinotenda sm1-pst-fall-CAUS-CAUS-FV 1.Tatenda 9.pot POSS-9.water
       'Tinotenda made Tatenda drop the water pot.' (Literally: 'Tinotenda
       made Tatenda make the water pot fall.')

    b. Tinotenda   a-ka-dy-is-is-a   mwana chipunhu.
       1.Tinotenda sm1-pst-eat-CAUS-CAUS-FV 1.child   7.spoon
       'Tinotends fed the child with a spoon.' (Literally: 'Tinotenda made
       spoon make the child eat.')

    c. ? Tinotenda   a-ka-tamba-is-is-a   Tatenda Tendai.
       1.Tinotenda sm1-pst-dance-CAUS-CAUS-FV 1.Tatenda 1.Tendai
       'Tinotenda made Tatenda make Tendai dance.'

Each of the sentences in (10) are double-causative constructions. Although *poto yemvura*, 'water pot' is the Causee of the first causative in (10a), it is also the internal argument of the verb and a prototypical Patient so its thematic value is 0. The second Causee *Tatenda* is a non-agentive Experiencer and its thematic value is 1, making the thematic weight of each complement acceptably light for both causatives to embed. (10b) demonstrates that Shona, like Kinyarwanda, exhibits causative-instrumental syncretism (Kimenyi 1980; 1995; Peterson 2007; Jerro 2013). I follow Jerro (2013) and assume that instrumental-causative constructions are not fundamentally different from other causatives. The verb in (10b) is transitive, but with its internal argument omitted, rendering the structure essentially identical to the doubly-causativized unegative in (10c). However, (10b) is completely grammatical, whereas (10c) is borderline acceptable at best. The problem is thematic weight. In (10b), the first Causee, *mwana*, 'the child,' is non-agentive and has a thematic value of 1, as does the second Causee, *chipunhu*, 'the spoon.' The first causative's complement has a thematic weight of 1, and the second causative's complement has a thematic weight of 2, so neither causative is overburdened and the sentence is grammatical and felicitous. In (10c), however, it is unintuitive to interpret an animate Causer such as *Tatenda*, as non-agentive, and if *Tatenda* is an Agent, then the thematic weight of the second causative's complement is 4, which is far too heavy for a Shona causative head to embed. Although it is unintuitive that *Tatenda* would be non-agentive, it is not impossible. Narrative context that firmly establishes both *Tatenda* and *Tendai* as non-agentive drastically improves the sentences' acceptability for my consultants,[5] which further supports my claim that causative selectional restrictions are thematically motivated. While thematic weight may not be the whole story, the sentences in (10) provide strong evidence that some formalized measure of thematic prominence is likely a significant part of the explanation.

2.4 i^*-bundling

In addition to complement selection, Pylkkänen's causatives are distinguished by a "Voice-bundling" toggle. I assert that this property, which I reconceive as i^*-bundling, is the product of the causative head merging directly with i^* before merging into the rest of the structure. The result is that the new compound CAUS-i^* possesses the selectional requirements of both the causative head and of i^*. The compound takes an initial complement according to its inherent thematic weight limit, and because i^* selects for the category D (Wood & Marantz 2017: 257) and has not yet had its selectional feature checked, an external argument must be introduced. It is not a property of i^* that it forces a merge with a nominal argument (Wood & Marantz 2017: 257), but I argue that when its features bundle with causatives, the resulting structure either mandates the introduction of an agentive external argument or closes off the extended projection of the verbal domain such that no other argument can be merged and semantically integrated. While complement selection constrains what causatives can embed, i^*-bundling essentially constrains what can embed causatives.

Pylkkänen (2008) classifies English causatives as "root-selecting" and "Voice-bundling", so under this analysis an i^*-bundling causative that can take complements with a maximum thematic weight of 0. An English causative cannot embed unergative or transitive roots, because once it has merged, there is no room for anything except the Causer. Because it is non-i^*-bundling, the Japanese causative can occur with unergative and transitive roots, despite it also having a maximum complement weight of 0:

(11) Japanese (Pylkkänen 2008: 120)
      John-ga   kodomo-o nak-asi-ta.
      John-NOM child-ACC cry-CAUS-PST
      'John made the child cry.'

Figure 3 demonstrates the proposed structure of the sentence in (11)

---

[5]I used a story where Tatenda was under a spell and Tendai was the name of a puppet.

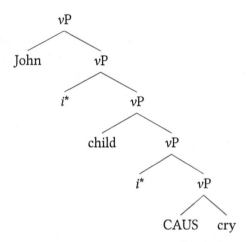

Figure 3: The structure of a causativized unergative in Japanese

Figure 3 reveals a problem: the current theory does not prevent the lower i^* from manifesting non-expletively and introducing an agentive Causee. Like in Shona, Causees in Japanese are non-agentive (Pylkkänen 2008: 107), so in order not to over-generate, this model needs an additional component. I suggest that the first agentive argument to merge above a causative head automatically saturates the Causer role it introduces, closing the structure off to possible Causees. The 'child' is therefore non-agentive, because in order to be the Causee and not the Causer, it must be.

Pylkkänen (2008) asserts that Bemba causatives cannot embed high applicative arguments because they are "verb-selecting" and high applicatives are phase heads, but this conclusion conflicts with the fact that Shona's "verb-selecting" causatives can embed high applicatives. Pylkkänen cites a Bemba construction where the causative scopes over the applicative and does not address whether or not Bemba also prohibits constructions in which the applicative scopes over the causative. My proposal can account for both of these possibilities, while also accounting for Shona.

If Bemba allows applicatives to embed causatives, but not vice-versa, its causative selects for complements with a maximum thematic weight of 1 and does not bundle with i^*. In this scenario, the causative can embed no more than its non-agentive Causee and a weightless Theme/Patient, which is why complements with Benefactives and co-occurring non-agentive Causees are too heavy. Because the occasion of the causative's merge does not mandate the immediate introduction of the Causer, however, high applicatives are able to scope over causatives.

If Bemba completely prohibits causative-applicative co-occurrence, its causative head selects for complements with a maximum thematic weight of 1 and bundles with i^*. The causative head is unable to embed applied objects for the same reason as before, but because this causative also necessarily triggers the introduction of an agentive Causer, there is no position for the high applicative to merge and embed it.

In Hiaki, an Uto-Aztecan language, causatives can embed high applicatives, but high applicatives cannot embed causatives (Jung 2014). An i^*-bundling causative head that takes complements with a maximum thematic weight of 2 would be consistent with this causative-applicative co-occurrence pattern. This causative head would be able to embed complements as large as a non-agentive Causee and an applied object together, but if it were also i^*-bundling, applicatives would not be able to embed it, because it would be immediately followed by the introduction of an agentive Causer. Since a thorough engagement with Jung (2014) would represent too large a digression, however, all this is merely conjecture, based solely on the scopal possibilities of cooccurring causative-applicative constructions.

Overall, my proposal, with its three main components, complement selection based on thematic weight, i^*-bundling, and the first-Agent-is-the-Causer rule, is both flexible and constrained enough to account for a range of causative variation.

3 Applicatives

3.1 Pylkkänen's typology

Since Pylkkänen first proposed her high-low typology of applicatives in 2002, many authors have suggested that this binary theory is not enough to capture the range of applicative argument introduction in the world's languages (Jeong 2007; Peterson 2007; Georgala et al. 2008; Cuervo 2003; 2010; 2012; 2015; Tsai 2009; Kim 2011; 2012; Georgala 2012). In Cuervo's overview at the beginning of this volume, she presents evidence that far more complexity is necessary to describe the world's dative and applicative diversity. She proposes a rich typology that takes into account the many kinds of structures that applicatives embed, as well as the many kinds of structures that embed applicatives. It is also my view that Pylkkänen's model is not fully comprehensive, and in this section, I argue that high and low merge locations are not sufficient to describe the range of applicative constructions in and outside of Bantu.

Pylkkänen (2008) proposes that there are HIGH and LOW applicatives. High applicatives are functional heads that introduce and license non-core arguments merged above the verb and below Voice, relating the applied argument to an event. High applicatives often convey the notion of a favor, where the applied object, prototypically (though not always) a Benefactive, is positively impacted by the entire set of circumstances described by the verb:

(12) Shona
Musikana a-ka-chek-er-a   baba   uswa.
1.girl   SM1-PST-cut-APPL-FV 1a.father 14.grass
'The girl cut grass for the father.'

Low applicatives introduce and license a non-core argument merged below the verb and relate the applied argument to the verb's DO. This structure is often interpreted as a transfer of possession:

(13) Shona
Mai   va-p-a   vana   bhuku.
2b.mother SM2b-give-FV 2.children 5.book
'The mother gave the children a book.'

For Wood & Marantz, low applicatives are the result of *i** merging with the internal argument of a verb and introducing another argument interpreted to be the internal argument's possessor. This merge location is wholly unique to low applicative constructions, so no disambiguating mechanics are necessary; if *i** merges directly with a nominal argument inside a VP, it always has a low applicative interpretation (see Figure 4).

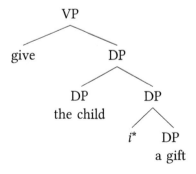

Figure 4: Partial structure of the low APPL *construction 'Miriam gave the children a gift.'*

High applicatives involve the root-adjunction structure I mentioned in my explanation of *i**-bundling in §2.2. Because the structural position of high applicatives is the same as Voice, Wood & Marantz distinguish external arguments with
high applicative interpretations from external arguments with agentive (or expletive) interpretations, by proposing that before merging with the verb, applicative
heads merge with a root that essentially has the meaning of the preposition *for*.
In another paper from this collection, Calindro, who also deploys the underspecified *i** head in her analysis, argues that a curious diachronic shift has occurred in
Brazilian Portuguese. The language lacks a lexical root of the kind described by
Wood & Marantz, but Calindro presents evidence that speakers have innovated a
construction where *i** merges with an existing preposition before that combined
constituent merges with the verb phrase, a structure nearly identical to the one
Wood & Marantz propose for applicatives (see Figure 5).

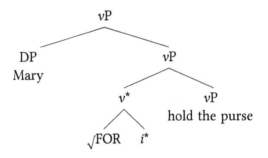

Figure 5: Partial structure of the high APPL *construction 'John held the
purse for Mary.'*

In §3.2, I discuss different interpretations of the same applicative surface structure.

3.2 Applicative allosemy

The sentence in (14) has three distinct interpretations.

(14)   Shona
    Mai   va-ka-bik-ir-a   mwana chikafu.
    2b.mother SM2b-PST-cook-APPL-FV 1.child 7.food
    i. 'The mother cooked the child food.'
    ii. 'The mother cooked food for the child.'
    iii. 'The mother cooked the food instead of the child.'

Distinguishing between all three meanings is difficult, but narrative context allows for clearer elicitation and explanation of the data. Below are three narratives I used with my consultant to determine that each of these interpretations are valid and possible.

(15)   **Recipient**
       The child was hungry and unable to feed herself. Her *mother cooked the child food* and she (the child) ate it.

In this interpretation, the applicative defines a relationship between the food the mother cooked and the child. The child receives and then possesses the food.

(16)   **Benefactive**
       The child was old enough to learn how to cook. She wanted to watch her mother prepare her favorite dish. The mother complied with this wish and *cooked the food for the child* so that she could learn.

In this interpretation, the applicative defines a relationship between the child and the event of the food being cooked. The child benefits from the event in a way that does not semantically necessitate the food entering her possession.

(17)   **Substitutive**
       The child was supposed to cook dinner for the family, but she was sick and unable to fulfill her responsibility. The mother helped and *cooked the food instead of the child*, such that she did not have to cook the food.

The allosemy in (15) and (16) is not well accounted for in the literature. Bantu languages have been analyzed as having both (high) applicative derivational morphology and (low) applicative lexical ditransitive constructions (van der Wal 2017). While it is true that all of Bantu's rare ditransitive roots have low applicative interpretations,[6] it is not true that all applicative morphology corresponds to high applicative semantics. I assume that low meaning coincides with low syntax, and that high meaning coincides with high syntax, regardless of surface level representation. Why some low applicative constructions have applicative morphology and some do not is an important question, one that I am unfortunately unable to answer in this paper. Despite these issues, the syntactic distinction between the Recipient and Benefactive meanings in (15) and (16) is commonly acknowledged. The structure behind the substitutive interpretation, however, is

---

[6]Rare because many canonical ditransitives such as 'show,' 'tell,' or 'send' are conveyed using applicative or causative constructions.

not well established in the literature, so I justify my choice to classify it as semantically and structurally distinct from other high applicatives in §3.3.

3.3 Super-high applicatives

Marten & Kula (2014) suggest a SUPER-HIGH applicative in Bemba with substitutive semantics, distinguished morphologically by the locative clitic =*kó*:

(18)   Bemba (Marten & Kula 2014: 22)
        Ábá-icé   bá-lée-tólók-el-a=kó   bá-mayó.
        2.children SM2-PROG-jump-APPL-FV=LC17 2.mother
        'The children are jumping for/on behalf of the mother.'

Shona is like Bemba and has a morphological strategy for indicating substitutive semantics:

(19)   Shona
        Tinotenda   a-ka-bik-ir-ir-a   Tatenda   chikafu.
        1.Tinotenda SM1-PST-cook-APPL-APPL-FV 1.Tatenda 7.food
        'Tinotenda cooked food instead of Tatenda.'

The doubled applicative affix in (19) is the clearest way to express this interpretation in Shona, but the substitutive meaning can be interpreted from a single
applicative (demonstrated in (14)). There are also double applicative structures
where each affix indicates a separate instance of applicativization, and two applicative arguments are introduced (see the discussion of (20) later in this section
for an example).

I adopt Marten's (2016) proposal that the substitutive applicative is super-high
because it merges above Voice. In Figure 6, I demonstrate this structure using i^*
to introduce all external arguments.

I assert that super-high applicatives merge first with the same 'for' root as high
applicatives. The semantic contributions of high and super-high applicatives are
similar, in that they both broadly designate the applicative arguments as entities
positively impacted by their complements. Therefore, in combination with the
fact that the structural positions of high and super-high applicatives are distinct,
I argue the same root is sufficient.

Kim (2011; 2012) also argues for an applicative merge location above Voice
(above the external most argument introduced by i^* in the terms of this analysis). Kim proposes that in Japanese adversity causatives (which I discussed in

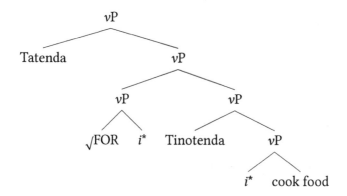

Figure 6: Structure of the super-high APPL construction in (19)

§2.2) and Korean adversity passives, which are very similar to Japanese adversity causatives, an applicative head she calls "peripheral APPL" merges very high above all other external arguments and introduces affectee arguments that are the syntactic subjects of their clauses. I assume that, given the similarity between the two structures, Wood & Marantz's account of Japanese adversity causatives is a suitable account of Korean adversity passives as well. Kim's proposed merge location for peripheral APPL is motivated primarily by word order: the affectee is the syntactic subject of the construction by virtue of preceding the verb (Korean and Japanese are SOV). In my analysis, the arguments introduced by super-high applicatives are not syntactic subjects and word order is a challenge for the theory, rather than supporting evidence. While I am not able to resolve the issue of word order here,[7] I do motivate my proposed structural position for super-high applicatives with a variety of evidence.

Empirical support for the super-high applicative's super-high merge location in Shona comes from three sources. First, the substitutive semantics relate the applied object, the Substitutee, to the Agent and the entire event in which it participates, indicating that the complement of the applicative root-adjoined i^* is large, including the verb phrase and its external argument. Second, binding data in double-applicative constructions where there is one substitutive applicative

---

[7]In addition to leaving the derivation of word order to future work, I also beg off the topic of affix ordering. Most Bantu languages have a strict templatic ordering of causative and applicative affixes (Good 2005), and many display causative-applicative co-occurrence with ambiguous scope (Baker 1985; Hyman 2002). It suffices to say that given variable semantic interpretations and the fact that the causatives and applicatives have to concatenate onto the verb stem apart from the arguments they introduce, movement is necessary to derive these surface structures. Movement is not, however, a part of this analysis.

and one high applicative support the structurally higher placement of the substitutive.

(20) Shona

    a. Shiri ya-ka-yimb-ir-ir-a   mai$_i$ wese ari mu-taundi
        9.bird SM9-PST-sing-APPL-APPL-FV 2b.mother$_i$ every in 18-9.town
        mwana wake$_i$.
        child   POSS$_i$
        'The bird sang for her$_i$ child instead of every mother$_i$ in town.'

    b. * Shiri ya-ka-yimb-ir-ir-a   mai   wake$_i$ mwana$_i$ wese
        9.bird SM9-PST-sing-APPL-APPL-FV 2b.mother POSS$_i$ child$_i$ every
        ari mu-taundi.
        in 18-9.town
        'The bird sang for every child$_i$ in town instead of her$_i$ mother.'

In (20), the Substitutee ('the mother') is able to bind the Benefactive ('the child') of the singing event enacted by the Substitute ('the bird'), but in (20), the Benefactive is unable to bind the Substitutee, indicating that the Substitutee is in a higher structural position than the Benefactive.

I discuss the third source of empirical evidence, which comes from scopal interactions in cooccurring causative-applicative construction, in §3.4.

3.4 Applicative-causative cooccurrence

Wechsler (2016) concludes that there are four hypothetical scopal interactions in a construction where both an applicative and a causative affix to an unergative stem. They are illustrated with English examples and tree diagrams in Figures 7–9.

Previously, I stated that the structural positions of high and super-high applicatives were complementary, but the implementation of i^* flattens the landscape of structural diversity that anchors the differentiation between the two structures. Super-high applicatives embed external arguments, but Figure 8 demonstrates that high applicatives can embed non-agentive Causees, which are also external arguments, so it is necessary to establish the structural or semantic context that distinguishes super-high from high. I assert that when applicative root-adjoined i^* merges directly above an agentive argument introduced by non-expletive i^*, it is interpreted as having substitutive semantics.

Three of the interpretations in Figures 7–10 are possible in Shona. The prohibited interpretation provides the additional evidence I promised in §2.3. Because

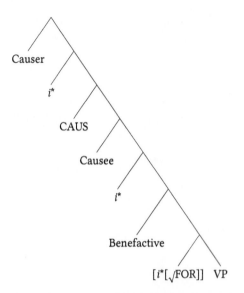

Figure 7: Causativized high applicative: Tinotenda made Chipo dance for Tatenda (such that Tatenda benefited from the dancing)

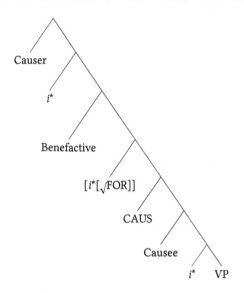

Figure 8: High applicativized causative: Tinotenda, for Tatenda, made Chipo dance (such that Tatenda benefited from the coercive action)[a]

---

[a]The interpretive difference between the scopes in Figures 7 and 8 may be difficult to untangle. Imagine, however, a situation where *Tatenda* needs to learn how to make someone dance and so watching *Tinotenda* direct *Chipo* is helpful.

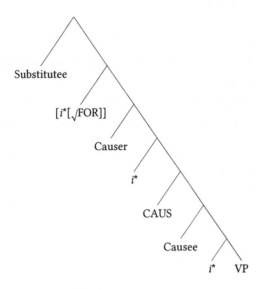

Figure 9: Super-high applicativized causative: Tinotenda, instead of Tatenda made Chipo dance (such that Tatenda did not have to make Chipo dance)

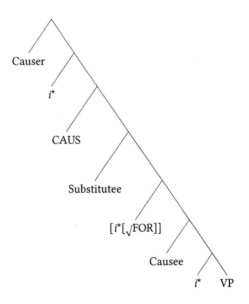

Figure 10: Causativized Super-high applicative: Tinotenda made Chipo dance instead of Tatenda (such that Tatenda did not have to dance)

Shona causatives can embed complements with a maximum thematic weight of only 2, and because applicative root-adjoined *i** can only be interpreted as substitutive when it embeds an agentive argument, it follows that Shona causatives would not be able to embed a substitutive applicative. (21) shows that this prediction holds.

(21) Shona

Tinotenda a-tamb-is-ir-a   Tatenda Chipo.

1.Tinotenda SM1-PST-dance-CAUS-APPL-FV 1.Tatenda 1.Chipo

i. 'Tinotenda made Chipo, for Tatenda, dance.' [CAUS[HI-APPL[vP]]]

ii. 'Tinotenda, for Tatenda, made Chipo dance.' [HI-APPL[CAUS[vP]]]

iii. 'Tinotenda, instead of Tatenda, made Chipo dance.'
[SH-APPL[CAUS[vP]]]

iv. *'Tinotenda made Chipo, instead of Tatenda, dance.'
[CAUS[SH-APPL[vP]]]

The Shona causative's inability to take a substitutive applicative construction as a complement, demonstrated in (21) by the impossibility of the fourth interpretation, provides robust support for the proposal that substitutive applicatives embed Agents and merge at a higher position than high applicatives.

Intriguingly, there is a structure in Shona where applicative root-adjoined *i** heads convey substitutive semantics in a position above a non-agentive argument, and are therefore able to exhibit the generally impossible causativized substitutive interpretation:

(22) Shona

Tinotenda a-zvi-nyu-dz-ir-a   Tatenda.

1.Tinotenda SM1-REFL-drown-CAUS-APPL-FV 1.Tatenda

'Tinotenda made herself drown instead of Tatenda.' (such that Tatenda did not have to drown)

I propose that in (22), when the external argument *Tinotenda* is introduced non-expletively as an Agent by *i**, it saturates three roles in its semantic integration with its complement. The reflexive morpheme *zvi-* merges in the internal argument position, but only as a placeholder that contributes reflexive semantics. When the causative enters the structure, it introduces a Causer and Causee role, and while the internal argument of 'drown', would usually saturate the Causee role, the internal argument role still requires saturation itself. Therefore, when *Tinotenda* merges, it saturates the Causer role, the Causee role, and the Patient role introduced internally by the verb. Because of the unique structure imparted by the reflexive, the applicative root-adjoined i^* embedded by the causative, though it does not embed an Agent, does embed an argument inextricably related to an Agent, enabling the substitutive interpretation and the usually prohibited scope. This analysis builds on Wood & Marantz's (2017) treatment of Icelandic figure reflexives, in which they also propose a structure where an external argument, integrated by non-expletive i^* as the agentive participant in the event, is identified with a semantic role merged lower in its complement.

In this section I have proposed a merge location for applicatives with substitutive semantics, and I have also provided empirical evidence for that structural position. Additionally, I have used the analysis to account for unusual data, showing the theory's flexibility and strength. Section §4 concludes.

4 Conclusion

4.1 Overgeneration

Overgeneration remains a problem for this analysis. If i^* is the sole non-core argument introducer in all languages, then why do some languages allow it to merge as a high applicative, and others do not? What about the languages in which i^* merges even higher with substitutive semantics? Moreover, the disappearance of lexical diversity previously used to formalize argument structure (AS) constraints is globally disruptive to the theory. I am unable to resolve these issues, but my analysis is not alone in retaining this gap.

4.2 Nominal licensing

Kim's (2011) proposal that unpronounced applicative heads introduce non-agentive Causees is, in some sense, correct, in that both arguments are introduced by i^* in what could be argued to be its expletive capacity. This begs a question that could provide a very promising seed for further research in the area of dative structures: in what ways is expletive i^* connected with dative case marking and Case assignment of dative arguments cross-linguistically?

Many authors build analyses on the assumption that all non-core argument introducers are also sources of abstract Case (Mchombo & Firmino 1999; Jeong 2007; Cuervo 2003; 2010; 2015; Sheehan 2013; van der Wal 2017) whereas others argue for some degree of decomposition between argument introduction and Case-licensing (Baker & Collins 2006; Georgala et al. 2008; Georgala 2012; Haddican & Holmberg 2012; Halpert 2012; Wechsler 2014; 2016). Additionally, some scholars propose variation in the direction of Case-assignment as another means of accounting for cross-linguistic diversity (Sheehan 2013; van der Wal 2017; Baker 2008).

Cuervo (2003; 2010) argues that dative subjects of Spanish psychological predicates are licensed by applicative heads, and Royo's paper in this collection offers a similar account of psych-verbs in Catalan. Kim's (2011) structurally similar affectee subjects introduced by peripheral APPL are nominative, however, with dative marked arguments present elsewhere in the construction. Does expletive *i** constitute a source of (dative) Case? Perhaps, expletive *i** introduces affectee subjects in Korean, assigns Case downwards, and licenses an argument it does not introduce, while in Spanish expletive *i** licenses upwards to reach its introducee. Royo (2020 [this volume]) argues that Catalan applicative heads can also optionally assign accusative Case (or maybe just license 'little c' accusative case), which complicates this hypothesis further.

If expletive *i** were a source of dative Case, it would make sense that the various types of dative arguments often bear little semantic resemblance to one another, even intralinguistically. Elsewhere in this volume, Fábregas & Marín (2020 [this volume]), who argue from a different theoretical perspective, contend that Spanish datives only appear dissimilar and that a single semantic structural property underlies all dative morphology. Were my speculation that dative Case might derive from expletive *i** true, however, the only semantic property dative-marked arguments would necessarily share is that of being non-agentive (which, it's worth noting, does not contradict any of the empirical evidence presented by Fábregas & Marín and especially reflects their data involving the subjects of psychological predicates).

The literature on applicatives describes a rich AS ecosystem of functional heads that vary with respect to whether they introduce arguments and/or assign Case, as well as whether they assign Case upwards, downwards, or in both directions. How *i** can be parameterized to capture the breadth of Case-licensing variation is a crucial line of inquiry, with many open questions.

4.3 Parameterization

One clear advantage that my proposal of causative complement selection has over prior analyses, is in the arena of parameterization and language acquisition. Rather than individually eliminate every impossible complement and acquire every possible one, my analysis is such that a child only has to attend to and remember the largest complement attested in their primary language data, because every smaller (thematically lighter) complement will be possible. This idea echoes previous work on "implicational hierarchies," which limit the number of distinct parameters necessary to describe cross-linguistic variation (Holmberg & Roberts 2009; Biberauer 2011; Biberauer & Roberts 2012; 2015; Sheehan 2013; Biberauer et al. 2013; van der Wal & Biberauer 2014; Biberauer et al. 2014; van der Wal 2017).

A potential complication for my proposal, however, is that the choice between expletive and non-expletive interpretation is decided, according to Wood & Marantz, "in the semantics, after syntactic structure is built and sent to spell-out" (2017: 266). Most of the theoretical stickiness here amounts to an order of operations problem: if the causative head merges before the relevant theta roles in its complement are assigned, then how can it distinguish based on thematic weight, as I have argued?

One possibility is that constituent pieces of the structure are sent to spell-out and then semantic interpretation in chunks, a proposal that reflects one of the major concepts of phase theory (Chomsky 1999). This solution represents a compromise between a syntactically-oriented theory of causative complement selection and a semantically-oriented one, in that the causative head still selects in the syntax, but based on a finalized semantic interpretation that has already been computed at the relevant interface. Another possibility is that what seems like complement selection is actually an interpretive property that operates after the syntactic derivation. If the latter possibility is correct, where in the grammar is this information stored, and at what point in the derivation does it operate? How is parametric variation in interpretive rules like this captured in the theory? While I do not possess the empirical evidence necessary to settle these issues, my thematic weight proposal ultimately accounts well for the data I have presented, and I leave further theoretical clarification to future work.

4.4 Summary

In §2, I argued in favor of a single non-core argument introducer, i^*. I also proposed an original model of complement selection for causative heads, which accommodates i^* and reduces the number of individual causative heads necessary to account for intra-linguistic variation.

In §3, I argued for an additional merge location and associated semantic interpretation for applicative root-adjoined i^* heads. I also provided empirical evidence for the structural position of super-high applicatives, and offered in-depth analysis of causative-applicative cooccurrence.

I have maintained reduction of argument introducers in the lexicon as a priority throughout this analysis. The necessity of more complex complement selection and a greater number of structural positions for causative and applicative heads does not entail lexical under-specification per se, but it does put into perspective the number of individual functional items that would be required to account for cross-linguistic and intra-linguistic variation in previous analyses.

I have ultimately provided significant theoretical motivation for a reduced inventory of non-core argument introducers in Bantu, demonstrating that both causative and applicative data can be accommodated by a sparser lexicon.

Abbreviations

In language data from Bantu, numbers and numbers followed by lowercase letters (e.g. 2b) refer to noun classes. Additional abbreviations: FV: final vowel; HI-APPL high applicative SM subject marker SH-APPL super-high applicative.

Acknowledgments

I want to thank Collence Nyazenga, my dear friend and Shona consultant. I also want to thank Theresa Biberauer for her co-supervision of my master's thesis (from which much of this analysis developed), and Jenneke van der Wal, who co-supervised my thesis and provided a great deal of feedback on these ideas when they were still in their conference poster infancy. Thank you as well to the editors of this volume for all their hard work, and to my anonymous reviewers for their helpful comments.

References

Baker, Mark C. 1985. The Mirror Principle and morphosyntactic explanation. *Linguistic Inquiry* 16(3). 373–415.

Baker, Mark C. 2008. *Parameters of agreement* (Cambridge Studies in Linguistics 115). Cambridge, UK: Cambridge University Press.

Baker, Mark C. & Chris Collins. 2006. Linkers and the internal structure of vP. *Natural Language & Linguistic Theory* 24. 307–354.

Belletti, Adriana & Luigi Rizzi. 1988. Psych-verbs and θ-Theory. *Natural Language & Linguistic Theory* 6(3). 291–352.   DOI:10.1007/BF00133902

Biberauer, Theresa. 2011. *In defence of lexico-centric parametric variation: Two 3rd factor-constrained case studies.* Paper presented at the Workshop on Formal Grammar and Syntactic Variation, Rethinking Parameters, Madrid, ES.

Biberauer, Theresa, Anders Holmberg, Ian Roberts & Michelle Sheehan. 2014. Complexity in comparative syntax: The view from modern parametric theory. In Frederick J. Newmeyer & Laurel B. Preston (eds.), *Measuring grammatical complexity*, 103–127. Oxford, UK: Oxford University Press.

Biberauer, Theresa & Ian Roberts. 2012. *On the significance of what hasn't happened.* Conference Presentation. Paper presented at the Diachronic Generative Syntax Conference, Lisbon.

Biberauer, Theresa & Ian Roberts. 2015. Rethinking formal hierarchies: A proposed unification. *Cambridge Occasional Papers in Linguistics* 7. 1–31.

Biberauer, Theresa, Ian Roberts & Michelle Sheehan. 2013. No-choice parameters and the limits of syntactic variation. In Robert E. Santana-LaBarge (ed.), *Proceedings of the 31st West Coast Conference on Formal Linguistics*, 46–55. Somerville, MA: Cascadilla Proceedings Project.

Chomsky, Noam. 1999. *Derivation by phase* (MIT Occasional Papers in Linguistics 18). Cambridge, MA: Massachusetts Institute of Technology.

Cuervo, María Cristina. 2003. *Datives at large.* Cambridge, MA: Massachusetts Institute of Technology. (Doctoral dissertation). https://dspace.mit.edu/handle/1721.1/7991.

Cuervo, María Cristina. 2010. Some dative subjects are born, some are made. In *Selected Proceedings of the 12th Hispanic Linguistics Symposium, 13. Somerville, MA.* Cascadilla Proceedings Project.

Cuervo, María Cristina. 2012. Remarks on argument structure. In María Cristina Cuervo & Yves Roberge (eds.), *The end of argument structure?*, 1–11. Bingley, UK: Emerald Group Publishing Limited.

Cuervo, María Cristina. 2015. Parameters and argument structure II: Causatives and applicatives. In Antonio Fábregas, Jaume Mateu & Michael Putnam (eds.), *Contemporary linguistics parameters*, 123–146. Norfolk, UK: Bloomsbury Publishing Plc.

Diercks, Michael. 2012. Parameterizing case: Evidence from Bantu. *Syntax* 15(3). 253–286.

Fábregas, Antonio & Rafael Marín. 2020. Datives and stativity in psych predicates. In Anna Pineda & Jaume Mateu (eds.), *Dative constructions in Romance and beyond*, 221–238. Berlin: Language Science Press. DOI:10.5281/zenodo.3776549

Georgala, Efthymia. 2012. Applicatives in their Structural & Thematic Function: Cornell University. (Doctoral dissertation).

Georgala, Efthymia, Waltraud Paul & John Whitman. 2008. Expletive and thematic applicatives. In Charles B. Chang & Hannah J. Haynie (eds.), *Proceed-*

ings of the 26th West Coast Conference on Formal Linguistics. Somerville, MA: Cascadilla Proceedings Project.

Givón, Talmy. 1969. *Studies in Chibemba and Bantu grammar.* Los Angeles, CA: University of California, Los Angeles. (Doctoral dissertation).

Good, Jeff. 2005. Reconstructing morpheme order in Bantu: The case of causativization and applicativization. *Diachronica* 22(1). 3–57.

Grimshaw, Jane B. 1990. *Argument structure* (Linguistic Inquiry Monographs 18). Cambridge, Mass: MIT Press.

Haddican, William & Anders Holmberg. 2012. Object movement (a)symmetries in British English dialects. In Jaehoon Choi, E. Alan Hogue, Jeffrey Punske, Deniz Tat, Jessamyn Schertz & Alex Trueman (eds.), *Proceedings of the 29th West Coast Conference on Formal Linguistics*, 72–80. Somerville, MA: Cascadilla Proceedings Project.

Halpert, Claire. 2012. *Argument licensing and agreement in Zulu.* Cambridge, MA: Massachusetts Institute of Technology.

Haspelmath, Martin. 2016. Universals of causative and anticausative verb formation and the spontaneity scale. *Lingua Posnaniensis* LVIII(2). DOI:https://doi.org/10.1515/linpo-2016-0009

Holmberg, Anders & Ian Roberts. 2009. Introduction: Parameters in minimalist theory. In Theresa Biberauer, Anders Holmberg, Ian Roberts & Michelle Sheehan (eds.), *Parametric variation: Null subjects in minimalist theory,* 1–57. Cambridge, UK: Cambridge University Press.

Hyman, Larry M. 2002. Suffix ordering in Bantu: A morphocentric approach. In Geert Booij & Jaap van Marle (eds.), *Yearbook of morphology 2002,* 245–281. Dordrecht, NL: Kluwer Academic Publishers.

Jackendoff, Ray. 1972. *Semantic interpretation in generative grammar* (Studies in Linguistics 2). Cambridge, MA: MIT Press.

Jeong, Youngmi. 2007. *Applicatives: Structure and interpretation from a minimalist perspective.* Vol. 104. Amsterdam: John Benjamins.

Jerro, Kyle Joseph. 2013. *Argument structure and the typology of causatives in Kinyarwanda: Explaining the causative-instrumental syncretism.* Austin, TX: University of Texas at Austin MA.

Jung, Hyun Kyoung. 2014. *On the syntax of applicative and causative construction.* Tucson, AZ: University of Arizona. (Doctoral dissertation).

Kim, Kyumin. 2011. *External argument introducers.* Toronto, ON: University of Toronto. (Doctoral dissertation). https://tspace.library.utoronto.ca/handle/1807/31805.

Kim, Kyumin. 2012. External argument-introducing heads: Voice and Appl. In María Cristina Cuervo & Yves Roberge (eds.), *The end of argument structure?*, 131–154. Bingley, UK: Emerald Group Publishing Limited.

Kimenyi, Alexandre. 1980. *A relational grammar of Kinyarwanda.* Berkeley & Los Angeles, CA: University of California Press.

Kimenyi, Alexandre. 1995. *Kinyarwanda applicatives revisited.* Boston, MA. Paper presented at the Niger-Congo syntax and semantics workshop on the applicative architectures.

Kittilä, Seppo. 2013. Causative morphemes as a de-transitivizing device: What do non-canonical instances reveal about causation and causativization? *Folia Linguistica* 47(1). 113–137.

Kulikov, Leonid. 2001. Causatives. In Martin Haspelmath (ed.), *Language typology and language universals: An international handbook*, vol. 2, 886–898. Berlin: Walter De Gruyter.

Marten, Lutz. 2016. *Benefactive and substitutive applicatives in Bemba.* Cambridge. Paper presented at the Syntax Research Cluster Event.

Marten, Lutz & Nancy C. Kula. 2014. Benefactive and substitutive applicatives in Bemba. *Journal of African Languages and Linguistics* 35(1). 1–44. DOI:10.1515/jall-2014-0001

Mchombo, Sam A. & Gregório Firmino. 1999. Double object constructions in Chichewa and Gitonga: A comparative analysis. *Linguistic Analysis* 29(1). 214–233.

Mylne, Tom. 1999. A feature-based system for classifying semantic roles. In *A feature-based system for classifying semantic roles.* Proceedings of the 1999 Conference of the Australian Linguistic Society.

Peterson, David A. 2007. *Applicative constructions* (Oxford Studies in Typology and Linguistic Theory). Oxford: Oxford University Press.

Pylkkänen, Liina. 2002. *Introducing arguments.* Massachusetts Institute of Technology. (Doctoral dissertation).

Pylkkänen, Liina. 2008. *Introducing arguments* (Linguistic Inquiry Monographs 49). Cambridge, MA: MIT Press.

Royo, Carles. 2020. The accusative/dative alternation in Catalan verbs with experiencer object. In Anna Pineda & Jaume Mateu (eds.), *Dative constructions in Romance and beyond*, 371–393. Berlin: Language Science Press. DOI:10.5281/zenodo.3776563

Sheehan, Michelle. 2013. *Towards a parameter hierarchy for alignment.* Paper presented at the West Coast Conference on Formal Linguistics (WCCFL), Tempe, AZ.

Sheehan, Michelle & Jenneke van der Wal. 2016. Do we need abstract case? In Kyeong-min Kim, Pocholo Umbal, Trevor Block, Queenie Chan, Tanie Cheng, Kelli Finney, Mara Katz, Sophie Nickel-Thompson & Lisa Shorten (eds.), *Proceedings of the 33rd West Coast Conference on Formal Linguistics*, 351–360. Somerville, MA: Cascadilla Proceedings Project.

Tsai, Wei-Tien D. 2009. *High applicatives are not high enough: A cartographic solution.* Taipei, Taiwan.

van der Wal, Jenneke. 2015. Evidence for abstract case in Bantu. *Lingua* 165. 109–132.

van der Wal, Jenneke. 2017. Flexibility in symmetry: An implicational relation in Bantu double object constructions. In Laura R. Bailey & Michelle Sheehan (eds.), *Order and structure in syntax II: Subjecthood and argument structure* (Open Generative Syntax), 115–152. Berlin, Germany: Language Science Press. DOI:10.5281/zenodo.1116761

van der Wal, Jenneke & Theresa Biberauer. 2014. *From macroparameters to nanoparameters: A comparative Bantu case study.* Paper presented at the International Workshop on Bantu Languages: Studies in East African Bantu and Microvariation, London, UK.

Wechsler, Mattie. 2014. *The stacking behavior of valence-increasing verbal extensions and their arguments in Shona.* Bryn Mawr: Bryn Mawr College. (Bachelor's thesis).

Wechsler, Mattie. 2016. *Case-assignment in applicative, causative, and double object constructions: A comparative analysis with emphasis on microvariation in Bantu.* University of Cambridge. (MPhil thesis).

Wood, Jim & Alec Marantz. 2017. The interpretation of external arguments. In Roberta D'Alessandro, Irene Franco & Ángel J. Gallego (eds.), *The verbal domain*, 255–278. Oxford: Oxford University Press. DOI:10.1093/oso/9780198767886.001.0001

Wunderlich, Dieter. 1997. Cause and the structure of verbs. *Linguistic Inquiry* 28(1). 27–68.

Chapter 11

When the applicative needs the antipassive

David Basilico

University of Alabama at Birmingham

In some languages, an antipassive morpheme feeds applicativization, in others, it bleeds it. The analysis of this asymmetry given here relies on two recent proposals: Pylkkänen's (2008) view that the low applicative must merge with a transitive verb and Basilico's (2012; 2017) claim that that the antipassive marker can introduce an internal argument. In those cases where the antipassive feeds the applicative, the antipassive marker introduces the internal argument, while in those cases where it bleeds it, the antipassive marker is the expected intransitivizer, disallowing an internal argument from appearing syntactically. This work provides a parsimonious account of the cross-linguistic differences in applicative formation with the antipassive.

1 Introduction

In a number of languages, an antipassive morpheme appears in cases of applicativization. A particularly interesting example comes from Chukchi (Dunn 1999). He considers that there is both an applicative and antipassive form of the *-ine* prefix. An example of the applicative use of *-ine* is seen in the following examples. Dunn (1999: 214) states "this applicative relates to the original transitive stem so that the O of the original stem is an oblique and another oblique argument of the original stem is the O."

(1) Chukchi (Dunn 1999)

   a. ətlʔa-ta   jəme-nenat   ewirʔ-ə-t.
      mother-ERG hang-3SGA.3PLO clothing-E-3PL.ABS
      'Mother hung up the clothes.'

David Basilico. 2020. When the applicative needs the antipassive. In Anna Pineda & Jaume Mateu (eds.), *Dative constructions in Romance and beyond*, 273–294. Berlin: Language Science Press. DOI:10.5281/zenodo.3776553

b. ətlʔa-ta   **ena**-jme-nen   tətəl   meniɣ-e.
mother-ERG **ANTIP**-hang-3SGa.3SGO door.3SG.ABS cloth-INS
'Mother hung the door with cloth.'

Note that the translations in the examples are different. In (a), the theme is an absolutive while in (b) it is an oblique, with the added argument in (b) being a location that appears as the absolutive. Note also that the morpheme *-ine* appears (as *-ena* as a result of phonological processes). The antipassive use of *-ine*, which is more well-known, is seen in the following example (2).

(2)   Chukchi (Kozinsky et al. 1988)

a. Qənwer ʔettʔ-e   rələpʔen-nin   gutil-ən.
finally   dog-ERG broke-AOR.3SG/3SG tether-ABS
'Finally the dog broke the tether.'

b. Qənwer ʔettʔ-ən **ine**=nləpʔet=gʔi   (gutilg-e).
finally   dog-ABS **ANTIP**-broke-AOR.3SG (tether-INS)
'Finally the dog broke the tether.'

In (2a), we see a transitive, ergative clause. The subject is in the ergative case, and the direct object in the absolutive, with the verb showing agreement with both the subject and object. In (2b), we have the antipassive clause. The subject in the absolutive case, with the object in an oblique case and agreement with the subject only.[1]

---

[1]There is also a use of the antipassive morpheme in Chukchi which has been dubbed the "spurious antipassive" by Hale (2002) and discussed in Bobaljik & Branigan (2006) and Bobaljik (2007). Here, we see the antipassive morpheme as a kind of "inverse agreement", when "a second or third person participant acts upon a first person participant" (Polinsky 2016). These examples are from Polinsky (2016).

(i) ə-nan ɣəm   ine-ɬʔu-ɣʔi.
3SG.ERG 1SG.ABS ANTIP-see-AOR.3SG
'S/he saw me.'

(ii) ɣət-nan muri   ɬʔu-tku-∅.
2sg.ERG 1sg.ABS see-ANTIP-AOR.2sg
'You saw me.'

Bobaljik & Branigan (2006) attempt to unify this use of the antipassive morpheme with its more general use. However, I follow Polinsky (2016) and treat these as agreement markers and not involved with argument addition or elimination/demotion. I do not treat these constructions in this work.

To explain this "applicative" use of the antipassive morpheme, I propose a different analysis. Rather than considering that *-ine* has both an antipassive and applicative use, I propose that *-ine* is an antipassive marker only. In those cases where we see an applicative use of *-ine*, we have the antipassive use of the suffix, with the antipassive feeding the appearance of a null applicative.

The explanation for the presence of the antipassive morpheme relies on an analysis of the low applicative construction given in Pylkkänen (2008), as well as an analysis of the antipassive construction given in Basilico (2012; 2017). In short, Pylkkänen (2008) requires that the low applicative merge with a verb that introduces an internal argument. Basilico (2017), building on Borer (2005); Lohndal (2014); Acedo-Matellán & Mateu (2014) and others, considers that verbs do not necessarily introduce any of their arguments. For Basilico (2017), the antipassive morpheme, rather than being a detransitivizing morpheme, is one way for an internal argument to be introduced. Thus, the antipassive morpheme merges with the verb that has no arguments and creates a verb that introduces an internal argument. In this way, the verb becomes the right type to serve as an argument of the applicative.

I turn to an overview of these two proposals next.

2 The low applicative and arguments within the VP

Pylkkänen (2008) extends Kratzer's (1996) analysis of external arguments to certain kinds of applied arguments. Her "high applicatives" are those extra arguments which can occur in the absence of a direct object. In these cases, the applied argument is introduced by a separate syntactic head, like the external argument in Kratzer's (1996) analysis, and introduces a thematic role predicate $\lambda x \lambda e[\text{benefactive}(x,e)]$, notated as BENE here. It integrates semantically by event identification (see Figure 1).

These "high applicatives" are contrasted to "low applicatives", which are extra arguments that occur only in the presence of a direct object. In these cases, the applicative head combines with both noun phrases, the direct object and then the applied (indirect) object before the entire applicative structure merges with the verb. The semantic representation of the applicative head in this case is more complex: $\lambda x.\lambda y.\lambda f.\lambda e.f(e,x)$ & THEME(e, x) & to-the-possession (x,y). The verb in this case must introduce an argument. I give the structure in Figure 2 with the corresponding semantics given below the structure.

The agent will be added by a separate Voice head and the thematic role predicate and argument will be integrated into the semantic representation through event identification (not shown).

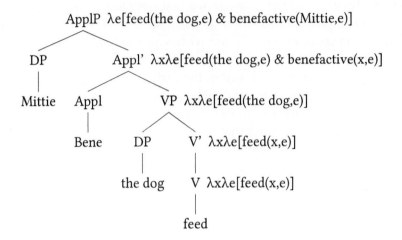

Figure 1: High applicative

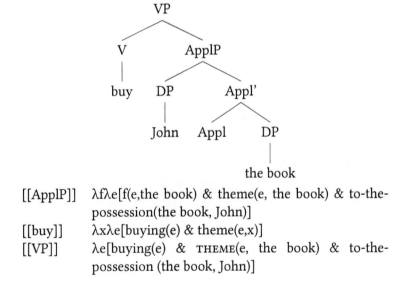

[[ApplP]] λfλe[f(e,the book) & theme(e, the book) & to-the-possession(the book, John)]

[[buy]] λxλe[buying(e) & theme(e,x)]

[[VP]] λe[buying(e) & THEME(e, the book) & to-the-possession (the book, John)]

Figure 2: Low applicative

The phenomenon of low applicatives interacts with the notion of transitivity and the introduction of internal arguments. For Pylkkänen (2008), low applicatives are possible only with transitive verbs, since they involve a relation between two DPs.

3 The antipassive as an argument introducer

Though the antipassive appears to be an intransitivization process, Basilico (2012; 2017) proposes, based in part on asymmetries in the appearance of antipassive morphemes in Eskimo-Aleut languages, that the antipassive morpheme actually adds an argument rather than demotes or saturates an argument. In these languages, core transitive, result verbs (CTV) (as discussed first in Levin 1999; Rappaport Hovav & Levin 1999 and subsequent work) such as 'break' and 'open' always occur with an overt antipassive morpheme in an antipassive construction.

(3)   Inuktitut (Spreng 2012)

    a. Piita-up   naalautiq surak-taa.
        Peter-ERG radio.ABS break-PART.3SG/3SG
        'Peter broke the radio.'

    b. Piita   surak-si-juq   (naalauti-mik).
        Peter.ABS break-ANTIP-PART.3SG (radio-MIK)
        'Peter is breaking the radio.'

    c. * Piita   surak-tuq   (naalauti-mik).
        Peter.ABS break-PART.3SG radio-MIK
        'Peter broke the radio.'

Non-core transitive manner verbs (NCTV) such as 'eat' and 'drink' appear in an antipassive frame with no special morphology.

(4)   Inuktitut (Spreng 2012)

    a. Anquti niri-vuq   (niqi-mik).
        man.ABS eat-IND.3SG meat-MIK
        'The man is eating meat.'

    b. Anguti-up niqi   niri-vaa.
        man-ERG   meat.ABS eat-IND.3SG/3SG
        'The man is eating meat.'

Basilico (2017) proposes that core transitive verbs do not introduce their internal argument, while non-core transitive verbs do. In this way, he builds from Rappaport Hovav & Levin's (1999) idea that the internal argument of a NCTV is introduced by the verbal root in a monoeventive event structure template, while the internal argument of a CTV is a "structure" argument of a bieventive event structure template, as seen in (5) and (6) below.

(5) $[x \text{ act}_{<manner>} y]$

(6) $[[x \text{ act}_{<manner>}] \text{ cause } [\text{become } [y <state>]]]$

In (5), the 'y' participant is licensed by the root component that fills in the <manner> element of the monoeventive activity template. In (6), the y component is actually part of the CTV change of state template itself and so it must be present whenever there is a change of state verb.

In the Eskimo language Iñupiak, Nagai (2006) describes the difference between two seemingly synonymous verbs which both mean 'wet to tan': *aŋula-*, which is an agentive verb and *imaq-*, which is patientive. Agentive verbs do not occur with an antipassive morpheme and in their single argument intransitive frame appear with the external argument only as the subject. Patientive verbs must occur with an antipassive morpheme and in their single argument intransitive frame appear with their internal argument as the subject; in this frame they are unaccusative. With respect to the agentive *aŋula-*

> [t]he focus, however, is not on the patient's changing state from not being wet to being wet, but on the agent's process of wetting the patient. Thus, even though it implies the agent's changing the state of the patient, the focus is not on the patient's change of state, but on the process of the agent's being engaged in the activity of wetting the patient. On the other hand, *imaq-* "wet to tan" focuses on the patient's changing state from not being wet to being wet. (Nagai 2006: 215)

This discussion of the difference between these two verbs recalls the manner/result distinction, in which the agentive verb focuses on what the agent does in carrying out the process (manner), while the patientive focuses on the result of the process. CTVs are typically result verbs, while manner verbs are NCTVs. In the framework adopted here, a CTV is a predicate of events only, while a NCTV is a relation between an event and an entity. A CTV in Eskimo-Aleut would be a patientive, result verb while a NCTV would be agentive, manner verb.

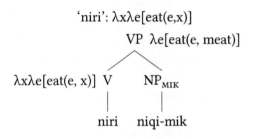

Figure 3: NCTV syntax

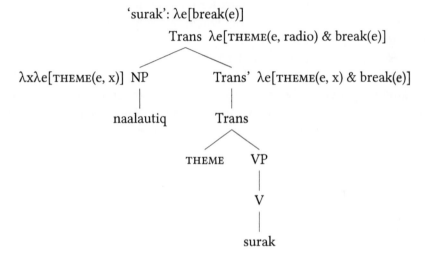

Figure 4: CTV syntax

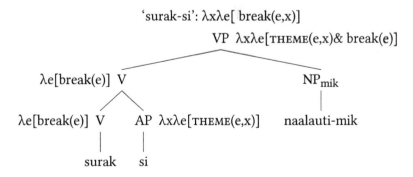

Figure 5: CTV + antipassive syntax

As can be seen in the above, the CTV in the transitive frame (Figure 4) has the internal argument introduced outside the VP by separate head, which I notate as Trans, which is the head of a Transitive Phrase. It is the counterpart of Voice for the internal argument. This Trans head introduces a thematic role predicate (the THEME thematic role) in its head. This thematic role predicate is integrated semantically through event identification. In this way, the internal argument is introduced very much like an external argument or a high applicative argument (Johns & Kučerová 2017). In the antipassive frame for the CTV (Figure 5), the antipassive morpheme, like Trans, introduces the internal theme argument through a thematic role predicate, but in this case it introduces the argument within the VP. In this way, the antipassive syntax for the CTV in terms of introducing the argument mirrors that of the NCTV, which lexically introduces its argument within the VP.

To these representations, we add a Voice head which introduces an external argument thematic role predicate, here agent. In the transitive, a transitive Voice head assigns ergative case to its subject, with Tense assigning absolutive case to the direct object. In the antipassive, an intransitive Voice head assigns no case, with the external argument assigned case from Tense.

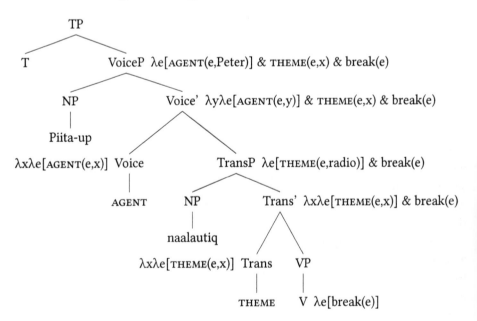

Figure 6: CTV with external argument

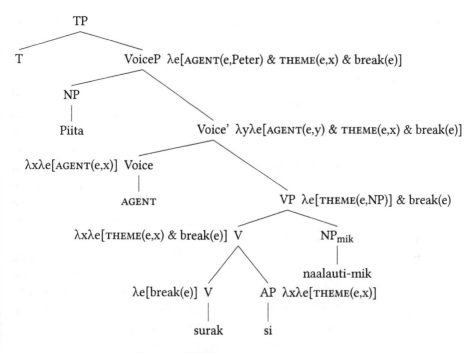

Figure 7: NCTV with external argument

4 The analysis: Putting it all together

Pylkkänen (2008) requires that a low applicative phrase merge with a verb that introduces its internal argument. If we consider that the verb itself does not introduce an argument, then it is not possible for a verb to be the argument for ApplP. Basilico (2017) considers that an antipassive morpheme can step in to turn the verb into one that does introduce its argument. Since the verb is now of the right semantic type, the applicative phrase can now merge with the verb. In this way, we explain why the antipassive morpheme appears in this applicative construction; the antipassive feeds the applicative by supplying the internal argument.

Moving to a concrete example, we can give an analysis for the argument rearrangement seen in the example with the verb 'hang' above in (1). In the basic form, the verb introduces no internal argument; the theme argument is introduced by a separate head outside of the VP, as in Figure 8.

With the "applicative" form, we can think of the 'door' coming to 'have' the cloth. By hypothesis, the verb *jame* 'hang' has no arguments. The antipassive morpheme *ine-* combines with the verb to add an argument position to the verb.

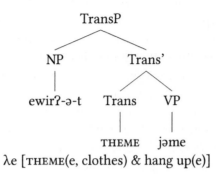

$$\lambda e \ [\text{THEME}(e, \text{clothes}) \ \& \ \text{hang up}(e)]$$

Figure 8: Syntax for transitive 'hang'

In this way, the verb becomes the right type to semantically compose with ApplP. The null applicative morpheme merges first with the theme/possessee *meniɣ* 'cloth' and then with the possessor *tətəl* 'door'. The whole ApplP then merges with the verb that is of the right semantic type after the merger of the antipassive morpheme. Note that the introduction of the Trans head comes too late to supply the internal argument. The Appl head must combine with a verb with an argument, and though the Trans head does supply a theme argument, creating a structure of the right semantic type, the phrase formed is not the right syntactic type for the ApplP because it creates a Trans functional phrase rather than a V.

Let me walk through a derivation here. First, the verb combines with the antipassive morpheme to introduce an internal argument.

(7) a. [$_V$ ena jme]
     b. $\lambda x \lambda e[\text{hang}(e) \ \& \ \text{THEME}(e, x)]$

The applicative head merges with the direct object and then with the indirect object to create the applicative phrase.

(8) a. [$_{ApplP}$ [tətəl] [$_{Appl'}$ Appl [$_{NP}$ meniɣ-e]]
     b. $\lambda f \lambda e$ f(e, the cloth) & THEME(e, the cloth) & to-the-possession-of (the cloth, the door)

Finally, the ApplP formed in (8) merges with the V from (7) to create the VP. The antipassive morpheme has adjoined to the V, allowing the V to project.

(9) a. [$_{VP}$ [$_V$ ena jme] [$_{ApplP}$ [tətəl] [$_{Appl'}$ Appl [$_{NP}$ meniɣ-e]]]
     b. $\lambda e[\text{hang}(e) \ \& \ \text{THEME}(e, \text{cloth}) \ \& \ \text{to-the-possession-of}(\text{door}, \text{cloth})]$

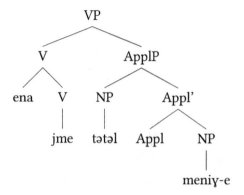

Figure 9: Applicative syntax

Thus, the applicative use of the antipassive morpheme is not an applicative use per se; antipassive formation is necessary to feed applicative formation. Here, the applicative morpheme is null. If this analysis is on the right track, as noted in Cuervo 2020 [this volume], a defining feature of an applicative morpheme need not be its overt exponence. Furthermore, note that in this analysis of applicatives, as with Pylkkänen's original (2008) analysis, the Appl head selects not only for a DP as a complement but the entire ApplP selects for a transitive verb. Thus, in terms of Cuervo's typology for applicatives (Cuervo 2020 [this volume]), these Appl heads that have non-verbal complements (in this case a NP or DP) can only appear within a clause that has a transitive verb. But the point in the configuration at which the internal argument is introduced is important. The analysis here posits two positions for the internal argument, one within the VP and one external to the VP within a functional projection. Thus, as in both Cuervo's (Cuervo 2020 [this volume]) and Wechsler's (Wechsler 2020 [this volume]) analyses, the point in the structure at which the applicative is introduced is important, especially in those theories which introduce arguments syntactically.

4.1 Not a case of "raising"

Support for the idea that these structures involve applicative formation and not a syntactic rearrangement of noun phrases as a result of movement comes from meaning differences in antipassive sentences in which there is "locative" advancement (Polinskaja & Nedjalkov 1987). I argue that these cases of advancement of the locative argument to absolutive position in the context of the antipassive are another instance in which we see antipassivization necessary for the addition of an applied argument. Consider the following.

(10) Chukchi (Polinskaja & Nedjalkov 1987)

    a. ətləg-e   mətqəmət (kawkaw-ək) kili-nen.
       father-ERG butter.ABS (bread-LOC) spread.on-3SG/3SG(AOR)

    b. ətləg-ən mətq-e   (kawkaw-ək) ena-rkele-g'e.
       father-ABS butter-INS (bread-LOC) ANTIP-spread.on-3SG(AOR)

    c. ətləg-ə   mətq-e   kawkaw ena-rkele-g'e.
       father-ERG butter-INS bread.ABS ANTIP-spread.on-3SG(AOR)
       'The father spread butter on the bread.'

In (a) we have the ergative, transitive clause, and in (b) we have the antipassive variant. The (c) example shows the placement of the location 'bread' as the absolutive argument but the verb still contains the antipassive morpheme. A second example is from Kozinsky et al. (1988).

(11) Chukchi (Kozinsky et al. 1988)

    a. ətləg-e   təkeč?-ən utkuč?-ək pela-nen.
       father-ERG bait-ABS   trap-LOC leave-3SG/3SG

    b. ətləg-en təkeč?-a utkuč?-ək ena-pela-g?e.
       father-ABS bait-INS trap-LOC ANTIP-leave-3SG

    c. ətləg-e   təkeč?-a utkuč?-ən ena-pela-nen.
       father-ERG bait-INS trap-ABS ANTIP-leave-3SG/3SG
       'The father left the bait by the trap.'

In the (a) example, we have a transitive, ergative structure with the noun phrase *təkeč?-ən* 'bait' as the absolutive (affixed with -*ən*) and the noun phrase *utkuč?-ək* 'trap' with a locative case marker (-*ək*) attached. The (b) example gives the antipassive counterpart of the (a) example, where the noun phrase *təkeč?-a* 'bait' is now in the instrumental case (affixed with -*a*) and the verb is affixed with the antipassive *ena*- morpheme. The subject is in the absolutive case and the verb shows agreement only with the subject. What is interesting is the (c) example. Here we have what looks like an antipassive clause; the verb is affixed with the antipassive morpheme *ena*- and the noun phrase 'the bait' is in the instrumental case—exactly as in (b). However, the location argument *utkuč?-ən* 'trap' is not affixed with the locative marker but appears in absolutive case, and the verb shows both subject and object agreement, agreeing with the absolutive 'trap'. We have a transitive clause here, with *ətləg-e* 'the father' as the subject and *utkuč?-ən* 'the trap' as the absolutive object. The "original" direct object still appears as a "demoted" object, and the verb still appears with antipassive morphology.

We might at first take the raising of the locative element to be movement of the locative element internal to the VP and adjoined to some other phrase, where it can receive absolutive case. However, there is a meaning difference between the (a) and (b) examples as contrasted to the (c) example in (11). Kozinsky et al. (1988) state that (c) means something quite different from (a), and derive this difference from a pragmatic suprapropositional meaning (SPM) difference between the two clauses. Kozinsky et al. (1988: 684) give the SPM for the (a) example as "the bait has changed its location," while that for (c) is not merely about a change in location but "implies that some bait is put in the trap which is, thus, ready for operation". They note that the two sentences have different truth conditions; they state that "the former [example (11a)] can be used if the trap and the bait are merely stockpiled in one and the same place for the time being, while the latter [example (11b)] can by no means denote such a situation".

While (a) and (c) are not truth conditionally equivalent, (b) and (a) are. Though Kozinsky et al. (1988) derive this denotational difference from a pragmatic difference, it seems unlikely that a pragmatic difference can lead to different denotational semantics. We need a representation in which we can explain why (a) and (c) are denotationally different.

I argue here that the promotion of the locative is a case of a low applicative. Thus, just like above, here the "promoted" object is in the specifier of a low applicative. The antipassive morphology is needed so there can be an argument position within the VP.

In the basic transitive case, we have a change of location structure. The location argument is projected within the VP, and the theme element, in this case 'the bait', appears within a Trans head. The structure of the verb phrase will be as in Figure 10, with its semantics shown beneath.

We can antipassivize this structure. The morpheme *ine-* introduces the theme argument within the verb phrase. This structure is denotationally synonymous with (11a) above because there is no difference in the roles that the participants play in the event. The only difference is where and how the theme argument is introduced. Figure 11 gives the antipassive syntax.

In the case of the promotion of the locative NP to absolutive, here I argue that the structure is different; there is a low applicative morpheme introduced and 'the trap' appears in the specifier of this applicative morpheme. I show the syntax in Figure 12. This applicative morpheme introduces a possession relation between 'the trap' and 'the bait'; thus, 'the trap' has 'the bait'. It is this difference—the presence of the applicative morpheme that introduces a possessive applicative relation—that accounts for the denotational difference between the (a)/(b) cases

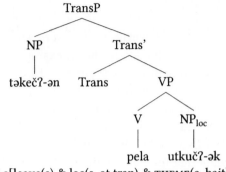

$\lambda e[\text{leave(e) \& loc(e, at trap) \& THEME(e, bait)}]$

Figure 10: Transitive syntax and semantics

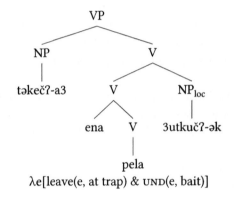

$\lambda e[\text{leave(e, at trap) \& UND(e, bait)}]$

Figure 11: Antipassive syntax and semantics

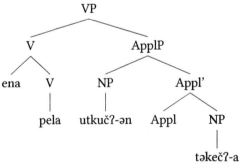

$\lambda e \ [\text{leave(e) \& THEME(e, bait) \& to-the-possession-of (trap, bait)}]$

Figure 12: Applicative syntax and semantics

and the (c) case. In the (c) case, the trap must come to have the bait at the end of the event, while in the (a)/(b) case we only have a change of location structure so 'the trap' and 'the bait' need only be spatially near each other at the end of the event. Perhaps a better translation for the "locative advancement" sentence is 'The father left the trap with bait'.

The notion that these examples of locative advancement involve an applicative element is also supported by impossibility of incorporating the locative nominal into the verb.

(12) Chukchi (Kozinsky et al. 1988)

    a. * ətləg-e   təkeč?-ən utkuč?ə-pela-nen.
       father-ERG bait-ABS   trap-leave-3SG/3SG

    b. * ətləg-en   təkeč?-a utkuč?ə-pela-g?e.
       father-ABS bait-INS trap-leave-3SG
       'The father left the bait by the trap.'

This lack of incorporation is somewhat surprising, since absolutive arguments usually can incorporate. But if we take the locative argument to be an applicative argument, then we can reduce the lack of incorporation to another well-known restriction in noun incorporation: goal/recipient/possessor (indirect object) arguments do not incorporate (Baker 1988).

A further reason to consider that antipassivization introduces an argument comes from cases of antipassivization feeding "dative shift". The following example shows "dative shift" with a change of state verb.

(13) Chukchi (Spencer 1995)

    a. ətləg-e   akka-gtə qora-ŋə təm-nen.
       father-ERG son-DAT deer-ABS kill-3SG.s/3SG.o

    b. ətləg-e   ekək   ena-nmə-nen   qora-ta.
       father-ERG son.ABS ap-kill-3SG.s/3SG.o deer-INS
       'The father killed a reindeer for the son.'

What is interesting in this case is that a change of state verb such as 'kill' appears to undergo the dative (really the benefactive) alternation. However in this case, as the (b) example shows, the verb must first be antipassivized before the benefactive argument can appear as the absolutive. Verbs of change of state such as 'kill' in English do not undergo this alternation, while verbs of creation can.

(14) English

    a. The father killed a reindeer for his son.

    b. * The father killed his son a reindeer.

    c. The father built a house for his son.

    d. The father built his son a house.

If a core transitive result verb such as 'kill' does not introduce its argument, then the verb is not the right type to serve as an argument of ApplP. However, a creation verb such as 'build' is a noncore transitive verb and does introduce its argument, so it can serve as the input to applicativization.[2] Thus, we explain the difference in English above. But in Chukchi, it is possible for this core transitive result verb to undergo the benefactive alternation, but only when the antipassive morpheme is present. So we see again that the addition of an applied object, in this case the benefactive, requires the antipassive. The verb 'kill' does not introduce an argument at the VP level, so the antipassive morpheme is necessary to introduce one. Though Trans does eventually introduce an internal argument, it is outside of the VP domain so it is merged too late for the ApplP, which must merge with a verb.[3] This contrast with the oblique marked location argument shows that the antipassive does not involve the loss of absolutive case (as in Baker 1988), since absolutive is available for the promoted argument. Thus, it is unlikely that the antipassive morpheme is the head of a special external argument introducing v head that does not assign case (Levin 2015), or blocks T from assigning case, thus forcing an oblique case for the undergoer argument.[4]

---

[2] Also, verbs of creation are agentive verbs in Eskimo-Aleut, as in this example from Central Alaskan Yup'ik (Miyaoka 2012), which is expected if creation verbs introduce their argument.

    (i)   kenir-tuq
           cook-IND.3SG

       'She is cooking something.'

[3] Spencer (1995) states that "dative shift" has not been reported to occur with intransitive verbs. Thus, it is unlikely that the phenomenon illustrated here is a high applicative, since high applicatives can occur with intransitive verbs.

[4] We could analyze the promotion of the location argument to absolutive as a case of an additional high applicative element, perhaps assigned some "affected" role. The denotational difference would come from this "affected" role. However, this analysis does not gain us much over the analysis presented above: there are still two "object" positions, one within the VP and there is still an applicative head. The analysis presented in the text is superior, though, in the sense that elements that generally are assigned only an "affected" role tend to be animate and/or sentient (Bosse et al. 2012).

4.2 Not just for case reasons

One final note concerns whether or not the addition of the antipassive argument with the applicative is necessary for argument structure reasons or simply case reasons. One potential alternative explanation for the presence of the antipassive is that there are not enough structural case positions for all the arguments. We might suggest that the promoted locative argument "steals" absolutive case from the undergoer argument, so there is no structural case for the undergoer argument. Antipassivization is then required in order to assign case to the undergoer if the location receives the only absolutive.

For Baker (1988), antipassivization absorbs the case assigning ability of the verb, so applicatives should be impossible with antipassivized verbs. He gives examples from Tzotzil which motivate this claim.

(15)   Tzotzil (Aissen 1983)

    a. č-i-ʔak'-van.
       ASP-A1-give-ANTIP
       'I am giving [someone] (i.e. my daughter, in marriage).

    b. * Taš-Ø-k-ak'-van-be   li Šune.
       ASP-A3-E1-give-ANTIP-to the Šun
       'I am giving [someone] to Šun.' (my daughter, in marriage)

Here, the antipassive suffix is -*van* and the applied suffix is -*be*.

So there is some cross-linguistic difference here in the ability of antipassives to have applied arguments. An explanation for this difference comes from the different types of antipassive markers. In this case, the antipassive marker in Tzotzil, unlike *ine-* in Chukchi, is not an argument introducer but an intransitivizer. Note that unlike the antipassive in Chukchi, these examples from Tzotzil are absolutely intransitive; Aissen (1983: 291) states that "verbs suffixed with -*van* have a reading like 'to do x to y or with respect to y' where y must be human, either a nonspecific human or a discourse referent. In either case, *verbs suffixed with –van never occur with an overt object*" [italics mine].

(16)   Tzotzil (Aissen 1983)

    a. Muk'bu š-i-mil-van.
       never ASP-A1-kill-ANTIP
       'I never killed anyone.'

b. ... š-k'-ot   sibtas-van-uk-Ø.
   ASP-come frighten-ANTIP-uk-A3
   '... he came to frighten [people].'

c. ʔAk'-b-at-Ø   s-veʔel, ʔi-Ø-veʔ lek. Ta ša la
   give-be-PASS-A3 his-meal ASP-A3-eat well ASP now PT
   š-Ø-mey-van,   ta ša la š-Ø-buɇ'-van   ti
   ASP-A3-embrace-ANTIP ASP now PT ASP-A3-kiss-ANTIP the
   kriarailetike.
   maids
   'He was given his meal, he ate well. The maids embraced [him] and
   kissed [him].'

These "absolutely intransitive" verbs do not introduce a syntactic argument,
not even an internal argument marked with oblique case or a null syntactic one.
Though their lexical-conceptual meaning has two participants, there is no argument in the syntax; rules of construal based on pragmatics and the lexical-
conceptual meaning of the verb derive the interpretation of a second event participant. If there is no internal argument introduced, then there can be no low
applicative formation.

An alternative to this analysis considers that this antipassive marker does introduce an argument, but that this argument comes existentially closed and thus
there is no open argument position. The verb, then, is still not of the right type to
combine with the ApplP, because the internal argument position has been satu-
rated. In this way, both types of antipassive markers introduce arguments, with
the difference attributed to whether or not that argument position is open or
closed. Furthermore, we can then make a parallel with the passive construction,
as some languages allow the external argument to be expressed as an oblique and
some do not. However, these "missing objects" in this absolutely intransitive constructions are not interpreted existentially, but either as a discourse referent or
generically. In fact, antipassive clauses with -*ine* in Chukchi and -*si* in Inuit with
no overt oblique argument can be interpreted existentially, unlike the examples
from Tzotzil given above.

In addition, another alternative is to consider that the antipassive morpheme
does suppress absolutive case, but the difference between Chukchi and Tzotzil is
that the Appl morpheme itself brings along absolutive case in Chukchi but not
Tzotzil. However, this alternative is unlikely since even in a simple antipassive
construction in Tzotzil with no applicative, the internal argument is not allowed.

Thus, the internal argument in Tzotzil is never possible.[5]

Thus, we see here how considering whether or not an antipassive morpheme introduces an argument can explain some of the cross-linguistic variation seen in applicativization and antipassivization.[6]

5 Conclusion

In some languages, antipassivization is necessary for applicativization. Following Basilico (2012; 2017), I argue that the antipassive morpheme can introduce an internal argument. This argument introduction allows for low applicative formation, given Pylkkänen's (2008) analysis that low applicatives require transitive verbs. In those cases where antipassivization does not support applicativization, these antipassive morphemes do not introduce an internal argument. These latter constructions allow no oblique internal argument to be present in the syntax. Case reasons alone cannot explain these facts.

By upending the standard notion that antipassivization always involves argument elimination or demotion, but can involve argument addition, this study accounts for a seemingly contradictory cross-linguistic relationship between antipassivization and applicativization.

We have further support for the view that internal arguments can be introduced in the syntax. In addition, this work shows that there are two different positions for the introduction of the internal argument, one internal to the VP and one external to the VP. This analysis asks us to revisit notions such as Baker's (1988) Uniformity of Thematic Assignment Hypothesis, as well as the syntactic characterization of the unaccusative and unergative distinction.

Abbreviations

The abbreviations used in the glosses of this chapter follow the Leipzig Glossing Rules. Additional abbreviations: ASP aspectual morphemes PART partitive mood PT particle.

---

[5] I thank an anonymous reviewer for both alternatives suggested here.

[6] A prediction of this approach to the antipassive is that verbs which introduce their arguments and thus do not appear with overt antipassive morphology in the antipassive construction (such as agentive verbs in Eskimo-Aleut) would not need antipassive morphology with a low applicative. Unfortunately, I do not have such data available to me which shows that this prediction is confirmed. Thank you to both reviewers for pointing out this prediction to me.

David Basilico

Acknowledgments

I would like to thank the audience at the *Dative structures and beyond* conference for helpful insights and comments, as well as two anonymous reviewers for their reading and comments. The usual disclaimers apply.

References

Acedo-Matellán, Víctor & Jaume Mateu. 2014. From syntax to roots: A syntactic approach to root interpretation. In Artemis Alexiadou, Hagit Borer & Florian Schäfer (eds.), *The syntax of roots and the roots of syntax*, 14–32. Oxford: Oxford University Press.

Aissen, Judith. 1983. Indirect object advancement in Tzotzil. In David M. Perlmutter (ed.), *Studies in relational grammar 1*, 272–302. Chicago, IL: University of Chicago Press.

Baker, Mark C. 1988. *Incorporation: A theory of grammatical function changing.* Chicago, IL: Chicago University Press.

Basilico, David. 2012. The antipassive and its relation to scalar structure. In María Cristina Cuervo & Yves Roberge (eds.), *The end of argument structure*, 75–104. Bingley, UK: Emerald Group Publishing Limited.

Basilico, David. 2017. *The antipassive adds an argument.* Austin, TX. Paper presented at the 2017 Annual Meeting of the Linguistic Society of America.

Bobaljik, Jonathan David. 2007. The limits of deponency: A Chukotko-centric perspective. In Matthew Baerman, Greville G. Corbett, David Brown & Andrew Hippisley (eds.), *Deponency and morphological mismatches*, 174–201. Oxford: Oxford University Press.

Bobaljik, Jonathan David & Phillip Branigan. 2006. Eccentric agreement and multiple case checking. In Alana Johns, Diane Massam & Juneval Ndayiragije (eds.), *Ergativity: Emerging issues*, 47–77. Dordrecht: Springer.

Borer, Hagit. 2005. *Structuring sense: The normal course of events.* Vol. 2. Oxford: Oxford University Press.

Bosse, Solveig, Benjamin Bruening & Masahiro Yamada. 2012. Affected experiencers. *Natural Language & Linguistic Theory* 30. 1185–1230. DOI:10.1007/s11049-012-9177-1

Cuervo, María Cristina. 2020. Datives as applicatives. In Anna Pineda & Jaume Mateu (eds.), *Dative constructions in Romance and beyond*, 1–39. Berlin: Language Science Press. DOI:10.5281/zenodo.3776531

Dunn, Michael. 1999. *A grammar of Chukchi*. Canberra: Australian National University. (Doctoral dissertation).

Hale, Ken. 2002. Eccentric agreement. In Beatriz Fernández & Pablo Albizu (eds.), *Kasu eta Komunztaduraren gainean [on case and agreement]*, 15–48. Vitoria-Gasteiz: Euskal Herriko Unibetsitatea.

Johns, Alana & Ivona Kučerová. 2017. On the morphosyntactic reflexes of the information structure analysis in the ergative patterning of the Inuit language. In Jessica Coonn, Diane Massam & Lisa Travis (eds.), *Oxford handbook of ergativity*, 397–418. Oxford: Oxford University Press.

Kozinsky, Ivan, Victor Nedjalkov & Maria Polinskaja. 1988. Antipassive in Chukchee: Oblique object, object incorporation, zero object. In Masayoshi Shibatanni (ed.), *Passive and voice*, 651–707. Amsterdam: John Benjamins.

Kratzer, Angelika. 1996. Severing the external argument from its verb. In Johan Rooryck & Laurie Zaring (eds.), *Phrase structure and the lexicon*, 109–137. Dordrecht: Kluwer.

Levin, Beth. 1999. Objecthood: An event structure perspective. In Sabrina J. Billings, John P. Boyle & Aaron M. Griffith (eds.), *Papers from the 35th Regional Meeting of the Chicago Linguistic Society (CLS), 1: The Main Session*, 223–247. Chicago, IL: Chicago Linguistic Society.

Levin, Theodore. 2015. *Toward a unified analysis of antipassive and pseudo noun incorporation constructions*. Portland, OR. Paper presented at the 2017 Annual Meeting of the Linguistic Society of America.

Lohndal, Terje. 2014. *Phrase structure and argument structure: A case study of the syntax-semantics interface*. 1st edn. (Oxford Studies in Theoretical Linguistics 49). Oxford, UK: Oxford University Press.

Miyaoka, Osahito. 2012. *A grammar of Central Alaskan Yupik CAY)* (Mouton grammar library 58). Berlin: De Gruyter Mouton. OCLC: ocn816279854.

Nagai, Tadataka. 2006. *Agentive and patientive verb bases in North Alaskan Iñupiaq*. Fairbanks, AK: University of Alaska Fairbanks. (Doctoral dissertation).

Polinskaja, Maria S. & Vladimir P. Nedjalkov. 1987. Contrasting the absolutive in Chuckchee: Syntax, semantics and pragmatics. *Lingua* 31(1–4). 239–269. DOI:10.1016/0024-3841(87)90074-X

Polinsky, Maria. 2016. *Deconstructing ergativity: Two types of ergative languages and their features* (Oxford Studies in Comparative Syntax). New York, NY: Oxford University Press.

Pylkkänen, Liina. 2008. *Introducing arguments*. Cambridge, MA: MIT Press.

Rappaport Hovav, Malka & Beth Levin. 1999. Building verb meanings. In Miriam Butt & Wilhelm Geuder (eds.), *The projection of arguments: Lexical and compositional factors*, 97–134. Stanford, CA: CSLI Publications.

Spencer, Andrew. 1995. Incorporation in Chukchi. *Language* 71(3). 439–489. DOI:10.2307/416217

Spreng, Bettina. 2012. *Viewpoint aspect in Inuktitut: The syntax and semantics of antipassives*. Toronto: University of Toronto. (Doctoral dissertation).

Wechsler, Mattie. 2020. The lexical underspecification of Bantu causatives and applicatives. In Anna Pineda & Jaume Mateu (eds.), *Dative constructions in Romance and beyond*, 241–271. Berlin: Language Science Press. DOI:10.5281/zenodo.3776551

Part IV

Case alternations involving datives

Chapter 12

Dative objects with novel verbs in Icelandic

Jóhannes Gísli Jónsson
Unversity of Iceland

Rannveig Thórarinsdóttir
Unversity of Iceland

This paper discusses the results of two online surveys testing object case with novel verbs in Icelandic. The results show that a novel transitive verb takes a dative direct object if the verb (a) encodes some kind of motion of the object referent, or (b) has a translational substitute that takes a dative object. If neither (a) nor (b) holds, the object gets the default accusative case. Thus, caused motion plays a major role in the licensing of dative case with direct objects in Icelandic.

1 Introduction

Dative case with direct objects in Icelandic has been widely discussed in the linguistic literature (see e.g. Yip et al. 1987; Barðdal 2001; 2008; Svenonius 2002; Maling 2002; and Jónsson 2013a). The central issue is the degree to which the dative is semantically predictable. As discussed by Maling (2002), verbs with dative objects are found in various verb classes in Icelandic, most of which also include verbs with accusative objects. Thus, it appears that dative is predictable only in a broad sense. However, it can be shown that dative objects are fully predictable in at least three closely related classes, verbs of ballistic motion (Svenonius 2002) verbs of emission (Maling 2002, Jónsson 2013a) and pour verbs (Jónsson 2013a).

One way of probing the semantics of dative objects in Icelandic is to examine novel transitive verbs since these verbs should reflect the regular aspects of dative case assignment. Indeed, the fact that new verbs never take genitive objects

 Jóhannes Gísli Jónsson & Rannveig Thórarinsdóttir. 2020. Dative objects with novel verbs in Icelandic. In Anna Pineda & Jaume Mateu (eds.), *Dative constructions in Romance and beyond*, 297–315. Berlin: Language Science Press. DOI:10.5281/zenodo.3776555

(Jónsson & Eythórsson 2011) suggests that they cannot assign truly idiosyncratic case. However, with the exception of Barðdal (2001; 2008), new verbs with dative objects have not been a central concern in the literature on the Icelandic case system.

We report here on the results of two online surveys testing object case with verbs that have become part of colloquial Icelandic in the last few decades (see Thórarinsdóttir 2015). The results show that a novel transitive verb takes a dative direct object if the verb (a) encodes motion of the object referent, or (b) has a translational substitute that takes a dative object. We will refer to (b) as isolate attraction, following Barðdal (2001), and take the term translational substitute to mean an established verb taking a dative object that can replace the new verb semantically. If neither (a) nor (b) applies, the object gets accusative case, the default case for direct objects in Icelandic. This holds not only for verbs selecting one object case but also for verbs displaying variation between dative and accusative. This means that some verbs may be ambiguous in whether they encode caused motion or not. Note, however, that case variation in Icelandic may also be purely formal and not reflect any semantic distinction between the variants (see Jónsson 2013b); for discussion of formal case variation in Romance, see Ledgeway et al. 2020 [this volume] and Royo 2020 [this volume]).

The strong link between caused motion and dative objects in Icelandic has often been discussed, e.g. by Barðdal (2001; 2008); Svenonius (2002); Maling (2002); and Jónsson (2013a). Our proposal is new in that caused motion is argued to be the crucial meaning component of new dative verbs in Icelandic that are not licensed by isolate attraction. That isolate attraction plays a role independent of caused motion is shown by novel verbs like *dílíta* 'delete electronically', which does not express any motion of the object. This verb takes a dative object just like its translational substitute *eyða* 'delete, spend, waste', which has a broader meaning than *dílíta*. Further examples of isolate attraction will be discussed in §3.2 below.

Since there are only two ways in which a novel verb can get a dative object and both of them are quite restricted, our proposal makes strong predictions about dative objects with novel verbs in Icelandic. As discussed in §3 and §4, these predictions are borne out by the data from the two online surveys. Importantly and in clear contrast to Barðdal (2001; 2008), we do not allow for the possibility that novel verbs take a dative object if they are attracted to specific classes of dative verbs with a similar meaning. Thus, the data from the two surveys will be accounted for without any recourse to this possibility, although various subclasses of verbs taking the same object case will be mentioned in our discussion.

2 Background

There is a fundamental unity to all dative objects in Icelandic in that dative is preserved under passivization. In this respect, dative differs sharply from accusative (Zaenen et al. 1985). Case preservation in passives applies equally to datives that are completely predictable, such as dative recipients or benefactives with ditransitive verbs (Jónsson 2000), and datives that are idiosyncratically associated with some monotransitive verbs. This latter type is exemplified by verbs like *anna* 'meet (demand), have time for', *gleyma* 'forget', *stríða* 'tease', *treysta* 'trust' and *unna* 'love'. This contrast between dative and accusative shows that dative is not a structural case in Icelandic, at least not in the same sense as accusative (see Thráinsson 2007: 181–192 and references cited there).

A further difference is that accusative is not associated with any specific semantics as transitive verbs of all kinds take accusative objects in Icelandic. In fact, as shown the by the ECM construction, accusative can even be assigned to a DP that is not an argument of the relevant verb. Although it has been observed that certain sublasses of transitive verbs in Icelandic only allow accusative objects (Jónsson 2013a), this is best understood as a constraint on the assignment of dative (and genitive) case. In §3 and §4, some verb classes that systematically exclude dative or genitive objects will be mentioned but this should not be taken to mean that accusative is semantically determined in these classes.

Despite the differences between accusative and dative discussed above, it has become fairly common in recent years to link both these cases to functional heads in the extended vP. Thus, the Icelandic dative is often associated with an applicative head inside VoiceP/vP. Wood (2015: 128–138) argues that this is correct for indirect objects but generally not for direct objects. His arguments are based e.g. on the fact that dative is preserved with indirect objects but not direct objects under suffixation of the "middle" suffix -*st* in Icelandic. His proposal is that direct object datives are licensed by a functional head that he labels v_{DAT}, following Svenonius (2006). The results discussed in §3 and §4 suggest that there is a functional head that licenses dative objects with verbs that express caused motion. Diachronic evidence from Faroese points in the same direction since dative has systematically disappeared with all such verbs but is preserved with various other monotransitive verbs in Faroese (Jónsson 2009). This diachronic development can be interpreted as the loss of the relevant functional head in the history of Faroese.

Svenonius (2002) shows that verbs of ballistic motion like *kasta* 'throw' always take a dative object in Icelandic. With these verbs, the agent applies force to cause an object to move but the motion of the object continues after the agent has done his/her part. Svenonius (2002) claims that dative objects in Icelandic are found with verbs where the subevent associated with the agent does not completely overlap temporally with the subevent associated with the theme object. This is correct as a one-way generalization as every verb that complies with it takes a dative object in Icelandic but it is not immediately obvious how far this generalization extends beyond verbs of ballistic motion. We cannot discuss this issue fully here, but it seems to us that it also comprises emission verbs, pour verbs and many of the verbs tested in the online surveys relating to information technology and expressing motion from one electronic location to another.

Another complicating factor is that dative case is found with various verbs of motion that involve complete temporal overlap of the two subevents associated with the agent and the theme. Thus, verbs of accompanied or directed motion may take a dative object (cf. *drösla* 'move (with difficulty)', *lyfta* 'lift, raise', *smeygja* 'slip, slide', and *ýta* 'push') or an accusative object (cf. *bera* 'carry', *draga* 'pull', *hækka* 'raise', and *lækka* 'lower'). However, the data discussed in §3 and §4 suggest that dative objects with novel verbs are licensed by caused motion, irrespective of any subclassification of the relevant verbs. Hence, it appears that dative is in the process of being generalized to all transitive motion verbs in Icelandic (Barðdal 2008).

The theoretical literature on motion verbs across languages is very much focused on intransitive verbs like *run* and *dance* and there is no standard definition of caused motion that we are aware of. Still, this does not turn out to be much of a problem for our purposes. As we will see, the crucial issue is to distinguish verbs that encode caused motion of the direct object from verbs where caused motion is not encoded but rather inferred from world knowledge. It is only novel verbs in the former class that take a dative object, i.e. if isolate attraction does not play a role.

3 The results

In the following two sections, the results of a large-scale study of direct object case with 40 novel verbs in Icelandic will be discussed. These verbs have become part of the Icelandic lexicon in the last few decades, mainly as borrowings from English or Danish but some as native neologisms. Most of these verbs are highly colloquial and not often found in writing, especially the loan verbs, but as far as we know this has no effect on object case.

3.1 The two surveys

The study to be discussed here consisted of two online surveys, with 393 and 402 participants, respectively (see Thórarinsdóttir 2015 for details). Each survey featured 50 sentences, 20 sentences testing object case with novel verbs and 30 fillers. For every sentence, the participants were asked to select four options presented to them in this order: (a) the accusative form of the direct object, (b) the dative form of the direct object, (c) both forms accepted, (d) neither form accepted. Option (d) was selected quite often, especially with verbs of low frequency, presumably because some of the participants were not familiar with these verbs. By contrast, very few opted for (c), even with verbs where we suspect that many speakers allow both accusative and dative.

The verbs tested in the two surveys are listed below. The glosses are based on the relevant test sentences in the surveys.

(1)   a. Verbs in the first survey:
      brodkasta 'broadcast', *dánlóda* 'download', *droppa* 'quit, drop', *drulla* 'get, put', *dömpa* 'dump', *farta* 'drive fast', *flexa* 'show off with, throw around', *gúgla* 'google', *hannesa* 'steal (a text)', *installa* 'install (a program)', *jáa* 'search for on ja.is', *jinxa* 'put a curse on', *krakka* 'unlock, crack', *krassa* 'cause to crash', *offa* 'turn off, shock', *rippa* 'copy (illegally)', *slaka* 'pass', *slumma* 'kick (a ball)', *smessa* 'send by sms', *sneika* 'sneak'

   b. Verbs in the second survey:
      átsorsa 'outsource', *bekka* 'bench press', *blasta* 'play loudly, blast', *bleima* 'blame', *domma* 'dominate', *fiffa* 'fix (illegally)', *gólfa* 'press (the pedal) to the floor', *gramma* 'put on Instagram', *græja* 'procure', *gúffa* 'eat greedily', *kikka* 'kick, hit', *meila* 'e-mail', *mæna* 'collect, mine', *neimdroppa* 'namedrop', *peista* 'paste', *pósta* 'post (online)', *sjera* 'share (online)', *skrína* 'screen, keep an eye on', *skúbba* 'be the first to tell (a piece of news)', *syngja* 'tell (a secret)'

Five verbs are not included in the following discussion here, either because the relevant test sentences allowed for too many possibilities for their semantic interpretation (*jinxa, kikka*) or because it can be argued that they are not really new (*drulla, slaka, skúbba*).

The two surveys were designed to test our hypothesis that dative case with novel transitive verbs in Icelandic is licensed by two factors: (a) caused motion of the object referent, or (b) a translational substitute taking a dative object (isolate attraction). The verbs were selected so that they would fall into three groups of roughly the same size: (a) verbs taking a dative object, (b) verbs taking an accusative object, and (c) verbs displaying variation between dative and accusative. A random selection of novel verbs would have produced a less balanced sample in view of Barðdal's (2008: 78–79) study of 107 novel verbs in Icelandic where accusative outscored dative by a ratio of approximately 2:1. Note that no effort was made to include verbs from all the subclasses of the dative verbs discussed by Maling (2002) as the right verbs would have been hard to find and this would have required a much bigger study.

The novel verbs tested in the study can be divided into three classes: (a) verbs that strongly favour dative, (b) verbs that strongly favour accusative, and (c) verbs that vary between dative and accusative object. For concreteness, classes (a) and (b) were defined such that the preferred case was selected at least five times more often than the other case. Verbs from the first two classes are discussed in §3.2 and §3.3 below but variation between dative and accusastive is the topic of §4.

3.2 Dative objects

Many verbs in the current study showed a strong preference for a dative object. This is true of the following verbs in the first survey:

Table 1: Verbs taking a dative object in survey 1

Verb	Gloss	DAT	ACC	Both	Neither
dánlóda	'download'	**93,1**	4,1	0,5	2,3
droppa	'quit, drop'	**90,6**	1,5	0,3	7,6
dömpa	'dump'	**87,8**	0,5	1,3	10,4
installa	'install'	**85,8**	6,6	2,5	5,1
brodkasta	'broadcast'	**85,2**	2,8	1,0	11,0
sneika	'sneak'	**55,0**	5,1	1,5	38,4
flexa	'throw around'	**54,7**	8,7	1,0	35,6
slumma	'kick (a ball)'	**47,8**	8,4	3,8	40,0

Although the acceptance rate for dative ranges from 47,8% to 93,1%, the dative was chosen at least five times more often than the accusative for every verb here. There were also significant differences with respect to the last option (neither), with high frequency verbs like *dánlóda*, *droppa*, and *installa* scoring below 8% but verbs of low frequency like *sneika*, *flexa* and *slumma* scoring above 35%. We take this to show that the lowest scoring verbs were the most familiar to the participants and vice versa. The same trend was also evident in other tables in this paper.

As discussed in more detail below, all the verbs listed in Table 1 encode some kind of motion of the object referent. This is also true of all the verbs in the second survey that showed a clear preference for a dative object:

Table 2: Verbs taking a dative object in survey 2

Verb	Gloss	DAT	ACC	Both	Neither
pósta	'post (online)'	**96,0**	2,0	0,5	1,5
gúffa	'eat greedily'	**87,1**	8,0	2,7	2,2
sjera	'share (online)'	**81,3**	6,0	0,7	12,0
blasta	'play loudly, blast'	**76,6**	12,4	3,0	8,0
átsorsa	'outsource'	**64,2**	11,2	5,5	19,1

The test sentences with the top three verbs in Table 1 are shown in (2) below:

(2) a. Ertu   búin að dánlóda nýju   myndinni   með Ryan
          are.you done to download new.DAT the.movie.DAT with Ryan
          Gosling?
          Gosling?
          'Have you downloaded the new movie with Ryan Gosling?'

     b. Ég held að   ég verði að droppa þessu   námskeiði.
          I   think that I   must to drop   this.DAT course.DAT
          'I think that I must drop this course.'

     c. Djöfull er bossinn duglegur að dömpa á þig verkefnum.
          bloody is the.boss relentless to dump on you tasks.DAT
          'How relentlessly the boss dumps tasks on you!'

The motion verbs *dánlóda*, *droppa* and *dömpa* can be replaced here by the dative verbs *hlaða niður* 'download', *sleppa* 'release, skip' and *demba* 'dump, pour', respectively, without any change in meaning. Hence, it is impossible to determine if the datives in (2a–c) are due to isolate attraction or caused motion. The same applies to *brodkasta*, a verb of emission which has a translational substitute in the dative verb *sjónvarpa* 'broadcast'. However, the dative object with *sneika* and *sjera* is presumably due to isolate attraction by *lauma* 'sneak' and *deila* 'share, divide', both of which take a dative object.

Other verbs in Tables 1 and 2 do not have a translational substitute taking a dative object in the traditional vocabulary of Icelandic, e.g. *installa*, *pósta*, and *gúffa*. All these verbs encode motion of the object, although not in a literal sense, except perhaps *gúffa*. The relevant test sentences are shown in (3):

(3)   a.   Þú   þarft að installa Office pakkanum.
           you need to install Office the.package.DAT
           'You need to install the Office package.'

      b.   Helga póstaði ótrúlega   skemmtilegu   myndbandi á   vegginn
           Helga posted incredibly entertaining.DAT video.DAT on the.wall
           minn áðan.
           my   just
           'Helga just posted an incredibly funny video on my wall.'

      c.   Af   hverju eru allir farnir að gúffa í   sig chiafræjum?
           from what   are all started to shovel in REFL chia.seeds.DAT
           'Why has everybody started to eat chia seeds like crazy?'

The sense of motion is quite clear with *pósta* since the meaning can be paraphrased roughly as 'place (text, picture, video etc.) on a website to make available to others'. Matters are more complicated with *installa* because this verb describes the process of getting a software program ready for use and that does not involve movement in any obvious way. However, most people have probably seen a progress bar when installing software and this creates the perception that there is movement from one location to another. Moreover, since programs are usually downloaded from the internet before they are installed, it seems that native speakers see *installa* as a process that includes downloading from the internet. This is supported by the fact that a directional PP like *á tölvuna þína* 'to your computer' can be added in (3a) to express the final location of the program. Hence, the object of *installa* gets dative case just like the object of *dánlóda*.

The verb *gúffa* is obligatorily accompanied by the directional preposition *í* 'in' plus a simple reflexive bound by the subject. Thus, it seems that the verb itself encodes caused motion whereas the directional PP denotes where the food ends up. Examples like (3c) describe putting food quickly and/or greedily into the mouth but the food is not necessarily consumed. This is shown in (4) below, which is not a contradiction in our judgment:

(4) Hann gúffaði í sig kökum en skyrpti þeim út í laumi.
he shovelled in REFL cakes.DAT but spat them.DAT out in secret
'He ate cookies like crazy but spat them out secretly.'

This is not possible with ingestion verbs like *éta* 'eat' or *borða* 'eat', both of which take an accusative object. Unlike *gúffa*, these verbs encode consumption of food but not movement into the mouth. Of course, a sentence like (3c) would generally be understood as saying that people eat a lot of chia seeds but this is through real world knowledge as it is not customary to put food into one's mouth without eating it. The contrast between *gúffa* and *éta* or *borða* suggests that motion vs. consumption of food may be the critical factor determining object case with verbs of ingestion, but this will have to be an issue for future investigation.

The verbs that still require some comment are *flexa*, *átsorsa*, *slumma* and *blasta*. The verb *flexa* means to throw money around to show off so the sense of motion is quite clear. The same is true of *átsorsa* which typically involves moving a task from one company to another. The verb *blasta* denotes sound emission and emission of all kinds is a type of ballistic motion (Jónsson 2013a). Finally, *slumma* is clearly a verb of ballistic motion so only dative is possible (see Jónsson 2013a for more examples and discussion of similar verbs).

3.3 Accusative objects

Some verbs in the study received a significantly higher score for accusative than dative. These verbs are listed in the following table:

Table 3: Verbs taking an accusative object

Verb	Gloss	DAT	ACC	Both	Neither
fiffa	'fix (illegally)'	1,5	**94,5**	0,0	4,0
gúgla	'google'	4,6	**93,6**	0,5	1,3
krakka	'unlock, crack'	1,3	**86,2**	2,3	10,2
gólfa	'press to the floor'	3,5	**74,9**	0,7	20,9
skrína	'screen, keep an eye on'	1,3	**74,1**	0,0	24,6
gramma	'put on Instagram'	8,5	**66,9**	3,0	21,6
jáa	'search for on ja.is'	7,1	**58,8**	0,3	33,8
offa	'turn off, shock'	9,4	**58,0**	0,5	32,1
domma	'dominate'	8,5	**52,5**	0,0	39,0

For most of these verbs, it is intuitively clear that the direct object does not undergo motion in any sense. Consider, for example, the following test examples of the verbs *krakka*, *offa* and *fiffa*:

(5)   a.   Geta þeir krakkað hvaða síma   sem er?
           can they hack   which phone.ACC that is
           'Can they hack any phone whatsoever?'

      b.   Þetta attitude offaði   mig   alveg.
           this attitude turned.off me.ACC completely
           'This attitude shocked me completely.'

      c.   Þau lentu   í   peningavandræðum og byrjuðu að fiffa
           they landed in money.trouble   and started to fix
           bókhaldið.
           the.book-keeping.ACC
           'They got into financial difficulties and started to fiddle with the numbers.'

The verbs *gramma* and *gólfa* stand out in Table 3 because they seem to express motion of the object. The test examples with these verbs are provided in (6):

(6)   a.   Hann gólfaði   bensíngjöfina   þegar hann var kominn út
           he   pushed.down the.foot.pedal.ACC when he   was come   out
           á   hraðbrautina.
           to the.highway
           'He started to speed when he entered the highway.'

      b.   Er einhver búinn að gramma   nýja tíuþúsundkallinn?
           is someone done to instagram new 10,000.krónur.bill.ACC
           'Has someone put the new 10,000 krónur bill on Instagram?'

These verbs are crucially different from the dative verb *pósta* discussed in §3.2 in that they name the final location of the object. By contrast, *pósta* does not specify the destination of the moved file and thus is compatible with a directional PP, as in (3b). The verb *gólfa* is derived from the noun *gólf* 'floor' and the meaning is literally 'push to the floor' and *gramma* derives from the noun *Instagram* and means 'put on Instagram'. Hence, the final location of the object is encoded rather than movement to that location. Verbs of this kind are referred to as pocket verb by Levin (1993) and they all take an accusative object in Icelandic, e.g. *axla* 'shoulder', *bóka* 'book', *fangelsa* 'imprison', *hýsa* 'house', *jarða* 'bury', *ramma* 'frame' and *slíðra* 'sheathe'.

4 Case variation

Some verbs in the present study displayed significant variation between accusative and dative. Under our hypothesis, case variation is expected whenever a verb is semantically ambiguous in a way that is linked to caused motion or the existence of a translational substitute taking a dative object. However, as we will see, this does not necessarily entail a difference in truth conditions.

For convenience, the verbs examined here will be referred to as DAT/ACC verbs. The discussion of these verbs is divided into two subsections below, monotransitive verbs and ditransitive verbs, since they give rise to somewhat different issues.

4.1 Monotransitive verbs

The following table lists monotransitive DAT/ACC verbs in the two surveys. As can be seen here, the dative outscored the accusative with six verbs but the reverse preference was found with four verbs:

Table 4: Monotransitive verbs taking both dative and accusative object

Verb	Gloss	DAT	ACC	Both	Neither
bleima	'blame'	**48,8**	32,3	1,2	17,7
krassa	'cause to crash, ruin'	**48,6**	27,0	2,3	22,1
neimdroppa	'namedrop'	**42,5**	30,9	3,2	23,4
mæna	'collect, mine'	**41,5**	17,9	2,5	38,1
syngja	'tell (a secret); sing'	**36,1**	15,2	1,5	47,2
farta	'drive fast'	**34,1**	13,0	0,5	52,4
rippa	'copy (illegally)'	19,3	**59,0**	1,8	19,9
hannesa	'steal (a text)'	19,1	**51,9**	3,3	25,7
peista	'paste'	44,8	**47,5**	4,7	3,0
bekka	'bench press'	32,1	**38,6**	7,2	22,1

All the DAT/ACC verbs listed here, except *peista*, scored over 15% for the last option (neither) and this reflects the low frequency of these verbs. Arguably, infrequent novel verbs have not been used enough to acquire an established meaning across speakers. As a result, they may have different intuitions about the meaning of these verbs, including the presence or absence of the factors that license a dative object. Admittedly, our data on the meaning of monotransitive

DAT/ACC verbs for different speakers is rather limited and our remarks below will inevitably be somewhat speculative. Still, we hope to show that these verbs are ambiguous in ways which affects object case, unlike the verbs discussed in §3 and listed in Table 3 and Table 4.

Under our analysis, the dative variant with DAT/ACC verbs that do not express caused motion must be due to isolate attraction. Speakers that select a dative object with *bleima*, *krassa*, and *mæna* do so because they see the dative verbs *kenna um* 'blame', *rústa* 'ruin', and *safna* 'collect' as translational substitutes. As for *rippa* and *hannesa*, these verbs have a translational substitute in the dative verb *stela* 'steal' for some speakers. For other speakers, these two verbs denote copying without stealing, in which case *stela* is not a translational substitute and consequently the object must be accusative.

The verbs *neimdroppa*, *peista*, and *bekka* are among the DAT/ACC verbs for which the dative variant is licensed by caused motion. The test examples with these verbs are shown in (7):

(7) a. Hún byrjaði strax   að neimdroppa einhverjum böndum   sem
         she started right.away to namedrop some.DAT   bands.DAT which
         hún hafði djammað með.
         she had partied with

     b. Hún byrjaði strax   að neimdroppa einhver   bönd   sem
         she started right.away to namedrop some.ACC bands.ACC which
         hún hafði djammað með.
         she had partied with
         'She started immediately to namedrop bands she had partied with.'

     c. Tölvan   frýs   alltaf þegar ég reyni að peista myndinni
         the.computer freezes always when I try to paste the.picture.DAT
         í   Word.
         into Word

     d. Tölvan   frýs   alltaf þegar ég reyni að peista myndina
         the.computer freezes always when I try to paste the.picture.ACC
         í   Word.
         into Word
         'The computer always freezes when I try to paste the picture into a Word document.'

    e. Þessi gella getur bekkað 150 kílóum/kíló.
       this chick can bench 150 kilos.DAT/ACC
       'This chick can bench 150 kilos.'

For some speakers, *neimdroppa* is more or less synonymous with the accusative verbs *nefna* 'mention' and *telja upp* 'recount, list'. As expected, only accusative is possible in this sense. For other speakers, *neimdroppa* means to mention something in a way that is similar to dropping, i.e. in a sneaky way as to show off by mentioning something or someone famous. This use is associated with a dative object. Thus, the variation between accusative and dative boils down to the presence or absence of caused motion in a metaphorical sense as part of the lexical semantics of *neimdroppa*.

The case variation with *peista* does not correlate with any obvious truth conditional difference between the two variants. Still, it is clear that the object must be dative if *peista* is interpreted as a verb of motion in the sense of moving a piece of text or a picture from one file to another or within the same file. Alternatively, if *peista* encodes the resulting attachment rather than motion, only accusative is possible. In the latter case, *peista* is very much like the accusative verb *líma* 'glue'. For discussion of other similar examples of case variation, see Jónsson (2013a).

The verb *bekka* takes a dative object if it encodes motion of the object, as reflected by the gloss 'bench press'. In that sense, *bekka* is similar to the dative verb *lyfta* 'lift'. Still, *lyfta* is not a translational substitute in (7e) because replacing *bekka* by *lyfta* would yield a slightly different claim. The accusative variant may be due to the fact that *bekka* in (7e) is not only about moving a weight in a specified direction but also exerting great physical force against gravity. The verb *bekka* can also be used with objects that do not undergo movement, e.g. *bekka heimsmet* (literally 'bench a world record'), in which case only accusative is possible.

That leaves us with *farta* and *syngja*. These verbs had the highest score of all the DAT/ACC verbs for the last option (neither), suggesting that many native speakers were not familiar with these verbs in the relevant meaning. The verbs were tested in the following examples:

(8) a. Þótt   þetta sé hálfgerður dótabíll er ekkert leiðinlegt að farta
        although this is halfmade toycar is not   boring   to drive.fast
        honum/hann.
        him.DAT/ACC
        'Although this is a kind of a toycar, it is fun to speed.'

b. Hann var ekki lengi að syngja þessu/þetta   að lögreglunni.
   he   was not long to sing   this.DAT/ACC to the.police
   'I did not take him long to tell the police the whole story.'

The dative variant with *farta* encodes caused motion of a vehicle but the accusative is more difficult to explain. Perhaps it signals that the agent steps on the accelerator so that the car produces a sound similar to farting. This does not necessarily involve caused motion because this sound can be produced even if the car is not moving, e.g. if it is stuck in snow.

In its basic sense, *syngja* 'sing' is a performance verb which takes an accusative object like all other such verbs in Icelandic, e.g. *blístra* 'whistle', *flytja* 'perform', *leika* 'play', *lesa* 'read', *raula* 'hum', *spila* 'play', *tóna* 'chant' and *þylja* 'recite'. This basic meaning may have lead some speakers to chose accusative with *syngja* in (8b). However, *syngja* describes a manner of speaking in (8b) and all such verbs take a dative object in Icelandic if they express the exchange of information. These verbs include *blaðra* 'babble', *gaspra* 'babble', *hreyta* 'toss (words)', *hvísla* 'whisper', *kjafta* 'tell (a secret)', *muldra* 'mumble' and *stynja upp* 'moan'. Thus, it can be argued that *syngja* in (8b) encodes motion of the message conveyed to the police.

4.2 Ditransitive verbs

Three ditransitive verbs were tested in the present study and they all displayed considerable variation between accusative and dative with the direct object. The participants were not asked about the indirect object since dative is the only possibility there for new verbs. As shown in Table 5, the ditransitive verbs had virtually the same acceptance rate for both cases:

Table 5: Ditransitive verbs taking both dative and accusative object

Verb	Gloss	DAT	ACC	Both	Neither
græja	'procure; take care of'	**40,6**	37,1	1,7	20,6
smessa	'send by sms'	**36,9**	34,1	4,6	24,4
meila	'e-mail'	36,3	**39,8**	3,5	20,4

Verbs taking a dative indirect object and an accusative direct object (DAT-ACC verbs) constitute by far the biggest class of ditransitive verbs in Icelandic (see Zaenen et al. 1985 and Jónsson 2000). This class also includes most of the canonical ditransitive verbs in Icelandic, e.g. *gefa* 'give', *lána* 'lend', *rétta* 'pass', *segja* 'tell', *selja* 'sell', *senda* 'send' and *sýna* 'show'. The DAT-DAT class is much smaller and contains only a handful of typical ditransitive verbs, including *lofa* 'promise', *skila* 'return' and *úthluta* 'allot'.

In view of this, one would expect new ditransitive verbs to exhibit only DAT-ACC, unless the verb in question has a translational substitute with DAT-DAT. However, as discussed in more detail below, the DAT-DAT class relates to caused motion in a way that is similar to what we have already shown for monotransitive verbs. This class is also theoretically interesting in that the double dative strongly suggests two different sources for the two datives, e.g. an applicative head for the indirect object and some other functional head for the direct object.

We will start our discussion with *græja* because it is more straightforward than the other two verbs. The relevant test examples are shown in (9) below:

(9) a. Þú græjar þér   bara útilegudrasli   ef þú átt það ekki.
    you procure you.DAT just camping.stuff.DAT if you own it not

    b. Þú græjar þér   bara útilegudrasl   ef þú átt það ekki.
    you procure you.DAT just camping.stuff.ACC if you own it not
    'You just get yourself camping stuff if you don't have it.'

For *græja*, the double dative is due to the fact that this verb has, at least for some speakers, a translational substitute in the DAT-DAT verb *redda* 'procure, take care of'. In that sense, *græja* indicates that something was obtained in a casual or hurried way. Speakers selecting DAT-ACC understand *græja* presumably more like *útvega* 'procure', a DAT-ACC verb which has a more general meaning than *redda* because it is completely neutral with respect to how the direct object is procured.

The test examples for the verbs *meila* and *smessa* are given in (10):

(10) a. Gætirðu meilað mér   þessu/þetta sem fyrst?
    could.you e-mail me.DAT this.DAT/ACC as first
    'Could you e-mail this to me as soon as possible?'

    b. Geturðu ekki bara smessað honum reikningsnúmerinu   okkar?
    can.you not just SMS   him.DAT the.account.number.DAT our

    c. Geturðu ekki bara smessað honum reikningsnúmerið   okkar?
    can.you not just SMS   him.DAT the.account.number.ACC our
    'Can't you just send him our account number by SMS?'

The verbs *meila* and *smessa* are verbs of instrument of communication and have no translational substitutes taking a dative object. Rappaport Hovav & Levin (2008) claim that verbs of instrument of communication in English encode caused motion and the same is true for Icelandic. Both *meila* and *smessa* entail that the direct object changes location in electronic space, although it need not reach its intended goal (see Beavers 2011 on *e-mail*). These verbs also encode caused possession as the indirect object must be capable of possession and thus cannot be a location. This is a standard diagnostic to show that the double object construction in English encodes caused possession (see Green 1974 and much subsequent work). Thus, the examples in (11a–b) are ungrammatical unless *Berlin* refers to the people working in an office in Berlin:

(11)   a. *Gætirðu meilað Berlín   þessu/þetta sem fyrst?
            could.you e-mail Berlin.DAT this.DAT/ACC as   first
            'Could you e-mail Berlin this as soon as possible?'

        b. *Geturðu ekki smessað Berlín   númerinu/númerið?
            can.you not SMS   Berlin.DAT the.number.DAT/ACC
            'Can't you send Berlin the number by SMS?'

This ambiguity means that native speakers are faced with two options when using *meila* and *smessa* as double object verbs, to treat them as DAT-DAT verbs encoding caused motion or DAT-ACC verbs encoding caused possession, apparently without any difference in truth conditions.

The intended goal of verbs of instrument of communication can be expressed not only as a dative DP but also as a PP headed by the preposition *til* 'to' (Barðdal 2008: 128–132) but this does not effect the case variation with the direct object:

(12)   a. Gætirðu meilað þessu/þetta til mín?
            could.you e-mail this.DAT/ACC to me.GEN
            'Could you e-mail this to me?'

        b. Geturðu smessað númerinu/númerið   til hennar?
            can.you SMS   the.number.DAT/ACC to her.GEN
            'Can you send her the number by SMS?'

This shows that *meila* and *smessa* encode caused motion in (12) because only such verbs allow the goal to be expressed in a PP headed by *til* in Icelandic. However, caused possession is also encoded in examples like (12) because the goal must be capable of possession:

(13) a. *Gætirðu meilað þessu/þetta til Berlínar?
          could.you e-mail this.DAT/ACC to Berlin.GEN
          'Could you e-mail this to Berlin?'

      b. *Geturðu smessað númerinu/númerið til Berlínar?
          can.you SMS   the.number.DAT/ACC to Berlin.GEN
          'Can you send the number by SMS to Berlin?'

In view of the discussion above, one remaining issue is why the traditional motion verb *senda* 'send' always takes an accusative direct object. While we cannot provide a definitive answer here, this may have to do with the fact that (a) this verb lacks a manner component and (b) it does not entail motion that starts with the agent of the action. For instance, a sentence like *Jón sendi Maríu bók* 'John sent Mary a book' may describe a situation where Jón orders a book from an internet company that delivers the book directly to Mary (see also Beavers 2011 on *send* in English). Thus, the verb *senda* appears to be more about causing something to reach some person or place in any conceivable way rather than motion per se.

5 Conclusions

The results from the two large-scale surveys discussed in this paper show that a novel transitive verb in Icelandic takes a dative object if it (a) encodes some kind of caused motion of the object referent, or (b) has a translational substitute that takes a dative object. If neither (a) nor (b) holds, the object gets the default accusative case.

It is usually rather straightforward to determine if condition (b) holds and our discussion of such cases has indeed been rather brief. It is more difficult to argue that caused motion licenses a dative object. Crucially, the concept of caused motion has to be understood very broadly to include not only movement of concrete objects but also various abstract objects, including electronic files or messages.

Some of the novel verbs discussed here vary between dative and accusative object. This applies to some monotransitive verbs as well as the three ditransitive verbs tested. Under our analysis, this is expected if the relevant verb is semantically ambiguous such that the dative variant encodes caused motion or has a translational substitute taking a dative object. As argued in §4, the predictions of our analysis are borne out although some questions remain concerning the meaning of some verbs for individual speakers.

Abbreviations

The abbreviations used in the glosses of this chapter follow the Leipzig Glossing Rules.

Acknowledgements

We wish to thank two anonymous reviewers for constructive feedback on an earlier version of this paper. The usual disclaimers apply. This study was financially supported by a grant from the Icelandic Research Fund (Rannís).

References

Barðdal, Jóhanna. 2001. *Case in Icelandic: A synchronic, diachronic and comparative approach.* Lund: University of Lund. (Doctoral dissertation).

Barðdal, Jóhanna. 2008. *Productivity: Evidence from case and argument structure in Icelandic.* Amsterdam: John Benjamins.

Beavers, John. 2011. An aspectual analysis of ditransitive verbs of caused possession in English. *Journal of Semantics* 28. 1–54.

Green, Georgia M. 1974. *Semantics and syntactic regularity.* Bloomington, IN: Indiana University Press.

Jónsson, Jóhannes Gísli. 2000. Case and double objects in Icelandic. *Leeds Working Papers in Linguistics and Phonetics* 8. 71–94.

Jónsson, Jóhannes Gísli. 2009. Verb classes and dative objects in Insular Scandinavian. In Jóhanna Barðdal & Shobhana Chelliah (eds.), *The role of semantic, pragmatic and discourse factors in the development of case*, 203–224. Amsterdam/Philadelphia: John Benjamins.

Jónsson, Jóhannes Gísli. 2013a. Dative versus accusative and the nature of inherent case. In Beatriz Fernández & Ricardo Etxepare (eds.), *Variation in datives: A microcomparative perspective*, 144–160. Oxford: Oxford University Press.

Jónsson, Jóhannes Gísli. 2013b. Two types of case variation. *Nordic Journal of Linguistics* 36(1). 5–25.

Jónsson, Jóhannes Gísli & Thórhallur Eythórsson. 2011. Structured exceptions and case selection in Insular Scandinavian. In Horst Simon & Heike Wiese (eds.), *Expecting the unexpected: Exceptions in the grammar*, 213–242. Berlin: Mouton de Gruyter.

Ledgeway, Adam, Norma Schifano & Giuseppina Silvestri. 2020. Microvariation in dative-marking in the Romance and Greek varieties of Southern Italy. In Anna Pineda & Jaume Mateu (eds.), *Dative constructions in Romance and beyond*, 317–349. Berlin: Language Science Press. DOI:10.5281/zenodo.3776557

Levin, Beth. 1993. *English verb classes and alternations: A preliminary investigation*. Chicago: University of Chicago Press.

Maling, Joan. 2002. Það rignir þágufalli á Íslandi [It rains dative in iceland]: Verbs with dative objects in icelandic]. *Íslenskt mál og almenn málfræði* 24. 31–105.

Rappaport Hovav, Malka & Beth Levin. 2008. The English dative alternation: The case for verb sensitivity. *Journal of Linguistics* 44. 129–167. DOI:10.1017/S00222267070049

Royo, Carles. 2020. The accusative/dative alternation in Catalan verbs with experiencer object. In Anna Pineda & Jaume Mateu (eds.), *Dative constructions in Romance and beyond*, 371–393. Berlin: Language Science Press. DOI:10.5281/zenodo.3776563

Svenonius, Peter. 2002. Icelandic case and the structure of events. *The Journal of Comparative Germanic Linguistics* 5. 197–225. DOI:10.1023/A:1021252206904

Svenonius, Peter. 2006. *Case alternations and the Icelandic passive and middle*. Unpublished manuscript, University of Tromsø.

Thórarinsdóttir, Rannveig B. 2015. *Fallstjórn slangursagna [The case government of slang verbs.]* Reykjavík: University of Iceland. (BA thesis).

Thráinsson, Höskuldur. 2007. *The syntax of Icelandic.* Cambridge: Cambridge University Press.

Wood, Jim. 2015. *Icelandic morphosyntax and argument structure.* Dordrecht: Springer.

Yip, Moira, Maling Joan & Ray Jackendoff. 1987. Case in tiers. *Language* 63. 217–50.

Zaenen, Annie, Joan Maling & Höskuldur Thráinsson. 1985. Case and grammatical functions: The Icelandic passive. *Natural Language & Linguistic Theory* 3(4). 441–483.

Chapter 13

Microvariation in dative-marking in the Romance and Greek varieties of Southern Italy

Adam Ledgeway
University of Cambridge

Norma Schifano
University of Birmingham

Giuseppina Silvestri
University of California, Los Angeles

Greek and Romance have been spoken alongside of one another for centuries in southern Italy. Even though the Greek-speaking areas have been dramatically reduced over the centuries such that today Greek is now only spoken by a small number of increasingly elder speakers in a handful of villages of Calabria and southern Apulia (Salentino), the influence of Greek is still undeniable in that it has left its mark on the structures of the surrounding Romance dialects. Indeed, in this respect Rohlfs aptly coined the phrase *spirito greco, materia romanza* (literally "Greek spirit, Romance material") to highlight the fact that in many respects the syntax of these so-called Romance dialects is underlying Greek, despite employing predominantly Romance lexis. In this paper we draw on two case studies from the Romance and Greek varieties spoken in Calabria to illustrate how the syntax of argument-marking has variously been subject to contact-induced change, giving rise to significant variation in the marking and distribution of RECIPIENT arguments in accordance with both pragmatic and structural factors. In both cases, it will be shown that contact-induced borrowing does not replicate the original structure of the lending language but, rather, produces hybrid structures which are ultimately neither Greek nor Romance in nature.

Adam Ledgeway, Norma Schifano & Giuseppina Silvestri. 2020. Microvariation in dative-marking in the Romance and Greek varieties of Southern Italy. In Anna Pineda & Jaume Mateu (eds.), *Dative constructions in Romance and beyond*, 317–349. Berlin: Language Science Press. DOI:10.5281/zenodo.3776557

1 Introduction: Greek-Romance contact in southern Italy

As is well known, Greek has been spoken as an indigenous language in southern Italy since ancient times (Falcone 1973: 12–38; Horrocks 1997: 304–306; Manolessou 2005: 112–121 Ralli 2006: 133). According to one, albeit now unpopular, view championed most notably by Rohlfs (1924; 1933; 1974; 1977), the Greek spoken in southern Italy, henceforth Italo-Greek, is to be considered a direct descendant of the ancient (mainly Doric) Greek varieties which were imported into *Magna Graecia* as early as the eighth century BC with the establishment of numerous Greek colonies along the coasts of southern Italy. The opposing – and now widely accepted – view, argued most vehemently by Battisti (1927) (cf. also Morosi 1870; Parlangèli 1953), sees the Greek of southern Italy as a more recent import dating from the Byzantine period of domination between the sixth and eleventh centuries (though see Fanciullo 2007, for a conciliatory approach to these apparently two opposing views). Whatever the correct view, it is in any case clear that by the beginning of the second millennium AD Greek was still widely spoken as a native language in north-western Sicily, Calabria and Apulia.

Today, by contrast, Italo-Greek survives precariously only in a handful of villages of southern Calabria and Salento in the respective areas of Bovesía and Grecía Salentina. In Bovesía, where the local variety of Greek is known as *Greko* (though usually known as *grecanico* in Italian), the language is today confined to five remote villages of the Aspromonte mountains (namely, Bova (Marina), Chorío di Rochudi, Condofuri (Marina), Gallicianò and Roghudi (Nuovo)), where it is reputed (Spano 1965; Martino 1980: 308–313; Stamuli 2007: 16-19; Remberger 2011: 126-127), at least according to some of the most generous estimates (cf. Katsoyannou 1995: 27-31; Katsoyannou 2001: 8-9), to be spoken by as many as about 500 speakers (cf. however Squillaci forthcoming). In Grecía Salentina, on the other hand, the language, locally known as *Griko*, appears to have fared somewhat better, in that it continues to be spoken in a pocket of seven villages of the Otranto peninsula (Calimera, Castrignano dei Greci, Corigliano d'Otranto, Martano, Martignano, Sternatia, Zollino) by as many as 20,000 speakers according to the most optimistic estimates (Comi 1989; Sobrero & Miglietta 2005; Manolessou 2005: 105; Marra 2008; Romano 2008: 52–53; Baldissera 2013: 3–4), though once again our recent investigations would indicate a considerably lower figure.

Now, although Greek was extensively spoken in southern Italy for centuries, following the gradual expansion first of Latin and then what were to become the local Romance varieties in this same area, Greek and Romance came to be used alongside of each other in a complex situation of diglossia with expanding bilingualism. As a consequence, the Romance dialects of these two areas, namely *Calabrese* and *Salentino*, display huge structural influences from Italo-Greek, since they first emerged among speakers whose mother tongue was Greek (the "substrate") and continued to develop and expand to the present day in the shadow of the surrounding, albeit shrinking, Italo-Greek dialects (the "adstrate"). In recent times these latter varieties also increasingly show some structural influences from the local Romance dialects and, in particular, from regional Italian which has also been thrown into the mix, at least among younger members of the speech community (cf. Martino 1980; Profili 1985; Marra 2008; Romano 2008: 338), as witnessed, for example, in causative constructions (Ledgeway et al. forthcoming; In preparation).

Consequently, it has become commonplace in the literature to claim that once extensive Greek-Romance bilingualism throughout the extreme south of Italy has given rise to an exceptional Hellenization of the local Romance dialects or, as Rohlfs (1933: 61) aptly put it, a case of *spirito greco, materia romanza* "Greek soul, Romance (lexical) material".[1] While accepting Rohlfs' general thesis that the Romance dialects of this area superficially appear to be nothing more than Greek disguised as Romance, such broad-brush generalizations obscure many subtle differences between Italo-Greek and the local Romance varieties which have largely gone unnoticed (for an overview, see Ledgeway 2013). In what follows we shall therefore consider two case studies in microvariation involving dative structures born of Greek-Romance contact in Calabria. More specifically, these case studies illustrate the influence of Grecanico on Calabrese involving the so-called Greek-style dative whereby the relevant Romance dialects have variously adopted and adapted an original Greek structure that highlights both significant diatopic and diachronic microvariation in the structural realization of dative marking within the DP, as well as in the structural positions in which dative-marked DPs are licensed. In both cases, the varieties in question marry together in still poorly explored and largely little understood ways facets of core Romance and Greek syntax to produce a number of innovative hybrid structures, the evidence of which can be profitably used to throw light on the nature of parametric variation and the proper formal characterization of convergence and divergence. Indeed, once we begin to peel back the layers, it soon becomes clear that convergence through grammars in contact does not necessarily lead to simple borrowing and transference through interference, but more frequently gives rise to new hybrid structures born of reanalysis of the original Italo-Greek structures within a Romance (or Italo-Greek) grammar instantiating "deeper" microparametric options.

---

[1]Cf. the distinction between PAT(tern) and MAT(erial) discussed in Matras & Sakel (2004; 2007).

2 Greek-style dative

Since at least Rohlfs (1969: §639),[2] it has been reported that many Romance dialects of southern Calabria, following an original Greek pattern (cf. Joseph 1990: 160) now widespread within the Balkan Sprachbund (Sandfeld 1930: 187; Pompeo 2012), extended the distribution of the genitive preposition *di* 'of' to mark many of the traditional uses of the dative (including benefactive and ethical datives in addition to core RECIPIENT arguments), the so-called *dativo greco* "Greek-style dative". Consequently, on a par with the Grecanico pattern in (1a) in which the indirect object *Goséppi* is Case-marked genitive, witness the genitive form of the definite article *tu*, in the Calabrese dialect of S. Ilario in (1b) the RECIPIENT argument is marked with the genitive preposition *d(i)* 'of'.

(1) a. Bova
       Ordínettse tu   Goséppi ná 'ne   meθéto.
       he.ordered of.the Giuseppe that he.be with.them
       'He ordered Giuseppe to stay with them.'

    b. S. Ilario
       Si   dissi d-u   figghiòlu 'u   si   ndi   vaci.
       DAT.3= I.said of-the boy   that self= therefrom= he.goes
       'I told the boy to go.'

This pattern of dative marking is attested in several dialects around Bova, witness the examples in (2a–c), although its use today in Bova itself can, at best, be described as moribund. By contrast, no such use of the genitive has been recorded for the Romance dialects of Salento, as further confirmed by our own fieldwork, witness (3) where the RECIPIENT argument is marked by the typical Romance preposition *a* 'to'.

(2) Calabrese

    a. Nci   lu dissi di lu párracu.
       DAT.3= it= I.said of the priest
       'I told the priest.'

    b. Nci   u mandai d-u   nonnu.
       DAT.3= it= I.sent of-the grandfather
       'I sent it to grandfather.'

---

[2]Cf. Rohlfs (1969: §639); Trumper (2003: 232–233); Vincent (1997: 209); Katsoyannou (1995: 243, 427–429); Katsoyannou (2001: 54–55); Ralli (2006: 140–141); Ledgeway (2013: 192–196).

   c. Nci   u   muštrai di lu mè vicinu.
      DAT.3= it= I.showed of the my neighbour
      'I showed it to my neighbour.'

(3) Scorrano, Salento
     Vene   cu lli   face lezione alla   fija.
     he.comes that DAT.3= does lesson to.the daughter
     'He comes to teach their daughter.'

Although there is undoubtedly some truth to these traditional descriptions of the Greek-style dative, they nonetheless conceal some non-trivial differences between Grecanico and Calabrese. In particular, a detailed examination of the distribution of the Greek-style dative highlights the need to distinguish between at least two varieties of Calabrese, henceforth Calabrese₁ and Calabrese₂, in which the distribution of the Greek-style dative not only displays some important differences with respect to Grecanico, but also in relation to each other.

2.1 Case study 1: Calabrese₁

From our fieldwork and investigations the varieties that come under the label of Calabrese₁ include, at least, the dialects of Bagaladi, San Lorenzo, Brancaleone, Palizzi, Bovalino, [†]Bova, Chorío, Roccaforte, Africo, Natile di Careri, San Pantaleone and S. Ilario.[3] In contrast to the traditional description of the Greek-style dative reviewed in §2 above, the distribution of the Greek-style dative in these varieties shows some major differences (cf. Trumper 2003; Ledgeway 2013: 193–196). First, Greek-style genitive marking of indirect objects is not obligatory in Calabrese. Indeed, in accordance with the typical Romance pattern, RECIPIENT arguments surface much more frequently in the dative marked by the preposition *a* 'to' (*a* 'to' + *u* 'the.MSG' > *ô* 'to the'), witness (4a) which forms a minimal pair with (4b).

(4) Africo

    a. Nci   dissi ô   figghiòlu 'i   ccatta u   latti.
       DAT.3= I.said to.the boy   that he.buys the milk

    b. Nci   dissi d-u   figghiòlu 'i   accatta u   latti.
       DAT.3= I.said of-the boy   that he.buys the milk
       'I told the boy to buy the milk.'

---

[3]For full details about the authors' fieldwork, see the project's website at https:// greekromanceproject.wordpress.com/the-project.

Second, in structures such as (4b) the genitive-marked indirect object DP is always obligatorily doubled by a dative clitic, witness the grammaticality judgments reported in (5a-c).

(5)   a. Africo
          *(Nci) dissi d-u   figghiòlu 'i   accatta u   latti.
          DAT.3= I.said of-the boy   that he.buys the milk
          'I told the boy to buy the milk.'

      b. Bagaladi
          *(Nci) lu scrissi di mè frati.
          DAT.3= it= I.wrote of my brother
          'I wrote it to my brother.'

      c. Bagaladi
          *(Nci) lu vindia di Don Pippinu.
          DAT.3= it= I.sold of Don Peppino
          'I was selling it to Don Peppino.'

It would appear then that we are not dealing with an autonomous genitive structure as in (Italo-)Greek, but, rather, with a hybrid structure in which the indirect object is referenced in part through dative marking on the verbal head and in part through genitive marking on the nominal dependent. This observation is even more striking when we consider that many of the same dialects have an independent genitive clitic (INDE >) *ndi* 'of it; thereof/-from' which, despite providing a perfect match for the genitive case of the nominal dependent, cannot double the indirect object in such examples:

(6)   a. Africo
          * Ndi dissi d-u   figghiòlu 'i   accatta u   latti.
          GEN= I.said of-the boy   that he.buys the milk

      b. Bagaladi
          * Ndi lu scrissi di mè frati.
          GEN= it= I.wrote of my brother

      c. Bagaladi
          * Ndi lu vindia di Don Pippinu.
          GEN= it= I.sold of Don Peppino

Finally, the use of the so-called Greek-style dative is not indiscriminate, but carries a marked pragmatic interpretation. Thus, despite appearances, (4a-b) are not entirely synonymous. By way of comparison, consider the English minimal pair in (7a-b), where the indirect object of the first example (*to someone*) has undergone so-called *dative shift* in the second example, instantiating the double object construction where it now appears without the dative marker *to* and comes to precede the underlying direct object (see the contributions in PART I of this volume for further detailed discussions of the double object construction).

(7)   a. I promised to rent every apartment in the building to someone.

     b. I promised to rent someone every apartment in the building.

As is well known, one of the pragmatico-semantic consequences of *dative shift* in English is to force a known or given interpretation of the RECIPIENT argument, as can be clearly seen by the contrast in (7a–b):[4] whereas the quantifier *to someone* in (7a) typically refers to an unknown individual or group of individuals (e.g. whoever I can find who is willing to pay the rent), dative-shifted *someone* in (7b) typically, though not necessarily unambiguously for all speakers, refers to a particular individual already known to the speaker (e.g. my father's best friend), but whom the speaker simply chooses not to name in this particular utterance (for discussion, see Aoun & Li 1993). By the same token, it is this same presuppositional reading of the RECIPIENT that is licensed by the Greek-style dative in Calabrese$_1$, witness the implied specific reading of *studenti* in (8b) when marked by the genitive *di* in contrast to its non-specific reading in (8a) when it surfaces with the dative *a*; similarly, the identity of 'the boy' in (4b) is assumed to be known to the addressee.[5]

(8)   Bova

    a. La machina, nci   la vindu a nu studenti.
       the car   DAT.3= it= I.sell to a   student
       'I'll sell the car to a student (= not known to me, any gullible student I
       can find).'

---

[4]For full discussion, see Larson (1988; 1990); Jackendoff (1990); Torrego (1998) and references cited there.

[5]An anonymous reviewer points out that the alternation between the analytic prepositional construction with σε 'to' and the synthetic genitive is not necessarily free in Standard Modern Greek where the difference between the non-specific and specific readings in (8a–b) finds an exact parallel (cf. Dimitriadis 1999; Michelioudakis 2012). Nonetheless, there still remains a significant difference between Calabrese$_1$ and Standard Modern Greek, in that the use of the genitive in Calabrese$_1$ is only ever employed as a marked strategy to signal the presuppositional reading, whereas in Standard Modern Greek the synthetic genitive can also mark non-presuppositional readings just like the analytic prepositional construction.

b. La machina, nci   la vindu di nu studenti.
   the car   DAT.3= it= I.sell of a   student
   'I'm selling a student the car (= specific student known to me).'

Integrating these observations with the results of the investigation of indirect object marking across Greek dialects carried out by Manolessou & Beis (2004) (cf. also Joseph 1990: 160; Horrocks 1997: 125–126; Horrocks 2007: 628–629; Ralli 2006: 140–141), Ledgeway (2013: 194–195) proposes a partial parameter hierarchy based on the marking of indirect objects (IOs) along the lines of (9) with representative examples in (10a–d), ultimately to be understood as part of a larger hierarchy related to argument marking and alignments (cf. Sheehan 2014).

(9)

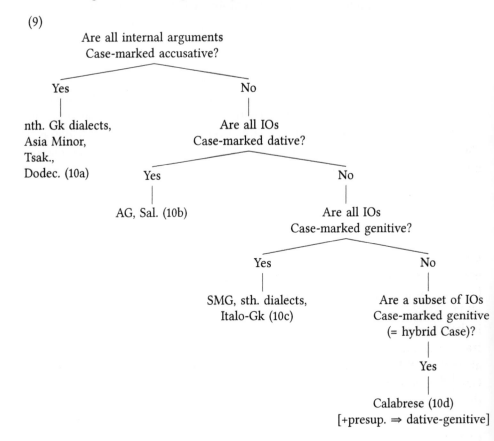

324

(10)   a.   Tsakonian (Manolessou & Beis 2004)
           επέτσε **τον**   όνε
           he.said the.ACC donkey.ACC
           'he said to the donkey.'

       b.   Ancient Greek (Xenophon, *Anabasis* 3.1.7)
           λέγει   τὴν   μαντείαν **τῷ**   Σωκράτει.
           he.says the.ACC oracle.ACC the.DAT Socrates.DAT
           'He reveals the oracle to Socrates.'

       c.   Martano, Griko
           Ce t' adrèffiatu **tù**   'pane.
           and the brothers=his him.GEN said
           'And his brothers said to him.'

       d.   Africo
           Nci   dissi ô   figghiòlu 'i ccatta u latti.
           DAT.3= I.said to.the boy   that he.buys the milk
           'I told the boy to buy the milk.'

The first option in (9) represents the least marked question that we can ask about the marking of indirect objects, namely whether they are formally distinguished at all from other internal arguments (cf. also the contribution by Manzini 2020 [this volume]). The positive reply to this question thus isolates a group of northern Greek dialects, Asia Minor dialects, Tsakonian and Dodecanese which, in contrast to all other Greek varieties, fail to mark a formal distinction between direct and indirect objects, witness the default accusative-marking of the RECIPI-ENT in (10a). We are thus dealing with a case of mesoparametric variation, in that in these varieties accusative, arguably the core object Case crosslinguistically and licensed by *v*, hence situated at the top of our hierarchy, indiscriminately marks all DP objects, a naturally definable class (namely, [-NOM] Ds). The next option is that exhibited by varieties such as ancient Greek and Salentino which, by contrast, unambiguously distinguish indirect objects by marking them dative (10b; cf. also (3) above), in contrast to varieties such as standard modern Greek, southern Greek dialects and Italo-Greek which are situated further down the hierarchy in that they conflate this category with the genitive (10c). The greater and increasing markedness of these latter two options follows from the observation that crosslinguistically dative, generally taken to be licensed by an Appl(icative) functional head (see, for example, Cuervo 2020 [this volume]; for an opposing view, see however Manzini 2020 [this volume]), represents the least marked distinctive Case for indirect objects, whereas genitive, at least in those languages with rich case systems, typically displays all the hallmarks of an inherent Case whose distribution is largely defined by not entirely predictable lexical factors, hence taken here to be assigned by a lexical V head. These two options reflect, respectively, micro- and nanoparametric variation. In the former case dative serves to uniquely mark a small, lexically definable subclass of functional heads, namely all Ds bearing the RECIPIENT feature (for arguments in favour of treating theta roles as formal features, see Hornstein 1999). In the latter case, by contrast, genitive is associated with a class of predicates whose membership can only be established on purely lexical grounds, inasmuch as the RECIPIENT feature is just one of many semantic roles associated with genitive marking.

The final option in (9) is represented by the *dativo greco* in Calabrese (10d), clearly the most marked option of all, insofar as the marking of RECIPIENT arguments in this variety is strictly context-sensitive, with the *dativo greco* serving to narrowly delimit individual RECIPIENT arguments in accordance with their [±presuppositional] reading. This more complex and non-uniform behaviour is further reflected in the surface form of the so-called *dativo greco* which, we have observed, involves a composite Case structure combining dative clitic marking on the verbal head with genitive prepositional marking on the nominal dependent, presumably reflecting the simultaneous intervention of $Appl_{DAT}$ and V_{GEN} heads in the licensing of such indirect objects. These facts highlight how convergence through grammars in contact does not necessarily lead to simple borrowing, but frequently yields new hybrid structures born of reanalysis. Below we shall explore the syntax of this instantiation of the Greek-style dative in greater detail to ascertain its significance for theoretical issues about argument structure and especially the mapping between morphological marking and syntactic configurations.

2.2 Case study 2: Calabrese₂

The second variety of Calabrese identified through our fieldwork that we must consider, henceforth Calabrese₂, is found in the villages of Gioiosa Ionica and San Luca. In contrast to Calabrese₁, the Greek-style dative in Calabrese₂ displays a much more restricted distribution subject to lexico-structural factors. In particular, the Greek-style dative in this variety only surfaces when the RECIPIENT argument is introduced by a definite article (11a), with the typically Romance prepositional marker *a* 'to' surfacing in all other contexts, witness (11b) where the RECIPIENT is headed by the indefinite article.[6]

(11) Gioiosa Ionica

    a. Nci   detti nu libbru d-u   figghjiolu.
       DAT.3= I.gave a book of-the kid
       'I gave a book to the kid.'

---

[6]The variety of San Luca dialect investigated by Chilà (2017) – henceforth San Luca$_2$ – appears to represent a more conservative variety in which all dative arguments are marked by *di* 'of', and not just those introduced by the definite article as shown by the examples in (i.a–b):

(i) San Luca$_2$

    a. Telefonanzi   'i zzìuta!
       telephone.IMP.2SG=DAT.3 of uncle=your
       'Ring your uncle!'
    b. 'A torta si   piacìu 'i tutti.
       the cake DAT.3= pleased of all
       'Everyone liked the cake.'

Although Chilà (2017: 4–5) argues that presuppositionality – or, in her terms, the feature [±known] – plays no role in the licensing of the Greek-style dative in San Luca$_2$, all her examples involve specific and definite referents, including those such as (ii.a–c) which she claims are [−known] but which are clearly presupposed (note that Chilà does not provide any examples with nominals introduced by the indefinite article).

(ii) San Luca$_2$

    a. Si   dissi d' u postinu 'u si   ndi   vai.
       DAT.3= I.said of the postman that self= therefrom= he.goes
       'I told the postman to leave.'
    b. Si   fici   'na telefunata   d' u funtaneri.
       DAT.3= I.made a   telephone.call of the plumber
       'I gave the plumber a call.'
    c. Si   telefonai   d' a putìca / 'u bonchettu.
       DAT.3= I.telephoned of the shop   the restaurant
       'I rang the shop / the restaurant.'

Pending further investigation, it might then be that San Luca$_2$ is not necessarily the most conservative Calabrian variety replicating the generalized distribution of the Greek-style genitive of Grecanico, but, rather, represents another variety to be included among those grouped under the label of Calabrese$_1$.

b. Nci   detti nu libbru a nu figghjiolu.
   DAT.3= I.gave a book to a kid
   'I gave a book to a kid.'

This contrast can be seen even more clearly through a comparison of the dialects of Gioiosa Ionica and San Luca in relation to the behaviour of proper names. As in many Romance varieties (cf. Ledgeway 2012: 103–104; 2015: 111–112), proper names do not co-occur with a definite article in the dialect of Gioiosa Ionica, whereas in the dialect of San Luca proper names are introduced by an expletive definite article just as in Greek (Mackridge 1985: 198; Holton et al. 1997: 276–278; Ledgeway 2013: 208–209). As a consequence, whenever a RECIPIENT is lexicalized by a proper name it is marked by *a* 'to' in Gioiosa Ionica (12a), but by *di* 'of' in San Luca since the presence of the definite article in this variety automatically triggers and licenses the use of the Greek-style dative (12b).

(12) a. Gioiosa Ionica
        Nci   detti nu libbru a Maria.
        DAT.3= I.gave a book to Maria
        'I gave a book to Maria.'

     b. San Luca
        Stamatina   si   detti nu pocu i pani d-u   Petru.
        this.morning DAT.3= I.gave a little of bread of-the Petru
        'This morning I gave a bit of bread to Petru.'

To sum up, we note then that in Calabrese$_2$ dative is marked by *a* 'to', and not by the Greek-style dative with *di* 'of', whenever the RECIPIENT surfaces as: (a) a proper name (12a; but cf. 12b), singular kinship term (13a) or tonic pronoun (13b); (b) an indefinite DP (13c); (c) a nominal introduced by a demonstrative (13d) or a bare quantifier (13e). In structural terms, what all three contexts have in common is that the D position is either not available to the definite article, since this position is already directly lexicalized by the nominal (e.g. pronoun) or through N-to-D movement (e.g. proper name, kinship term), or the D position is simply not lexicalized, as happens with indefinite DPs, where the cardinal lexicalizes the head of a lower functional projection (variously termed CardP/NumP), and with demonstratives and bare quantifiers where the DP is embedded within a DemP and a QP, respectively.

(13)   Gioiosa Ionica

    a. Non nci   telefonari a ziuma!
       not DAT.3= phone.INF to uncle=my
       'Do not phone my uncle!'

    b. Maria m' u detti   a mia.
       Maria me= it= gave.3SG to me
       'Maria gave it to me.'

    c. Ajeri   nci   telefonau a nu previte.
       yesterday DAT.3= I.phoned to a priest
       'Yesterday I phoned a priest.'

    d. Ajeri   nci   telefonava a iju previte i Messina.
       yesterday DAT.3= I.phoned to that priest of Messina
       'Yesterday I phoned that priest from Messina.'

    e. Non telefonari a nuju!
       not phone.INF to nobody
       'Don't phone anybody!'

2.3 Interim conclusions and questions

We have seen that the Romance dialects of Calabria have been in centuries-old contact with Grecanico as the sub- and adstrate contact language. As a consequence, Calabrese has adopted and, in turn, adapted a number of original Greek structural traits, including the Greek-style genitive-dative syncretism which has led to a certain degree of competition in the marking of RECIPIENT arguments which may variously surface in conjunction either with *di* 'of' or *a* 'to' in accordance with the competing Greek and Romance patterns, respectively. In particular, in Calabrese$_1$ the Greek-style dative is pragmatically restricted, in that it has been shown to be intimately linked to presuppositionality, marking just those RECIPIENTS which are interpreted as being highly individuated and specific. By contrast, in Calabrese$_2$ the Greek-style dative is structurally restricted, in that its distribution has been shown to be strictly linked to the availability of the definite article and, by implication, the lexicalization or otherwise of the D position, with the Greek-style dative occurring just in those contexts in which the D position is realized by the definite article.

Against these considerations, we must consider a number of related questions. First, are the distributions of the Greek-style dative witnessed in Calabrese₁ and Calabrese₂ related, or should they be seen as separate developments arising from the reanalysis of the original underlying Greek pattern? Second, if they are related, as we shall argue below, how then does one develop from the other and, what is their diachronic relationship? Third, we have superficially observed how in both varieties of Calabrese the Greek-style dative (*di*) variously alternates with a Romance-style dative (*a*), but it remains to be understood how this alternation is to be interpreted in structural terms. Finally, we must also ask what these competing structures tell us about the structural positions in which dative DPs are licensed, and about the locus of dative-marking in DPs.

3 Calabrese₁ revisited

With these considerations in mind, we now return to Calabrese₁. The basic facts which need to be accounted for include why: (i) the use of the Greek-style dative gives rise to a presuppositional reading of the RECIPIENT; (ii) the DP has to be clitic-doubled; (iii) the doubling clitic has to be marked dative, rather than genitive; (iv) there is an apparent Case mismatch between the dative-marked clitic on the verbal head and the genitive-marked DP dependent, giving rise to an apparently hybrid Case structure; and (v) canonical datives are marked with (AD >) *a* 'to'. Superficially, then, one might be tempted to propose a double object analysis for the Calabrese₁ facts,[7] since, on a par with the double object construction reported in many languages, the RECIPIENT necessarily receives a presuppositional reading, is animate, and is clitic-doubled (for futher discussion, see also Cuervo 2020 [this volume]). Furthermore, double object constructions have previously been independently reported for other dialects of southern Italy (cf. Ledgeway 2000: ch.2; 2009: 844–847), witness the representative examples in (14a–d).

(14)　a.　Naples
'A　　　purtaie　a　　Maria o　　rialo (*a　Maria).
her.ACC= I.brought DOM Maria the.M gift.M DOM Maria
'I took Maria the present.'

---

[7]Cf. a.o. Barss & Lasnik (1986); Larson (1988; 1990); Jackendoff (1990); Collins & Thráinsson (1993); Marantz (1993); Demonte (1995); Pesetsky (1995); Collins (1997); Torrego (1998); Harley (2002); Pylkkänen (2008); Anagnostopoulou (2003); Cuervo (2003); Jeong (2007); Bruening (2010b,a); Ormazabal & Romero (2010); Harley & Jung (2015); Pineda (2016).

b. Curti, Caserta
’O   facettero n’ ata   paliata.
him.ACC= they.did   an other.F thrashing.F
‘They gave him another thrashing.’

c. Calvello, Potenza
La   ˈrakə nu kaˈvaddə.
her.ACC= I.give a.M horse.M
‘I’ll give her a horse.’

d. Mattinata, Foggia
Lu   turˈʧi   lu   ˈkuəddə.
him.ACC= he.wrung the.M neck.M
‘He wrung its neck.’

In the Neapolitan example (14a), for instance, the RECIPIENT argument *a Maria* has been "shifted" such that it obligatorily surfaces, as in the corresponding English sentence, to the left of the THEME argument marked by the prepositional accusative *a* (< AD) and doubled by the accusative clitic *’a*. Similarly, in examples (14b–d) the RECIPIENT surfaces as a pronominal clitic, but is marked accusative, not dative (for further discussion, see also the chapter by Cornilescu 2020 [this volume]) .

Although the parallels between the Greek-style dative in Calabrese₁ and the double object construction initially appear quite compelling, a closer look at the relevant facts reveals a number of problems with such an analysis. First, the RECIPIENT in the Greek-style dative is not, at least superficially, "shifted" to a position in front of the THEME (cf. 14a), although this does not necessarily appear to be a precondition for the RECIPIENT in the double object construction, witness, for example, the position of the RECIPIENT in the Spanish construction (Demonte 1995; see also the discussions in the chapters Cuervo 2020 [this volume], by Calindro 2020 [this volume], and by Cépeda & Cyrino 2020 [this volume]). Second, there is no requirement that the subject in a Greek-style dative construction be interpreted as a causer (cf. 13a–d), a reading which is standardly taken to be characteristic of the subject in the double object construction. Third, an analysis in terms of a double object construction fails to offer any explanation for the apparent mismatch between the dative and genitive Case-marking borne by the clitic and coreferent DP, respectively. Fourth, unlike what happens in the double object construction (cf. Barss & Lasnik 1986; Larson 1988), where the asymmetrical binding of the dative-marked RECIPIENT by the accusative-marked THEME in the prepositional dative construction (cf. 15a) is reversed allowing the accusative-

marked RECIPIENT to bind into the THEME (cf. 15b), the use of the Greek-style
dative does not engender a reversal in the asymmetrical c-command relations
between the THEME and RECIPIENT (cf. 16a–b; see Cornilescu 2020 [this volume]
for discussion of the binding facts in Romanian ditransitives).

(15) a. I sent every book to its author.

    b. I sent every author his book.

(16) Africo

    a. A   sarta   (nci)   mandau ogni vesta â   so patruna.
       the dressmaker DAT.3= sent   each dress to.the its owner

    b. A   sarta   nci   mandau ogni vesta d-a   so patruna.
       the dressmaker DAT.3= sent   each dress of-the its owner

    'The dressmaker sent each dress to its owner.'

Finally, a very clear piece of evidence that the Greek-style dative in Calabrese₁
is not amenable to a double object analysis comes from the observation that
the Greek-style dative is not limited to ditransitive clauses, but is also found
with monotransitives (cf. 17a–b) that otherwise canonically select for dative arguments.

(17) a. Natile di Careri
       Non si   gridari   d-u   figghiolu!
       not   DAT.3= shout.INF of-the son
       'Don't shout at the child!'

    b. Palizzi
       Nci   parrai / scrivia / telefunai d-u   sindacu.
       DAT.3= I.spoke / I.wrote / I.phoned of-the mayor
       'I spoke to / wrote to / rang the mayor.'

In what follows, we thus exclude the possibility of a double object analysis for
the Greek-style dative in Calabrese₁. Instead we adopt the view here that, on a
par with other Romance varieties (though not Romanian), dative is canonically
marked in Calabrese₁ with the preposition *a* 'to', giving rise to a structure like
that in (18a) and exemplified in (19a). The RECIPIENT DP thus constitutes a core
argument which in Calabrese₁ is very frequently, though not obligatorily, doubled by a dative clitic. By contrast, we analyse the Greek-style dative exemplified
in (19b) along the lines of (18b), where we take dative once again to be assigned to

a core argument, here instantiated by pro and obligatorily referenced by a dative clitic on the verb. Consequently, we interpret the DP introduced by *di* 'of' to be an adjunct, albeit coreferential with the clitic-pro argument chain.[8]

(18)   a. $(Cl_i)...T\text{-}V...(DP_{ACC})...[a\ DP_{DAT}]_i$

       b. $*(Cl_i)...T\text{-}V...(DP_{ACC})...[pro_{DAT}]_i,\ [di\ DP]_i$

(19)   a. (Nci)   la vindu a nu studenti.
          DAT.3= it= I.sell to a   student
          'I'll sell it to a student.'

       b. $*(Nci_i)$ la vindu pro_i di nu studenti.
          DAT.3= it= I.sell   of a   student
          'I'll sell a student it.' (lit. 'I'll sell it to him, a student.')

Under this analysis we can now capture the principal characteristics of the Greek-style dative. First, the obligatory presuppositional reading of the RECIP-IENT argument follows immediately from the fact that the dative argument is instantiated by a pro licensed and referenced by a dative clitic, inasmuch as clitic-pro chains invariably yield presuppositional readings of their pronominal referents which are interpreted as known, specific and highly salient in the discourse. This is not the case in the canonical Romance-style dative construction (18a; but cf. 19b), where the dative argument is realized by a lexical DP and hence not pragmatically restricted.

Second, we now have a straightforward explanation for the obligatory presence of the dative clitic in the so-called Greek-style dative construction, since the clitic is part of a clitic-pro argument chain and is therefore necessary to reference and license pro. Despite appearances, there is then no doubling as such involved, inasmuch as the clitic licenses pro rather than doubling the coreferential DP adjunct.

Third, and by the same token, the observed Case mismatch between the clitic, marked dative, and the full DP, marked genitive, is only apparent, since dative Case is exhausted by the clitic-pro argument chain, whereas the coreferential DP represents an adjunct licensed by the canonical marker of obliques/non-arguments, namely the genitive preposition *di* 'of'.

---

[8] Observe that this analysis comes very close to, and indeed is compatible with, the idea in many analyses of the double object construction that the RECIPIENT argument is not a core argument but, rather, is an adjunct licensed by an Appl head.

Fourth, the rightmost position of the DP in examples such as (19b) now follows without further stipulation, since the DP is an adjunct and hence occurs in extra-sentential positions (whether to the right or to the left) outside of the sentential core, thereby also excluding any form of "dative shift". Indeed, when the RECIPIENT is marked by *a* 'to' it can bind into the THEME in examples such as (20a), where the latter presumably involves a case of marginalization occupying its in situ position within the *v*-VP, witness the absence of a resumptive accusative clitic, and the RECIPIENT has been raised to a focus position within the lower left periphery crossing the THEME (Frascarelli 2000; Cardinaletti 2002; Cruschina 2012: 42–47). However, when the RECIPIENT occurs in the so-called Greek-style dative (20b), such binding is not possible. Given our (topical) adjunct interpretation of DPs marked by the Greek-style dative, the ungrammaticality of (20b) is fully expected since the RECIPIENT is merged in an extra-sentential right-peripheral position from where it cannot precede the THEME in its in situ position within the *v*-VP.

(20) Africo

> a. A sarta   nci   mandau a ogni patruna a so vesta.
>   the dressmaker DAT.3= sent   to each owner the her dress

> b. *A sarta   nci   mandau di ogni patruna a so vesta.
>   the dressmaker DAT.3= sent   of each owner the her dress

'The dressmaker sent each owner her dress.'

Fifth, the stability of the binding facts observed in (16) now follows straightforwardly since, even when the Greek-style dative is employed (cf. 16b), the RECIPIENT is still realized by a core DP argument (viz. pro) Case-marked dative and licensed in the same argument position as a lexical DP in the so-called Romance-style dative (cf. 16a) from where it can be bound by the c-commanding THEME argument. The presence or otherwise of a coreferential topic adjunct introduced by *di* 'of' therefore proves irrelevant to the basic binding facts, which are invariably determined within the sentential core by the two internal arguments whose licensing positions, and hence also their binding relations, remain unchanged. However, one respect in which the two sentences in (16a–b) differ concerns the availability of the individual and distributive scopal readings of *patruna*. Whereas both readings of *patruna* are available in (16a) where both scope relations can be reconstructed within the *v*-VP between the QP *ogni* and the possessive anaphor *so*, only the individual reading is possible in (16b) in accordance with the characteristic presuppositional reading of the so-called Greek-style dative noted above.

The absence of this distributive reading in (16b) highlights how the adjunct *d-a so patruna* takes scope over the THEME *ogni vesta*, but not vice versa, providing further proof for the fact that right-peripheral (familiar) topics like *d-a so patruna* are merged in extra-sentential positions from where quantifiers like *ogni* 'each' cannot scope over them at LF (cf. Cardinaletti 2002; Frascarelli 2004; Frascarelli & Hinterhölzl 2007).[9]

Finally, the analysis outlined in (18b) correctly predicts that the distribution of the Greek-style dative should equally occur in monotransitives as in ditransitives, inasmuch as its distribution is not linked to the presence of a THEME argument. Furthermore, the use of the Greek-style dative with monotransitives also highlights the weakness of functionalist accounts which take the obligatory use of the dative clitic as a means of distinguishing between the dative-RECIPIENT and genitive-POSSESSOR readings of the lexical DP in examples such as (21a). However, the evidence of monotransitives such as (21b), where there is no ambiguity regarding the dative-RECIPIENT interpretation of the lexical DP but the dative clitic continues to be obligatory, excludes any such functionalist interpretation of the facts.

(21) a. Bova
          Nci   vindu la machina di lu studenti.
          DAT.3= I.sell the car   of the student
          'I'll sell the student the car.' (*'I'll sell the student's car.')

      b. Natile di Careri
          Non *(si)   gridamu d-i   nostri figghioli!
          not DAT.3= we.shout of-the our   children
          'Let's not shout at our children!'

To conclude, we have established that in Calabrese₁ the dative is invariably marked by *a* 'to' as in most other varieties of Romance. By contrast, the use of *di* 'of' in the so-called Greek-style dative has been shown to mark right-peripheral adjuncts, with the dative-marked RECIPIENT still licensed as a core argument (pro) in association with a coreferential dative clitic (cf. pronominal argument hypothesis developed in Jelinek 1984). It thus appears that Greek-Romance contact in the case of Calabrese₁ has given rise to an imperfect replication of the

---

[9]In fact, in (16a) when the dative clitic is absent both the individual and distributive readings are possible, although the distributive interpretation is strongly preferred, whereas only the individual reading is possible when the clitic is present. Thus, just as in (16b), it would appear that the presence of the clitic in (16a) forces a right-dislocated topical interpretation of the RECIPIENT DP which takes scope over the THEME licensing the individual reading.

corresponding Grecanico genitive-marked RECIPIENT structure. In particular, in Calabrese₁ dative is canonically marked by *a* 'to', with Greek-style marking of RECIPIENTS by means of *di* 'of' having been reanalysed as a marked structure pressed into service as a last resort option to Case-mark adjunct DPs whenever dative Case has been otherwise exhausted within the sentential core. Indeed, as argued in Ledgeway (2013), such exaptive outcomes are far from infrequent in the Greek-Romance contact situation of southern Italy where contact-induced borrowing typically does not replicate the original structure of the lending language but, rather, produces hybrid structures which are ultimately neither Greek nor Romance in nature.

4 Calabrese₂ revisited

We now return to Calabrese₂ where the facts to be accounted for include: (i) why the Greek-style dative only occurs in conjunction with the definite article (cf. 22a); (ii) why the dative is marked by *a* 'to' (cf. 22b) if the definite article is absent; and (iii) what the relationship, if any, is between the distribution of the Greek-style dative in Calabrese₂ and Calabrese₁ (cf. 19a–b).

(22)   Gioiosa Ionica

    a. Ajeri   nci   telefonau d-u   previte.
       yesterday DAT.3= I.phoned of-the priest
       'Yesterday I phoned the priest.'

    b. Ajeri   nci   telefonau a nu previte.
       yesterday DAT.3= I.phoned to a priest
       'Yesterday I phoned a priest.'

We begin with the last question regarding the diachronic relationship between the distribution of the Greek-style dative in Calabrese₁ and Calabrese₂, which, we will see, also provides an answer to our first question regarding the restriction of the Greek-style dative to nominals introduced by the definite article. In particular, we argue that the use of the Greek-style dative in Calabrese₂ represents a development from the more conservative distribution observed in Calabrese₁ where it was seen to license a presuppositional reading of the DP adjunct. In such cases, the DP is typically headed by the definite article, the archetypal marker of presuppositionality, thereby creating a strong association between the definite article and the Greek-style genitive. It is therefore entirely plausible to suppose that this frequent pairing of the definite article with the Greek-style dative under the presuppositional reading eventually led in Calabrese$_2$ to a distributional reanalysis of the Greek-style dative which came to be restricted to the definite article. We thus also have a highly natural explanation for our first question regarding the distributional restriction of the Greek-style dative to nominals headed by the definite article.

Further proof for this diachronic development comes from the observation that while most speakers of Calabrese$_2$ today restrict the Greek-style genitive to definite DPs introduced by the definite article, some speakers of the dialect of San Luca (but not the dialect of Gioiosa Ionica) are less restrictive in that they optionally extend the use of the Greek-style genitive to definite DPs situated higher up the animacy/definiteness hierarchy (Silverstein 1976; Aissen 2003) to also include, for example, kinship terms (23).

(23)   San Luca
       Aieri   u   Petru si   talefunau   'i / a frati=ma.
       yesterday the Peter 3.DAT= telephoned of / to brother=my
       'Yesterday Pietro rang my brother.'

In this respect, it is not coincidental that San Luca is also the variety that employs the definite article with proper names, hence also systematically marked by the Greek-style dative (cf. 12b) and therefore extending its distribution higher up the animacy/definiteness hierarchy. Evidence like this highlights how the pragmatico-semantic category of presuppositionality has been subject to formal reinterpretation and reanalysis in the passage from Calabrese$_1$ to Calabrese$_2$, such that today the distribution of the Greek-style dative variously maps onto different subgroupings of nominals characterized by differing degrees of animacy and definiteness, but ultimately all interpreted in some sense as presupposed.

Unlike in Calabrese$_1$ where *di*-marked DPs were shown to be adjuncts that occur in extra-sentential positions (24a), in Calabrese$_2$ RECIPIENT DPs introduced by *di* 'of' therefore represent genuine dative arguments integrated and licensed within the sentential core, as further witnessed by the optionality of the doubling dative clitic *nci* on the verb in (24b), although it proves extremely common.

(24)   a.   Calabrese$_1$
            (Nci$_i$) lu dissi pro$_i$, di lu párracu.
            DAT.3= it= I.told   of the priest

b. Calabrese$_2$

(Nci) u dissi d-u previte.

DAT.3= it= I.told of-the priest

'I told the priest.'

We turn finally to consider the formal alternation between *a* 'to' and *di* 'of' in the marking of RECIPIENT arguments in Calabrese$_2$. Above we noted that *a* 'to' surfaces whenever D° is lexicalised by a pronominal D (25a) or a raised N (25b) and whenever D° is not lexicalised (25c–e).

(25) Gioiosa Ionica

a. Maria m' u detti a mia.
   Maria to.me= it= gave.3SG to me
   'Maria gave it to me.'

b. Non nci telefonari a ziuma!
   not DAT.3= phone.INF to uncle=my
   'Do not phone my uncle!'

c. Ajeri nci telefonau a nu previte.
   yesterday DAT.3= I.phoned to a priest
   'Yesterday I phoned a priest.'

d. Ajeri nci telefonava a iju previte i Messina.
   yesterday DAT.3= I.phoned to that priest of Messina
   'Yesterday I phoned that priest from Messina.'

e. Non telefonari a nuju!
   not phone.INF to nobody
   'Don't phone anybody!'

Consequently, we concluded that *di* 'of' surfaces uniquely in conjunction with nominals introduced by the definite article (26a). While this descriptive generalization captures the core distributional facts of the Greek-style dative in Calabrese$_2$ it is not entirely correct and needs to be revised in the light of evidence such as (26b).

(26) Gioiosa Ionica

a. Ajeri nci telefonau di cuggini mei.
   yesterday DAT.3= I.phoned of-the cousins my
   'Yesterday I phoned my cousins.'

b. Ajeri   nci   telefonau a /*di tutti i   cuggini mei.
   yesterday DAT.3= I.phoned to of all   the cousins my
   'Yesterday I phoned all my cousins.'

Although example (26b) involves a nominal introduced by the definite article, just as in (26a), it is also preceded by the universal quantifier *tutti* 'all' and
dative is marked by the preposition *a* 'to' rather than *di* 'of'. This seems to suggest that the correct descriptive generalization is that the Greek-style dative in
Calabrese₂ only occurs in conjunction with the definite article (cf. 26), but that
it does not necessarily always occur whenever the definite article is employed
(cf. 26b). Indeed, the contrast witnessed in (26a–b) highlights how morphosyntactic variation in dative-marking through the formal alternation between *a* 'to'
and *di* 'of' crucially depends on whether K(ase) is realized in a scattered or syncretic fashion (cf. Giorgi & Pianesi 1997). In particular, as illustrated structurally
in (27a) and exemplified in (28a–c) we see that whenever lexical material intervenes between the K° and D° positions, whether the latter is lexicalized (cf. 28a)
or not (cf. 28b–c), then these two positions are independently projected and the
two heads are realized in a scattered fashion with the K° head lexicalized by *a* 'to'.
When, however, the two heads are adjacent and the D° position is lexicalized, as
in examples (29a–b), then a syncretic K/D head obtains in which both Case and
definiteness are inextricably bound together and morphologically spelt out as a
single head *d-u/-a/-i* 'of-the.MSG/FSG/PL'.

(27) a.

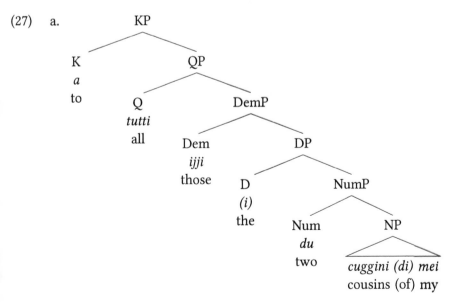

b.

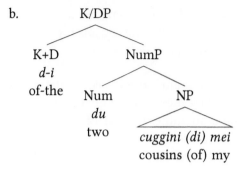

(28)   Gioiosa Ionica

a. Ajeri   nci   telefonau a tutti i   cuggini mei.
    yesterday DAT.3= I.phoned to all   the cousins my
    'Yesterday I rang all my cousins.'

b. Ajeri   nci   telefonau a (tutti) ijji   cuggini mei.
    yesterday DAT.3= I.phoned to (all)   those cousins my
    'Yesterday I rang (all) those cousins of mine.'

c. Ajeri   nci   telefonau a du cuggini di   mei.
    yesterday DAT.3= I.phoned to two cousins of.the my
    'Yesterday I rang two of my cousins.'

(29)   Gioiosa Ionica

a. Ajeri   nci   telefonau di   cuggini mei.
    yesterday DAT.3= I.phoned of.the cousins my
    'Yesterday I rang my cousins.'

b. Ajeri   nci   telefonau di   du cuggini di   mei.
    yesterday DAT.3= I.phoned of.the two cousins of.the my
    'Yesterday I rang my two cousins.'

In conclusion, we have seen that in Calabrese$_2$ the Romance-style dative *a* represents the scattered spell-out of a single [Kase] feature in contrast to the Greek-style dative *d-u/-a/-i* which instantiates the syncretic spell-out of a feature bundle [Kase, Definite]. As argued above, this latter development represents the outcome in Calabrese$_2$ of a progressive association of the definite article with the Greek-style genitive under its original presuppositional reading (as still preserved in Calabrese$_1$), yielding the portemanteau morphs *du/da/di*. In this respect, it is revealing to note that in conjunction with the genitive preposition *di* 'of' we find in Calabrese$_1$, where there is no necessary structural association of the definite article with the Greek-style dative, both full forms of the definite article preserving the initial lateral as well as aphaeresized forms, namely bisyllabic *di lu/la/li* and monosyllabic *du/da/di*. In Calabrese$_2$, by contrast, the definite article forms a syncretic head with the genitive preposition and only the aphaeresized forms *du/da/di* are found.

5 Conclusion

The detailed discussion of Grecanico and Calabrese argument marking above has shown how, at least on the surface, the grammars of the these two linguistic groups are in many respects very similar, to the extent that the observed structural parallels are far too striking for them to be dismissed as accidental but, rather, must be considered the result of centuries-old structural contact between Greek and Romance, ultimately to be placed towards the upper end of the five-point scale of contact intensity proposed by Thomason & Kaufman (1988). The direction of such contact has consistently been shown to be unidirectional, involving the transfer and extension of original Greek structural features into the surrounding Romance varieties. At the same time, however, we have seen that a detailed examination of the Greek-style dative reveals how the finer details of such structural parallels often differ in subtle and unexpected ways once adopted in Romance: this highlights how speakers have not so much borrowed actual Greek forms but, rather, reshaped and reanalysed, often in a process of replication (Heine & Kuteva 2003; 2005), already existing Romance categories (e.g. dative and genitive marking) to approximate the superficial Greek models and patterns. Indeed, data from argument marking highlight how the varieties in question marry together in still poorly explored and largely little understood ways facets of core Romance and Greek syntax to produce a number of innovative hybrid structures, the evidence of which can be profitably used to throw light on parametric variation and, in our particular case, on the nature and licensing of dative, as well as the proper formal characterization of convergence and divergence.

In the case of Grecanico and Calabrese, which it must not be forgotten independently share a common Indo-European ancestry that is in large part responsible for their shared macro- and mesoparametric settings (e.g. head-initial, nominative-accusative alignment, pro-drop), observed Greek-biased convergence between the two can typically be reduced to a surface effect of shared microparametric settings. By way of illustration, consider once again the case of the Greek-style dative. Specifically, we saw that Calabrese patterns not with standard Romance varieties such as Italian, but, rather, with Grecanico in exhibiting varying degrees of syncretism in the marking of dative and genitive, the manifestation of which was argued to be ultimately understood as a case of microparametric variation in the marking of RECIPIENT arguments (cf. 9). On the other hand, the more subtle nature of divergence between Calabrese and Grecanico can be reduced to the surface effect of different settings in relation to hierarchically "deeper" microparametric options and, above all, in relation to nanoparametric differences. Returning again to the Greek-style dative, although Grecanico and Calabrese share the same parametric setting in relation to dative and genitive syncretism, we have seen how only distinct deeper microparametric settings can provide the key to understanding the more restricted distribution of the syncretism in Calabrese licensed by specific structural and pragmatic features associated with different functional heads (namely, $K°$ and $D°$).

Finally, the preceding discussion has provided and reviewed significant evidence to demonstrate that ultimately the local Romance varieties of southern Calabria cannot be regarded as Greek disguised as Romance. Although such a view has traditionally enjoyed a great deal of acceptance since Rohlfs' now classic slogan *spirito greco, materia romanza*, it is based on rather superficial structural similarities deriving from retained macro- and mesoparametric settings and, above all, from shared "shallow" microparametric settings. However, as soon as one begins to peel back the layers, it soon becomes clear that convergence through grammars in contact does not necessarily lead to simple borrowing and transference through interference, but more frequently gives rise to new hybrid structures born of reanalysis of the original Greek structures within a Romance grammar instantiating "deeper" microparametric options. This observation goes against the general prediction (cf. Biberauer & Roberts 2012) that, all things being equal, syntactic change should proceed "upwards" within parametric hierarchies as acquirers strip away features in their attempt to postulate the simplest featural analyses compatible with the PLD (Roberts & Roussou 2003). In the particular cases at hand, however, we are dealing with convergence where speakers are not so much trying to provide the best fit with the PLD, but, rather, are striving to accommodate fully acquired structures from an increasingly less native/attrited L1 (viz. Grecanico) in a native L2 (viz. Calabrese), frequently introducing competing and additional options within the contact grammar. Within this scenario, one possibility that presents itself to speakers is to reanalyse such optionality as meaningful variation, thereby enriching the contact grammar with new choices and concomitant distinctions. This appears to have been the case with the Greek-style dative, where the introduction of Greek-style genitive marking of Recipient arguments does not replace Romance-style dative marking wholesale, but, rather, emerges in Calabrese$_1$ as a marked context-sensitive option that is specialized in the marking of individual Recipient arguments in accordance with their [±presuppositional] reading,[10] a development, in turn, reanalysed in Calabrese$_2$ as a structurally-conditioned alternation in accordance with the syncretic realization or otherwise of Case and definiteness.

Abbreviations

The abbreviations used in the glosses of this chapter follow the Leipzig Glossing Rules.

Acknowledgments

This work is part of the Leverhulme Research Project RPG-2015-283 *Fading voices in southern Italy: investigating language contact in Magna Graecia.*

References

Aissen, Judith. 2003. Differential object marking: Iconicity vs. Economy. *Natural Language & Linguistic Theory* 21(3). 435–483.

Anagnostopoulou, Elena. 2003. *The syntax of ditransitives: Evidence from clitics.* Berlin: Walter de Gruyter.

Aoun, Joseph & Yen-hui Audrey Li. 1993. *Syntax of scope.* Vol. 21. Cambridge: MIT Press.

Baldissera, Valeria. 2013. *Il dialetto grico del Salento: Elementi balcanici e contatto linguistico.* Università Ca' Foscari Venezia. (Doctoral dissertation).

Barss, Andrew & Howard Lasnik. 1986. A note on anaphora and double objects. *Linguistic inquiry* 17(2). 347–354.

Battisti, Carlo. 1927. Appunti sulla storia e sulla diffusione dell'ellenismo nell'Italia Meridionale (avec 3 cartes). *Revue de linguistique romane* 3. 1–91.

---

[10]The [±presuppositional] distinction also plays a crucial role in the licensing of differential object marking in Calabrese, as fully demonstrated in Ledgeway et al. (forthcoming).

Biberauer, Theresa & Ian Roberts. 2012. Towards a parameter hierarchy for auxiliaries: Diachronic considerations. *Cambridge Occasional Papers in Linguistics* 6(9) (Article 9). 267–294.

Bruening, Benjamin. 2010a. Ditransitive asymmetries and a theory of idiom formation. *Linguistic Inquiry* 41(4). 519–562. DOI:10.1162/LING_a_00012

Bruening, Benjamin. 2010b. Double object constructions disguised as prepositional datives. *Linguistic Inquiry* 41(2). 287–305. DOI:10.1162/ling.2010.41.2.287

Calindro, Ana Regina. 2020. Ditransitive constructions: What sets Brazilian Portuguese apart from other Romance languages? In Anna Pineda & Jaume Mateu (eds.), *Dative constructions in Romance and beyond*, 75–95. Berlin: Language Science Press. DOI:10.5281/zenodo.3776535

Cardinaletti, Anna. 2002. Against optional and null clitics. Right dislocation vs. marginalization. *Studia linguistica* 56(1). 29–57.

Cépeda, Paola & Sonia Cyrino. 2020. Putting objects in order: Asymmetrical relations in Spanish and Portuguese ditransitives. In Anna Pineda & Jaume Mateu (eds.), *Dative constructions in Romance and beyond*, 97–116. Berlin: Language Science Press. DOI:10.5281/zenodo.3776539

Chilà, Annamaria. 2017. Il sincretismo genitivo-dativo nella varietà reggina di S. Luca. *L'Italia dialettale* LXXVIII. 57–71.

Collins, Chris. 1997. *Local economy*. Cambridge: MIT press.

Collins, Chris & Höskuldur Thráinsson. 1993. Object shift in double object constructions and the theory of case. *Papers on Case and Agreement II, MITWPL* 19. 131–174.

Comi, Pasquale. 1989. *Un'indagine sulla vitalità attuale del griko a Castrignano dei Greci (Lecce)*. University of Zurich. (MA thesis).

Cornilescu, Alexandra. 2020. Ditransitive constructions with differentially marked direct objects in Romanian. In Anna Pineda & Jaume Mateu (eds.), *Dative constructions in Romance and beyond*, 117–142. Berlin: Language Science Press. DOI:10.5281/zenodo.3776541

Cruschina, Silvio. 2012. *Discourse-related features and functional projections*. Oxford: Oxford University Press.

Cuervo, María Cristina. 2003. *Datives at large*. Cambridge, MA: Massachusetts Institute of Technology. (Doctoral dissertation). https://dspace.mit.edu/handle/1721.1/7991.

Cuervo, María Cristina. 2020. Datives as applicatives. In Anna Pineda & Jaume Mateu (eds.), *Dative constructions in Romance and beyond*, 1–39. Berlin: Language Science Press. DOI:10.5281/zenodo.3776531

Demonte, Violeta. 1995. Dative alternation in Spanish. *Probus* 7(1). 5–30. DOI:10.1515/prbs.1995.7.1.5

Dimitriadis, Alexis. 1999. On clitics, prepositions and case licensing in Standard and Macedonian Greek. In Artemis Alexiadou, Geoffrey Horrocks & Melita Stavrou (eds.), *Studies in Greek syntax*, 95–112. Dordrecht: Kluwer. DOI:10.1007/978-94-015-9177-5_5

Falcone, Giuseppe. 1973. *Il dialetto romaico della Bovesia*. Milano: Istituto lombardo di scienze e lettere.

Fanciullo, Franco. 2007. Greco e grecismi nel diasistema italo-romanzo. Alcune considerazioni. In Marcello Aprile (ed.), *Nuove riflessioni sulla lessicografia. Presente, futuro e dintorni del lessico etimologico italiano*, 233–245. Galatina: Congedo.

Frascarelli, Mara. 2000. *The syntax-phonology interface in focus and topic constructions in Italian*. Vol. 50. Dordrecht: Kluwer.

Frascarelli, Mara. 2004. Dislocation, clitic resumption and minimality: A comparative analysis of left and right topic constructions in Italian. In Bok-Bennema Reineke, Bart Hollebrandse, Brigitte Kampers-Manhe & Petra Sleeman (eds.), *Romance languages and linguistic theory 2002: Selected papers from "Going Romance," Groningen 2002*, vol. 256, 99–118. Amsterdam: John Benjamins.

Frascarelli, Mara & Roland Hinterhölzl. 2007. Types of topics in German and Italian. In Kerstin Schwabe & Susanne Winkler (eds.), *On information structure, meaning and form. Generalizations across languages*, 87–116. Amsterdam: John Benjamins. DOI:10.1075/la.100.07fra

Giorgi, Alessandra & Fabio Pianesi. 1997. *Tense and aspect: From semantics to morphosyntax*. Oxford: Oxford University Press.

Harley, Heidi. 2002. Possession and the double object construction. *Linguistic Variation Yearbook* 2(1). 31–70.

Harley, Heidi & Hyun Kyoung Jung. 2015. In support of the PHave analysis of the double object construction. *Linguistic Inquiry* 46. 703–730.

Heine, Bernd & Tania Kuteva. 2003. On contact-induced grammaticalization. *Studies in Language* 27(3). 529–572. DOI:10.1075/sl.27.3.04hei

Heine, Bernd & Tania Kuteva. 2005. *Language contact and grammatical change*. Cambridge: Cambridge University Press. DOI:10.1017/CBO9780511614132

Holton, David, Peter Mackridge & Irene Philippaki-Warburton. 1997. *Greek: A comprehensive grammar of the modern language*. London: Routledge.

Hornstein, Norbert. 1999. Movement and control. *Linguistic inquiry* 30(1). 69–96.

Horrocks, Geoffrey. 1997. *Greek: A history of the language and its speakers*. London: Longman.

Horrocks, Geoffrey. 2007. Syntax: From classical Greek to the Koine. In Anastasios Phoivos Christidis (ed.), *A history of ancient Greek: From the beginnings to late antiquity*, 618–631. Cambridge: Cambridge University Press.

Jackendoff, Ray. 1990. On Larson's treatment of the double object construction. *Linguistic inquiry* 21(3). 427–456.

Jelinek, Eloise. 1984. Empty categories, case, and configurationality. *Natural Language & Linguistic Theory* 2(1). 39–76.

Jeong, Youngmi. 2007. *Applicatives: Structure and interpretation from a minimalist perspective*. Vol. 104. Amsterdam: John Benjamins.

Joseph, Brian D. 1990. Greek. In Bernard Comrie (ed.), *The major languages of Eastern Europe*, 144–173. London: Routledge.

Katsoyannou, Marianne. 1995. *Le parler gréco de Gallicianò (Italie): Description d'une langue en voie de disparition*. Paris: Paris 7. (Doctoral dissertation).

Katsoyannou, Marianne. 2001. Le parler grec de Calabre: Situation linguistique et sociolinguistique. *Lalies* 21. 7–59.

Larson, Richard K. 1988. On the double object construction. *Linguistic Inquiry* 19(3). 335–391.

Larson, Richard K. 1990. Double objects revisited: Reply to Jackendoff. *Linguistic Inquiry* 21(4). 589–632.

Ledgeway, Adam. 2000. *A comparative syntax of the dialects of Southern Italy: A minimalist approach*. Oxford: Blackwell.

Ledgeway, Adam. 2009. *Grammatica diacronica del napoletano* (Beihefte zur Zeitschrift für romanische Philologie 350). Tübingen: Max Niemeyer Verlag.

Ledgeway, Adam. 2012. *From Latin to Romance: Morphosyntactic typology and change*. Vol. 1. Oxford: Oxford University Press.

Ledgeway, Adam. 2013. Greek disguised as Romance? The case of southern Italy. In Mark Janse, Brian D. Joseph, Angela Ralli & Metin Bagriacik (eds.), *Proceedings of the 5th International Conference on Modern Greek Dialects and Linguistic Theory (MGDLT)*, 184–228. Patras: Laboratory of Modern Greek Dialects, University of Patras. http://hdl.handle.net/1854/LU-4211390.

Ledgeway, Adam. 2015. Parallels in Romance nominal and clausal microvariation. *Revue Roumaine de Linguistique* LX(2–3). 105–127. https://www.repository.cam.ac.uk/handle/1810/249244.

Ledgeway, Adam, Norma Schifano & Giuseppina Silvestri. In preparation. Greek–romance contact in southern italy.

Ledgeway, Adam, Norma Schifano & Giuseppina Silvestri. Forthcoming. Variazione nella codifica degli argomenti verbali nelle varietà romanze e greche della calabria meridionale: "dativo greco" e marca differenziale dell'oggetto diretto. In Patrizia Del Puente (ed.), *Atti del IV Convegno internazionale di dialettologia - Progetto A. L. Ba.* Calice Editore.

Mackridge, Peter. 1985. *The modern Greek language: A descriptive analysis of standard modern Greek.* Oxford: Oxford University Press.

Manolessou, Io. 2005. The Greek dialects of southern Italy: An overview. *KAMPOS: Cambridge Papers in Modern Greek* 13. 103–125.

Manolessou, Io & Stamatis Beis. 2004. Syntactic isoglosses in modern Greek dialects: The case of the indirect object. *Modern Greek Dialects and Linguistic Theory* 2(1). 220–235.

Manzini, M. Rita. 2020. Romance *a*-phrases and their clitic counterparts: Agreement and mismatches. In Anna Pineda & Jaume Mateu (eds.), *Dative constructions in Romance and beyond*, 351–370. Berlin: Language Science Press. DOI:10.5281/zenodo.3776561

Marantz, Alec. 1993. Implications of asymmetries in double object constructions. In Sam A. Mchombo (ed.), *Theoretical aspects of Bantu grammar*, 113–150. Stanford, CA: CSLI Publications.

Marra, Piersaverio. 2008. Un'indagine sociolinguistica nella Grecìa salentina: 'speculazioni' su una lingua in agonia. In Antonio Romano & Piersaverio Marra (eds.), *Il griko nel terzo millennio: 'speculazioni' su una lingua in agonia*, 49–100. Il Laboratorio.

Martino, Paolo. 1980. L'isola grecanica dell'Aspromonte: Aspetti sociolinguistici. In Federico Albano Leoni (ed.), *I dialetti e le lingue delle minoranze di fronte all'italiano. Atti dell'XI congresso internazionale di studi. Cagliari 27-30 maggio 1977*, 305–341. Roma: Bulzoni.

Matras, Yaron & Jeanette Sakel. 2004. Investigating the mechanisms of pattern replication in language convergence. *Studies in Language* 31(4). 829–865.

Matras, Yaron & Jeanette Sakel. 2007. Introduction. In Yaron Matras & Jeanette Sakel (eds.), *Grammatical borrowing in cross-linguistic perspective*, vol. 38, 1–13. Berlin: Walter de Gruyter.

Michelioudakis, Dimitris. 2012. *Dative arguments and abstract case in Greek.* Cambridge: University of Cambridge. (Doctoral dissertation).

Morosi, Giuseppe. 1870. *Studi sui dialetti greci della Terra d'Otranto.* Bologna: A. Forni.

Ormazabal, Javier & Juan Romero. 2010. The derivation of dative alternations. In Maia Duguine, Susana Huidobro & Nerea Madariaga (eds.), *Argument structure and syntactic relations from a crosslinguistic perspective*, 203–232. Amsterdam: John Benjamins.

Parlangèli, Oronzo. 1953. *Sui dialetti romanzi e romaici del Salento.* Milano: Congedo.

Pesetsky, David. 1995. *Zero syntax: Experiencers and cascades.* Cambridge, MA: MIT Press.

Pineda, Anna. 2016. *Les fronteres de la (in)transitivitat: Estudi dels aplicatius en llengües romàniques i basc.* Barcelona: Institut d'Estudis Món Juïc. Published and revised version of the doctoral dissertation.

Pompeo, Flavia. 2012. Il sincretismo di genitivo e dativo nella lega balcanica. Una convergenza multipla? *Studi Italiani di Linguistica Teorica e Applicata* 41. 531–544.

Profili, Olga. 1985. La romanisation d'un parler grec de l'Italie du sud par les parlers romans environnants. In *Actes du XVIIe congrès international de linguistique et de philologie romanes,* 129–139. Aix-en-Provence: Université de Provence.

Pylkkänen, Liina. 2008. *Introducing arguments.* Cambridge, MA: MIT Press.

Ralli, Angela. 2006. Syntactic and morphosyntactic phenomena in modern Greek dialects: The state of the art. *Journal of Greek Linguistics* 7(1). 121–159.

Remberger, Eva-Maria. 2011. Morfosintassi verbale dei dialetti neogreci in Calabria. In Walter Breu (ed.), *L'influsso dell'italiano sul sistema del verbo delle lingue minoritarie: Resistenza e mutamento nella morfologia e nella sintassi,* 123–148.

Roberts, Ian & Anna Roussou. 2003. *Syntactic change: A minimalist approach to grammaticalization.* Cambridge: Cambridge University Press.

Rohlfs, Gerhard. 1924. *Griechen und Romanen in Unteritalien.* Firenze: LS Olschki.

Rohlfs, Gerhard. 1933. *Das Fortleben des antiken Griechentums in Unteritalien.* Köln: Petrarca-Haus.

Rohlfs, Gerhard. 1969. *Grammatica storica della lingua italiana e dei suoi dialetti.* Vol. 3, Sintassi e formazione delle parole. Torino: Einaudi.

Rohlfs, Gerhard. 1974. *Scavi linguistici nella Magna Grecia (nuova edizione interamente rielaborata ed aggiornata).* Lecce: Congedo.

Rohlfs, Gerhard. 1977. *Grammatica storica dei dialetti italogreci (Calabria, Salento):(traduzione del manoscritto tedesco di Salvatore Sicuro). Nuova edizione interamente rielaborata ed aggiornata.* München: CH Beck.

Romano, Antonio. 2008. Riflessioni preliminari sulla situazione linguistica della Grecìa salentina. In Antonio Romano & Piersaverio Marra (eds.), *Il griko nel terzo millennio: 'speculazioni' su una lingua in agonia,* 13–47. Il Laboratorio.

Sandfeld, Kristian. 1930. *Linguistique balkanique: Problèmes et résultats.* Paris: E. Champion.

Sheehan, Michelle. 2014. Towards a parameter hierarchy for alignment. In Robert Santana-LaBarge (ed.), *Proceedings of the 31st West Coast Conference on Formal Linguistics (WCCFL)*, 399–408.

Silverstein, Michael. 1976. Hierarchies of features and ergativity: Grammatical categories in Australian languages. In Robert M. W. Dixon (ed.), *Ergativity: Towards a study of grammatical relations*, 112–171. Canberra: Australian Institute of Aboriginal Studies.

Sobrero, Alberto A. & Annarita Miglietta. 2005. Politica linguistica e presenza del grico in Salento, oggi. In Cristina Guardiano, Emilia Calaresu, Cecilia Robustelli & Augusto Carli (eds.), *Lingue, istituzioni, territori. Riflessioni teoriche proposte metodologiche ed esperienze di politica linguistica. Atti del XXXVIII congrsso internazionale di studi della società di linguistica Italiana, (modena, 23-25 settembre 2004)*, 209–226. Roma: Bulzoni.

Spano, Benito. 1965. *La grecità bizantina ei suoi riflessi geografici nell'Italia meridionale e insulare*. Vol. 12. Trieste: Libreria goliardica.

Squillaci, Maria Olimpia. Forthcoming. When a language becomes old: The case of Calabrian Greek. In *Selected papers from the XV International Conference on Minority Languages*. Belgrade: University of Belgrade.

Stamuli, Maria. 2007. *Morte di lingua e variazione lessicale nel greco. Tre profili dalla Bovesìa*. Naples: University of Naples. (Doctoral dissertation).

Thomason, Sarah Grey & Terrence Kaufman. 1988. *Language contact, creolization, and genetic linguistics*. Berkeley: University of California Press.

Torrego, Esther. 1998. *The dependencies of objects*. Cambridge, MA: MIT Press.

Trumper, John B. 2003. The misunderstood double marking of indirect objects and new infinitive strategies in unexpected places: A brief study of Romance variation. In Christina Tortora (ed.), *The syntax of Italian dialects*, 229–249. Oxford: Oxford University Press.

Vincent, Nigel. 1997. Prepositions. In Martin Maiden & Mair Parry (eds.), *The dialects of Italy*, 208–213. London: Routledge.

Chapter 14

Romance *a*-phrases and their clitic counterparts: Agreement and mismatches

M. Rita Manzini

Università di Firenze

DOM (Differential Object Marking) arguments in Romance are associated with the *a*/dative morphology typical of goal arguments, because both have the same syntactic structure of embedding (§1). Clitics do not necessarily share the case alignment of full pronouns/lexical DPs. Indeed clitics and lexical DPs are separately merged each in their domain. The case array may therefore be set differently (§2). DOM objects give rise to a number of patterns under cliticization, including the standard Spanish one, *leísmo* and *loísmo/laísmo* (the latter typical also of South Italian). This variation depends on the fact that lexical DPs may be associated with DOM though clitics aren't (standard Spanish, *loísmo/laísmo*) or both may be associated with DOM (*leísmo*) (§3).

1 DOM and inherent datives

In examples like (1), from a South Italian dialect, the *a*-phrase *a iddu* '(to) him' is traditionally described as instantiating Differential Object Marking (DOM) when co-occurring with *viðinu* 'they see', and as instantiating a dative goal when co-occurring with *parlanu* 'they speak'.[1] In other words, the morphological similarity is seen to conceal two different underlying syntactic structures.

---

[1]DOM is a widespread phenomenon (Bossong 1985) whereby referentially high ranked objects and referentially low ranked objects have different morphosyntactic realizations. Ranking is determined by notions of animacy/definiteness, hence by a referentiality scale along the lines of the D-hierarchy of Kiparsky (2008).

M. Rita Manzini. 2020. Romance *a*-phrases and their clitic counterparts: Agreement and mismatches. In Anna Pineda & Jaume Mateu (eds.), *Dative constructions in Romance and beyond*, 351–370. Berlin: Language Science Press. DOI:10.5281/zenodo.3776561

(1) Celle di Bulgheria (Manzini & Savoia 2005)
     Parlanu/Viðinu   a   iddu.
     they.speak/they.see to/DOM him
     'They speak to/they see him.'

A few recent generative works argue that the morphological similarity between DOM and dative arguments externalizes a deeper syntactic similarity,
specifically in the Romance languages. Torrego (1998) insists that the coincidence
of dative and DOM *a* cannot be accidental, given cross-linguistic evidence such
as the coincidence of dative and DOM postpositions in Hindi. More explicitly,
Torrego (2010), discussing sentences like (2), provides the structural representation in (3). Thus "agentive verbs such as Spanish *contratar* 'hire' also have a
hidden Appl selected by the light verb v_{DO}" – in other words *contratar a DP*
is *CAUSE a contract to DP*. Therefore, "the single animate object of a transitive
accusative verb will *always* be marked with dative morphology, simply because
it is dative. The animate object will be in Spec, Appl, hence a Goal/Beneficiary
receiving inherent Case from Appl" (Torrego 2010: 462).

(2) Spanish (Torrego 2010)
     Han   contratado *(a) una amiga/Julia/mi amiga.
     they.have hired   (to) a   friend/Julia/my friend
     'They hired a friend/Julia/my friend.'

(3) [$_{vP}$ Agent [$_{v'}$ v_{DO} [$_{ApplP}$ *a* DP [$_{Appl'}$ Appl [$_N$ *contrato*]]]]]

Pineda (2016: 359–360) essentially adopts Torrego's structure for Catalan (4),
where the verb can occur either with an *a* argument (dative) or with a bare argument (accusative). According to Pineda, the case alternation is a parametric
choice, independently needed to account for the difference between Romance
ditransitives (with dative goals) and English ditransitives (with dative-shift objects)[2] (see also Pineda 2014).

(4) Catalan (Pineda 2016)
     L'Anna   telefona (a) l'Andreu.
     the Anna phones   (to) the Andreu
     'Anna phones Andreu.'

---

[2]This raises the question why Romance lacks dative shift in ditransitives (see Lima-Salles 2016
for what it might look like in some Brazilian Portuguese dialects). Note that no Appl need
be involved in English dative shift, see Kayne (1984); Pesetsky (1995); Harley (2002); Beck &
Johnson (2004).

(5) [$_{VoiceP}$ Agent [$_{vP}$ v_{DO} [$_{ApplP}$ (*a*) DP [$_{Appl'}$ Appl [$_N$ *telefonada*]]]]]

Manzini & Savoia (2010); Manzini (2012); Manzini & Franco (2016) reject the idea that Romance languages, or more in general Indo-European languages, have an Appl projection.[3] Rather, in these languages relational content is carried directly by adpositions or by dative/oblique case inflections.[4] This line of work further individuates the fundamental relational content of *a*/dative case in the inclusion or part/whole relation (cf. Belvin & den Dikken 1997), which is taken to underlie inherent and material possession, possession of a mental state (experiencers) and also location (inclusion in location). Additionally, this approach makes use of the standard idea that transitive predicates are decomposable into two event layers, in the most typical instance a causation event and a result event, and adopts the standard minimalist structuring of the transitive predicate into a *v* and a V layer.

On these grounds, Southern Italian examples like (1) are associated with the structure in (6). The *a* preposition/dative case, labelled ⊆, carries the inclusion/-possession content (see also Franco & Lorusso 2020 [this volume]). The two arguments of ⊆ are the pronoun *him* and the VP event – so that the overall interpretation of *They speak to him* is 'they cause him speech'; and *They see him* is close to 'they have sight of him'.

(6)

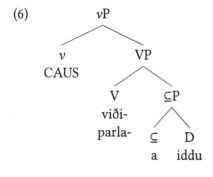

[3]Their approach goes back to Manzini & Savoia (2005: II: 517), according to whom "prepositional accusatives, like locatives/datives introduced by *a*, are interpreted in terms of denotational properties fundamentally of a locative type". Manzini & Savoia (2005) take location to be primitive, while here location is taken to be a derived form of inclusion/possession, see below and especially fn. 6.

[4]The theoretical point is that there is no advantage in enforcing what Culicover & Jackendoff (2005) call Interface Uniformity, namely that the same meaning always maps to the same syntactic structure. Interface Uniformity leads to the adoption of complex functional architectures of the cartographic type, which raise issues of evolvability and learnability in the sense of Chomsky et al. (2019).

In turn, the structure of embedding of bare accusative objects is simply as shown in (7).

(7) Celle di Bulgheria

  a. Camu na fimmina.
      I.call a woman
      'I call a woman.'

  b. ... [$_{vP}$ CAUS [$_{VP}$ *camu* [$_{DP}$ *na fimmina*]]]

The most serious problem for the unification of DOM and inherent datives is generally held to be passivization. Objects of *call* in (7) or of *see* in (1) passivize, independently of their referential ranking, hence independently of whether they are associated with structure (6) or with structure (7b) in the active. Objects of *speak* in (1) never passivize. Manzini & Franco (2016) argue that the *a* preposition/dative case with *speak* in (6) is selected by the verb. Under passive, selected dative case must be preserved, barring raising to nominative position. In other words *John was spoken to* would be well-formed but is unavailable in Romance; **John was spoken* is ungrammatical exactly as in English and for the same reasons (violation of the selection properties of the verb).

On the contrary, the *a* preposition/dative case with *see* in (6) is structural, since it depends not on the selection properties of the verb, but on the DOM configuration. More explicitly, I assume that under DOM, a highly ranked referent cannot be embedded as a theme, but must be embedded with a role at least as high as that of possessor/locator of the VP subevent, as schematized in (8).

(8) DOM
     [$_{VP}$ V [*(P⊆) DP]]
     where DP = 1/2P > pronoun > proper name etc.

According to Manzini & Franco, passive voids the context for the application of DOM, since the internal argument is raised out of its VP-internal position to [Spec, IP]. Therefore, no ⊆ preposition or case need be present in the derivation, and passivization is well-formed.

An important point made by Pineda (2016) is that given the identical structural realization of DOM and inherent datives, one may expect that some inherent datives are reanalyzed as DOM and end up being passivized. Apulian varieties like (9) are a case in point (see Loporcaro 1988; Ledgeway 2000 for independent attestations). This kind of reanalysis further supports the unification of DOM and inherent datives.

(9)   Minervino Murge

   a.   Jaɟɟə skrittə a jiddə.
         I.have written to him
         'I have written to him.'

   b.   Jiddə jɛ statə skrittə (da la suərə).
         he   is been written (by the sister)
         'He has been written to by his sister.'

   In what follows, I concentrate on a classical empirical aspect of the discussion
of Romance DOM/dative arguments, namely the clitics that double or pronominalize them. Note that I will not be discussing the conditions under which clitic
doubling is possible or necessary; my topic is just the morphological form of the
clitics that double/pronominalize DOM and inherent datives. In addressing this
matter, I adopt one of the two frameworks laid out above, namely the Relator P
one, rather than the Appl one. One reason is that adopting an abstract Appl projection for languages that manifestly have no applicative morphology introduces
additional structural complexity. Everything else equal, it is simpler to hold that
the *a* preposition, or the dative case, are elements endowed with semantic content, supporting the inclusion/possession predication. Whether there is a way of
stating the conclusions of §2–§3 in Appl terms or not remains an open question.

2 Clitics and full DPs may be associated with different case arrays

Manzini & Savoia (2014) find that in Albanian varieties, the case array of 1/2P
pronouns does not match that of lexical DPs or 3P pronouns. Thus lexical DPs
and 3P pronouns distinguish a nominative, an accusative and an oblique (da-
tive/ablative) case. On the other hand, 1/2P pronouns distinguish the nominative
case from an objective case that encompasses accusative and dative contexts, as
well as an ablative case. In the examples in (10a)–(10b) the first object of *see* and
the second object of *give* are lexicalized by the same 1/2P pronoun, while the
prepositional object has a separate ablative form in (10c). This contrasts with the
two distinct forms of the 3P pronoun in (10a) and (10b), accusative and oblique
respectively; the latter also occurs in the prepositional object position in (10c).

(10)   Shkodër, Albanian (Manzini & Savoia 2014)

   a.   ɛ/mə/na   ʃɔfin   atɛ/mu/ne.
         3SG.ACC/1SG/1PL see.3PL 3SG.ACC/1SG.OBL/1PL.OBL
         'They see him/me/us.'

b. j/m/n   a   japin   atii/mu/ne.
3SG.OBL/1SG/1PL 3SG.ACC give.3PL 3SG.OBL/1SG.OBL/1PL.OBL
'They give it to him/me/us.'

c. pɾei/poʃt/para   mejɛt/nɛʃ/atii
from/behind/before 1SG.LOC/1PL.LOC/3SG.OBL
'from/behind/before him/me/us'

Data of the type in (10) are traditionally dismissed in descriptive accounts as instances of morphological irregularity. In these terms, Albanian has a four-case system (nominative, accusative, oblique, ablative) – and while 3P displays dative/ablative syncretism, 1/2P displays accusative/dative syncretism. However, still following Manzini & Savoia (2014), there is a different way of looking at the pattern in (10). Despite the fact that Albanian is not usually recognized as a DOM language, the 1/2P case system could depend on the fact that 1/2P pronouns are in fact subject to DOM.[5]

Recall that in the South Italian and Ibero-Romance languages in §1, or in Hindi as quoted by Torrego (1998), DOM takes the form of dativization. The fact that the context in (10a) displays dative forms, exactly like the context in (10b), can then be construed as indicating that 1/2P pronouns are DOMed and that DOM takes the form of dativization/obliquization.[6]

---

[5]This way of looking at things presupposes that 1/2P vs 3P is an independently attested referential cut for the application of DOM. Center-South Italian varieties provide evidence that this is so, as in (i).

(i)   Colledimacine (Manzini & Savoia 2005)

     a. A   camatə a   mme/a nnu.
       he.has called   DOM me/DOM us

       'He called me/us.'

     b. A   camatə frattə   tiə/kwiʎʎə.
       he.has called   brother yours/him

       'He called him/my brother.'

[6]The dative realization of DOM is found not only in the Italic/Romance family and in the Indo-Aryan family, but also in the Iranian family, for instance in the Vafsi language, as well as in Armenian (Manzini & Franco 2016). Importantly, Romance *a* also introduces location/direction, as does the Hindi dative/DOM postposition *-ko*. This provides a bridge with the other major descriptive strategy of DOM marking in Indo-European, roughly a locative one. Thus in Eastern Romance (Romanian), where dative is inflectional, DOM takes the form of prepositional marking by locative *pe*; Persian *-ro* is also a directional. The common lexicalization of dative and locative, as seen in Romance *a*, Hindi *-ko*, is accounted for by Franco & Manzini (2017) by treating locative as a specialization of the inclusion relation, roughly inclusion in location. Following this line of argumentation to its logical conclusion, DOM in Indo-European languages would seem to involve the embedding of highly ranked referents under the ⊆ relator without exception.

Recall that I am interested in the reflexes of DOM and inherent dative on the clitic system. Several properties distinguish 1/2P clitics from 3P clitics in Romance, which I will illustrate just with Italian. From the data in Table 1 it is evident that 3P clitics are differentiated by gender (masculine/feminine) and by case (accusative/dative) – but 1/2P are insensitive to either distinction, as shown in Table 2.[7]

Table 1: 3P Italian clitics

	ACC.M	ACC.F	DAT.M	DAT.F
3SG	lo	la	gli	le
3PL	li	le	(loro)	(loro)

Table 2: 1/2P Italian clitics

	ACC/DAT
1SG	mi
2SG	ti
1PL	ci
2PL	vi

As already discussed for Albanian, the classical approach to asymmetries like those in Table 2 between 1/2P and 3P clitics is to postulate a single underlying φ-features and case system, namely a system rich enough to be able to account for 3P, and to assume that morphological mechanisms are responsible for the surface syncretisms observed in 1/2P. Note, however, that the different morphological make-up in Table 1–Table 2 correlates with a different positioning in the clitic string. Thus 1/2P clitics have the same position as 3P dative clitics in dative contexts such as (11a). However, in (11b) it can be seen that the 3P accusative follows the locative clitic; the 1/2P clitic precedes it, as in (11c). This means that dative and accusative 1/2P clitics are not distinguished syntactically.

(11)   Italian

    a. (Sulla ferita) gli/mi   ci   mette   la   pomata.
       on.the wound 3DAT/1SG LOC put.3SG the pomade
       'He put the pomade on my/his wound.'

---

[7]In Table 1 the plural form *loro* is parenthesized because it is not a clitic – but a non-clitic oblique pronoun (with a special distribution) suppletive for the clitic.

b. Mi ci mette vicino.
   1SG LOC put.3SG close
   'He puts me close to there.'

c. Ce lo mette vicino.
   LOC 3SG put.3SG close
   'He puts it/him close to there.'

There is a third phenomenon with respect to which 1/2P and 3P clitics differ, besides different morphological make-up (Table 1–Table 2) and different positioning (11). As shown by Kayne (1989), in Italian (French, etc.) perfect participles agree with D(P) complements placed to their left, hence with accusative clitics. This is illustrated in (12a); the 3P feminine accusative clitic cannot co-occur with a masculine inflection on the participle. By contrast, 3P dative clitics do not agree with the perfect participle, as in (12b); the latter must surface in the (default) masculine form, even if the clitic is overtly feminine.

(12)   Italian

    a. La   ha   aiutata/*aiutato.
       3.MPL.ACC has.3SG helped-FSG/helped-MSG
       'He helped her.'

    b. Le   ha   parlato/*parlata.
       3.FSG.DAT has.3SG talked-MSG/talked-FSG
       'He talked to him/her.'

Accusative 1/2P clitics may agree with the perfect participle, as illustrated in (13a). However, lack of agreement is also possible in (13a), leading to the masculine singular form of the participle. Agreement is impossible with 1/2P clitics in dative contexts in (12b).

(13)   a. Mi/ti   ha   aiutata/aiutato.
          1SG/2SG has.3SG helped-FSG/helped-MSG
          'He helped me(f.)/you(f.).'

       b. Mi/ti   ha   parlato/*parlata.
          1SG/2SG has.3SG spoken-MSG/spoken-FSG
          'He spoke to me(f.)/you(f.).'

In short, notionally accusative 1/2P clitics in (13a) may behave like dative clitics (irrespective of Person) in not triggering perfect participle agreement. Importantly, if the intrinsic features of 1/2P pronouns, such as the lack of overt gender, were at stake, we would expect them to always display optional agreement. However, agreement is obligatory in contexts where the 1/2P pronoun has been moved to subject position as in (14). This supports the view that the optionality of 1/2P object agreement depends not on the intrinsic features of the 1/2P forms, but rather on their structure of embedding.

(14)   Italian
       (Io) sono   arrivata/*arrivato.
       1SG be.1SG arrived-FSG/-MSG
       'I(f.) have arrived.'

Let us then go back to what is traditionally construed as the accusative/dative syncretism of Italian 1/2P object clitics in Table 2. Suppose that this syncretism is properly described as 1/2P clitics having an oblique (dative) but not an accusative form. The next step of the analysis is the observation that obliquization and specifically dativization of highly ranked referents characterizes DOM in Indo-European languages and specifically in Romance (cf. also fn. 5). If so, one may reasonably surmise that what appear to be idiosyncratic morphological properties of 1/2P clitics in Italian are in reality due to the fact that Italian 1/2P clitics undergo DOM.

Under this analysis, the optionality of agreement with 1/2P clitics in (13) replicates at a smaller scale a well-known independent parameter concerning the optionality of agreement with DOM objects. Given a language where DP objects agree with the verb and inherent datives do not, in principle two configurations may arise with DOM datives, as indicated in (15).

(15)   Object agreement configurations with DOM arguments.

       a. DOM arguments, like object DPs, agree with the verb.
       b. DOM arguments, like inherent datives, do not agree with the verb.

Indo-Aryan languages verify the existence of both patterns in (15). These languages present agreement of the perfect participle with the internal argument, for instance in Punjabi (16a), where the internal argument is absolutive and the external argument ergative. Furthermore, they are characterized by DOM, generally opposing animates/humans to inanimates/non-humans, realized by means of a postposition, which in Punjabi is -*nu*, as in (16b). What is relevant here is that the DOM object in (16b) does not agree with the perfect participle, which shows up in the masculine singular (similarly in Hindi).

(16) Punjabi (Manzini et al. 2015)

    a. O-ne   kutt-e   peddʒ-e.
       s/he-ERG dog-MPL send.PRF-MPL
       'S/he sent the dogs.'

    b. Mɛ: o-nu/una-nu   dekkh-ea.
       I   s/he-DOM/they-DOM see.PRF-MSG
       'I saw him/her/them.'

In other Indo-Aryan languages, DOM objects, also realized by an oblique postposition, agree with the perfect participle exactly as absolutive objects do (Masica 1991: 342). Thus in Marwari/Rajasthani the perfect participle always agrees with the object, whether it is DOM or not. In (17) I illustrate agreement of the perfect participle with DOM objects (-*nai*).

(17) Rajasthani (Khokhlova 2002)
    Raawan giitaa-nai maarii   hai.
    Rawan.M Gita.F-DOM beat.PRF.F be.PRS.3SG
    'Rawan beat Gita.'

Recall that if the present line of reasoning is correct, it is not possible to explain the 1/2P clitic paradigm in Italian in terms of morphological idiosyncrasy. Rather, 1/2P clitics are subject to DOM, hence they are externalized by oblique case. This in turn predicts two possible grammars for object agreement, given in (15). In one grammar, object agreement characterizes direct and DOM objects; in the alternative grammar agreement is restricted to direct objects. Given the Indo-Aryan data, we can safely conclude that nothing stands in the way of analysing Romance 1/2P clitics as subject to the DOM constraint (rather than as displaying the accusative/dative morphological syncretism) – and that this treatment may actually be advantageous in understanding their optional agreement.

In conclusion, clitics can be associated with a case array not matching that of lexical DPs/full pronouns, exactly like full pronouns may have a case alignment different from that of lexical DPs.[8]

Thus for instance 1/2P clitics in Italian undergo DOM, even though full pronouns/DPs do not. Note that if the clitic moved from a so-called 'big DP' hosted in the predicative domain, we would expect case uniformity. Therefore movement analyses of clitics are disfavoured by the present conclusions, and base generation analyses correspondingly favoured. In the rest of the article, I assume that clitics are base generated within their own field in the sentence (Sportiche 1996).

3 DOM and inherent datives under cliticization and clitic doubling

In this section, I turn to the question of which clitics pronominalize DOM objects. The conditions under which clitic doubling is possible/required are outside the scope of the present work. Hence, in what follows, I will alternate doubling and non-doubling (simple cliticization) data without further comment.

Traditional approaches hold that DOM objects are syntactically accusatives, though they may be morphologically syncretic with datives/obliques; therefore, one may expect that they are doubled/pronominalized by accusative clitics, even though goal datives are doubled/pronominalized by dative clitics, as schematized in (18a). However, if DOM arguments share the syntactic structure of inherent datives, as argued here in §1, we may expect that both are doubled (or more

---

[8]As an anonymous reviewer notes, the framework I adopt leads one to expect that there could be other case mismatches between DPs and the clitics that pronominalize (or perhaps double) them, within the boundaries imposed by UG. For instance, the anonymous reviewer notices that in French dative clitics are often reported to have a wider distribution than *à*-phrases, in causatives (see Sheehan 2020 [this volume]) and in benefactives/malefactives. A banal example in Italian is (ia), where two datives are inadmissible within the embedded predicate, but a matrix dative clitic is a possible lexicalization for the embedded external argument in (ib).

(i)   Italian

    a. Ho fatto scrivere (*a) mio fratello alla sua fidanzata.
        I.have made write (to) my brother to his fiancee
        'I made my brother speak to his fiancee.'

    b. Gli/lo   ho   fatto scrivere alla sua fidanzata.
        3DAT/3MSG.ACC I.have made write to his fiancee
        'I made him speak to his fiancee.'

generally pronominalized) by the same clitics, as in (18b). In turn, the option in (18b) may be taken to imply that both DOM and goal datives correspond to dative clitics, as in (18b-i). However one may also consider the possibility that both correspond to accusative clitics, as in (18b-ii).

(18) Cliticization configurations with DOM and goal arguments

    a. Clitics doubling/ pronominalizing DOM arguments belong to the accusative series, clitics doubling/ pronominalizing goal datives belong to the dative series;

    b. Clitics doubling/pronominalizing DOM and goal datives belong to the same series:

       i. both belong to the dative series

      ii. both belong to the accusative series.

All three possibilities in (18) are attested by the data. Pattern (18b-ii), in which accusative clitics lexicalize both theme and goal arguments, is known as *loísmo/laísmo* in the Spanish descriptive tradition and is robustly attested in Central and Southern Italian varieties (Rohlfs 1969: §633), as exemplified in (19a). Dialects like (19) do have a morphological dative clitic, but it regularly shows up only in ditransitive contexts, for instance (19c), as opposed to (19b). I agree with Pineda (2016) that *loísmo/laísmo* in the traditional sense of the term, i.e. an accusative 3P clitic doubling or pronominalizing a dative DP, must be kept separate from progressive varieties like Minervino in (9), which allow the goal argument of *write* to be passivized. Indeed in the corpus of Manzini & Savoia (2005), dialects like Celle in (19) (or Tempio in (20) below) do not display passivization.

(19) Celle di Bulgheria (Manzini & Savoia 2005)

    a. U   parlanu/viðinu   a   iddu.
       3MSG.ACC speak.3PL/see.3PL to/DOM him
       'They speak to/they see him.'

    b. U/a   ʃkrivu   (a idu/a   issa).
       3MSG.ACC/3FSG.ACC write.1SG to him/to her
       'I write him/her.'

    c. Li   ʃkrivu   na littira.
       3.DAT write.1SG a   letter
       'I write him/her/them a letter.'

Agreement with the perfect participle, which is absent from Ibero-Romance but present in Italo-Romance, shows that true accusative clitics are involved. Because of the phonological neutralization of final vowels to schwa, these data are difficult or impossible to find in Central and Southern varieties and are therefore briefly illustrated in (20) with a variety of Northern Sardinia.

(20)   Tempio Pausania (Manzini & Savoia 2005)
        l   aɟɟu   vaiḍḍat-u/-a/-i   / vist-u/-a/-i
        3.ACC have.1SG spoken-M.SG/-F.SG/-PL / seen-M.SG/-F.SG/-PL
        'I have seen/spoken to him/her/them.'

Next, under the uniform treatment of DOM and inherent datives proposed here, one would normally expect the pattern (18b-i) to be instantiated, whereby both inherent datives and DOM objects are lexicalized by dative clitics. This is robustly documented in Spanish dialects, under the traditional label of *leísmo*, for instance in Basque varieties, as illustrated in (21). Within the present analysis, it is natural to conclude that the clitics in (21) reflect the same case organization as their doubled DP counterparts – hence goal and DOM datives coincide in the dative clitic *le*.

(21)   Spanish, Basque dialect (Ormazabal & Romero 2013)

        a. Lo   vi   (*el libro).
            3M.SG.ACC saw.1SG   the book
            'I saw it/the book.'

        b. Le   vi   (al   niño/a   la niña).
            3DAT saw.1SG   DOM.the boy/DOM the girl
            'I saw him/her/the boy/the girl.'

Going back to the schema in (18) once more, we must finally consider the possibility that DOM and goal arguments have different clitic counterparts, as in (18a). This possibility is instantiated in some of the best-known varieties of Spanish, including the standard. In standard Spanish, animate internal arguments are pronominalized by an accusative clitic, as in (22a). By contrast, a DP lexicalizing a goal dative is doubled by a dative clitic, as in (22b). In the Rioplatense variety, though not in the standard one, (22a) is also grammatical as an instance of doubling.

(22)   Spanish (standard/Rioplatense)

    a. Lo   vio (*/^{OK} a   Juan).
        3M.SG.ACC   saw.3SG DOM Juan
        'He saw him/Juan.'

    b. Le   dio   el libro (a Juan).
        3DAT gave.3SG the book to Juan
        'He gave him the book (to John).'

The pattern in (22) appears to favour the view that the a-phrase in (22a) is an underlying accusative, determining doubling by an accusative clitic. But *loísmo* and *leísmo* dialects provide equally strong *prima facie* evidence in favour of the view that DOM and inherent datives have the same structure of embedding, so that they are treated alike under cliticization. As stated at the end of §2, I adopt the view that clitics and DPs are each separately merged in their relevant domains (Sportiche 1996), and eventually connected by Agree when cooccurring.[9] At the same time, the clitic and the doubled DP do not necessarily agree in Case, which is again part of the conclusion of §2.

Consider then the *leísmo* pattern again, as exemplified in (21) above. From the point of view of the analysis of DOM in §1, the clitic and the DP it doubles/pronominalizes actually agree in case, namely in dative case. More formally, the clitic and the DP share the $\subseteq$ property, lexicalized by P in front of the lexical DP and by dative case on the clitic, as schematized in (23). In other words, varieties like (23) can be described simply by saying that the conditions attaching on VP-internal embeddings of full DPs, also hold for the insertion of D heads in the clitic domain.

---

[9] Adopting Agree as the operation that connects the clitic and doubled DP implies that all of the structural conditions on Agree, as defined by Chomsky (2000), hold in the doubling configuration. As for the Phase Impenetrability Condition (PIC), the simplest way to insure that it is met is to adopt the conclusion of Sportiche (1996), that clitics are Merged in a clitic field located in the periphery of vP, from where they move the short step to IP. On the other hand, if clitics are base generated in IP, additional or alternative assumptions may be needed. The other major condition is c-command (and in fact minimal c-command, i.e. Minimality). If clitics are heads adjoined to v/I, then c-command of vP/VP-internal arguments follows. Nevertheless, a delicate issue arises because we have adopted the view that object clitics may alternate between a $\subseteq$ and a D form, and so do object DPs/$\subseteq$Ps, according to whether they do or not undergo DOM. The simplest thing to say is that φ-features label the root node in any event. The anonymous reviewer raises more complex issues yet, such as Long Distance Agreement, which are beyond the scope of the present article.

(23) $[_{IP} [_{\subseteq} \text{ } le] [_{I} \text{ } vi \text{ } [_{VP} \text{ } \bcancel{vi} \text{ } [_{CP} \text{ } a \text{ } la \text{ } niña]]$ (cf. (21b))

The *loísmo* pattern is schematized in (24). In present terms, there is a $\subseteq$ case mismatch in (24) both when the DP argument corresponds to an inherent dative (with the verb *speak (to)*) and when it corresponds to a DOM dative (with the verb *see*). Recall that inherent dative and DOM arguments can be distinguished, among others, on the basis of passivization; DOM datives with *see* passivize, while inherent datives with *speak (to)* do not passivize. Needless to say, the parallel behavior of goal and DOM *a*-phrases under *loísmo* tendentially supports their unification, though not as directly as the *leísmo* pattern in (23). Assume as before that DPs and clitics are each separately merged in their domains (predicative and inflectional, respectively), and that each domain may have its own case pattern. In the predicative domain in (24), highly ranked DPs (including 3P full pronouns) are introduced by the oblique $\subseteq$ relator under DOM, as are goal arguments selected by the verb. By contrast, in the clitic domain, all 3P internal arguments are simply lexicalized as Ds, i.e. as accusative.

(24) $[_{IP} [_{D} \text{ } u] [_{I} \text{ } parlanu/viðinu \text{ } [_{VP} \text{ } \bcancel{parlanu/viðinu} \text{ } [_{CP} \text{ } a \text{ } iddu]]$ (cf. 19a)

In the ditransitive counterparts to (24), goal clitics surface in the dative, as in structure (25). In a functionalist vein, one could account for (25) by invoking the need for disambiguation. There are formal means to implement the same basic idea. In an Agree configuration, the clitic effectively acts as a probe for its DP argument goal. If the clitic was embedded as a bare D in (25), its closest goal would be the direct object, namely *na littira* 'a letter', yielding a reading different from the intended one. In other words, the right reading is achieved only by having recourse to the specialized dative clitic. Economy considerations privilege the simpler lexicalization in (24) where possible.

(25) $[_{IP} [_{\subseteq} \text{ } li] [_{I} \text{ } \bcancel{ʃkrivu} \text{ } [_{VP} \text{ } ʃkrivu \text{ } na \text{ } littira \text{ } [_{CP} \text{ } a \text{ } iddu]]$ (cf. 19c)

The most problematic configuration from the present point of view of DOM arises in the standard variety of Spanish or in Rioplatense dialects, where DOM obliques are doubled by accusative clitics, while goal datives are doubled by dative clitics, along the lines of (26). It is a fact that in languages like (26) cliticization distinguishes lexical datives and DOM objects, while the present approach says that they have the same structure. However, recall that I assume that the case array of clitics in the inflectional domain does not necessarily match the case array of lexical DPs in the predicative domain. If so, we can describe (26) by saying that in the clitic domain, themes and goals are assigned accusative and dative respectively, and no DOM applies – even though DOM applies to lexical DPs in the predicative domain.

(26)   a. $[_{IP} [_D lo] [_I vio [_{VP} \text{vio} [_{PP \subseteq} a \text{ } Juan]]$
       b. $[_{IP} [_{D \subseteq} le] [_I dio [_{VP} \text{dio} el libro [_{PP \subseteq} a \text{ } Juan]]$

Let us then take stock. In §1 and 2 I have briefly argued for two main conclusions, which form the basis of the discussion in this section, namely (27).

(27)   In Romance

       a.   DOM and goal arguments are both embedded by $\subseteq$ (§1)
       b.   Clitic and full DP arguments are both first-merged in their respective domains, each with their own case alignment (§2).

In this section, I only considered Romance varieties where arguments of the predicative domain display DOM. Let us call this the DOM=Dat case alignment. In the clitic domain, we can find the same alignment (Table 3bi). However, DOM may be missing, yielding the case pattern Acc≠Dat (Table 3a). Finally, the clitics may display a single accusative realization for all direct or indirect object, in Table 3bii. Obviously, the numbering of the schemas in Table 3 is meant to match those in (18).

Table 3: Case patterns of clitics and DPs

		Clitics	DPs
a.		ACC≠DAT	DOM=DAT
b.	i	DOM=DAT	DOM=DAT
	ii	ACC	DOM=DAT

Suppose DOM in the predicative domain results from embedding of the argument under the same elementary predicate as the dative (27a). Suppose further that clitics can have their own independent case alignment (27b). Then there are at least three logical possibilities – namely that clitics have the same DOM pattern as the predicative domain (*leísmo*), or that they have a non-DOM pattern (standard Spanish) or that finally they have accusative for all internal arguments (*loísmo*). [10]

If the variation spread matches the logically possible outcomes, then parametrization is simply seen to correspond to the choices left open by Universal Grammar. In a sense, one might say that there is no explanation for the observed variation, but only descriptive statements, as (23)–(26) are. In another sense, the best of explanations actually turns out to hold, namely that variation, in this instance, does not require any additional statement. No parameter specifies the open choices, which simply follow from the structure of grammar and the lexicon. [11]

4 Conclusions

DOM arguments are associated with the *a*/dative morphology typical of goal arguments, because they share the same syntactic structure of embedding, namely the relational content ⊆ associated with the preposition *a* or with the dative case inflection (§1). Pronouns, especially 1/2P pronouns, do not necessarily share the

---

[10] If both object clitics and object DPs can be ±DOM, and they freely mix and match, we expect a fourth configuration – namely that there may be languages where a DOM 3P clitic corresponds to non-DOM DP objects. The closest match to this fourth predicted possibility arises in Quiteño Spanish, where "the DO-CLs have been almost universally replaced by *le(s)*... This replacement applies irrespective of the features [±animate] and [±masc] ...Thus, it could be said that QS has carried *leísmo* to conclusion" (Suñer 1989: 387–388), cf. (i). Importantly, "if there is an IO phrase, the CL refers unambiguously to the IO argument, and the DO automatically goes to ø" (Suñer 1989: 389), cf. (ii).

    (i)   Ya   le vendió. (where *le* = *el carro* 'the car')
            already it sold.3SG
            'He already sold it.'

    (ii) Al   chófer   le   ø di.   (where ø = *los papeles* 'the papers')
           to.the chauffeur to.him   gave.1SG
           'I gave them to the chauffeur.'

[11] In recent work, Manzini & Franco (2019) formalize the Object agreement parameter in (15) in terms of labelling. Thus, DOM objects can project both a D(P) label and a P(P)/K(P) label. Bare direct objects project only DP and inherent datives project only PP/KP (see Cornilescu 2020 [this volume] for similar ideas applied to partially overlapping data). The Cliticization parameter in (18) can perhaps be resolved in the same way. In any event, this is beyond the scope of the present paper, whose aim was solely to display the actual extent of variation in Romance and draw some conclusions about the free crossing of parameter values.

same case alignment as lexical DPs. In §2 I have concluded that though a language like Italian has no DOM with lexical DPs/full pronouns, the presence of a single object form of 1/2P clitics is to be interpreted as evidence of the presence of DOM in the clitic domain, and not as a mere morphological syncretism.

In §3, I assumed that clitics and lexical DPs are separately merged each in their domain. The case array may then be differently set. I interpreted standard/Rioplatense Spanish as instantiating the pattern in which 3P clitics are not sensitive to DOM, though DOM is enforced by lexical DPs and full pronouns. The traditional name of *leísmo* describes configurations in which animate 3P clitics are always dative, whether DOMed or inherent goals. The equally traditional label of *loísmo/laísmo* describes the pattern in which 3P object clitics corresponding to animate referents (subject to DOM in the predicative domain) or to inherent datives are both in the accusative.

References

Beck, Sigrid & Kyle Johnson. 2004. Double objects again. *Linguistic Inquiry* 35(1). 97–124.

Belvin, Robert & Marcel den Dikken. 1997. There, happens, to, be, have. *Lingua* 101(3–4). 151–183.

Bossong, Georg. 1985. *Empirische Universalienforschung. Differentielle Objektmarkierung in der neuiranischen Sprachen.* Tübingen: Narr.

Chomsky, Noam. 2000. Minimalist inquiries: The framework. In Roger Martin, David Michaels & Juan Uriagereka (eds.), *Step by step: Essays on Minimalist Syntax in honor of Howard Lasnik*, 89–155. Cambridge, MA: MIT Press.

Chomsky, Noam, Ángel Gallego & Dennis Ott. 2019. Generative grammar and the faculty of language: Insights, questions, and challenges. *Catalan Journal of Linguistics* Special Issue: Generative syntax. Questions, crossroads, and challenges: *Generative syntax: Questions, crossroads, and challenges.*

Cornilescu, Alexandra. 2020. Ditransitive constructions with differentially marked direct objects in Romanian. In Anna Pineda & Jaume Mateu (eds.), *Dative constructions in Romance and beyond*, 117–142. Berlin: Language Science Press. DOI:10.5281/zenodo.3776541

Culicover, Peter & Ray Jackendoff. 2005. *Simpler syntax.* Oxford: Oxford University Press.

Franco, Ludovico & Paolo Lorusso. 2020. Aspectual datives (and instrumentals). In Anna Pineda & Jaume Mateu (eds.), *Dative constructions in Romance and beyond*, 175–194. Berlin: Language Science Press. DOI:10.5281/zenodo.3776545

Franco, Ludovico & M. Rita Manzini. 2017. Instrumental prepositions and case: Contexts of occurrence and alternations with datives. *Glossa: A Journal of General Linguistics* 2(1) (Article 8). 1–47. DOI:10.5334/gjgl.111

Harley, Heidi. 2002. Possession and the double object construction. *Linguistic Variation Yearbook* 2(1). 31–70.

Kayne, Richard S. 1984. *Connectedness and binary branching.* Dordrecht: Foris.

Kayne, Richard S. 1989. Facets of Romance past participle agreement. In Paola Benincà (ed.), *Dialect variation and the theory of grammar,* 85–103. Dordrecht: Foris.

Khokhlova, Ludmila. 2002. *Syntactic peculiarities of Rajasthani.* Heidelberg. Paper presented at the 17th European Conference on Modern South Asian Studies.

Kiparsky, Paul. 2008. Universals constrain change, change results in typological generalizations. In Jeff Good (ed.), *Linguistic universals and language change,* 23–53. Oxford: Oxford University Press.

Ledgeway, Adam. 2000. *A comparative syntax of the dialects of Southern Italy: A minimalist approach.* Oxford: Blackwell.

Lima-Salles, Heloisa M. 2016. The syntax of (ditransitive) predicates of transference in Dialectal Brazilian Portuguese. *Quaderni di Linguistica e Studi Orientali* 2. 79–96.

Loporcaro, Michele. 1988. *Grammatica storica del dialetto di Altamura.* Pisa: Giardini.

Manzini, M. Rita. 2012. From Romance clitics to case: Split accusativity and the Person Case Constraint. In Irene Franco, Sara Lusini & Andrés Saab (eds.), *Romance languages and linguistic theory 2010: Selected papers from 'Going Romance' Leiden 2010,* 1–20. Amsterdam: John Benjamins.

Manzini, M. Rita & Ludovico Franco. 2016. Goal and DOM datives. *Natural Language and Linguistic Theory* 34. 197–240.

Manzini, M. Rita & Ludovico Franco. 2019. 'Agreement of Structural Obliques' parameter: DOM and pseudopartitives. *Lingvisticae Investigationes* 42(1). Monica Irimia & Anna Pineda (eds.). 82–101.

Manzini, M. Rita & Leonardo M. Savoia. 2005. *I dialetti italiani e romanci: Morfosintassi generativa.* Alessandria: dell'Orso.

Manzini, M. Rita & Leonardo M. Savoia. 2010. Case as denotation: Variation in Romance. *Studi Italiani di Linguistica Teorica e Applicata* XXXIX(3). 409–438.

Manzini, M. Rita & Leonardo M. Savoia. 2014. Person splits in the case systems of Geg Albanian (Shkodër) and Arbëresh (Greeks). *Studi Italiani di Linguistica Teorica e Applicata* XLIII(1). 7–42.

Manzini, M. Rita, Leonardo M. Savoia & Ludovico Franco. 2015. Ergative case, aspect and person splits: Two case studies. *Acta Linguistica Hungarica* 62(3). 1–55.

Masica, Colin. 1991. *The Indo-Aryan languages.* Cambridge: Cambridge University Press.

Ormazabal, Javier & Juan Romero. 2013. Object agreement, clitics and dialectal variation. *Probus* 25(2). 301–344.

Pesetsky, David. 1995. *Zero syntax: Experiencers and cascades.* Cambridge, MA: MIT Press.

Pineda, Anna. 2014. What lies behind dative/accusative alternations in Romance. In Stefania Marzo & Karen Lahousse (eds.), *Romance languages & linguistic theory 2012*, 123–139. Amsterdam: John Benjamins.

Pineda, Anna. 2016. *Les fronteres de la (in)transitivitat: Estudi dels aplicatius en llengües romàniques i basc.* Barcelona: Institut d'Estudis Món Juïc. Published and revised version of the doctoral dissertation.

Rohlfs, Gerhard. 1969. *Grammatica storica della lingua italiana e dei suoi dialetti.* Vol. 3, Sintassi e formazione delle parole. Torino: Einaudi.

Sheehan, Michelle. 2020. The Romance Person Case Constraint is not about clitic clusters. In Anna Pineda & Jaume Mateu (eds.), *Dative constructions in Romance and beyond*, 143–171. Berlin: Language Science Press. DOI:10.5281/zenodo.3776543

Sportiche, Dominique. 1996. Clitic constructions. In Johan Rooryck & Laurie Zaring (eds.), *Phrase structure and the lexicon*, 213–276. Dordrecht: Kluwer.

Suñer, Margarita. 1989. Dialectal variation and clitic-doubled direct objects. In Carl Kirschner & Janet DeCesaris (eds.), *Studies in Romance linguistics: Selected proceedings from Linguistic Symposium on Romance Languages XVII*, 377–395. Amsterdam: John Benjamins.

Torrego, Esther. 1998. *The dependencies of objects.* Cambridge, MA: MIT Press.

Torrego, Esther. 2010. Variability in the case patterns of causative formation in Romance and its implications. *Linguistic Inquiry* 41(3). 445–470.

Chapter 15

The accusative/dative alternation in Catalan verbs with experiencer object

Carles Royo
Universitat Rovira i Virgili

Various Catalan psychological verbs that are part of causative sentences with an accusative experiencer (*Els nens van molestar la Maria* or *La van molestar* 'The kids annoyed Maria' or 'They annoyed her') alternate with stative sentences that change the sentence order and have a dative experiencer (*A la Maria li molesta el teu caràcter* 'lit. To Maria your character is annoying'). Other psychological verbs, however, can form both types of sentence without changing the accusative morphology of the experiencer (*Els nens van atabalar la Maria* or *La van atabalar* 'The kids overwhelmed Maria or They overwhelmed her'; *A la Maria l'atabala el teu caràcter* 'lit. To Maria your character is overwhelming'). I argue that in stative sentences of all these verbs the experiencer is a real dative, regardless of its morphology (dative or accusative). Differential indirect object marking (DIOM) explains why accusative morphology is possible in these constructions.

1 Introduction

Since the first half of the 20th century (cf. Ginebra 2003: 16, Ginebra 2015: 147), some Catalan psychological verbs belonging to Belletti & Rizzi (1988)'s type II – which make sentences with an accusative experiencer or AcExp (1a)/(2a) – have appeared with some frequency in both the written and spoken language with a change in sentence order and a dative experiencer (1b)/(2b). This accusative/dative alternation has generated considerable academic debate. In most instances, the rules of the Institute of Catalan Studies (IEC) governing the Catalan language do not countenance this change in case marking, although the IEC's new normative grammar (GIEC 2016) and the changes introduced on 5 April 2017 to its online normative dictionary (DIEC2 2007) accept the dative case marking – as well

Carles Royo. 2020. The accusative/dative alternation in Catalan verbs with experiencer object. In Anna Pineda & Jaume Mateu (eds.), *Dative constructions in Romance and beyond*, 371–393. Berlin: Language Science Press. DOI:10.5281/zenodo.3776563

as the accusative – in some particular predicates: including the verbs *encantar* 'delight', *estranyar* 'surprise', *molestar* 'annoy' and *preocupar* 'worry'.[1]

(1) a. Els nens van   molestar la Maria   (*o* la   van
         The kids AUX.3PL annoy.INF the Maria.ACC or 3FSG.ACC AUX.3PL
         molestar).
         annoy.INF
         'The kids annoyed Maria (or They annoyed her).'
    b. A la Maria   li   molesten els nens.
         to the Maria.DAT 3SG.DAT annoy.3PL the kids
         (lit.) 'To Maria kids are annoying.'

(2) Cabré & Mateu 1998: 77

    a. Les teves paraules la   van   *sorprendre, preocupar,*
         the your words   3FSG.ACC AUX.3PL surprise.INF worry.INF
         molestar molt.
         annoy.INF a_lot
         'Your words surprised, worried, annoyed her a lot.'
    b. Li   *sorprèn, preocupa, molesta* que la joventut d' avui fumi
         3SG.DAT surprises worries annoys that the youth   of today smoke
         tant.
         so_much
         (lit.) 'To him/her that the youth of today smoke so much is surprising, worrying, annoying.'

This change has not had a uniform impact on Catalan dialects. Moreover, notable differences often occur within each dialect and even in the use that a specific speaker makes of these predicates (cf. Cabré & Mateu 1998: 70). Indeed, some predicates have become more entrenched than others, something that is irregularly reflected in several lexicographical collections in the Catalan language. It is common for AcExp verbs in Spanish to present this argument alternation (cf. Mendívil Giró 2005; Marín & McNally 2011, among others). For this reason, psychological verbs that are used with dative constructions in Catalan, when they have traditionally been used with accusative constructions (AcExp), have often

---

[1]Before publication of the GIEC (2016), the IEC accepted the intransitive nature of the verb *interessar* 'interest' as well as an accusative case marking.

been regarded as syntactic calques of the Spanish; yet, some studies describe the change as being inherent to the Catalan language.

This paper argues that in a stative sentence containing these verbs the experiencer is a real dative, not only when it presents the dative morphology, but also when it presents the accusative form (see also Cabré & Fábregas 2020 [this volume] and Ledgeway et al. 2020 [this volume], about the different natures of datives). I also argue that the accusative morphology of such stative sentences is facilitated by a mechanism of differential indirect object marking (DIOM).

2 Syntactico-semantic configuration of sentences with accusative and dative

Ynglès (1991) and Cabré & Mateu (1998) point out that the syntactico-semantic configuration differs when some AcExp verbs are used with the accusative and when they are used with the dative: see the contrast in (3).[2] In (1a) and (2a), three components of causative verbs imply a change of state: cause + process (change) + resulting state (cf. Levin & Rappaport Hovav 1995; Cabré & Mateu 1998; Rosselló 2008). The verb needs to be followed by an accusative in an eventive sentence of external causation and a neutral subject-verb-object (SVO) order. On the other hand, (1b) and (2b) do not have these three components, and the verb requires the dative in a stative sentence and a neutral object-verb-subject (OVS) order and clitic doubling (see also Fábregas & Marín 2020 [this volume]).

(3) a. Els nens van   molestar la Maria   *expressament* i   els
       The kids AUX.3PL annoy.INF the Maria.ACC on_purpose and the
       mestres també *ho van   fer.*
       teachers also   it AUX.3PL do.INF
       'The kids annoyed Maria on purpose and the teachers also did.'

    b. *A la Maria   li   molesten els nens *expressament* i   els
       to the Maria.DAT 3SG.DAT annoy.3PL the kids on_purpose and the
       mestres també *ho fan.*
       teachers also   it do

Two mechanisms help differentiate the causative structure in (1a)/(2a) from the stative structure in (1b)/(2b). On the one hand, their verbal aspect: the per-

---

[2]For further information on the proof and examples that show that sentences such as that in (1a)/(2a) are configured differently from those illustrated in (1b)/(2b), see Royo (2017: Section 4.1).

fective aspect contributes to a causative interpretation while the imperfective aspect contributes to a stative interpretation; hence, there is a relation between the lexical aspect of the sentence (eventive or stative) and the verbal aspect of the predicate (perfective or imperfective). And, on the other, the sentence order: a neutral SVO order will be interpreted as causative and a neutral OVS order will be interpreted as stative.

In line with Ynglès (1991); Cabré & Mateu (1998); Rosselló (2008) and GIEC (2016: Section 21.5b-c) for Catalan, Pesetsky (1995) for English, Bouchard (1995) for French and Acedo-Matellán & Mateu (2015) for Spanish, I consider that Catalan psychological verbs with an accusative experiencer (AcExp) generally cause a change of state:[3] in these sentences subjects are agents or inanimate causes and accusative experiencers are strictly speaking patients, even though conceptually they can be regarded as experiencers. I also concur with several authors who point out that the OVS stative construction of some AcExp Catalan verbs is the same as that of psychological verbs with a dative experiencer (DatExp, for example *agradar* 'to like'; cf. Cabré & Mateu 1998; Ramos 2004; Rosselló 2008; Cuervo 2010, among others): the subject is a stimulus or source of the psychological experience and the dative experiencer is not a patient, it does not undergo a change of state. What is more, clitic doubling occurs when the experiencer phrase appears in preverbal position.[4]

These data suggest that many speakers need to change both the syntactical pattern of AcExp verbs and the sentence order when they use these verbs in a stative construction: the different semantic or lexical-aspectual interpretation of these sentences is reflected in the different syntactic configuration of constructions that contain Catalan AcExp verbs.[5] According to (Ginebra 2003: 14, 29–30),

---

[3] According to other authors, the characterization of these sentences is different or allows different structures: cf. van Voorst (1992); Arad (1999); Landau (2010); Marín & McNally (2011) and Fábregas (2015). Several authors, including Fábregas & Marín (2012); Fábregas et al. (2012); Marín & Sánchez Marco (2012); Ganeshan (2014) and Viñas-de-Puig (2014), study these constructions in their general analyses of the stative and eventive nature of Spanish sentences with psychological verbs (note Viñas-de-Puig do the same also with Catalan psychological verbs). Acedo-Matellán & Mateu (2015: 83 (4)) also accept that these verbs cause a change of state in Spanish but point out that there is a less common construction of AcExp verbs with the accusative, that is, stative causative transitive (*Este problema la ha preocupado desde siempre*).

[4] Acedo-Matellán & Mateu (2015) have questioned this assumption in psychological verbs in Spanish and draw a distinction between DatExp verbs (unaccusative statives) and AcExp verbs that are constructed with the dative (unergative statives). For a discussion of this issue, see Royo (2017: Section 6.2.4.1).

[5] Several authors claim that the change between causative and stative interpretation implies a change in the Spanish case marking, between accusative and dative respectively: cf. Fábregas (2015); Viñas-de-Puig (2017) and Ganeshan (2019).

however, the examples in (4) show that Catalan can also denote a stative OVS construction without changing from the accusative to the dative with some predicates. These can be AcExp verbs (4a) or non-psychological causative verbs that become psychological by means of a metaphorical expansion of the meaning (4b) (the *psych constructions* described by Bouchard 1995). Therefore, the lexical nature of the verb plays an important role in the alternation since some verbs tend not to construct stative sentences with the dative.

(4) Ginebra 2003: 29–30

    a. Al   seu germà l'   atabala   la nova responsabilitat.
       to.the his brother 3MSG.ACC overwhelms the new responsibility
       (lit.) 'To his brother the new responsibility is overwhelming.'

    b. Al   Xavier el   destrossa aquesta tensió contínua.
       to.the Xavier 3MSG.ACC destroys this   tension constant
       (lit.) 'To Xavier this constant tension is destroying.'

What is more, with AcExp verbs such as those identified by Cabré & Mateu (1998) – *molestar, preocupar, sorprendre* (see (2)) – speakers may hesitate between accusative and dative case marking in OVS stative sentences. Some examples of this hesitation in a Catalan/Spanish bilingual newspaper are shown in (5). The print edition of the paper includes an OVS sentence with the verb *preocupar* 'worry' that governs the accusative in Catalan (5a) and the dative in Spanish (5b); on the other hand, in the Catalan online edition the same sentence appears with a dative (5c). Examples (6) and (7) show the same hesitation with the verb *molestar* 'annoy', in the same news item reported by six media in Catalan on 5 December 2012: three use the accusative (6) and three the dative (7).[6]

(5) *La Vanguardia*, 15 May 2015, p. 15 (headline)

    a. Catalan, printed version
       Per_què a CiU la   preocupa Ciutadans
       why   to CiU.F 3FSG.ACC worries Ciutadans.SG

    b. Spanish, printed version
       Por_qué a CiU le   preocupa Ciutadans
       why   to CiU.F 3SG.DAT worries Ciutadans.SG

---

[6]The three sentences in the accusative use direct speech while the three in the dative use indirect speech, which may indicate that the person making the statement conceptualizes the verb differently from the journalists who report it.

    c. Catalan, online version
        Per_què a CiU li   preocupa Ciutadans
        why   to CiU.F 3SG.DAT worries Ciutadans.SG
        (lit.) 'Why to CiU Ciutadans is worrying.'

(6) a. VilaWeb (headline)
        Rigau: 'A Wert el   molesta l' èxit   del   model d'
        Rigau to Wert 3MSG.ACC annoys the success of.the model of
        immersió'
        immersion
        (lit.) 'Rigau: "To Wert the model of immersion's success is annoying".'

    b. *El Periódico de Catalunya* (headline)
        Rigau: "A Wert el   molesta l' èxit   de la immersió
        Rigau to Wert 3MSG.ACC annoys the success of the immersion
        lingüística"
        language
        (lit.) 'Rigau: "To Wert the language immersion's success is annoying".'

    c. *Ara* (headline)
        Rigau: "A Wert, el_que el   molesta és l' èxit   del   model
        Rigau to Wert what 3MSG.ACC annoys is the success of.the model
        educatiu   català"
        educational Catalan
        (lit.) 'Rigau: "What is annoying to Wert is the Catalan educational model's success".'

(7) a. 3/24, www.ccma.cat (headline)
        Rigau creu   que a Wert li   molesta "l' èxit" del
        Rigau believes that to Wert 3SG.DAT annoys the success of.the
        model català
        model Catalan

    b. diaridegirona.cat (headline)
        Rigau creu   que a Wert li   molesta "l' èxit" del   model
        Rigau believes that to Wert 3SG.DAT annoys the success of.the model
        català
        Catalan
        (lit.) 'Rigau believes that to Wert the Catalan model's "success" is annoying.'

  c. *El Punt Avui*
     La titular d' Ensenyament, creu   que a Wert li
     the minister of Education   believes that to Wert 3SG.DAT
     "molesta" el model "d' èxit"   de l' escola catalana.
     annoys the model of success of the school Catalan
     (lit.) 'The minister of Education believes that to Wert the model "of
     success" of the Catalan school is annoying.'

In fact, if in (1b) and (2b) we replace the dative clitic with the accusative clitic –
*A la Maria **la** molesten els nens*; *(A ella) **La** sorprèn, preocupa, molesta que la joventut d'avui fumi tant* – our discussion above about distinguishing these sentences from those in (1a) and (2a) is still valid: they are useful ways of characterizing both constructions differently, but they do not help determine the case marking.

The ability of Catalan to construct a stative sentence with an AcExp verb and an accusative experiencer makes it necessary to analyse this accusative in those cases of hesitation with the dative (that is, in OVS stative sentences). We need to know whether the order of the sentences and clitic doubling in Catalan are sufficient to denote a lexical-aspectual change in the sentence or whether a change in case marking is also required.

3 Nature of the accusative and dative experiencer in OVS stative sentences

In the sentences in (1b)/(2b) and (4)-(7), whether the verb governs the accusative or the dative, the subject is a stimulus of the emotion and the object is not a patient but an experiencer of the whole event in a more prominent structural position than that occupied by the stimulus. It can be shown that this experiencer argument, regardless of whether it is accusative or dative, is not a topicalized element and that it has properties of a subject: cf. examples a and b in (8)-(13). It behaves just like the experiencer in sentences with DatExp verbs such as *agradar* 'like' (see the c examples in (8)-(13)) and other canonical subjects (see the d examples in (8) and (12) and example (10e)): it behaves quite differently from topicalized objects (see the d examples in (9)-(11) and (13)).[7]

The experiencer can link an anaphora in the subject (cf. Demonte 1989; Eguren & Fernández Soriano 2004) (8), be modified with the adverb *només* 'only' (cf.

---

[7]In examples (8)-(13), as in the other examples employed in this paper, I conduct a descriptive rather than a prescriptive assessment.

Cuervo 1999) (9), allow *Wh*-extraction (cf. Belletti & Rizzi 1988) (10), be an indefinite generalized quantifier in initial position (cf. Belletti & Rizzi 1988; Masullo 1992; Cuervo 1999) (11), control the subject of an infinitive clause (cf. Campos 1999; Alsina 2008) (12) and it cannot be separated, in Catalan, by a comma from the rest of the sentence (cf. Ginebra 2003; 2005) (13).

(8) a. OVS AcExp, **dative/accusative**
A l' Albert$_i$ {**li**$_i$ / **el**$_i$} molesta aquesta fotografia de
to the Albert **3SG.DAT** / **3MSG.ACC** annoys this photo of
si_mateix$_i$.
himself
(lit.) 'To Albert this photo of himself is annoying.'

b. OVS AcExp, **accusative**
A l' Albert$_i$ **el**$_i$ neguiteja aquesta fotografia de si_mateix$_i$.
to the Albert **3MSG.ACC** disturbs this photo of himself
(lit.) 'To Albert this photo of himself is disturbing.'

c. DatExp, **dative**
A l' Albert$_i$ **li**$_i$ agrada aquesta fotografia de si_mateix$_i$.
to the Albert **3SG.DAT** likes this photo of himself
'Albert likes this photo of himself.'

d. Subject, dative
L' Albert$_i$ envia una fotografia de si_mateix$_{i/*j}$ a la Núria$_j$.
the Albert.SBJ sends a photo of himself to the Nuria.DAT
'Albert sends a photo of himself to Nuria.'

(9) a. OVS AcExp, **dative/accusative**
Només a l' Albert {**li** / **el**} molesta aquesta situació.
only to the Albert **3SG.DAT** / **3MSG.ACC** annoys this situation
(lit.) 'Only to Albert this situation is annoying.'

b. OVS AcExp, **accusative**
Només a l' Albert **el** neguiteja aquesta situació.
only to the Albert **3MSG.ACC** disturbs this situation
(lit.) 'Only to Albert this situation is disturbing.'

c. DatExp, **dative**
Només a l' Albert **li** agrada la cervesa.
only to the Albert **3SG.DAT** likes the beer
'Only Albert likes beer.'

    d. Topicalized dative

        $^?$Només a l' Albert **li**   vaig   prendre el bolígraf.[8]

         only   to the Albert 3SG.DAT AUX.1SG take.INF the pen

(10) a. OVS AcExp, **dative/accusative**

         La situació que a l' Albert {**li**   / **el**}   molesta és

         the situation that to the Albert 3SG.DAT / 3MSG.ACC annoys is

         aquesta.

         this

         (lit.) 'The situation that to Albert is annoying is this.'

    b. OVS AcExp, **accusative**

         La situació que a l' Albert (**el**)   neguiteja és aquesta.

         the situation that to the Albert 3MSG.ACC disturbs is this

         (lit.) 'The situation that to Albert is disturbing is this.'

    c. DatExp, **dative**

         Els llibres que a l' Albert (**li**)   han   agradat són aquests.

         the books that to the Albert 3SG.DAT have.3PL liked   are these

         'The books that Albert liked are these.'

    d. Topicalized dative

         $^{??}$Els llibres que a l' Albert (**li**)   he   donat són aquests.

         the books that to the Albert 3SG.DAT have.1SG given are these

    e. Preverbal subject

         Els llibres que l' Albert   m'   ha donat són aquests.

         the books that the Albert.SBJ 1SG.DAT has given are these

         'The books that Albert gave me are these.'

(11) a. OVS AcExp, **dative/accusative**

         A ningú (no) {**li**   / **el**}   molesta aquesta situació.

         to nobody NEG 3SG.DAT / 3MSG.ACC annoys this   situation

         (lit.) 'To nobody this situation is annoying.'

    b. OVS AcExp, **accusative**

         A ningú (no) (**el**)   neguiteja aquesta situació.

         to nobody NEG 3MSG.ACC disturbs this   situation

         (lit.) 'To nobody this situation is disturbing.'

---

[8]This sentence is acceptable with a stressed intonation: *Només A L'ALBERT...*

    c. DatExp, **dative**
       A ningú (no) **li** va agradar la pel·lícula.
       to nobody NEG 3SG.DAT AUX.3SG like.INF the film
       'Nobody likes the film.'

    d. Topicalized dative
       *A ningú (no) **li** vaig donar el quadre.
       to nobody NEG 3SG.DAT AUX.1SG give.INF the painting

(12) a. OVS AcExp, **dative/accusative**
       A l' Albert$_i$ {**li**$_i$ / **el**$_i$} molesta PRO$_i$ parlar en públic.
       to the Albert 3SG.DAT / 3MSG.ACC annoys PRO speak.INF in public
       (lit.) 'To Albert speaking in public is annoying.'

    b. OVS AcExp, **accusative**
       A l' Albert$_i$ **el**$_i$ neguiteja PRO$_i$ parlar en públic.
       to the Albert 3MSG.ACC disturbs PRO speak.INF in public
       (lit.) 'To Albert speaking in public is disturbing.'

    c. DatExp, **dative**
       A l' Albert$_i$ **li**$_i$ agrada PRO$_i$ parlar en públic.
       to the Albert 3SG.DAT likes PRO speak.INF in public
       'Albert likes speaking in public.'

    d. Subject
       L' Albert$_i$ vol PRO$_i$ arribar aviat.
       the Albert.SBJ wants PRO arrive.INF early
       'Albert wants to arrive early.'

(13) a. OVS AcExp, **dative/accusative**
       A l' Albert$_{(*,)}$ {**li** / **el**} molesta aquesta situació.
       to the Albert 3SG.DAT / 3MSG.ACC annoys this situation
       (lit.) 'To Albert this situation is annoying.'

    b. OVS AcExp, **accusative**
       A l' Albert$_{(*,)}$ **el** neguiteja aquesta situació.
       to the Albert 3MSG.ACC disturbs this situation
       (lit.) 'To Albert this situation is disturbing.'

   c. DatExp, **dative**

      A l' Albert_(*,) **li**   agrada aquesta situació.

      to the Albert   **3sg.dat** likes this   situation

      'Albert likes this situation.'

   d. Topicalized object

      (A) L' Albert_(,) l'   he   vist que plorava.

      dom the Albert   **3msg.acc** have.1sg seen that cried.3sg

      'Albert, I saw that he cried.'

4 OVS sentences with AcExp verbs and an accusative experiencer

The analysis conducted in section §3 highlights the similarity between the dative experiencer in sentences with DatExp verbs and the experiencer object in OVS stative sentences with AcExp verbs, whether the morphology is dative or accusative. When the experiencer has accusative morphology, there is evidence to show that it is in fact a dative if we place it in sentence-initial position by using a relative pronoun ((14a)-(14b)) (adjectival relative clause and noun relative clause),[9] an interrogative pronoun ((14c)-(14d)) (direct and indirect interrogative) or a determiner phrase (14e). In this context, the experiencer can optionally take either accusative or dative morphology in the corresponding agentive sentences with AcExp verbs (16), which is similar to how the person semantic object behaves in transitive sentences of non-psychological verbs, whether they are causative or not (17). But in stative sentences with AcExp verbs (14), the experiencer in initial position behaves like the dative experiencer in the corresponding sentences with DatExp verbs (15): it can only be dative, even though in (14) the morphology is still an accusative clitic within the sentence (cf. Royo 2017: Section 4.3.4).

To illustrate this contrast, the examples below are of stative sentences with imperfective verbal aspect (14)-(15) and causatives and non-causative transitives with perfective aspect (16)-(17). What is more, in (14) and (16) I use an AcExp verb that can easily be conceived of as causative of change of state, such as *atabalar* 'overwhelm', unlike other AcExp verbs such as *molestar* 'annoy', which in some contexts can have the meaning of *desagradar molt* ('displease a lot').

---

[9]In the examples, I do not consider the use of the relative often referred to as the *relatiu popular* (cf. Ginebra 2005: 154–155), which is always marked with an asterisk.

(14) a. És   una persona {a **qui**   / *que}   (l')   atabala
           is.3SG a.F person.F to whom.DAT / who.ACC 3FSG.ACC overwhelms
           el   record d' aquell fracàs.
           the memory of that   failure
           (lit.) 'He/She is a person to whom the memory of that failure is
           overwhelming.'

      b. {A **qui**   / *Qui}   (l')   atabala   el   record d' aquell
           to whom.DAT / who.ACC 3SG.ACC overwhelms the memory of that
           fracàs és *(a) la   Maria.
           failure is to the Maria.DAT
           (lit.) 'To whom the memory of that failure is overwhelming it is to
           Maria.'

      c. {A **qui**   / *Qui}   (l')   atabala   el   record d'
           to whom.DAT / who.ACC 3SG.ACC overwhelms the memory of
           aquell fracàs?
           that   failure
           (lit.) 'To whom the memory of that failure is overwhelming?'

      d. Voldria   saber   {a **qui**   / *qui}   (l')
           would_like.1SG know.INF to whom.DAT / who.ACC 3SG.ACC
           atabala   el   record   d' aquell fracàs.
           overwhelms the memory of that   failure
           (lit.) 'I would like to know to whom the memory of that failure is
           overwhelming.'

      e. * (A) la   Maria(*,)   l'   atabala   el   record d' aquell
           to the Maria.DAT 3FSG.ACC overwhelms the memory of that
           fracàs.[10]
           failure
           (lit.) 'To Maria, the memory of that failure is overwhelming.'

(15) a. És   una persona {a **qui**   / *que}   no (li)   agrada el
           is.3SG a   person to whom.DAT / who.ACC NEG 3SG.DAT likes   the

---

[10]In examples (14e) and (15e) the asterisk indicates that these sentences cannot be constructed
without the preposition *a* at the beginning of the sentence. With the preposition *a*, they are
fully acceptable sentences.

      record   d' aquell fracàs.
      memory of that   failure
      'He/She is a person who doesn't like the memory of that failure.'

b.   {A qui   / *Qui}   no (li)   agrada el record d' aquell
      to whom.DAT / who.ACC NEG 3SG.DAT likes   the memory of that
      fracàs és *(a) la Maria.
      failure is to   the Maria.DAT
      'Maria is the one who doesn't like the memory of that failure.'

c.   {A qui   / *Qui}   no (li)   agrada el record d' aquell
      to whom.DAT / who.ACC NEG 3SG.DAT likes   the memory of that
      fracàs?
      failure
      'Who doesn't like the memory of that failure?'

d.   Voldria   saber   {a qui   / *qui}   no (li)
      would_like.1SG know.INF to whom.DAT / who.ACC NEG 3SG.DAT
      agrada el record   d' aquell fracàs.
      likes   the memory of that   failure
      'I would like to know who doesn't like the memory of that failure.'

e.   * (A) la Maria$_{(*,)}$ no li   agrada el record   d' aquell fracàs.
      to the Maria.DAT NEG 3SG.DAT likes   the memory of that   failure
      'Maria doesn't like the memory of that failure.'

(16) a. És   una persona {a qui   (l')   / que}   han
        is.3SG a.F person.F to whom.DAT 3FSG.ACC / who.ACC have.3PL
        atabalat   contínuament amb insídies.
        overwhelmed continuously with malicious_acts
        'He/She is a person who somebody has overwhelmed continuously
        with malicious acts.'

     b. {A qui   (l')   / Qui}   han   atabalat
        to whom.DAT 3SG.ACC / who.ACC have.3PL overwhelmed
        contínuament amb insídies   és (a) la   Maria.
        continuously with malicious_acts is DOM the Maria.ACC
        'Maria is the one who somebody has overwhelmed continuously with
        malicious acts.'

     c. {A qui   (l')   / Qui}   han   atabalat   amb
        to whom.DAT 3SG.ACC / who.ACC have.3PL overwhelmed with

aquestes insídies?
these   malicious_acts
'Who has somebody overwhelmed with these malicious acts?'

d. Voldria   saber   {a qui   (l')   / qui}   han
would_like.1SG know.INF to whom.DAT 3SG.ACC / who.ACC have.3PL
atabalat   amb aquestes insídies.
overwhelmed with these   malicious_acts
'I would like to know who somebody has overwhelmed with these
malicious acts.'

e. (A) la Maria(,) l'   han   atabalat   contínuament
DOM the Maria.ACC 3FSG.ACC have.3PL overwhelmed continuously
amb insídies.
with malicious_acts
'Somebody has overwhelmed Maria continuously with malicious
acts.'

(17) a. És   una persona {a qui   (l')   / que}   han
is.3SG a.F person.F to whom.DAT 3FSG.ACC / who.ACC have.3PL
{mullat / vist} amb una mànega.
wet   / seen with a   hose
'He/She is a person who somebody has {wet / seen} with a hose.'

b. {A qui   (l')   / Qui}   han   {mullat / vist} amb una
to whom.DAT 3SG.ACC / who.ACC have.3PL wet   / seen with a
mànega és (a)   la   Maria.
hose   is DOM the Maria.ACC
'Maria is the one who somebody has {wet / seen} with a hose.'

c. {A qui   (l')   / Qui}   han   {mullat / vist} amb una
to whom.DAT 3SG.ACC / who.ACC have.3PL wet   / seen with a
mànega?
hose
'Who has somebody {wet / seen} with a hose?'

d. Voldria   saber   {a qui   (l')   / qui}   han
would_like.1SG know.INF to whom.DAT 3SG.ACC / who.ACC have.3PL
{mullat / vist} amb una mànega.
wet   / seen with a   hose
'I would like to know who somebody has {wet / seen} with a hose.'

e. (A) la Maria$_{(,)}$ l'   han   {mullat / vist} amb una
   DOM the Maria.ACC 3FSG.ACC have.3PL wet   / seen with a
   mànega.
   hose
   'Somebody has {wet / seen} Maria with a hose.'

Bearing in mind that stative sentences of AcExp verbs are constructed with a real dative, regardless of the morphology of the experiencer clitic, I use the abbreviation Dat(>|<Ac)Exp to differentiate these constructions from both AcExp causatives and DatExp statives. The abbreviation can be used in cases of hesitation between the accusative and the dative form and, at the same time, to differentiate Dat(>Ac)Exp when the morphology is dative and Dat(<Ac)Exp when the morphology is accusative.

5 Argument structure of stative sentences with AcExp verbs

According to Rosselló (2008: Sections 13.3.6.2a-b and 13.3.7.2b) and the GIEC (2016: 21.2.2b and 21.5a), one characteristic of Catalan psychological verbs with an experiencer object (AcExp and DatExp) is that they can elide their object in the absolute use of the verb. Sentences with the absolute use of these predicates can express the property of a stimulus to affect a hypothetical experiencer, a stative construction with both DatExp verbs (18a) and AcExp verbs (18b), which in this case does not express an action.[11]

(18) a. La xocolata agrada ('és agradable'); La família importa ('és
         the chocolate likes   is pleasant   the family matters   is
         important').
         important
         (lit.) 'Chocolate is pleasant.' (lit.) 'Family is important.'

      b. Els nens molesten ('són molestos'); El teu caràcter atabala
         the kids annoy   are annoying   the your character overwhelms

---

[11]The GIEC (2016: 21.2.2b and 21.5a) points out that in absolute use those verbs that have an instrumental value (*tallar* 'cut', *obrir* 'open', *tancar* 'close', *tapar* 'cover', etc.), which like AcExp verbs are generally causative of change of state, express a property of the subject rather than a particular action.

('és atabalador').
 is overwhelming
(lit.) 'Kids are annoying.' (lit.) 'Your character is overwhelming.'

Following Cuervo's proposal (2003: Section 1.3.3.2) for verbs that she calls *predicational statives*, all the sentences in (18) have an underlying stative unaccusative structure. For sentences with an experiencer, we need a functional head that introduces a dative with experiencer semantics and the characteristics of a subject in a hierarchically superior position and which relates it to the whole event that indicates a property of the stimulus: a high applicative head (external argument), with the dative in the position of specifier (cf. Pylkkänen 2008; Cuervo 2003; 2010; see also Cuervo 2020 [this volume]) (19).[12]

(19) a. DatExp
        A la Maria li   agrada la xocolata.
        to the Maria 3SG.DAT likes   the chocolate
        (lit.) 'To Maria chocolate is pleasant.'

    b. Dat(>|<Ac)Exp
        A la Maria {li   / la}   molesten els nens.
        to the Maria 3SG.DAT / 3FSG.ACC annoy.3PL the kids
        (lit.) 'To Maria kids are annoying.'

The unaccusative structure of (19a) for DatExp verbs matches Belletti & Rizzi's (1988) characterization of type-III predicates. The construction of (19b), however, requires some additional clarifications. Apparently, we should reject an unaccusative structure with an accusative experiencer – and in Catalan we do not expect an accusative to be an external argument – but if we bear in mind that it is a superficial accusative and that it is really a dative (cf. §3 and §4), this objection disappears. We also need to explain how some verbs can optionally use the accusative and dative forms (5)-(7), and other verbs the accusative form in OVS stative sentences, whether they are AcExp (4a) or causative predicates with a metaphorical psychological meaning (4b).

In these sentences, the experiencer is a non-topicalized element with subject properties and a real dative, regardless of the form it takes. The syntactic mechanism that can explain sentences in which the experiencer has apparent accusative

---

[12] Other authors explain the variability between the stative and the causative reading of these verbs without a high applicative head that introduces the experiencer in the stative construction (see Viñas-de-Puig 2014; 2017, and references therein). For example, Viñas-de-Puig proposes that in both readings the experiencer is licensed for a Sv_{EXP} head above the root, in a basic stative structure, which will take a causative reading by adding a Sv_{CAUS} above the Sv_{EXP}.

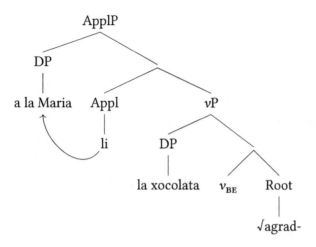

Figure 1: Structure of DatExp verb sentence

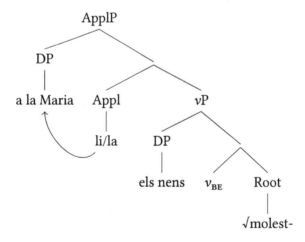

Figure 2: Structure of Dat(>|<Ac)Exp verb sentence

morphology (20b) is differential indirect object marking or DIOM (cf. Bilous 2011; Pineda 2016, 2020; Pineda & Royo 2017), which is not necessary when the clitic takes dative morphology (20a).

(20) a. Dat(>)Exp
        A la Maria   li   molesten els nens.
        to the Maria.DAT 3SG.DAT annoy.3PL the kids
        (lit.) 'To Maria kids are annoying.'

    b. Dat(<Ac)Exp
        A la Maria   l'   atabala   el teu caràcter.
        to the Maria.DAT 3FSG.ACC.DIOM overwhelm the your character
        (lit.) 'To Maria your character is overwhelming.'

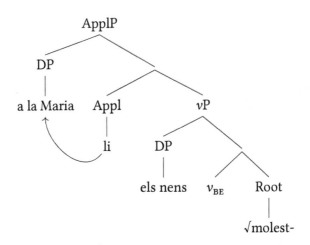

Figure 3: Structure of Dat(>Ac)Exp verb sentence

The dative case marking of these sentences is congruent with the semantic and syntactic characteristics of the experiencer and with the function of the high applicative heads in a Romance language like Catalan. A DIOM accusative morphology would allow speakers to use these constructions with verbs that are difficult to conceive of as stative, because in the minds of speakers they are closely related to verbs that cause a change of state (4). The morphological aspect of the experiencer depends on the lexical characteristics of the verb: even though the sentence is always stative, we can regard DIOM as being an anti-stativization mechanism in the minds of speakers. In this sense, it is significant that non-psychological causative verbs with a metaphorical psychological meaning present the superficial accusative form in OVS stative sentences (*destrossar* 'destroy', *enfonsar*

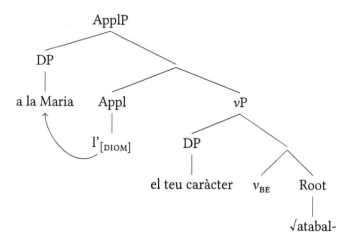

Figure 4: Structure of Dat(<Ac)Exp verb sentence

'sink'). Like some psychological verbs (*commoure* 'move, touch', *esparverar* 'terrify'),[13] they are verbs that speakers conceptualize habitually as being causative of change of state, unlike other verbs that more readily permit a stative conceptualization in certain contexts: for example, *molestar* 'annoy', which can sometimes have the meaning of *desagradar molt* ('displease a lot').[14]

This explanation takes into account the conceptual mechanisms that can, according to several authors, affect the construction of sentences and syntactic change: the speakers' conception of the world (cf. Ramos 2002), the linguistic conception of particular communicative contexts (cf. Rosselló 2008) and the different conceptualization of transitivity (cf. Ynglès 2011; Pineda 2012).

6 Conclusions

The main argument presented in this article is that in stative sentences of Catalan AcExp predicates, the experiencer is a real dative. In stative sentences of some AcExp verbs and other non-psychological causative verbs with metaphorical psychological semantics, the experiencer may present an external accusative morphology by means of differential indirect object marking (DIOM). DIOM is the manifestation in the minds of speakers of their difficulty to conceive certain

---

[13]Ginebra (2003: 14, 29–30) offers more examples of OVS stative sentences of this type with a superficial accusative in both verb types, that is, psychological and non-psychological verbs with metaphorical psychological meaning.

[14]For an explanation of other factors that intervene so that an AcExp verb can participate in sentences such as Dat(<Ac)Exp or Dat(>Ac)Exp, see Royo (2017: Section 5).

verbs as being stative or, in other words, of their tendency to conceive of them as being causative of change of state.

Abbreviations

The abbreviations used in the glosses of this chapter follow the Leipzig Glossing Rules. Additional abbreviations: DOM differential object marking.

Acknowledgments

This study has been supported by research project FFI2014-56258-P (Ministerio de Economía y Competitividad). I would like to thank Jaume Mateu for specific comments made in relation to this paper and Anna Pineda for encouraging me to present this research in public and to have it published.

References

Acedo-Matellán, Víctor & Jaume Mateu. 2015. Los verbos psicológicos: Raíces especiales en estructuras corrientes. In Rafael Marín (ed.), *Los predicados psicológicos*, 81–109. Madrid: Visor.

Alsina, Àlex. 2008. L'infinitiu. In Joan Solà, Maria-Rosa Lloret, Joan Mascaró & Manuel Pérez Saldanya (eds.), *Gramàtica del català contemporani*, 4th edn., 2389–2454. Barcelona: Editorial Empúries.

Arad, Maya. 1999. On "little v". *MIT Working Papers in Linguistics* 33. 1–25.

Belletti, Adriana & Luigi Rizzi. 1988. Psych-verbs and θ-Theory. *Natural Language & Linguistic Theory* 6(3). 291–352. DOI:10.1007/BF00133902

Bilous, Rostyslav. 2011. *Transitivité et marquage d'objet différentiel.* Toronto: University of Toronto. (Doctoral dissertation).

Bouchard, Denis. 1995. *The semantics of syntax: A minimalist approach to grammar.* Chicago, IL: University of Chicago Press.

Cabré, Teresa & Jaume Mateu. 1998. Estructura gramatical i normativa lingüística: A propòsit dels verbs psicològics en català. *Quaderns: Revista de traducció* 2. 65–81.

Cabré, Teresa & Antonio Fábregas. 2020. Ways of being a dative across Romance varieties. In Anna Pineda & Jaume Mateu (eds.), *Dative constructions in Romance and beyond*, 395–411. Berlin: Language Science Press. DOI:10.5281/zenodo.3776565

Campos, Héctor. 1999. Transitividad e intransitividad. In Ignacio Bosque & Violeta Demonte (eds.), *Gramática descriptiva de la lengua española*, vol. 2, 1519–1574. Madrid: Espasa Calpe.

Cuervo, María Cristina. 1999. Quirky but not eccentric: Dative subjects in Spanish. *MIT Working Papers in Linguistics* 34. 213–227.

Cuervo, María Cristina. 2003. *Datives at large*. Cambridge, MA: Massachusetts Institute of Technology. (Doctoral dissertation). https://dspace.mit.edu/handle/1721.1/7991.

Cuervo, María Cristina. 2010. La estructura de expresiones con verbos livianos y experimentante. In Marta Luján & Mirta Groppi (eds.), *Cuestiones gramaticales del español: Últimos avances*, 194–206. Santiago de Chile: ALFAL.

Cuervo, María Cristina. 2020. Datives as applicatives. In Anna Pineda & Jaume Mateu (eds.), *Dative constructions in Romance and beyond*, 1–39. Berlin: Language Science Press. DOI:10.5281/zenodo.3776531

Demonte, Violeta. 1989. *Teoria sintáctica: De las estructuras a la rección*. Madrid: Síntesis.

DIEC2 – Institut d'Estudis Catalans. 2007. *Diccionari de la llengua catalana*. 2nd edn. Barcelona: Institut d'Estudis Catalans, Enciclopèdia Catalana, Edicions 62. http://dlc.iec.cat.

Eguren, Luis & Olga Fernández Soriano. 2004. *Introducción a una sintaxis minimista*. Madrid: Gredos.

Fábregas, Antonio. 2015. No es experimentante todo lo que experimenta o cómo determinar que un verbo es psicológico. In Rafel Marín (ed.), *Los predicados psicológicos*, 51–79. Madrid: Visor Libros.

Fábregas, Antonio & Rafael Marín. 2012. State nouns are Kimian states. In Irene Franco, Sara Lusini & Andrés Saab (eds.), *Romance languages & linguistic theory 2010: Selected papers from 'going Romance' Leiden 2010*, 4, 41–64. Amsterdam, Philadelphia: John Benjamins.

Fábregas, Antonio, Rafael Marín & Louise McNally. 2012. From psych verbs to nouns. In Violeta Demonte & Louise McNally (eds.), *Telicity, change, and state: A cross-categorial view of event structure*, 162–185. New York, NY: Oxford University Press.

Fábregas, Antonio & Rafael Marín. 2020. Datives and stativity in psych predicates. In Anna Pineda & Jaume Mateu (eds.), *Dative constructions in Romance and beyond*, 221–238. Berlin: Language Science Press. DOI:10.5281/zenodo.3776549

Ganeshan, Ashwini. 2014. Revisiting Spanish ObjExp psych predicates. In Claire Renaud, Carla Ghanem, Verónica González López & Kathryn Pruitt (eds.), *Proceedings of WECOL 2013 (held at Arizona State University, Tempe Campus,*

November 8-10, 2013), 73–84. Fresno, CA: Department of Linguistics, California State University, Fresno.

Ganeshan, Ashwini. 2019. Examining animacy and agentivity in Spanish reverse-psych verbs. *Studies in Hispanic and Lusophone Linguistics* 12(1). 1–33.

GIEC – Institut d'Estudis Catalans. 2016. *Gramàtica de la llengua catalana*. Barcelona: Institut d'Estudis Catalans.

Ginebra, Jordi. 2003. *El règim verbal i nominal.* Manuscript.

Ginebra, Jordi. 2005. *Praxi lingüística: III. Criteris gramaticals i d'estil* (6). Tarragona: Servei Lingüístic de la Universitat Rovira i Virgili. Textos de normalització lingüística.

Ginebra, Jordi. 2015. Neologia i gramàtica: Entre el neologisme lèxic i el neologisme sintàctic. *Caplletra* 59. 137–157.

Landau, Idan. 2010. *The locative syntax of experiencers.* Cambridge, MA: MIT Press.

Ledgeway, Adam, Norma Schifano & Giuseppina Silvestri. 2020. Microvariation in dative-marking in the Romance and Greek varieties of Southern Italy. In Anna Pineda & Jaume Mateu (eds.), *Dative constructions in Romance and beyond*, 317–349. Berlin: Language Science Press. DOI:10.5281/zenodo.3776557

Levin, Beth & Malka Rappaport Hovav. 1995. *Unaccusativity: At the syntax-lexical semantics interface.* Cambridge, MA: MIT Press.

Marín, Rafael & Louise McNally. 2011. Inchoativity, change of state and telicity. *Natural Language and Linguistic Theory* 29. 467–502.

Marín, Rafael & Cristina Sánchez Marco. 2012. Verbos y nombres psicológicos: Juntos y revueltos. *Borealis: An International Journal of Hispanic Linguistics* 1(2). 91–108.

Masullo, Pascual J. 1992. Quirky Datives in Spanish and the Non-Nominative Subject Parameter. In Andrea Kathol & Jill Beckman (eds.), *Proceedings of the 4th Student Conference in Linguistics (SCIL 4), MITWPL 16*, 89–104. Cambridge, MA.

Mendívil Giró, José Luis. 2005. El comportamiento variable de "molestar": A Luisa le molesta que la molesten. In Gerd Wotjak & Juan Cuartero Otal (eds.), *Entre semántica léxica, teoría del léxico y sintaxis*, 261–272. Frankfurt: Peter Lang.

Pesetsky, David. 1995. *Zero syntax: Experiencers and cascades.* Cambridge, MA: MIT Press.

Pineda, Anna. 2012. Transitividad y afectación en el entorno lingüístico romance y eusquérico. In Xulio Viejo Fernández (ed.), *Estudios sobre variación sintáctica peninsular*, 31–73. Oviedo: Trabe.

Pineda, Anna. 2016. *Les fronteres de la (in)transitivitat: Estudi dels aplicatius en llengües romàniques i basc*. Barcelona: Institut d'Estudis Món Juïc. Published and revised version of the doctoral dissertation.

Pineda, Anna. 2020. From dative to accusative: An ongoing syntactic change in Romance. *Probus: International Journal of Romance Linguistics* 32(1). 129–173.

Pineda, Anna & Carles Royo. 2017. Differential Indirect Object Marking in Romance (and how to get rid of it). *Revue Roumaine de Linguistique* 4. 445–462.

Pylkkänen, Liina. 2008. *Introducing arguments* (Linguistic Inquiry Monographs 49). Cambridge, MA: MIT Press.

Ramos, Joan Rafael. 2002. Factors del canvi sintàctic. In M. Antònia Cano, Josep Martines, Vicent Martines & Joan J. Ponsoda (eds.), *Les claus del canvi lingüístic (Symposia Philologica 5)*, 397–428. Alacant: Institut Interuniversitari de Filologia Valenciana, Ajuntament de Nucia, Caja de Ahorros del Mediterráneo.

Ramos, Joan Rafael. 2004. El règim verbal: Anàlisi contrastiva català-castellà. In Cesáreo Calvo, Emili Casanova & Fco. Javier Satorre (eds.), *Lingüística diacrònica contrastiva*, 119–139. València: Universitat de València.

Rosselló, Joana. 2008. El SV, I: Verbs i arguments verbals. In Joan Solà, Maria-Rosa Lloret, Joan Mascaró & Manuel Pérez Saldanya (eds.), *Gramàtica del català contemporani*, 4th edn., 1853–1949. Barcelona: Editorial Empúries.

Royo, Carles. 2017. *Alternança acusatiu/datiu i flexibilitat semàntica i sintàctica dels verbs psicològics catalans*. Barcelona: Universitat de Barcelona. (Doctoral dissertation). https://www.tdx.cat/handle/10803/523541.

van Voorst, Jan. 1992. The aspectual semantics of psychological verbs. *Linguistics and Philosophy* 15(1). 65–92. DOI:10.1007/BF00635833

Viñas-de-Puig, Ricard. 2014. Predicados psicológicos y estructuras con verbo ligero: Del estado al evento. *Revista de Lingüística Teórica y Aplicada* 52(2). 165–188.

Viñas-de-Puig, Ricard. 2017. Psych predicates, light verbs, and phase theory: On the implications of case assignment to the experiencer in non-leísta experience predicates. In Juan J. Colomina-Almiñana (ed.), *Contemporary advances in theoretical and applied Spanish linguistics variation*, 201–224. Columbus, OH: The Ohio State University Press.

Ynglès, M. Teresa. 1991. Les relacions semàntiques del cas datiu. In Jane White Albrecht, Janet Ann DeCesaris, Patricia V. Lunn & Josep Miquel Sobrer (eds.), *Homenantge a Josep Roca-Pons: Estudis de llengua i literatura*, 271–308. Barcelona: Publicacions de l'Abadia de Montserrat, Indiana University.

Ynglès, M. Teresa. 2011. *El datiu en català: Una aproximació des de la lingüística cognitiva*. Barcelona: Publicacions de l'Abadia de Montserrat.

Chapter 16

Ways of being a dative across Romance varieties

Teresa Cabré

CLT-Universitat Autònoma de Barcelona

Antonio Fábregas

University of Tromsø-Norway's Arctic University

In this article, we argue that the term *dative* can correspond to objects of a very different linguistic nature, even in typologically close languages. Specifically, in syntactic terms datives can be different from accusatives or identical to them at some point in the derivation; in the latter case, clashes between 3rd person clitics emerge. Our approach, then, argues that clitic incompatibilities are best explained through syntactic tools.

1 Introduction: the nature of datives

In a non-trivial sense, advancing our understanding of language frequently involves learning that objects that we previously took to be primitive, underived units in fact are built through the combination of independent elements. The analysis of passives is a prime example of this, as noted by Williams (2015): we have moved away from a view where passive is a type of construction to a view where passives emerge from the conspiracy of several factors, some of them independent of each other. Also very frequently, noting that a linguistic object is a derived notion also implies realising that a single, unified definition of that object is just wrong, and that in different languages there are distinct procedures to build it — and again, passives come to mind (see Croft 2017), since they vary with respect to the availability of accusative objects, the types of predicates that can be subject to them or their relation with aspect.

Teresa Cabré & Antonio Fábregas. 2020. Ways of being a dative across Romance varieties. In Anna Pineda & Jaume Mateu (eds.), *Dative constructions in Romance and beyond*, 395–411. Berlin: Language Science Press. DOI:10.5281/zenodo.3776565

This chapter starts out with the observation that 'dative' is another notion that, like passive, is best understood merely as a traditional label which in reality can correspond to entities with very different properties across languages. This automatically predicts that in some languages what we call a dative is syntactically different from accusatives, while in other languages they will share some properties, in derivational or representational terms. From here, we will state the hypothesis that 3rd person clitic clashes between accusative and dative, in fact, depend on whether the dative in that particular language shares with accusatives a property that makes them compete to be licensed by one head or not (§2). We will then illustrate the situation with only a few languages, for reasons of space: Valencian Catalan (VC), non-Valencian Catalan (nVC) and Spanish (Sp.), ending the article with a short note on French and Italian (§3). But we will begin with some initial evidence that datives should be regarded as a derived object.

In her detailed cross-linguistic overview of datives, Næss (2009) adopts a functional or conceptual criterion to identify something as dative: something is called *dative* in a language if it is the marking assigned to prototypical goals. This criterion is probably the only one that allows a systematic comparison across typologically unrelated languages, but note that one function can be performed by means of different devices. And if we look briefly at the literature, it does seem that researchers agree that what we call dative corresponds to different objects across languages. Cuervo (2003) treats dative as a structural case — one that only appears within a specific structural configuration, in her case Spec, Applicative Phrase; by contrast, Woolford (2006) treats it as inherent case. Some languages allow dative-marked subjects (Zaenen et al. 1985), while others reject them (German: Bayer 2004) and others allow only some datives in subject position (Russian: Moore & Perlmutter 2000). Some treat datives as cases (Spanish: Ormazabal & Romero 2013), while others treat datives as the spell-out of possessive structures (Swiss German: Leu 2015). See also Ledgeway et al. (2020 [this volume]) and Royo (2020 [this volume]), for similar observations about the different natures of datives.

All these authors have compelling arguments to make their points. Our claim here is that they are all essentially right for the specific instances of dative they analyse. What is wrong, however, is the underlying assumption that the term *dative*, taken from descriptive traditional grammars, corresponds to a uniform phenomenon across languages. In the rest of this article we will argue that the idea that datives are derived objects, in fact, makes interesting predictions for the properties of clitic incompatibilities in Romance languages.

2 Clitic wars and what it means to be too similar in syntax

The example in (1) is one instance of a clitic clash within a cluster, a very frequent situation across Romance languages (Rezac 2010). The general format of the situation is that two clitic pronouns — and they must be clitics — are incompatible with each other when they are adjacent in the same sequence (see Cuervo 2020 [this volume] for a detailed analysis of different syntactic positions for datives; as far as we see, the dative clitic occupies the same structural position independently of the syntactic position of its related applicative phrase).

(1) Spanish
    * María le   lo   dio.
      María him.DAT it.ACC gave.3SG
      Intended: 'María gave it to him.' (cf. *María gave him it.)

Languages react in different ways to this situation, sometimes with different solutions for different clashes in the same language: one of the two clitics may disappear, or one may be replaced by another clitic from the system. In the case of (1), Spanish follows the latter pattern and replaces the dative with a reflexive form *se*.

(2) Spanish
    María se   lo   dio.
    María REFL it.ACC gave.3SG
    'María gave it to him.'

An overwhelming majority of the analyses of such clashes treats them as a morphological phenomenon, meaning that the clash and its repair are assumed to take place at a 'surface' level where the syntax and semantics of the structure are not affected by it — and by the same token not involved in triggering it. Perlmutter (1971), Bonet (1991), Bonet (1993), Bonet (1995), Grimshaw (1997), Pescarini (2007), Nevins (2012) are among the noteworthy authors that have adopted this view. Though their analyses differ from each other in very crucial details, they share several intuitions beyond their morphological treatment of the phenomena.

First, they propose that the clash is due to a form of morphological Obligatory Contour Principle (OCP) infraction (see especially Nevins 2012): the clash is caused by the morphological shape of the two clitics being identical or semi-identical. Note that using an OCP violation in itself involves complicating the architecture of grammar by allowing it to contain filters that exclude well-formed representations in syntax or phonology.

Second, they agree that, when the OCP is resolved by replacing one clitic with another, the clitic used in the repair is always more underspecified than the infringing clitic — in their analyses, because the repair involves removing some features from the representation. In the case of (2), the Spanish clitic *se* is more featurally impoverished than the dative *le*: as can be seen in (3), *le* contrasts in number — but not in gender — while *se* contrasts neither in gender nor in number.

(3)   a.   le [dative singular masculine / feminine] / les [dative plural masculine / feminine]

      b.   se [reflexive 3rd person, singular / plural, masculine / feminine]

In Italian, Pescarini (2007) notes that a clash between two instances of reflexive *si* is solved by substituting the first one with the form *ci*, used in locative contexts (4). This form *ci* is less specified than *si* because it can be used in locative contexts but also as a 1PL pronoun (see Ferrazzano 2003).

(4)   Italian

      a.   * Nel   medioevo   si   si   lavava   raramente.
           in.the Middle Ages REFL REFL washed.3sG seldom

      b.   Nel   medioevo   ci   si   lavava   raramente.
           in.the Middle Ages DEIC REFL washed.3sG seldom
           'In the Middle Ages they [people] rarely washed.'

Third, they also agree that when the clash involves two or more instances of the most underspecified clitic, the only repair possible is to erase one of them. This is illustrated for *ci* in (5).

(5)   Italian

      a.   * A Roma ci   ci   porta Mario.
           to Rome us.ACC there brings Mario

      b.   A Roma ci   porta Mario.
           to Rome us.ACC brings Mario
           'To Rome, Mario brings us.'

Our claim in this paper is that the second and third observation are right, but that they can be recast in a better way within a syntactic system where there is no need to propose a morphological OCP. Instead, the situations we see in the previous examples are an effect of standard syntactic competition for licensing by the same head or set of heads. In other words, the problem of (4) and (5) is the same as what we see in (6), which is wrong according to every theory because there are two DPs that compete for the same position in the derivation.

(6) * [Mary] [our family] arrives today.

Specifically, we will assume that Sportiche (1996) is right in his claim that the functional structure of a clause (at least in the languages we are dealing with here) includes a Clitic Area above *v*P. The clitics must be licensed in this area, which in turn — as we will see — can be split into several regions that are determined by microparametric choices in each (variety of a) language. In this system, the clitic clash is due to the descriptive principle in (7), which replaces the OCP.

(7) Two clitics produce a clash when they must occupy the same position at some point of the syntactic derivation.

(7) covers two types of cases. The first type of case is a situation where the competition involves the base-generation position. In less technical terms, the first type of clash arises in situations where one clitic is built using the exact same pieces as a second clitic. We will illustrate this situation with non-Valencian Catalan (§3.1).

The second type of case is the situation where, even though one clitic is not directly derived from the other, the grammatical properties of case assignment and checking of arguments in the specific language force them to compete to be licensed by the same head. We will illustrate this for Spanish (§3.2).

Let us now move on to the specific case studies.

3 Different datives, different clashes

Our main proposal is that Sportiche's clitic area can be split into different regions, each one designated for a different type of clitic (8). Specific languages make the split in different ways, following the general principle that, within a (universal) domain, languages have the freedom to select a subset of formal properties that they grammaticalise (Ramchand & Svenonius 2014; Wiltschko 2014).

(8) $[_{XP}$ X $[_{YP}$ Y $[_{ZP}$ Z   ...]]]
     clitic type 1   clitic type 2   clitic type 3 ...

The clash happens when the two clitics compete for a single region; the repair depends on how many other available regions — if any — there are in the language. Let us illustrate this with several cases.

3.1 Valencian Catalan and non-Valencian Catalan

The literature on the different clitic systems across Catalan varieties, and the corresponding clashes, is very abundant (Bonet 1993; Martin 2012). For reasons of space we will concentrate here on the opposition between two general varieties, abstracting away from more fine-grained subvarieties. Consider (9), which compares the Valencian (VC) system with the Non-Valencian (nVC) system.

(9)   a.   VC datives
      Li   / els   porta-ré   un regal.
      3SG.DAT / 3PL.DAT bring-FUT.1SG a   present
      'I will give him/her/them a present.'

   b.   nVC datives
      Li   / els hi [əlzi] porta-ré   un regal.
      3SG.DAT / 3PL.DAT   bring-FUT.1SG a   present
      'I will give him/her/them a present.'

One important difference between the two is that in nVC there is a component /i/ that is contained in both the singular and the plural dative. This component is identical to the locative clitic *hi* /i/, which — crucially — nVC has but VC lacks. Following Martin (2012), we propose that this is a sign that nVC builds the dative pronoun by combining the locative clitic with a DP layer identical to the accusative clitic (as represented in 10, abstracting away from morphophonological reordering). We part ways with Martin (2012) in that we consider this *hi* a real locative (a noun denoting regions of space, *pace* Rigau 1978; 1982), not an element expressing general deixis independent of any conceptual dimension.[1]

---

[1]Note that in view of the Catalan contrast between *aqu-í* 'here' and *aqu-est* 'this', it seems more plausible to propose that *aqu-* corresponds to the deictic part of the word and *-i* acts as a restrictor that provides place as the dimension where deixis applies. As one anonymous reviewer notes, probably the most controversial part of our analysis is to treat /i/ as the spell out of a locative N layer, given the existence of cases of *hi* where it substitutes for predicates or is used with an apparent expletive function. See Cabré & Fábregas (2019) for a more detailed presentation of how we deal with cases where *hi* behaves in Catalan like what seems to be a non-locative element: in short, we propose that the clitic still denotes space in a more metaphorical way, and is used to replace elements that correspond to the personal sphere of the subject, or to properties within whose set the subject is included.

(10)   nVC dative clitics

    a. $[_{DP}$ $(ə)l$ $[_{NumP}$ $\varnothing$ $[_{NP}$ $i]]]$

    b. $[_{DP}$ $(ə)l$ $[_{NumP}$ z $[_{NP}$ $i]]]$

As VC lacks a locative, it follows that it cannot build its dative pronouns with a locative noun. This perforce means that accusative and dative clitics must be differentiated by a specific property (given that they are spelled out differently, see (11)). At this point, just for the sake of argument, we will assume that they are different through case marking in the form of a KP assigning them inherent case (12), but that the specific property is irrelevant provided that one clitic is not derived from the other.

(11)   a. el 'accusative singular masculine'

    b. la 'accusative singular feminine'

    c. li 'dative singular, masculine / feminine'

(12)   a. $[_{KP}$ Dative $[...$NumP Sing$]]$ $\longleftrightarrow$ li

    b. $[_{KP}$ Dative $[...$NumP Plural$]]$ $\longleftrightarrow$ els

Let us now consider the behaviour of accusative and dative third person clitics inside the cluster. The sequence of two 3rd person clitics in nVC is ungrammatical, and gets resolved by the forms /li/ and /əlzi/; that is, in practice the surface result is identical to a single dative (see 13–14).[2]

(13)   a. * Li   (e)l   dona-ré.
          him.DAT it.ACC give.FUT.1SG

    b. L'hi dona-ré.
         L-HI give.FUT.1SG
         'I will give it to him.'

(14)   a. * Li   (e)ls   dona-ré.
          him.DAT them.ACC give-FUT.1SG

    b. Els hi dona-ré.
         ELS HI give-FUT.1SG
         'I will deliver them to him.'

---

[2]Note that the orthography *l'hi* (just like *els hi*) is pronounced identically to the singular clitic, /li/.

In contrast, VC does not display a clash in such sequences.

(15) a. Li'-l   dona-ré.
          him.DAT-it.ACC give-FUT.1SG
          'I will give it to him.'

      b. Li'-ls   dona-ré.
          him.ACC-them.ACC give-FUT.1SG
          'I will give them to him.'

To put it simply, there is a correlation between building the dative from the locative and not allowing a sequence of dative + accusative third person clitics. This is precisely what we expect if the clash emerges in syntax, through the licensing by heads within Sportiche's area. In nVC, the dative is in actuality an accusative containing a locative, so in a sequence that — using the traditional terminology — contains an accusative and a dative, there are in fact two accusative layers that will compete for licensing in the same position. The two cannot be licensed at the same time, so the resulting sequence is 'impoverished' on the surface (16b). Our claim is that within ZP there is only syntactic space for one D layer, one Number layer and one NP layer. The D layer is occupied by /l/, the number layer by /z/ and the noun layer by /i/.[3]

(16) a. $[_{XP}$ X $[_{YP}$ Y $[_{ZP}$ Z   ...]]]
          clitic type 1 clitic type 2 clitic type 3 ...
          $*li + (e)ls$
      b. $[_{XP}$ X $[_{YP}$ Y $[_{ZP}$ $(e)l^{D}\text{-}s^{Num}\text{-}i^{N}$]]]

By contrast, in VC, the dative is not derived from the accusative; each clitic is distinct, and therefore each one of them can be licensed in a different region of

---

[3] Interestingly, nVC uses a similar strategy to repair standard Person Case Constraint infractions: the dative is reduced to *hi* (*Al director, m'hi ha recomanat la Mireia* To-the director me-LOC has recommended Mireia 'Mireia has recommended me to the director'). Although we will not develop the argument here, our suggestion is that YP is an area where all arguments interpreted as affected must be licensed. The dative clitic is interpreted as referring to an affected participant (Adger & Harbour 2010), so 'dative' clitics must rise to YP. Person-marked clitics like *me* 'me' are affected by default, so they are base-generated in YP — which, as an anonymous reviewer has pointed out to us, explains the connection between person-marked clitics and datives in, for instance, marking through a 'to' and the absence of gender contrasts. As at some point in the derivation datives and person clitics compete for the same area. This explains the clash, which is resolved in the same way as before.

Sportiche's area: the clash does not emerge in (17) because their datives are not derived from their accusatives.[4]

(17) [$_{XP}$ X   [$_{YP}$ Y   [$_{ZP}$ Z   ...]]]
      clitic type 1   clitic type 2   clitic type 3 ...
      li (e)ls

3.2 Spanish spurious *se*

Another famous case of 3RD person clitic clash is provided by Spanish spurious *se*. Here we will argue that this clash is due to the same type of competition, and that the repair follows from the regions that Spanish defines in its Sportiche's area.

As can be seen in (18), there is no obvious evidence that the Spanish dative and the Spanish accusative are built one from the other; in particular, Spanish lacks any clitic /e/ which would allow one to segment the dative into the accusative layer plus a morphosyntactically significant unit. At least at first glance, then, the situation is different from Catalan.

(18)   Spanish clitics
       a. lo 'accusative masculine singular'
       b. la 'accusative feminine singular'
       c. le 'dative singular, masculine / feminine'

However, there is an important sense in which datives and accusatives are syntactically non-distinct in Spanish: Differential Object Marking in some "accusatives" is identical to dative marking (19), and in fact within the same *v*P the two markings cannot occur at the same time (20) (Ormazabal & Romero 2013; see also Cornilescu 2020 [this volume]).

(19)   a. Le   di   un libro a María.   [dative]
          her.DAT gave.1SG a book A María
          'I gave a book to María.'

---

[4] At this point, we lack sufficient evidence of whether there is a correlation between carrying KP and being spelled out by a non-analytical form, as perhaps the contrast between VC and nVC suggests. We are forced at this point to treat it as a lexical accident which does not follow from independent principles. Further research is necessary to determine whether the correlation is real or an accident of VC.

b. Vi   a María.   [accusative]
    saw.1sg A María
    'I saw María.'

(20)   Entregué   (*a) los prisioneros al   enemigo.
       delivered.1SG A   the prisoners   A-the enemy
       'I delivered the prisoners to the enemy.'

This pattern has motivated analyses where Spanish *v*Ps assign only one real case, "internal object case" (Romero 2012; Ormazabal & Romero 2013), which is manifested through *a*-marking. (20) is ungrammatical with double *a*-marking simply because the *v*P can only assign one case, and the two internal arguments compete with each other in order to get that case.[5] Our claim is, then, that (21) is ungrammatical for the same reason as (20): in both cases, two elements compete to be licensed by the same head, the one that assigns DOM in (20) and the one that licenses 3rd person clitics in (21).[6] Irrespectively of whether they are generated in different regions, at some point they will have to establish a case-relation with a head, and given that accusatives and datives both compete for this — because the only real case in Spanish is "internal argument case" — only one of them will remain.

(21)   * Le   lo   di.
       him.DAT it.ACC gave
       Intended: 'I gave it to him.'

In other words, like nVC datives, Spanish datives are 'fake datives', but for different reasons. To consider the repair strategy, and to be more explicit about the competition, let us say a bit more about the clitic regions in Spanish. We assume Kayne's (2010) proposal about the relevant regions in Spanish (22).[7]

---

[5] See Romero (2012) for the relation between the non *a*-marked "accusative" argument and case assignment.

[6] We assume that the presence of an object clitic (*lo* or *le*) implies that the pronoun has been checked in the ZP area at some point in the derivation. Our approach implies that objects not carrying DOM are case-licensed in a different way from DOM-objects (see also López 2012), but the distinction dissolves from the perspective of the clitic, which requires them to be generated in ZP.

[7] Among Kayne's (2010) arguments for this ordering, he observes that it reproduces the natural ordering of clitics inside the cluster and that one can establish an implicational hierarchy in terms of which clitics can intervene across varieties between subject agreement morphology and the verbal stem.

(22) [$_{WP}$ *se* [$_{XP}$ *me/te* [$_{YP}$ *le*   [$_{ZP}$ *lo*   ... [*vP*]]]]
       REFL   *me/you*   3SG.DAT   3SG.ACC

Interestingly, the sequence follows a logical ordering from two perspectives: first, the lowest type of clitics are those that are defined by the maximal number of interpretable phi features: accusative pronouns contrast in gender and number; datives contrast just in number; and reflexive pronouns lack interpretable phi features (Reuland 2011). Second, person-marked pronouns are higher than third person pronouns — perhaps defined by absence of person features — thus matching the observation that speaker and addressee are defined high in the clausal structure as a form of deixis (see Giorgi 2009, among many others).

Once we assume this sequence, it is striking that the incompatibilities attested in Spanish always involve pronouns in adjacent areas, and the repair involves using a clitic that belongs to a higher area: 3rd accusative and 3rd dative occupy adjacent regions,[8] and the repair involves using a reflexive pronoun rather than a dative (see Alcaraz 2017 for syntactic arguments that spurious *se* behaves as a real reflexive, which we do not reproduce for lack of space).

(23) [$_{WP}$ *se* [$_{XP}$ [$_{YP}$ *le* [$_{ZP}$ *lo* ... [*vP*]]]]

We have argued that *le* and *lo* are incompatible with each other due to case competition—in other words, because Spanish lacks a real dative case. To be more specific, we can assume that even though they end up in different regions, they are base-generated in the same position, which checks internal case (assume that is ZP).

Crucially, the repair involves removing one of the two clitics. The first question is, which one? In a morphologically-oriented theory with OCP, in principle either of the two clitics could be the one replaced. In our proposal, we correctly predict that the one replaced is the first one, because that is the highest one: if the repair involves using a clitic that belongs to a higher region, replacing the lowest one would produce a standard intervention effect because the long distance relation established between WP and ZP has another clitic in YP that is closer to WP than ZP.

(24) *[$_{WP}$ *se* [$_{XP}$ [$_{YP}$ *le* [$_{ZP}$ *lo* ...[*vP*]]]]

Second, why should it be *se*? On the assumption that a third person pronoun does not contain person features, the XP area — for 1st and 2nd person pronouns — is not available for 3rd person clitics; the closest available area is therefore

---

[8]See Sheehan 2020 [this volume] for further details about PCC effects.

the reflexive pronoun area. Given that the height correlates with the number of interpretable features, this also captures the intuition that the repairs always involve less specified clitics. In our account, this is just an epiphenomenon of the fact that syntactic structure is built from bottom to top and not vice versa.

Third, our approach also explains why a clash between two adjacent *se* pronouns cannot be resolved through substitution. (25) is ungrammatical; in our approach, it is so because the two *se* pronouns want to be licensed in the WP region, and there is place for only one of them. Given that the clitic area finishes here in Spanish, there is no other region to license the reflexive not licensed in WP.

(25) * Se   se   arrepiente mucho aquí.
      REFL REFL repent   a lot here
      Intended: 'Here it is very common to regret something.'

In Italian, on the other hand, such a repair strategy is possible, essentially because in this language the clitic area contains a region that precedes reflexives where *ci* (as an underspecified deictic element) is located. (4), repeated below as (26), is explained through an area such as (27); note that our approach also correctly predicts that (5), repeated as (28), can only be repaired through total erasure of one clitic.[9]

(26)   Italian
       a. * Nel   medioevo   si   si   lavava.
            in.the Middle Ages REFL REFL washed.3SG

       b. Nel   medioevo   ci   si   lavava.
          in.the Middle Ages DEIC REFL washed.3SG
          'In the Middle Ages they [people] washed.'

(27)   a. [$_{HP}$ *ci* [$_{WP}$ *si* [$_{XP}$ *mi* [$_{YP}$ *gli* [$_{ZP}$ *lo* ...[vP]]]]]
       b. [$_{HP}$ [$_{WP}$ **si si* [$_{XP}$ [$_{YP}$ [$_{ZP}$ ...[vP]]]]]
       c. [$_{HP}$ *ci* [$_{WP}$ *si si* [$_{XP}$ [$_{YP}$ [$_{ZP}$ ...[vP]]]]]

---

[9] An independent question is what specific features Italian *ci* spells out so that it can be used for both the 1pl and the locative. In this respect, we follow Ferrazzano (2003), who argues that Italian *ci* in fact stands for proximal deixis, irrespective of whether it applies to participants — where the closest participant is the speaker — or place. This approach is also compatible in principle with Pescarini's proposal that *ci* is featurally underspecified, introduced as a default. Note that an account based on homophony begs the question of why first person and place happen to be spelled out by exactly the same sequence.

(28)   * A Roma ci   ci   porta Mario.
        to Rome us.ACC there brings Mario

Again, note that in the case of (26b) our approach also correctly predicts that the clitic that will be replaced will be the first one in the series: on the assumption that structure is built bottom-up, necessarily the deictic clitic will precede the reflexive. As far as we can tell, the morphological approach cannot make this prediction.

3.3 A short note on French

At first sight, French is a surface counterexample to our proposal. It is plausible to speculate that at least the dative form *lui* contains the locative *y* /i/. This impression is confirmed, following our own logic, by the observation made by Rezac (2010) that *lui* cannot occur in a sequence with *y*, as illustrated in (29).

(29)   * Je lui   y   parle.
        I   him.DAT LOC talk.1SG
        Intended: 'I talk to him there.'

We would then predict that a 3rd accusative should be incompatible with a 3rd dative in French, for the same reasons as in nVC: the dative is a fake dative involving the locative layer. And yet, French seems to allow the sequence seen in (30).

(30)   Je   le   lui   ai   donné.
        I.NOM it.ACC him.DAT have.1SG given
        'I have given it to him.'

We argue that this is not a real counterexample, essentially because the apparent compatibility is purely orthographic, an artefact of the writing system. Schwarze (2001) notes that although the orthographic representation in French insists on keeping the two clitics, the natural pronunciation of the sequence written as *je le lui* is [ʒɥi] or [ʒlɥi], where crucially what is preserved, at most, is the shape of the fake dative [lɥi], as in nVC. In our view, pending a deeper typological study in French, this language confirms our predictions.

4 Conclusions

In this short contribution we have argued that what has been labelled *dative* in typologically related languages corresponds to very different types of entities. In the set of languages considered, only Valencian Catalan can be argued to have a real dative integrated as a distinct case in the system. Fake datives can be obtained — perhaps among other ways — by building them with locatives and DP layers (as in non-Valencian Catalan, possibly French), or inside languages which only assign one internal argument case and therefore do not make a real distinction between dative and accusative case.

We have furthermore argued that there is a correlation between whether the dative is fake or not and whether it will display a clash with accusative 3rd clitics or not. Specifically, we have argued that whenever the dative is fake, it competes with the accusative for licensing at the syntactic level.

We have thus sketched an account of "clitic wars" which treats the phenomenon as syntactic rather than morphological. We have shown that our account, based on a standard notion of "competition for licensing by a syntactic head", manages to capture the correct intuitions of the morphological approach (underspecification, alternation between substitution and erasure), while managing to make additional correct predictions not made by the morphological account (the highest clitic is substituted, erasure happens when there is no higher region in the clitic area). This makes the resort to generalised OCP solutions (or Richards's (2010) Distinctness) redundant. We hope that even though our study is limited in empirical scope we have convincingly shown that the syntactic route is worth exploring in accounting for these facts.

Abbreviations

The abbreviations used in the glosses of this chapter follow the Leipzig Glossing Rules. Additional abbreviation: DEIC: deictic.

Acknowledgements

The authors would like to thank the audience at and organisers of the *Dative Structures and Beyond* conference (Barcelona, January 2017) and the *Romanistentag* (Zurich, October 2017) for illuminating comments and suggestions. All disclaimers apply.

References

Adger, David & Daniel Harbour. 2010. Syntax and syncretisms of the Person Case Constraint. *Syntax* 10(1). 2–37.

Alcaraz, Alejo. 2017. *Spurious vs. Dative*. lingbuzz/003293.

Bayer, Josef. 2004. Non-nominative subjects in comparison. In Peri Bhashakarao & Karumuri V. Subbarao (eds.), *Non nominative subjects*, 31–58. Amsterdam: John Benjamins.

Bonet, Eulàlia. 1991. *Morphology after syntax: Pronominal clitics in Romance.* Cambridge, MA: MIT. (Doctoral dissertation).

Bonet, Eulàlia. 1993. 3rd person pronominal clitics in dialects of Catalan. *Catalan Working Papers in Linguistics* 3(1). 85–111.

Bonet, Eulàlia. 1995. Feature structure of Romance clitics. *Natural Language & Linguistic Theory* 13(4). 607–647.

Cabré, Teresa & Antonio Fábregas. 2019. 3rd person clitic combinations across Catalan varieties: Consequences for the nature of the dative clitic. *The Linguistic Review* 36(2). 151–190. DOI:10.1515/tlr-2018-2010

Cornilescu, Alexandra. 2020. Ditransitive constructions with differentially marked direct objects in Romanian. In Anna Pineda & Jaume Mateu (eds.), *Dative constructions in Romance and beyond*, 117–142. Berlin: Language Science Press. DOI:10.5281/zenodo.3776541

Croft, William. 2017. *Verbs: Aspect and causal structure.* Oxford: Oxford University Press.

Cuervo, María Cristina. 2003. *Datives at large.* Cambridge, MA: Massachusetts Institute of Technology. (Doctoral dissertation). https://dspace.mit.edu/handle/1721.1/7991.

Cuervo, María Cristina. 2020. Datives as applicatives. In Anna Pineda & Jaume Mateu (eds.), *Dative constructions in Romance and beyond*, 1–39. Berlin: Language Science Press. DOI:10.5281/zenodo.3776531

Ferrazzano, Lisa Reisig. 2003. *The morphology of* ci *and its 'distal' relative,* vi. Manuscript.

Giorgi, Alessandra. 2009. *About the speaker.* Oxford: Oxford University Press.

Grimshaw, Jane B. 1997. Projection, heads, and optimality. *Linguistic Inquiry* 28(3). 373–422.

Kayne, Richard S. 2010. Toward a syntactic reinterpretation of Harris and Halle (2005). In Brigitte Kampers-Manhe, Reineke Bok-Bennema & Bart Hollebrandse (eds.), *Romance languages and linguistic theory 2008: Selected papers from 'Going Romance' Groningen 2008*, 145–170. Amsterdam: John Benjamins.

409

Ledgeway, Adam, Norma Schifano & Giuseppina Silvestri. 2020. Microvariation in dative-marking in the Romance and Greek varieties of Southern Italy. In Anna Pineda & Jaume Mateu (eds.), *Dative constructions in Romance and beyond*, 317–349. Berlin: Language Science Press. DOI:10.5281/zenodo.3776557

Leu, Tom. 2015. *The architecture of determiners*. Oxford: Oxford University Press.

López, Luis. 2012. *Indefinite objects: Scrambling, choice functions, and differential marking*. Cambridge, MA: MIT Press.

Martin, Jesús. 2012. *Deconstructing Catalan object clitics*. New York, NY: New York University. (Doctoral dissertation).

Moore, John & David M. Perlmutter. 2000. What does it take to be a dative subject? *Natural Language and Linguistic Theory* 18(2). 373–416.

Næss, Åshild. 2009. Varieties of dative. In Andrej L. Malchukov & Andrew Spencer (eds.), *The Oxford handbook of case*, 572–581. Oxford: Oxford University Press.

Nevins, Andrew. 2012. Haplological dissimilation at distinct stages of exponence. In Jochen Trommer (ed.), *The morphology and phonology of exponence: The state of the art*, 84–116. Oxford: Oxford University Press.

Ormazabal, Javier & Juan Romero. 2013. Object agreement, clitics and dialectal variation. *Probus* 25(2). 301–344.

Perlmutter, David M. 1971. *Deep and surface structure constraints in syntax*. New York, NY: Holt Rinehart & Winston.

Pescarini, Diego. 2007. Types of syncretism in the clitic systems of Romance. *Anuario del seminario de filología vasca Julio de Urquijo* 41(2). 285–300.

Ramchand, Gillian & Peter Svenonius. 2014. Deriving the functional hierarchy. *Language Sciences* 46(Part B). 152–174. DOI:10.1016/j.langsci.2014.06.013

Reuland, Eric. 2011. *Anaphora and language design* (Linguistic Inquiry Monographs). Cambridge, MA: MIT Press.

Rezac, Milan. 2010. Ineffability through modularity: Gaps in the French clitic cluster. In Matthew Baerman, Greville G. Corbett & Dunstan Brown (eds.), *Defective paradigms: Missing forms and what they tell us*, 151–180. Oxford: Oxford University Press.

Richards, Norvin. 2010. *Uttering trees*. Cambridge, MA: MIT Press.

Rigau, Gemma. 1978. 'hi' datiu inanimat. *Els Marges* 12. 99–102.

Rigau, Gemma. 1982. Inanimate indirect objects in Catalan. *Linguistic Inquiry* 13(1). 146–150.

Romero, Juan. 2012. Accusative datives in Spanish. In Beatriz Fernández & Ricardo Etxepare (eds.), *Variation in datives: A microcomparative perspective*, 283–300. Oxford: Oxford University Press.

Royo, Carles. 2020. The accusative/dative alternation in Catalan verbs with experiencer object. In Anna Pineda & Jaume Mateu (eds.), *Dative constructions in Romance and beyond*, 371–393. Berlin: Language Science Press. DOI:10.5281/zenodo.3776563

Schwarze, Christoph. 2001. On the representation of French and Italian clitics. In Myriam Butt & Tracy Holloway King (eds.), *Proceedings of the LFG'01 conference*, 1–24. Chicago, IL: CSLI Publications.

Sheehan, Michelle. 2020. The Romance Person Case Constraint is not about clitic clusters. In Anna Pineda & Jaume Mateu (eds.), *Dative constructions in Romance and beyond*, 143–171. Berlin: Language Science Press. DOI:10.5281/zenodo.3776543

Sportiche, Dominique. 1996. Clitic constructions. In Johan Rooryck & Laurie Zaring (eds.), *Phrase structure and the lexicon*, 213–276. Dordrecht: Kluwer.

Williams, Alexander. 2015. *Arguments in syntax and semantics*. Cambridge: Cambridge University Press.

Wiltschko, Martina. 2014. *The universal structure of categories*. Cambridge: Cambridge University Press.

Woolford, Ellen. 2006. Lexical case, inherent case, and argument structure. *Linguistic Inquiry* 37(1). 111–130.

Zaenen, Annie, Joan Maling & Höskuldur Thráinsson. 1985. Case and grammatical functions: The Icelandic passive. *Natural Language & Linguistic Theory* 3(4). 441–483.

Name index